TAKING SIDES

Clashing Views in

Family and Personal Relationships

SEVENTH EDITION

Selected, Edited, and with Introductions by

Elizabeth Schroeder, EdD, MSW
Professional Trainer/Consultant

Contemporary Learning Series
2460 Kerper Blvd., Dubuque, IA 52001

Visit us on the Internet
http://www.mhcls.com

*For Matthew, who could teach lots of adults
about what's truly important
in family relationships.*

Photo Acknowledgment
Cover image: Getty Images

Cover Acknowledgment
Maggie Lytle

Library of Congress Cataloging-in-Publication Data
Main entry under title:
Taking sides: clashing views on controversial issues in family and
personal relationships/selected, edited, and with introductions
by Elizabeth Schroeder, MSW.—7th ed.
Includes bibliographical references and index.
1. Family—United States. 2. Interpersonal relationships. I. Schroeder, Elizabeth, *comp.*
306.85'973

MHID: 0-07-339714-8
ISBN: 978-0-07-339714-6
ISSN: 96-85806

Printed on Recycled Paper

Preface

As human beings, we relate to each other on a range of levels. We are acquaintances and friends, colleagues and supervisors—partners, spouses, and family members. The issues that affect us in our lives, regardless of the roles we are playing at any given time, are as diverse as they are complex. These are issues that affect us on the personal level, as well as on the political and public policy levels. We receive messages from peers, family members, religious institutions, and the media about how we should and can act within the contexts of our family and personal relationships, and we experience very specific repercussions for going with or against these messages.

The seventh edition of *Taking Sides: Clashing Views in Family and Personal Relationships* contains 38 dynamic points of view separated into 19 challenging, often contentious questions, some of which have never been debated within the pages of a *Family and Personal Relationships* issue before. Each issue features an *introduction,* which provides the context in which each debate is waged. At the end of each issue is a *postscript,* designed to encourage ongoing thought and discussions about the topic. *Suggested readings* offer additional resources you can consult for further information about each issue, and the *Internet References* lists online resources that can continue to enhance your knowledge and challenge your values and beliefs on any and all of these topics.

Taking Sides: Clashing Views in Family and Personal Relationships will push you to look at a variety of relationships and how human beings interact in new and different ways. You will be asked to think about the extent to which parents have the right to make decisions for their children. You will be pressed to reflect on whether you think that lesbian, gay, and bisexual individuals have the right to marry or adopt children. You will be *encouraged* to examine your beliefs on the effects that various public policies have on families and individuals seeking to start families, and on the extent to which the government has the right to legislate parental and caregiver decision-making.

A word to the instructor An *Instructor's Resource Guide with Test Questions* (multiple-choice and essay) is available through the publisher for the instructor using *Taking Sides* in the classroom. A general guidebook, *Using Taking Sides in the Classroom,* which discusses methods and techniques for integrating the pro/con approach into any classroom setting, is also available. An on-line version of *Using Taking Sides in the Classroom* and a correspondence service for *Taking Sides* adopters can be found at http://www.mhcls.com/usingts/.

Taking Sides: Clashing Views in Family and Personal Relationships is only one title in the Taking Sides series. If you are interested in seeing the table of contents for any of the other titles, please visit the Taking Sides Web site at http://www.mhcls.com/takingsides/.

128387

Acknowledgments The first individual I need to thank, as always, is Jill Peter. From the first edition I put together for McGraw-Hill Contemporary Learning Series, she has maintained a truly collaborative relationship with me, in which we made decisions together about topics, edits, and more. Also, thanks to Susan Brusch for her guidance and patience during Jill's brief absence, as well as everyone else at McGraw-Hill Contemporary Learning Series who may have had a hand in putting this edition together.

I also wish to thank:

- William J. Taverner, director of the Center for Family Life Education at Planned Parenthood of Greater Northern New Jersey, for being such a generous colleague. I would not have had the ongoing pleasure of working on Taking Sides had it not been for Bill.
- Rebecca Moore, for her valuable assistance in researching articles for this edition.
- The authors of the articles listed in this book. Their writings enable us to discuss and debate vital issues relating to our lives and our entire society.

As you read, do your best to remain open to different points of view. Avoid reading only the side with which you agree; be sure to review carefully the side with which you disagree. Understanding the viewpoint of a person with whom you disagree could help you to strengthen your own argument. (Then again, it could also change your mind.)

Elizabeth Schroeder, EdD, MSW
Professional Trainer/Consultant; Montclair, New Jersey

Contents In Brief

Contents

Walter L. Larrimore, vice president of medical outreach at Focus on the Family, explains that parents have always spanked their children, and believes that what we see in the media are only examples of times when parents have become abusive rather than using spanking appropriately. Irwin A. Hyman, director of the National Center for Study of Corporal Punishment and Alternatives, argues that there is never any reason to hit a child. Focusing on the emotional effects of spanking, he asserts that spanking is much more likely to teach children to tolerate and perpetuate violence than it is to correct disobedience.

Leslie Doty Hollingsworth, an associate professor of social work at the University of Michigan, offers a history of transracial adoption that has involved primarily white adoptive parents and Black or African American children. She argues that children are best served if they are adopted by families of their same racial background, and that systematic changes—such as adoption services and programs better geared towards adults of color—would enable more families to adopt children from their own backgrounds. Ezra Griffith and Rachel Bergeron, both faculty members of the Yale University School of Medicine's psychiatry department, argue that requiring racial and ethnic matching, while an appropriate effort, would leave too many children of color languishing in the foster and adoption systems. By maintaining that only in-race adoption is the best and idea situation, they ask rhetorically, does our society actually do more to reinforce cultural stereotypes or to truly serve children needing homes?

In reviewing Constance Ahrons' book, *We're Still Family: What Grown Children Have to Say About Their Parents' Divorce,* Elizabeth Marquardt, director of the Center for Marriage and Families at the Institute for American Values, argues that the manner in which Ahrons' questions were asked in her study yielded comments from participants in which they minimized the negative effects that their parents' divorce had on them. Through a combination of her own personal experience as a child of divorce and her work in the field, she maintains that divorce is a "tragedy" that dramatically and negatively impacts children for the rest of their lives. Constance Ahrons, author of *What Grown Children Have to Say About Their Parents' Divorce* and founding co-chair of the Council on Contemporary Families, found in her research findings that the ideas that children of divorced families end up much more troubled and unable to form adult relationships themselves are myths, that many adults whose parents divorced emerged from the experience stronger, wiser, and with closer relationships with their fathers, remaining connected to their families of origin even when the parent with whom they lived created a new stepfamily.

Chris Jeub, writer and president of Training Minds Ministries, is a former public school teacher with 11 children, all of whom he and his wife have homeschooled. Naming several famous homeschooled individuals, such as Winston Churchill, Benjamin Franklin, and Florence Nightingale, he argues that the home is the best environment in which to teach children, for social, academic, family strengthening, and religious reasons. Homeschooling, he maintains, frees parents to impart their own values to their children without concern for how these beliefs might clash with what is presented in the public school system. Carole Moore, a freelance writer, discusses how she weighed the options of home vs. public schooling and argues that even though homeschooling might offer some benefits to children, in the end, children who are homeschooled provides a distorted view of the world at large. Children will, she writes, make good decisions and bad decisions as a part of growing up, and whether they are home schooled or public schooled is not the determining factor in whether they grow up healthy and well-adjusted.

Child developmentalists Jeanne Brooks-Gunn, Wen-Jui Han, and Jane Waldfogel assert that their findings show many types of negative effects from maternal employment on the later cognitive and educational outcomes of children. Professor of sociology and anthropology Thomas M. Vander Ven and his colleagues argue that their studies show that the qualities or quantities of a mother working have relatively little or no influence on the social, emotional, and behavioral functioning of her children.

Bridget E. Maher, an analyst on marriage and family issues at the Family Research Council, argues that far too much funding has gone into programs that teach young people about sexuality and contraception—programs that she asserts are ineffective. She points out that most teens say they and their peers should receive strong messages about abstinence. Sue Alford, editor and director of public information services at Advocates for Youth, argues that young people are receiving sexuality information and messages from so many sources that it is irresponsible to restrict sexuality and other educators from discussing only abstinence. She maintains that the programs taught under the Abstinence Until Marriage funding often provide factually inaccurate information and hyperbolic assertions pertaining to the potential consequences of sexual relationships outside of marriage.

Ferdinand Yates, Jr. supports routine childhood immunizations, and offers an array of research demonstrating their efficacy and relative low risk of harm. He argues that society needs to be able to think beyond its own family structure, and consider that not vaccinating a child puts that child at higher risk for several contagious diseases, which could then be transmitted to others. Jini Patel Thompson speaks from her position as a parent who had to decide whether to vaccinate her child, and based on her own research, decided against it. She, too, cites a variety of research sources to demonstrate that the potential negative side effects of vaccinations, both long- and short-term, are not worth the potential positive outcomes for children.

Professor John A. Robertson of the University of Texas at Austin's School of Law argues that preconception gender selection of infants in utero for medical purposes should be allowed, and that insufficient data exist to demonstrate that any clear harm exists in allowing parents to do so. Norman Daniels (Tufts University), Carson Strong (University of Tennessee), Mary B. Mahowald (University of Chicago), and Mark V. Sauer (Columbia University) each take one aspect of Professor Robertson's arguments to demonstrate why preconception gender selection should not be allowed, including, for example, the socio-economic status inequity that allowing such a procedure, which likely would not be covered by health insurance, would create.

Amicur Farkas, B. Chertin, and Irith Hadas-Halpren, faculty of the Ben-Gurion University in Jerusalem, Israel, see ambiguous genitalia as a true emergency. They assert that feminizing surgery should be done on an infant with congenital adrenal hyperplasia to ensure that as an adult woman she will have sexual functioning and be able to give birth. Paul McHugh argues that a person's sense of gender identity is biologically based—that by changing an infant's or child's body before that child has a sense of who they are and risking being wrong about that sex assignment can do much more damage than good.

Teresa Stanton Collett, professor at South Texas College of Law, testifies in front of the U.S. House of Representatives in support of the federal Child Custody Protection Act. She advocates parental involvement in a minor's pregnancy, regardless of the girl's intention to carry or terminate the pregnancy. Parental involvement, Collett maintains, is not punitive; rather, it offers the girl herself additional protection against injury and sexual assault. Minors tend to have less access to information and education than adults; without this information and education, they are not able to provide truly "informed" consent, concludes Collett. Planned Parenthood Federation of America, Inc., the oldest and largest reproductive health organization in the United States, argues that parental notification and consent laws keep girls from exercising their legal right to access abortion. Notifying parents of their daughter's intent to terminate a pregnancy puts many girls at risk for severe punishment, expulsion from the home, or even physical violence. Planned Parenthood contends that, just as minors have the power to give their consent for other surgical procedures, they should be able to give their own consent to terminate a pregnancy.

Joan Biskupic, legal affairs correspondent for *USA Today*, discusses both the personal challenges for same-gender couples attempting to adopt in states that are not friendly to them, and provides an update of legal issues and options available to lesbian and gay couples, indicating a changing tide of acceptance toward couples of the same gender, as well as lesbian and gay individuals, adopting children. Timothy J. Dailey, senior research fellow at the Center for Marriage and Family Studies, provides an overview of state laws pertaining to adoption by lesbian or gay parents. He points to studies showing that children do much better in family settings that include both a mother and a father, and that the sexual behaviors same-sex parents engage in make them, by definition, inappropriate role models for children.

UNIT 4   TWENTY-FIRST CENTURY SEXUALITY ISSUES   223

Stephen O. Watters shares personal experiences of several women whose marriages have been unsatisfying and who have sought connection with men online. He argues that the type of connection people can establish via the Internet can be extremely powerful, and that the significance of these relationships can be just as damaging to a marriage as a live affair—perhaps even more so, since these online sexual relationships can, he says, lead to an addiction. CBSNEWS.com reports that while Internet relationships may not be healthy for a relationship, they are not the same thing as, and should not be equated with, an actual affair. A sexual relationship maintained only in print is nowhere near as intense as a relationship that is consummated in person.

Counselor and nurse Kathy Labriola argues that our society has a very limited view of what can be seen as "healthy" when it comes to relationship structures by offering several possible models of non-traditional relationships involving various relationship compositions. If society did not exclusively sanction the heterosexual monogamous marriage as the ideal relationship structure, more people would realize that they have other options and potentially have more fulfilling relationships. Stanley Kurtz, a writer and senior fellow at the Ethics and Public Policy Center, argues against what he sees as some people's passivity to the reality of open relationships by discussing the Netherlands in which plural marriage is allowed. He believes that same-sex marriage is wrong, will lead to the acceptance of plural marriage, and that the institution of marriage as a whole will disintegrate.

Professor of law Anthony D'Amato highlights statistics from the most recent National Crime Victimization Survey that demonstrate a correlation between the increased consumption of pornography over the years with the decreased incidence of rape. Some people, he argues, watch pornography in order to push any desire to rape out of their minds, and thus have no further desire to go out and actually do it. Judith Reisman president of the Institute for Media Education, asserts that sex criminals imitate what they see depicted in the media, providing examples of serial rapists and killers who had large stores of pornography in their possession, and research in which approximately 33% of rapists said that they had viewed pornography immediately prior to at least one of their rapes.

Journalist and medical writer Bob Roehr believes that the 30-year blood donation policy that continues to ban men who have sex with other men is irrational, because it discriminates based on a behavior, not on risk factors. Why, for example, is a heterosexual woman who has unprotected intercourse with many male partners is allowed to donate blood but a man who is in a monogamous relationship with only one other man in which they use condoms consistently is not? Dr. Marc Germain, medical director of microbiology and epidemiology at Héma-Québec, and Graham Sher, chief executive officer of the Canadian Blood Services, cite data that show a small increase in risk of transmitting HIV between men who have sex with other men, and that even this small increase merits restricting who can donate blood in order to serve the safety of the greater society. The expectation of the people receiving a blood donation that their blood will be disease-free outweighs, they say, the rights of those who are seen as high risk for HIV and other transfusion-transmitted diseases.

Sherry F. Colb, columnist and law professor, uses a case study involving a statutory rape case to raise concerns about whether rape and assault cases would be prosecuted sufficiently without statutory rape laws. Although not perfect, statutory rape laws can be assets in such cases as when the older partner denies the rape occurred or denies any responsibility for a resulting pregnancy or infection. Marc Tunzi, a family physician, believes that statutory rape laws are ineffective because people can get around them too easily. These laws, he argues, require that an otherwise healthy relationship between two people of different ages be criminalized, solely because there is some kind of sexual activity involved. As a result, medical and other licensed professionals do not want to break up these relationships that, in their professional opinion, are not problematic solely because of the age difference between the two partners.

Introduction

The Different Voices of Debate

Elizabeth Schroeder, EdD, MSW
Professional Trainer/Consultant

The Taking Sides series asks readers to evaluate opposing viewpoints on specific topics. In some settings, readers will be asked to respond either verbally or in writing to a particular viewpoint. In other settings, readers will simply evaluate an issue on their own, examining their own values and beliefs as they pertain to each topic. Regardless of how you will be using this volume, it is important to reflect on the ways in which we can express our opinions effectively. It is also important to be aware of how language is used to express these views, at times clearly revealing the politics behind an argument and at other times cleverly obscuring the political agenda. Finally, it is vital to reflect on how differences of opinion affect our lives—in particular, when these differences involve issues relating to family and personal relationships.

Negotiation Versus Debate: Finding a Place on the Continuum

The most successful negotiations are between people of opposing viewpoints who are able to be flexible, compromising to the extent that they believe they can while still remaining true to the goals of the particular negotiation process. We see this in the workplace when an employee is requesting a higher salary. We see this in educational settings when a student disagrees with an instructor's assessment of a paper or project. We see this globally in the international peace process. A supervisor may say, "I can't give you a 10 percent raise, but I can give you 5 percent." An instructor may not be able to raise a student's grade, but may be willing to offer the student an extra-credit assignment. A leader of one country may not be able to offer as much land to the leader of another country, but may be able to offer an increase in import/export relations. Both sides in any negotiation know how much power it has to leverage. If both sides have done their homework, they know how much the other has to leverage, as well.

Progress cannot be made, and a conclusion cannot be reached, without both sides giving in at least a little. When either side interprets "a little" to be "too much," the tendency is to shut down—to retreat to a less flexible vantage point in order to protect whatever advances may have already been made. In addition, as in a poker game, there is often an amount of forcing one's hand that goes on from either side. The same employee may say that she has a job offer from another company that can pay the 10 percent increase, thereby forcing her current employer to decide whether to meet her demands. A student may have a comparable assignment written by a classmate that received a higher grade, thereby revealing instructor bias against the student. A leader of one country can issue an ultimatum to a leader of another country. All of these are examples of negotiations.

A debate, however, is quite different. The most successful debates are between people who have diametrically opposing views on a given subject, and who are well versed in their opponents viewpoint. An absolutist view, with no room for questioning one's tenets or beliefs, may be judged as inflexible in social circles, yet is quite effective when one is involved in a debate. Political candidates, for example, emphasize this quite well during a campaign. A candidate who is clear and consistent in her viewpoints will be likely to be seen as a clear and consistent policymaker. A candidate who changes his mind on one or more issues is often accused of "waffling." As a society we want to hear that another person has made up her or his mind and intends to stay true to her or his word. Otherwise, we do not feel that we can trust that person.

It can be helpful to think of how people express their views in terms of a continuum. At one end of this continuum are staunchly conservative views, at the other are steadfast liberal views. In the center are what can be considered to be moderate views. It is important to note a few things about this continuum concept. First, there are many lines between liberal and moderate, and there are many between moderate and conservative. This means, for example, that not all people who identify themselves as liberal agree with everything that might be outlined in a liberal agenda. Second, how we label our own views may be different from how others label us. It is important to note the difference between a person's views and a person's identity. A person may identify with a particular political ideology or party, yet hold views that may not match those of that ideology or party. For example, a person can have moderate views about social policies, liberal views about government involvement, and conservative views about financial issues. Third, everything is relative. One person may be seen as moderate until someone more conservative comes along. The first person may then be seen as liberal rather than moderate. Finally, expressing views from a particular ideology can have both positive and negative consequences, depending on the audience in front of which one airs these views.

Desire and Reality: The "Should Be" Versus the "Is"

In debate, there is an inherent concept about which we are often not even aware—the "should be" versus the "is." Simply put, the "should be" is what we would like the outcome to be in a particular situation. The "is" refers to what the current state of that situation truly is.

We express our views in terms of what we think is, or would be, best. When this reflects the reality of a given situation, it is thought to be congruent with the "is"—or what is actually happening. However, "congruent" is not synonymous with "right." For example if a person were to say, "I think that only men should be president of the United States," his opinion would be congruent with the current reality. A viewpoint can often carry additional weight because the opposing viewpoint, that a woman should be president, has never happened and may not happen for some time. As a result, the "underdog" opinion is often seen as less valid or lacking in strength. Do not fall into this trap! Compelling arguments that are based in sound logic can gain widespread support and can have the power to change society. A little over 80 years ago women could not vote. Forty years ago an interracial couple would never have considered holding hands in public. Thirty years ago (and for some, still today) a same-sex couple risked losing family, friends, and their lives by publicly sharing their relationship status with others. In these and other cases, people arguing for the "should be" overthrew the people supporting the "is"—much to some people's delight, and to others' chagrin.

Basically, the "is" should not trump the "should be"—nor should it trump the "was." You may have heard someone argue a point based solely in past experience, explaining that if something "has always been this way," it should not change. Many of us have had the experience of parents or grandparents beginning a statement with, "In my day, we. . . ." It is tempting to discount these statements as outdated or otherwise inapplicable—yet it is important to remember that our values and beliefs are based very strongly and solidly in how we were raised. Our "was," as it were.

An example of the whole "should be" versus "is" debate centers around abstinence-only-unless-married education and comprehensive sexuality education, a topic that is discussed in this volume. Each side of the argument has a vehement "should be" that must be measured against the common "is" of our society. Consider the "should be" beliefs and expectations within each viewpoint as expressed in Table 1.

Interestingly enough, the two sides agree on a number of things:

- Young people should avoid behaviors that put them at risk for contracting sexually transmitted infections.
- Young people should avoid too-early pregnancy.

Table 1

Comprehensive Sexuality Education	Abstinence-Only-Unless-Married Education
• Young people should have access to age-appropriate information about sexuality in order to make well-informed decisions.	• Information about sexuality should focus exclusively on postponing sexual behaviors until a person is married.
• Young people should postpone sex until they are older, but information about contraception should be provided in case they do not.	• Providing information about contraception is the same thing as telling young people that it is okay to have sex.
• Sexual information should include information on a range of behaviors, experiences, and orientations.	• Heterosexuality is the norm and lessons should not be provided that have information about or for lesbian, gay, and bisexual individuals.

- Young people should be able to feel good about themselves, including feeling good about their bodies.
- Young people should be able to say "no" to anything that they do not feel comfortable doing sexually, and avoid pressuring others to do things sexually that they do not wish to do.

Aside from these points, there is much less common ground between the two sides. Each side believes itself to be in the right and the other to be wrong.

Regardless of the viewpoint, here is a sample of an "is" against which both sides need to be measured:

- Approximately three million teenagers contract a new Sexually Transmitted Infection (STI) every year in the United States.
- There are approximately 900,000 teen pregnancies every year in the United States.
- The average age of first intercourse in the United States is 16, depending on the demographics of the young person.

As you can see, neither side's beliefs, whether those on which they may agree or those on which they may disagree, impact the true reality of the world today. This introduces a third and vital concept when debating an argument—the "because."

The "because" is the justification for an argument or viewpoint and is at times regardless of the justification for the opponents' views. This is a fascinating aspect of debate. Quite simply, even though a person may have a strong justification, a listener can choose whether or not to believe that person. For example, comprehensive sexuality education supporters have peer-reviewed studies showing that abstinence-only programs, in their current formats, are ineffective. Their "because" is research—something one might consider to be a persuasive argument. Yet the U.S. government found this research irrelevant and instead has provided hundreds of millions of dollars in funding to programs that teach abstinence-only-until-marriage as the expected norm for all people. This is because the conservative supporters of the abstinence-only movement and many in the government believe that young people *should be* abstinent until marriage because that is the morally "right" thing to do. Thus, a factual "because" does not always carry the weight that a religious or moral "should be" does. Nowhere is this seen more clearly than when debating issues of family and personal relationships.

Recognizing the Language of Political Viewpoints

Oftentimes, we will read or listen to an opinion that we may believe to be mainstream, but that is actually coming from either conservative or liberal ideology. How do we sort through the language to know whose viewpoint we are actually reading? If we are reading a piece on the Internet that is written by a particular organization, selecting the "who we are" or "about us" link will often reveal conservative ideology that is based on religious teachings. When this language talks explicitly about God or Christianity, for example, the bias of the group is clear. However, there is more subtle language that also tends to express a conservative ideology. For example, a group whose mission operates around "concern for the American family," who "champions marriage and family as the foundation of civilization," who talks about being "pro-family" and its opponents as being "pro-abortion," who discusses "traditional American values," and who identifies itself as "pro-life" is most likely going to represent more conservative viewpoints.

A group whose ideology is more liberal will use language reflecting its views, as well. If the group's mission uses language that consists of having the "right to choose," protecting people's "civil rights," helping people "make informed and responsible decisions," and if it identifies itself as "pro-choice" and its opponents as "anti-choice," chances are it is more mainstream to liberal. Organizations that talk about "empowering women" and "religious freedom" will also be more likely to be seen as liberal.

This is important to note. Being identified as a particular ideology, regardless of whether that person identifies that way, can pigeonhole a person. Just as an actor who plays a particular role over and over again can become typecast, a person who uses certain language may be labeled as liberal or conservative and can have certain opinions attributed to her or him. A good example of this is the nonprofit organization, People for the American Way. Based on the descriptions and language examples discussed earlier, one might hear or read this organization's name and assume that it is conservative. However, it is much more liberal, focusing on freedom and democracy for all people living in the United States. This is why it is vital to separate the message from the person unless that person identifies her or himself in a particular way.

The Language of Debate Around Family and Personal Relationships

Discussing family and personal relationships, and the issues surrounding each, is much different from talking about one's favorite sports player, preferred political candidate, or any other topic. The word *family* itself is loaded, meaning different things to different people. "Personal" relationships involve people. Discussing family and personal relationships, therefore, is by definition more personal. As a result, people often debate topics from a visceral rather than an intellectual viewpoint, with the lines between the two occasionally being blurred. Inherent in debates about family and personal relationships are morals and values, which make any debate more challenging than one that is based on facts. Morals and values are rooted for many people in spiritual and religious beliefs. Once a higher being or entity enters the picture, ideologies shift. An argument that begins with "I think" will carry different weight from one that begins with "the church says," or "Buddha teaches us," or "according to the Torah," or anything else that is faith-based.

When you read the word *family,* what image comes to your mind? Some will see their own family, whether that is their family of origin or their current family system. Others will see a family as it may have been or as it is currently being portrayed in the media. Still others will see a family within the context of how it is defined in their religious settings. The definition of the word *family* is quite clear to some and much more diverse to others. In fact, if you were to ask different individuals what the word *family* means to them, you would very likely receive a number of different answers. However, when you are watching the news or listening to a political debate and the word *family* is tossed around, it is almost certain that the definition of family is quite clear: It is a man and a woman, legally married, with one or more children, living together in the same household. Some newscasters and politicians may have the parenthetical concept in their head about the religion of the ideal family, as well as the family's cultural or ethnic makeup.

For other people, those who were raised by a single parent, by an adult or adults who were other members of their family but not their own parents, by adoptive parents, by lesbian or gay parents, or by any other significant adult or adults, the use of the word *family* means something altogether different. Therefore, it is interesting to note that even with so much diversity of individuals, experience, and family systems, we still have a societal assumption in the United States that when someone in public discourse uses the word *family*, it is still within the context of a two-parent, one-or-more-child context—another social "should be" that does not always match the "is".

Among the ways in which Merriam-Webster's Collegiate Dictionary defines a family are:

a group of individuals living under one roof and usually under one head

a group of persons of common ancestry

a group of people united by certain convictions or a common affiliation

the basic unit in society traditionally consisting of two parents rearing their own or adopted children; *also:* any of various social units differing from but regarded as equivalent to the traditional family, [such as] a single-parent family

These definitions are similar, yet make interesting distinctions within each variation. Clearly, each of these definitions conveys values. It is up to the reader, however, to determine what that value is. For example, in the first definition it is implied that there is one leader in a family. Although the gender of that person is not specified, our society often makes the assumption that this is a male since the accompanying assumption is that the ideal home (the "should be" home) would have a mother and a father as parents. Yet later, an additional definition refers to "two parents" raising children. Once again, the gender or genders of the parents are not specified, yet we still make assumptions based on experience, values, and ideals. How interesting that one word can be defined in so many ways, simultaneously reflecting such different values within each definition.

Similarly, when someone refers to a relationship, what comes to mind for you? Is this a romantic relationship? If so, who are the people involved?

Merriam-Webster's offers these definitions of relationship:

the relation connecting or binding participants in a relationship; kinship; a romantic or passionate attachment

For some people, a relationship equals marriage, or a courtship that has marriage as its eventual outcome. For others, a relationship does not include marriage because the couple chooses not to marry. For others, a relationship does not include marriage because marriage is not legally available to them. As with the word *family,* the word *relationship* can conjure up different values for different individuals.

Conclusion

Regardless of the ideology we espouse of the language we use in expressing this ideology, our arguments must have reason behind them. Many people can recall asking for a reason why they had to do something their parents said and receiving the infuriating response, "Because I said so." This response worked solely because of the power difference between parent and child. However, two people who are closer in age and debating a topic should much more thoroughly explore their reasons.

For some, "I think" or "I believe" will suffice. Others will justify their arguments from an experiential standpoint, as in, "I have learned from my 15 years as a public school teacher that . . ." Some people need simply to identify themselves within a category; for example, as a father of two or as a bisexual womam. Still others will use religion and religious doctrine, as mentioned earlier. For some, the New Testament, Qu'ran, Torah, or other religious text is brought out to "trump" any other argument, challenging one's opponents to argue with God—or, at least, with the debater's definition of God. A Christian will be more likely to discount an argument that is based on the teachings of the Qu'ran than one that is based on the teachings of the New Testament because it is not congruent with her or his beliefs. Still others do not take religious texts literally, instead they interpret them within the context of daily life.

No matter what we believe, we must listen to people whose views are different from our own. We need to think before expressing ourselves. We need to do so confidently, yet respectfully.

Mother Teresa was quoted as saying, "Peace and war begin at home. If we truly want peace in the world, let us begin by loving one another in our own families. If we want to spread joy, we need for every family to have joy." She did not define family, nor did she define joy. Yet each person who reads this quote will have a different picture in her or his mind of exactly what a family is and what kind of joy would create peace. As you read this volume, you will see that the issues that relate to family and personal relationships are far-reaching and diverse. Family and interpersonal relationships are not exclusively about what goes on at home—they are about what happens in the legislature, in court rooms, in our communities, in the bedroom, in the United Nations, and beyond. Emotions run high when discussing family and personal relationships. Watch carefully, and you will see how often emotion, rather than intellect, dictates the course of these discussions.

Internet References . . .

National Adoption Center

The National Adoption Center works to expand adoption opportunities for children living in foster care throughout the United States, and to be a resource to families and to agencies who seek the permanency of caring homes for children.

http://www.adopt.org

National Association of Black Social Workers

The National Association of Black Social Workers was established in 1968 to "advocate and address important social issues that impact the health and welfare of the Black community." Their affiliate chapters, including student chapters, are spread throughout the United States.

http://www.nabsw.org

National Home Education Network

The National Home Education Network (NHEN) works to encourage and facilitate the grassroots efforts of state and local home-schooling organizations and individuals by providing information, fostering networking, and promoting public relations on a national level. The NHEN supports "the freedom of all individual families to choose home education and to direct such education."

http://www.nhen.org/

National Association of Social Workers

The National Association of Social Workers (NASW) is the largest membership organization of professional social workers in the world. NASW works to enhance the professional growth and development of its members, to create and maintain professional standards, and to advance sound social policies.

http://www.naswdc.org

Parental Decision Making: What's Best for Children . . . Or What's Best for Parents?

*U*se of the oft-quoted "it takes a village to raise a child" is still met with understanding, thoughtful nods as we appreciate the concept that many people beyond the family structure play key roles in raising children. There are, however, numerous factors that contribute to, interfere with, detract from, and otherwise affect how parents raise their children. Parenting styles vary. The so-called village includes the government, which is met with open arms by some, and skepticism and mistrust by others. This section examines five questions that society often asks relating to parenting issues:

- Is It Ever Appropriate to Spank a Child?

- Should Adoptive Parents Adopt Only within Their Own Racial/Ethnic Group?

- Does Divorce Create Long-Term Negative Effects for Children?

- Should Parents Homeschool Their Children?

- Do Mothers Who Work Outside of the Home Have a Negative Effect on Their Children?

ISSUE 1

Is It Ever Appropriate to Spank a Child?

YES: Walter L. Larrimore, from "Is Spanking Actually Harmful to Children?" *Focus on the Family* (Focus on the Family, 2002)

NO: Irwin A. Hyman, from *The Case Against Spanking: How to Discipline Your Child Without Hitting* (Jossey-Bass, 1997)

ISSUE SUMMARY

YES: Walter L. Larrimore, vice president of medical outreach at Focus on the Family, explains that parents have always spanked their children, and believes that what we see in the media are only examples of times when parents have become abusive rather than using spanking appropriately.

NO: Irwin A. Hyman, director of the National Center for Study of Corporal Punishment and Alternatives, argues that there is never any reason to hit a child. Focusing on the emotional effects of spanking, he asserts that spanking is much more likely to teach children to tolerate and perpetuate violence than it is to correct disobedience.

While a number of European countries have completely outlawed corporal punishment at home and at school, spanking one's child is legal in the United States. The laws in each state are different, but the recurring theme is that it is for the parent, guardian, or teacher to determine what their boundaries are.

According to the American Academy of Pediatrics, spanking is a commonly used disciplinary technique, with more than 90 percent of parents in the United States spanking their child or children at least once over the course of a given year. Yet public opinion about spanking is equally divided, and it is a topic that continues to be hotly debated by parents, young people, teachers, and policymakers alike.

Anti-spanking proponents call spanking child abuse—even child sexual abuse, based on the fact that spankings tend to be delivered to the buttocks. Murray Straus, co-director of the Family Research Laboratory at the University of New Hampshire in Durham, explains that whether spanking is child abuse under the law tends to be determined by the extent of the physical damage done. Therefore, an open-handed swat to the buttocks would be equivalent to a crack on the knuckles with a wooden hairbrush—as long as neither caused the child to require medical attention.

When it comes to legislating the rights of parents, our country is also divided. One court case in Massachusetts involved a man who felt he had biblical justification for hitting his son with a belt. While doing so did not break Massachusetts state law, social services removed the child from his home because they believed that his father's disciplinary actions could place him at risk for future injury. The man appealed this decision, saying that this removal violated his right to raise his son according to his religious beliefs. In Michigan, a man was arrested for spanking his girlfriend's four-year-old daughter and was charged with fourth degree child abuse. He struck her backside three times, and then again three times about a half hour later when she continued the disobedient behavior.

Opponents to spanking cite research demonstrating that children who are punished physically are more likely to be aggressive to others, including their own children once they become parents themselves. Concerns have been raised about the effects spanking can have on a child's emotional development and on his or her future ability to relate to others in intimate relationships.

Other experts believe that the anti-spanking research and equating spanking to child abuse blows the issue completely out of proportion. They maintain that there is a difference between spanking and child abuse—between a disciplinary measure that is controlled, delivered with love, and clearly explained to a child as the consequence of disobedient behavior, and beating a child out of anger or frustration. Pro-spanking advocates also cite research in order to show that spanking can be an effective disciplinary tactic without negatively affecting a child's emotional development or creating a greater tolerance for aggression. If the child knows and understands that she or he is loved, then the negative effects of spanking are minimized.

As you read these selections, think about how each author presents his viewpoint. Do you feel that each has sufficiently refuted the other? Think about your own experience of growing up as a child. How does that affect how you respond to each viewpoint? If you are strongly opposed to spanking, are there any circumstances under which you believe that a spanking is ever justified? If you believe that spanking is an effective disciplinary tactic, are there any conditions you would want to place on the type of spanking or how it is delivered?

Another point to think about is how and whether our local and federal governments should be involved on legislating parental behavior. A few years ago, the city of Oakland, California, recently voted down a resolution to make the entire state a "no-spanking zone." Should similar legislations be introduced in other states? Or should the government stay away from the family unit?

In the following selections, Irwin Hyman provides bullet-point summaries of the more than 30 years of research highlighting the harmful effects of spanking. He explains that, in addition to the physical and emotional harm to the child, spanking also perpetuates racism, classism, and sexism on a societal level. Walter Larrimore cautions readers to not jump to conclusions about the effectiveness of corporal punishment based on limited and, in his opinion, greatly flawed research. He further mentions research that demonstrates that spanking is not harmful to children, as long as it is administered in appropriate ways.

YES

Walter L. Larrimore

Is Spanking Actually Harmful to Children?

We've all seen the surveillance tape. Madelyne Gorman Toogood exits the department store. She looks around to see if anyone is watching and then begins to shake and pummel her 4-year-old daughter inside the car, hidden from the camera's view. We can't get it out of our heads. And can't really believe that any parent would do such a thing.

Incidents like this beg the question: should a reasonable and civilized country ban parental spanking?

Psychologist Elizabeth Thompson Gershoff of the National Center for Children in Poverty at Columbia University recently analyzed 88 studies involving corporal punishment, spanning 62 years of collected data, and concluded corporal punishment encourages negative behaviors in children.

But what if a medical study were released on the dangers of eating apples, and media outlets nationwide championed the banishment of oranges instead? Wouldn't that be absurd? Well, apples are magically being turned into oranges when it comes to the subject of child discipline.

However, Gershoff's study (and, for that matter, the Toogood incident) is *not* about spanking. It was about corporal punishment—of which spanking is only a small subset. Corporal punishment includes spanking along with many forms of training or discipline that are *inappropriate*. Children in some of Gershoff's analyzed studies, as in the Toogood case, were beaten or slapped. In other studies children were abused with sticks or injured in other ways. In fact, 65 percent of the studies included overly severe punishment.

Since the Gershoff study was released, it has grown into another anti-spanking tantrum by virtually every major media outlet. Headlines emblazoned across papers have touted breakthrough news on the negative effects of *spanking*. Apples suddenly turned into oranges.

Is it any surprise to anyone that child abuse and severe punishment would be associated with negative outcomes? Of course not. Any civilized parent would be shocked by these types of abuse, as most Americans are shocked by Mrs. Toogood's apparent actions. But this is a far cry from judiciously used mild spanking employed by many, if not most, loving parents. The excessive punishment of some misguided, angry or cruel parents should not become an argument to not discipline at all.

Not only was Gershoff's work misrepresented, many articles ignored reports countering Gershoff's review, including one by a prominent trio of researchers that was published in the same edition of the Psychological Bulletin of the American Psychological Association. The group, including two researchers from the University of California at Berkley and one from the University of Nebraska, concluded "the evidence presented in Gershoff's (review) does not justify a blanket injunction against mild to moderate disciplinary spanking."

What is appropriate spanking? The issue is not whether parents should spank, but how they spank. An important scientific conference defined spanking as physically non-injurious, intended to modify behavior, and administered to the extremities or buttocks. We would add that such discipline is never administered in anger. Used with children from approximately 18 months to 6 years of age (never later than puberty), spanking has been shown to be effective, especially when used *in conjunction with* other forms of discipline, such as time-outs, reasoning and other disciplinary tools.

Further, when studies that isolate mild spanking from abusive behaviors are analyzed, results have proven repeatedly that the practice is not harmful. Why have we not seen these findings reported in the press?

Proper spanking is often a necessary tool in parenting. Studies have shown an increase in child abuse in homes where appropriate spanking does *not* occur, as eliminating spanking takes away a strong, useful and suitable tool from a parent. Equating appropriate spanking with punishment that includes child abuse is inaccurate, unfair and misleads parents who are striving to properly raise their children.

Based upon the best evidence available, we would support the many parents who believe in spanking, when necessary. But we also believe it must be administered wisely and only when appropriate. The evidence does not show that spanking is a disciplinary cure-all.

Not all children need to be spanked, and not all parents should spank their children—especially parents prone to anger, hostility, abuse or outbursts. However, a parent that does not teach that there are consequences to behaviors will leave it to the police and others to do that later in the child's life.

Parents, for millennia, in virtually every recorded culture, have spanked their young children, when necessary, to teach them and to shape and mold their character—to ultimately benefit their children. Now parents are being fed confusing information—apples turned into oranges—by what appear to be anti-spanking advocates. Perhaps some discipline is in order for those guilty of fictionalized reporting.

Irwin A. Hyman  **NO**

Why We Hit and What
It Does to Kids

There is much debate about the actual effects of corporal punishment. These debates center on issues of age at the time of hitting, the force with which children are hit, and the effects on long-term behavior and personality development. Rather than bore you with numerous statistics, arguments about the validity of various studies, and the fine points of each debate, I will summarize what I believe are the major effects of corporal punishment on children. But first let me share with you the results of a recent and very important scientific conference on spanking.

In February 1996, I was fortunate to be a part of a panel of experts convened by the American Academy of Pediatrics, with support from New York's Montefiore Medical Center and the U. S. Maternal and Child Health Bureau, to develop a consensus statement about the short- and long-term consequences of corporal punishment. Sharing the panel with me were distinguished social scientists and physicians representing both sides of the spanking issue. Despite heated debate and some slippage into rhetoric reflecting personal biases, we were able to produce a final statement of compromise with which we could all live. The individual papers and the consensus statement are published in a supplement to *Pediatrics*. Despite our care in crafting an objective statement of our findings, the results will most likely be distorted in the media.

In essence, the thirteen-point statement released by the group refers to spanking as defined as the use of an opened hand on the extremities or buttocks that is physically noninjurious. I believe force which causes redness, soreness or bruising is injurious and would not be acceptable to most members of the group. While the group admitted that there was little pro or con scientific evidence on the spanking of two- to five-year-olds, there was agreement that surveys and studies of older children suggest that spanking is not advisable. Even the researchers in favor of spanking admitted that noncorporal methods of discipline have been shown to be effective with children of all ages, that prevention of misbehavior should be stressed, that excessive spanking is one of many risk factors for poor outcomes in the lives of children, and that parents should never spank in anger. This may be an oxymoron, since studies of spankers and spankees indicate that some level of anger is almost always associated with spankings. Finally, the group rejected spanking and paddling in schools.

While the prospankers interpret the lack of research on the harmful effects of spanking with preschoolers as proof that it is OK, I disagree and maintain that there is no reason to ever hit a child. My summary of the research and clinical experience over 30 years follows:

- Corporal punishment should not be used in schools, since there is convincing evidence that it is a significant contributing factor to emotional, legal, and social problems.
- Frequent and harsh spanking is consistently found to be present in the lives of boys who are aggressive and disobedient, who lie, cheat, are destructive with their own and others' belongings, and who associate with friends prone to delinquency.
- Frequent and harsh spanking can cause young children to bottle up their feelings of fear, anger, and hostility. In later life these children are unusually prone to suicidal thoughts, suicide, and depression.
- Despite the age or gender of the child, the family's social class or ethnicity, whether the child was hit frequently or rarely, severely or mildly, whether there were high or low levels of interaction and affection in the home, and regardless of the degree to which specific situational variables may have mitigated the effects of the punishment, spanking consistently contributes to lowered self-esteem.
- In toddlers, many punitive approaches, including spanking, do not result in compliance, but end simply with the administration of punishment. (Studies show that preschoolers who are hit are more likely to be more impulsive and aggressive than those who are not spanked. Furthermore, toddlers can be taught, using behavioral techniques such as associating their word for pain with the street or electrical outlets, to avoid those dangerous situations. Childproofing the house and monitoring toddlers will avoid the so-called necessity of spanking to teach children to avoid danger.)
- Children who are physically punished are more likely to grow up approving of it and using it to settle interpersonal conflicts. Even children who have experienced "normal" spankings are almost three times as likely to have seriously assaulted a sibling, compared to children who were not physically disciplined.
- Contrary to popular belief, studies of corporal punishment in schools indicate that it is not used as a last resort. In fact, it is too often the first punishment for nonviolent and minor misbehaviors. Beatings for minor misbehaviors can cause many stress symptoms in children.
- Younger children are hit most often; spanking slowly decreases until late adolescence. This contributes to feelings of helplessness, humiliation, and resentment that may lead to withdrawal or aggression toward caregivers.
- Boys are hit much more frequently than girls, thereby sustaining sexual stereotypes.
- In schools, minority and poor white children receive "lickings" four to five times more frequently than middle- and upper-class white children. This contributes to racism and classism in our society.

- Regional comparisons show that the highest proportion of corporal punishment in America occurs in states in the South and Southwest. Florida, Texas, Arkansas, and Alabama have consistently been among the leaders in the frequency of hitting schoolchildren. It is unreasonable and unfair that children's location should determine the degree to which they may be legally victimized.
- Corporally punished schoolchildren, especially those with emotional and academic disabilities, have suffered all types of injuries including welts, hematomas, damage to almost all external and many internal body parts, and death.
- Studies demonstrate that eliminating corporal punishment does not increase misbehavior in home or school. Systematic use of positive alternatives, however, has been shown to decrease misbehavior significantly.

POSTSCRIPT

Is It Ever Appropriate
to Spank a Child?

The term "spare the rod, spoil the child" has been used throughout history to justify corporal punishment of children. In the 1960s and 1970s, spanking was not only widely practiced, it could be delivered by any adult with authority over a child—whether the adult was the child's family member, teacher, house-keeper or babysitter, or the parent of a child's friend. The assumption was that adults, across the board, knew what was inappropriate behavior, and had the right to intervene as necessary.

There are many rules children must live by as they negotiate through childhood. However, problems arise when children receive conflicting messages about these rules. A child may overhear a parent using profanity, then be confused when he is punished for using it himself. A child might watch her parent smoke and ask why she cannot. And a child may not understand why he is being punished for hitting another child by being spanked himself. Parents can justify many of the rules that are necessary to impose upon a child to ensure her or his safety, particularly when a child asks to do an "adult" behavior, such as smoke cigarettes or speak freely. However, "Do as I say, not as I do" and "Because I say so," are not sufficient explanations for the child. Parents must provide consistent lessons, including explaining why a rule is being enforced. They should acknowledge that, indeed, some rules may not feel fair—but that they must be adhered to all the same. Providing explanations does not rule out appropriate strictness in parenting. However, rules are much more effective when delivered by parents who model these rules themselves.

Regardless of one's viewpoint, this issue is a highly personal one. A great deal of this debate centers around one's own experiences. Some pro-spanking proponents will say, "I was spanked as a child, and it didn't hurt me at all." Others remember the fear and humiliation of spankings without any recollection whatsoever of what they did to deserve them. While the frequency of corporal punishment has been decreasing over the years, there are many more discussions that need to take place about this highly sensitive topic.

ISSUE 2

Should Adoptive Parents Adopt Only within Their Own Racial/Ethnic Group?

YES: Leslie Doty Hollingsworth, from "Promoting Same-Race Adoption for Children of Color," *Social Work* (vol. 43, no. 2, 1998)

NO: Ezra E. H. Griffith and Rachel L. Bergeron, from "Cultural Stereotypes Die Hard: The Case of Transracial Adoption," *The Journal of the American Academy of Psychiatry and the Law* (vol. 34, no. 3, 2006)

ISSUE SUMMARY

YES: Leslie Doty Hollingsworth, an associate professor of social work at the University of Michigan, offers a history of transracial adoption that has involved primarily white adoptive parents and Black or African American children. She argues that children are best served if they are adopted by families of their same racial background, and that systematic changes—such as adoption services and programs were better geared towards adults of color—would enable more families to adopt children from their own backgrounds.

NO: Ezra Griffith and Rachel Bergeron, both faculty members of the Yale University School of Medicine's psychiatry department, argue that requiring racial and ethnic matching, while an appropriate effort, would leave too many children of color languishing in the foster and adoption systems. By maintaining that only in-race adoption is the best and ideal situation, they ask rhetorically, does our society actually do more to reinforce cultural stereotypes or to truly serve children needing homes?

T he practice of adopting children is nothing new; adoptions have been documented in the United States going back to the late nineteenth century. In the twentieth century, international adoptions in the United States increased at the end of World War II, a logical response to the number of children orphaned when families were uprooted or eradicated by the war's violence. This increase was also documented after the Korean and Vietnam wars, and more recently as violence continues to mar various countries world-wide and the number of children needing homes grows.

This means that many of the adults who have adopted and are currently adopting children are from a different racial or ethnic group than their adoptive children. In the most recent U.S. census, just over 17 percent of the adopted children under age 18 had adoptive parents of a different racial background than theirs (www.census.gov/prod/cen2000/doc/sf3.pdf).

While adoption as a practice is much less stigmatized today, adopting children outside of one's own racial or ethnic group remains controversial. Some believe that raising a child in a family outside of the child's racial group impedes the child from forming a healthy identity and from coping effectively in the world. In 1972, in response to the increase in transracial adoptions, the National Association of Black Social Workers (NABSW) produced a resolution stating, in part, that "[B]lack children belong physically and psychologically and culturally in black families where they can receive the total sense of them-selves and develop a sound projection of their future. Only a black family can transmit the emotional and sensitive subtleties of perceptions and reactions essential for a black child's survival in a racist society." While this statement is specifically about Black and African American children, the National Associa-tion of Social Workers (NASW)'s 2003 position statement about foster care and adoption includes all racial and ethnic backgrounds. Others argue that love is the most important component of any family, that parents of any racial or ethnic background can invest time and resources to teach their children about their racial or ethnic heritage and history, and connect them with social supports to ensure that their children integrate whatever identity best fits them. It is better, these individuals argue, to give a child a home, regardless of the different racial or ethnic backgrounds of the family members, than to let a child languish in foster care. Another controversial aspect about this debate is that these same individuals argue that there is an implicit bias in the NABSW and NASW guidelines; that they assume an adoptive family that is white; there are no guidelines or discussions around placing white children with families of color.

In the following selections, Leslie Doty Hollingsworth emphasizes the importance of placing children in families of the same racial background as theirs as the only way of truly providing the child with an opportunity to develop a solid, clear racial identity. Ezra Griffith and Rachel Bergeron cite research demonstrating, they assert, that children of transracial adoptions can develop strong identities and high self-esteem, the difference between their and their family's backgrounds notwithstanding.

YES ⬅

Leslie Doty Hollingsworth

Promoting Same-Race Adoption for Children of Color

Opponents of policies to protect same-race adoption for children of color assert that it is necessary to lift all restrictions on transracial adoption (alternately referred to as "interracial," "interethnic," or "transethnic" adoption) of the many children of color believed to be "languishing" in foster homes, residential programs, and institutional settings. This article briefly presents the history of the transracial adoption controversy and discusses its current status; counters assertions typically used to oppose same-race adoption policies for children of color; summarizes the positions of several social work organizations regarding adoption and race; and makes recommendations for education, policy, research, and practice.

History of Transracial Adoption

The adoption of orphaned children from other countries by U.S. families began in the 1940s with the end of World War II (Simon & Alstein, 1977). A rise in the number of such adoptions accompanied later wars, including the Korean and Vietnam Wars (Silverman, 1993). In the 1960s, widespread use of artificial birth control, the legalization of abortion, and decreased social stigma associated with bearing a child outside of marriage were accompanied by a substantial decrease in healthy white infants available for adoption. There was, however, no corresponding decrease among African American and other children of color (although foreign countries began to establish rules that limited some adoptions in those countries).

It has been suggested that adoption agencies, feeling the pressure of reduced fee income, found in the availability of children of color an opportunity to increase adoption fees (McRoy, 1989). One writer (Bartholet, 1991) suggested that as the United States became accustomed to children of color from other countries in its communities, it became easier to accept the transracial adoption of African American children. By 1971 transracial adoptions had reached an annual high of 2,574 (Simon & Alstein, 1987). Responding to this increase, a 1972 meeting of the National Association of Black Social Workers (NABSW)

From *Social Work*, Vol. 42, Issue 2, 1998, pp. 104–116. Copyright © 1998 by NASW Press. Reprinted by permission.

ended with a resolution opposing transracial adoption:

> Black children belong physically and psychologically and culturally in black families where they can receive the total sense of themselves and develop a sound projection of their future. Only a black family can transmit the emotional and sensitive subtleties of perceptions and reactions essential for a black child's survival in a racist society. Human beings are products of their environment and develop their sense of values, attitudes, and self-concept within their own family structures. Black children in white homes are cut off from the healthy development of themselves as black people. (quoted in McRoy, 1989, p. 150)

In response to that resolution, and to the Indian Child Welfare Act of 1978 giving tribal courts exclusive jurisdiction over American Indian child custody proceedings, some states established policies and procedures limiting transracial adoption and requiring that serious efforts be made to place children of color with adoptive parents of their own racial or ethnic group. Agencies specializing in same-race placements were established, and many traditional agencies modified their programs in the same direction.

Some parents who had adopted transracially were offended, however, by the NABSW resolution, perceiving it as not based in truth and disagreeing with the assertion that they were not capable of parenting their adoptive children of color adequately (Hermann, 1993). White foster parents began to file legal suits to prevent children of color who were in their care from being placed with same-race adoptive parents and to be allowed to adopt the children themselves (Elias, 1991). Advocates of transracial adoption, some of them transracial adoptive parents themselves (Bartholet, 1991; Mahoney, 1991), began to speak and write publicly in its support and in opposition to same-race protective policies. Criticism of protective policies for same-race adoption has included the following assertions:

- that same-race placement policies result in retention of children in foster care for longer than necessary, which may result in delay or denial of placement for children of color and therefore in long-term harm
- that there is no systematic recruitment of white parents to correspond to that of families of color, and therefore families of color are being given unfair advantage
- that same-race policies give families of color an edge in receipt of adoption subsidies, because children of color (whom same-race parents adopt) are eligible for such subsidies by nature of their "special-needs" status
- that agencies apply differential screening criteria to prospective black parents than to prospective white families (such as socioeconomic status, age, and marital status requirements), even though these have not been ruled out as viable criteria for selection
- that empirical studies have been biased toward studying the negative aspects of transracial adoption
- that in spite of such biases, studies have failed to document a negative effect of transracial adoption in areas such as general adjustment and self-esteem and, in some instances, have indicated a possible benefit

with regard to the transracial adoptee's ability to get along with and in a white world
- that there is no empirical support for the contention that parents of color do a better job at socializing their children ethnically
- that racial matching policies are in conflict with antidiscrimination legislation, such as the U.S. Constitution and Title IV of the Civil Rights Act of 1964 (Bartholet, 1991; Mahoney, 1991; National Coalition to End Racism in America's Child Care System, cited in McRoy, 1994).

A result of the opposition to same-race policies has been that "states have begun to reassess their policies which include race as a viable consideration in placement decision making" (National Coalition to End Racism in America's Child Care System, cited in McRoy, 1994). Subsequently, transracial adoptions began to increase in the early 1980s (McRoy, 1989). Bill Pierce, president of the National Council for Adoption, estimated that 12,000 children were transracially adopted in 1992 (Richman, 1993). Accurate national data on the numbers of transracial and same-race adoptions are not available because after 1971 the federal government no longer required states to maintain and report such data.

On December 22, 1995, the U.S. Department of Health and Human Services published final rules implementing the Adoption and Foster Care Analysis and Reporting System, a mandatory system of data collection on all children covered by Title IV-B of the Social Security Act, Section 427 ("Foster Care," 1997). Included are rules requiring states to collect data on all adopted children who were placed by the state child welfare agency or by private agencies under contract with the public child welfare agency. However, national adoption data are not yet available.

The recent increase in transracial adoptions has been influenced by a trend among child welfare agencies toward greater flexibility in eligibility to adopt. Such changes have included less rigidity regarding age, income, housing, family composition, and infertility examination requirements; attempts to make application procedures and agency locations and hours more convenient for prospective adopters; less emphasis on the need for matching the characteristics of child and parent (which may have facilitated same-race placements); a willingness to select single parents or those who already have birth or adopted children; openness to adoption by foster parents, caretakers, and relatives of the child; use of adoption resource exchanges; use of active and ongoing recruitment methods, often using the mass media and featuring specific children; and expansion of adoption subsidy programs (Child Welfare League of America, 1988). Although some of these changes may facilitate same-race adoptions, they have also opened the way for increases in transracial adoptions. People interested in adopting transracially typically either originally desired a white infant or preschool child and became willing to adopt a child of a different race or were the child's foster parents (Child Welfare League of America, 1988).

The Multiethnic Placement Act of 1994 prohibited agencies or entities engaged in adoption or foster care placements that receive federal assistance from "categorically deny[ing] to any person the opportunity to become an adoptive or foster parent, solely on the basis of the race, color, or national origin of the adoptive or foster parent or the child" and "from delay[ing] or deny[ing] the placement of a child solely on the basis of race, color, or national origin of the adoptive or foster parent or parents involved" (p. 4056). However, this law allowed "an agency or entity to which [the preceding applied to] consider the cultural, ethnic, or racial background of the child and the capacity of the prospective foster or adoptive parents to meet the needs of a child of this background as one of a number of factors used to determine the best interests of a child" (p. 4056).

Opponents of same-race protective policies criticized the qualification in the Multiethnic Placement Act that allowed race, culture, and ethnicity to be considered at all and the absence of penalties for failure to conform to the requirements of the act. Advocacy efforts with regard to federal and state adoption policy continued, and in August 1996 legislation was signed that modified the Multiethnic Placement Act of 1994. This legislation, which was enacted as a part of the Small Business Job Protection Act of 1996, had two sections: Section 1807 (Adoption Assistance), which allowed a tax credit to adoptive families with incomes not exceeding $75,000 of up to $5,000 ($6,000 in the case of children with "special needs") annually for qualified adoption expenses, and Section 1808 (Removal of Barriers to Interethnic Adoption), which removed the qualification provided by the earlier act and simply prevented any entity that receives federal funds from denying any person the opportunity to adopt or provide foster care and from delaying or denying the placement of a child on the basis of the race, color, or national origin of the adoptive or foster parent or the child involved.

Alternative Considerations

Given the history of transracial adoption, social workers need to be aware of alternative considerations to those that resulted in the current legislation. Delays in moving children of color out of the out-of-home care system are caused by factors other than restrictions on transracial adoption and can be resolved by actions other than lifting such restrictions. Improvements in six areas would alleviate such delays and lessen the need for transracial adoptions. First, because there are insufficient non-kin foster families of color, policies favoring adoption by foster parents are increasing the numbers of transracial adoptions. Second, there are indications that sufficient numbers of families of color are available to adopt healthy infants of color if such families are sought out and if traditional barriers to adoption are eliminated. Third, many children of color in the child welfare system are not available for adoption or have special needs. Fourth, overrepresentation of children of color in the child welfare system has been linked to disparities in services related to ethnic group. Fifth, children of color may be counted as being in foster placements when they are actually in permanent kinship care. Finally, poverty, which disproportionately affects families of color, has been associated with the abuse and neglect that often result in the out-of-home placement of children.

Policies Favoring Adoption by Foster Parents

Many children of color are placed with non-kin foster families (as many as 52 percent in California, according to Meyer & Link, cited in Barth, Courtney, Berrick, Albert, & Needell, 1994). Barth, Courtney, Berrick, Albert, and Needell noted that among the California children they studied, only two-thirds of African American children were placed in African American foster homes, and only 31 percent of Hispanic children were placed with Hispanic caregivers. (Because the figures for children of color include kinship placements, the actual proportion of placements of children of color with same-race, non-kin foster families is much lower than they found.) In contrast, 92 percent of selected white children in foster homes were placed with white foster families. The researchers noted that "when children were not placed with ethnically similar foster parents, they were almost always placed with Caucasians [and that] nearly one-half of Caucasian foster parents were caring for children of color" (Barth, Courtney, Berrick, Albert, & Needell, 1994, p. 245).

What has come to be known as the "fost adoption" program (Barth, Courtney, Berrick, & Albert, 1994) emerged in the mid-1970s (Meezan & Shireman, 1985) to promote the placement of children in foster homes with the explicit expectation that the foster parents will adopt the child if reunification with the birth parents fails. Before this program was implemented, foster placements were established in such a way that they would interfere neither with the reunification of the child with her or his birth parents nor with the permanent placement of the child in an adoptive home. Foster parents were considered temporary substitutes, and they were urged not to become attached to the child. If they did become attached, the child was often removed to another placement. With the advent of the "fost adoption" program, white foster families began to seek adoption of children of color placed in their homes, sometimes from birth, even when the children were not placed with the intention of their future adoption by those foster parents.

Thus, insufficient numbers of foster families of color reduce the likelihood that children of color will be adopted by a family of their same racial or ethnic group and gives an advantage to transracial placements. There is evidence that even children of mixed racial parentage tend to be confronted with racism or problems of racial identity while they are in placement, and researchers have recommended that these factors be considered in the selection and preparation of potential foster parents (Folaron & Hess, 1993). Increasing the numbers of available foster families of color has the potential, therefore, for increasing same-race adoptive placements (Rezendes, 1994).

Barth, Courtney, Berrick, and Albert (1994) compared children who were adopted within two years of entering foster care with children who remained in foster care for longer than two years before being adopted. Although they found no effect of ethnicity on "the odds of a timely adoption," an item consistently related to length of time until adoption was whether the child welfare worker and the foster family with whom the child was placed planned, at the time of the placement, that the child would be adopted by the family. The authors added, "the fact that an adoption is planned at the time of foster placement or that a child is under one month of age both decrease the odds that a child will stay in foster care more than two years" (p. 167). Because there was no effect for ethnicity, it can be concluded that the effect of age and planned placement occurs for children of color as well as for other children. If the pool of foster parents is less likely to contain foster parents of color, and if adoption plans continue to be made at the point of initial foster placement, especially within the context of the increased restrictions on same-race adoption protective policies, the likelihood that a child of color will be adopted by someone of her or his own race or ethnic group is diminished and the odds of a transracial adoption are increased.

Availability of Adoptive Families of Color

Evidence indicates that the number of families of color who are willing to adopt healthy infants may be sufficient if agency recruitment and eligibility policies are responsive to the cultures and lifestyles of such families. Early studies documented the failure of adoption agencies to implement culturally sensitive recruitment strategies and eligibility standards for potential adoptees of color (Day, 1979; Herzog, Sudia, Harwood, & Newcomb, 1971). Although many states and agencies took action to correct these circumstances, a recent survey by the North American Council on Adoptable Children (Gilles & Kroll, 1991) found that 83 percent of agencies in the 25 states studied acknowledged that organizational barriers continued to exist that prevented or discouraged families of color from adopting. The most frequently cited barriers were "institutional/systemic racism; lack of people of color in managerial positions; fees; 'adoption as business' mentality; communities' of color historical tendencies toward 'informal' adoption; negative perceptions of agencies and their practices; lack of minority staff; inflexible standards; general lack of recruitment activity and poor recruitment techniques; and 'word not out'" (pp. 7–8). With regard to the "adoption as business" mentality, one agency head was quoted as saying, "If your agency relied on fees, where would you place a minority kid . . . with a white family that can afford to pay, or a black family that can't?" (p. 14).

When adoption services and programs have become more responsive to families of color, such families have come forward to adopt. Haring reported in 1975 (cited in McRoy, 1989) that following changes in public and private adoption practices to encourage same-race adoptions, 70 families of color were approved for every 100 available children of color, reflecting an increase from 1971 (Herzog et al., 1971) of 39 families of color approved for every 100 children of color (and 116 white families approved for every 100 white children). More recently, a study by the North American Council on Adoptable Children (Gilles & Kroll, 1991) of 17 agencies specializing in finding same-race adoptive placements for children of color found that these agencies located same-race placements for 94 percent of their 341 African American children and 66 percent of their 38 Hispanic children; nonspecializing agencies obtained an average of 51 percent of same-race placements of 806 African American children and 30 percent of 168 Hispanic children (p. 8).

A number of sources have identified agencies that are exemplars in successfully engaging same-race adoptive families ("Adoption," 1992; Gant, 1984; Hairston & Williams, 1989; "Homes," 1993; Jackson-White, Dozier, Oliver, & Gardner, 1997; McRoy, Oglesby, & Grape, 1997). Hairston and Williams (1989) found that more than half of the 58 African American adoptive families they surveyed viewed the services they had received from exemplary national African American adoption agencies or programs as having led to their decision to adopt. Others (Gant, 1984; Gilles & Kroll, 1991) have similarly identified agency characteristics associated with successful recruitment of same-race families.

Availability for Adoption and Special Needs

Many children in out-of-home placements either are not available for adoption or have characteristics that make them difficult to place. Thus, they should not be included in numbers of children "languishing" in the system who are considered easily adoptable. Regarding availability for adoption, the Voluntary Cooperative Information System (VCIS) (cited in Flango & Flango, 1994), using figures received from states reporting, estimated that nationally 71,000 children had a permanency plan for adoption at the end of fiscal year 1992, meaning that their child welfare workers expected that parental rights would be voluntarily or involuntarily terminated and that the children would then become eligible for adoption. Of that number, it was estimated that 17,000 adoptions had been finalized and that another 17,000 adoptions were in the process of finalization. VCIS estimated that 21,000 children were in substitute care and still awaiting a decision regarding a final disposition. (The plight of the remaining 16,000 children was not clarified by VCIS, but because they were not included in one of the three categories mentioned above, they are assumed to not be imminently available for adoption.)

Two conclusions may be drawn from these data. First, half of children in the child welfare system may not be available for adoption (21,000 in out-of-home care awaiting final disposition and 16,000 not included in the statistics). Second, there is a difference between a child's having a permanency plan for adoption and actually being available for adoption. Child welfare workers, on assessing a family, may record adoption as the permanency plan without that ever becoming a reality, leading to incorrect assumptions among the public and among policymakers that children in such instances are actually available for adoption. Although these data are not restricted to children of color, they point to the inaccurate conclusions on which policy decisions may be made. With regard to children with special needs, the Child Welfare League of America (1988) observed that "there is a surplus of potential parents seeking to adopt white infants and preschool children and a shortage of those applying for those children who are available and need families" (p. 5); available children are "minority, severely handicapped, . . . age 12 or over; and in foster care four or more years" (p. 5). Thus, although the latter children are heavily counted among those who are languishing in out-of-home care, they are not the children that potential parents are seeking to adopt. Transracial adoption laws that are more liberal would not be expected, therefore, to decrease the numbers of these children substantially.

Inequities in Services

Disparities related to ethnic group have been observed in the prevention and intervention services that children in the child welfare system receive (Barth, Courtney, Berrick, & Albert, 1994). The implication is that prevention and intervention services are associated with children's successful exit from the child welfare system, although the authors do not speak directly to this point.

Mech (cited in Gould, 1991) found that African American children "were more likely to have no contact with workers than were white or Hispanic children" (p. 64). Similarly, African American families studied in the first three months after placement of their children were found to have experienced a mean number of agency contacts of 2.9, compared with a mean of 7.2 for white families (Close, cited in Williams, 1991). In Connecticut white children and foster families received more services and supports than children and foster families of color (Fein, Maluccio, & Kluger, cited in Barth, Courtney, Berrick, & Albert, 1994).

The issue of inequities in provision of services is especially important in family preservation, the process of providing intensive services and resources to families at risk of a child's removal from the home, usually because of real or threatened abuse or neglect. Williams (1991) noted that placement was avoided in more than three-fourths of families who received family preservation services and that children were able to remain in their own homes, safely, for one year after intervention. Recent research (Fraser, Pecora, & Haapala, 1991) has suggested that family preservation services may result in fewer placements for families of color compared to white families. Among families in Washington State, only 18.2 percent (10 of 55) of families of color who received family preservation services required the out-of-home placement of children, compared with 29.8 percent (75 of 252) of white families who received these services. These results suggest that intensive services can keep children of color out of out-of-home care.

Kinship Foster Care as Permanent Care

One of the most potentially misleading elements in the argument surrounding children of color in the out-of-home care system is the presentation of foster care statistics. Such statistics seldom distinguish kinship foster placements (placement of dependent children in the homes of relatives who have been formally approved, and subsidized, as foster parents for this purpose) from non-kinship foster placements. This distinction is important. Barth, Courtney, Berrick, Albert, and Needell (1994) noted that in California, two-thirds of the growth in the foster care caseload from 1984 to 1989 could be accounted for by the rise in kinship foster care. (This increase represents children who may otherwise have been placed in group homes or residential settings.) They also cite figures indicating that in 1990 kinship foster care accounted for 48 percent of all placements in New York (Meyer & Link, cited in Barth, Courtney, Berrick, Albert, & Needell, 1994). In New York City alone, the number of children in kinship foster homes rose from 151 in April 1985 to 14,000 in June 1989 (Thornton, 1991).

Children of color are widely represented in kinship foster placements. Forty-six percent of selected children in kinship foster care in California were African American, compared with 32 percent white children, 14 percent Hispanic children, and 9 percent children of other ethnic groups (Barth, Courtney, Berrick, & Albert, 1994). Ninety percent of kinship foster families in a Baltimore study were African American and 10 percent were white (Dubowitz, Feigelman, & Zuravin, 1993).

Two issues are important here. First, many kinship foster placements are considered permanent placements. In interviews with kinship foster parents in 20 homes, none of the children had a permanency goal of return to their parents (Thornton, 1991). In 19 of the 20 cases, the children were expected to be discharged to independent living when they became eligible (typically at age 17 or 18 years); in contrast, independent living was a goal for only 42 percent of children who were in nonrelative foster placements. When the kinship foster parents were asked "How long are you willing to provide care for your related foster child?" 100 percent of those who responded indicated they expected the children to remain with them until they were independent, until they no longer needed to be there, or as long as the foster parents were able to care for them. Similar findings were reported by Barth, Courtney, Berrick, Albert, and Needell (1994).

Second, kinship foster placements frequently do not result in formal adoption. Therefore, placement in relative foster care has consistently been linked to a corresponding decrease in the odds of adoption, especially for children of color, as if these were permanency failures. Barth, Courtney, Berrick, and Albert (1994) noted that "other things being equal, entering foster care under one year of age more than doubles a child's odds of being adopted but being placed initially in a kinship home cuts the odds by one-half" (p. 161). Thornton (1991) found that kinship foster parents were not interested in adopting the children in their care. Even when they were aware of available adoption subsidies, 85 percent of kinship foster parents stated that they would not adopt; one additional kinship foster parent stated that she would adopt only if she was pressured by the agency. Ninety-one percent of foster care case-workers indicated awareness of this mindset on the part of kinship foster parents.

The reluctance to adopt formally among African American kinship foster caregivers is based in cultural definitions of family and attitudes about family relationships. For example, the reason given by 70 percent of kinship foster parents for their unwillingness to adopt was that they already considered the child and themselves as being a part of the same family and that it was therefore unnecessary to adopt and would be confusing to the child (Thornton, 1991). They were content to maintain a grandparent-to-grandchild caregiving relationship. (In most instances, kinship foster parents are grandparents or great aunts or uncles.) Also, 30 percent of kinship foster parents were concerned that adopting the child formally would result in conflict in their relationship with the child's biological parents.

In summarizing factors associated with the likelihood of being adopted, Barth, Courtney, Berrick, and Albert (1994) asserted that kinship foster care should not be considered a substitute for adoption. At the same time, they pointed out that it must, under law (Adoption Assistance and Child Welfare Act of 1980), be understood as an option for adoption. In spite of this, foster care statistics may continue to combine relative and nonrelative foster placements, inflating the number of children who are in out-of-home care and appear to be available for adoption. If kinship foster caregivers are accepted as a part of the child's family, and the child's planned long-term placement with them considered an acceptable alternative to adoption, the numbers recorded for children who are available for or requiring adoption, especially children of color, should decrease dramatically.

Effects of Poverty

An overriding issue to be addressed is the circumstances that cause children of color to be in out-of-home placement in such large numbers. Living in poverty is one such circumstance, and it disproportionately affects children of color. Over 46 percent of all African American children lived in poverty in 1993, as did 41 percent of all Latino children; only 14 percent of white children lived in poverty (Children's Defense Fund, 1995). Fifty-six percent of children living with their mothers only were poor, compared with 12 percent of those living with married parents, and children of color were more likely than white children to live in mother-only households.

Poverty has been linked to the circumstances that result in out-of-home placements. A recently released National Incidence Study of Child Abuse and Neglect ("Survey Shows," 1996) showed that "children from families with annual incomes below $15,000 were over 22 times more likely to experience maltreatment than children from families whose incomes exceeded $30,000. They were also 18 times more likely to be sexually abused, almost 56 times more likely to be educationally neglected, and over 22 times more likely to be seriously injured" (p. 3). Children of single parents had an 87 percent greater risk of being harmed by physical neglect and an 80 percent greater risk of suffering serious injury or harm from abuse and neglect. Thus, children of color may be at greater risk of abuse and neglect, which may be associated with the inadequate resources and resulting stresses their parents confront. Poor children are at risk of permanent removal from their families simply because of their economic position in society.

The direction of public policies currently is to speed up the transracial adoption of children of color without first correcting the resource deficiencies that cause the children to be in out-of-home care. Such policies ignore the complexities of this situation and risk giving one group (those desiring to adopt a young child) an advantage while failing to protect those who are among the most vulnerable (poor children and families). Social programs originating under the Family Preservation Act of 1992 (Omnibus Budget Reconciliation Act of 1993) are examples of corrective efforts. For example, most states have programs modeled after the original Homebuilders, Inc., of Tacoma, Washington (Kinney, Madsen, Fleming, & Haapala, 1977). In such programs, child welfare workers are available to families on a 24-hour basis to provide immediate services and resources to facilitate the child's safe presence within the family. Wraparound programs (VanDenBerg & Grealish, 1996) coordinate the provision of services and resources to families, but on an ongoing rather than time-limited basis and as a collaborative community effort. These two programs are examples of how states may invest in families in attempting to prevent their breakdown.

Social Work Organization Positions

The formal positions of social work and related organizations serve as a guide to social work practice in the context of considerations of race and ethnicity in adoption. There is some variability in these positions, and this article briefly summarizes several.

In its most recent policy statement, NASW (1997) included the following: "Placement decisions should reflect a child's need for continuity, safeguarding the child's right to consistent care and to service arrangements. Agencies must recognize each child's need to retain a significant engagement with his or her parents and extended family and respect the integrity of each child's ethnicity and cultural heritage" (p. 137). The policy statement continues, "The social work profession stresses the importance of ethnic and cultural sensitivity. An effort to maintain a child's identity and her or his ethnic heritage should prevail in all services and placement actions that involve children in foster care and adoption programs, including adherence to the principles articulated in the Indian Child Welfare Act" (p. 138). With regard specifically to principles related to adoption, the statement reads, "The recruitment of and placement with adoptive parents from each relevant ethnic or racial group should be available to meet the needs of children" (p. 140).

In the concluding paragraph to its current position statement, the National Association of Black Social Workers (1994) stated,

> In conclusion, family preservation, reunification and adoption should work in tandem toward finding permanent homes for children. Priority should be given to preserving families through the reunification or adoption of children with/by biological relatives. If that should fail, secondary priority should be given to the placement of a child within his own race. Transracial adoption of an African-American child should only be considered after documented evidence of unsuccessful same race placements has been reviewed and supported by appropriate representatives of the African-American community. Under no circumstance should successful same race placements be impeded by obvious barriers (i.e., legal limits of states, state boundaries, fees, surrogate payments, intrusive applications, lethargic court systems, inadequate staffing patterns, etc.). As such, it will be mandatory that national policies with adequate funding be adopted as part of any new legislation. (p. 4)

The most recent standards of the Child Welfare League of America (1988) include an emphasis on the preservation of the birth family:

> When children's rights to the care and protection of those who gave them birth are jeopardized, society should, through its appropriate designated agencies, provide support to birth parents to make it possible for children to remain in their own homes. Children should not be deprived of their birth parents solely because of economic need, or the need for other forms of community assistance to reinforce parental efforts to maintain a home for them. (p. 2)

With regard to the role of the extended family, the standards read, "When children's parents are unable or unwilling to rear them, efforts should be made to have members of the extended family assume the parenting role and responsibility, providing they can offer the care and protection that the children need and that this is the desire of the birth parents" (p. 3). Finally, with regard to considerations of race and ethnicity, "Children should not be deprived of the opportunity to have a permanent family of their own by reason of age, religion, racial, or ethnic group identification, nationality, residence, or handicap" (p. 4). The standards include the clarification that federal legislation is perceived as safeguarding the rights of children.

The North American Council on Adoptable Children (NACAC) (Gilles & Kroll, 1991) has reaffirmed its original position, established in 1981, which stated as follows:

> Placement of children with a family of like ethnic background is desirable because such families are likely to provide the special needs of minority children with the strengths that counter the ill effects of racism. . . . The special needs of minority children who are of mixed ethnic background, school age, sibling groups or who have handicapping conditions should be considered in order to prevent unnecessary delays in placement. NACAC supports inclusion of multiethnic adoption as an option for children. (p. 37)

In 1988 NACAC (Gilles & Kroll, 1991), in addition to encouraging federal, state, and local officials to "fully utilize family resources in minority communities through aggressive and culturally sensitive recruitment and retention programs" (p. 38), decided to "direct [its] resources to the development, growth, and empowerment of minority adoptive parent groups" (p. 38). In 1990 it resolved the following: "Recognizing that fees charged prospective adoptive families present barriers to the most culturally appropriate placement for children in need of adoption, NACAC advocates that all child-placing agencies have as a goal working to develop alternative funding sources to cover all costs related to adoption services by working with both private and public sectors" (Gilles & Kroll, 1991, p. 38).

Five themes can be noted from among the position statements of these professional organizations regarding transracial adoption: (1) that ethnic heritage is important; (2) that children be raised preferably by their biological parents or, when not possible, by other biological relatives; (3) that economic

need alone is not an acceptable reason for children to be deprived of their biological parents; (4) that efforts should be made to ensure that adoptive parents
of the same race as the child are available and systemic barriers should not
interfere; and (5) that placement with parents of a different race is acceptable
and even preferable when the alternative means a child is deprived of a permanent home and family. It is important that social work organizations publi-
cize these positions to their members and advocate for public policies that
facilitate these themes.

Conclusions and Recommendations

Inequities exist in the eligibility and recruitment of non-kin foster families
and adoptive families of color, in services provided to children and families in
the child welfare system, and in the increased tendency of poor children to be
in out-of-home care. Statistics on the numbers and characteristics of children
of color who are in foster care and who are available for adoption may be misleading. Public policies that disallow the consideration of race and ethnicity
in adoption give an advantage to families who desire to adopt transracially. At
the same time, they fail to correct the circumstances that cause children of
color to require out-of-home placement, and they fail to eliminate methods of
maintaining or interpreting statistical data that may be misleading.

The following recommendations are made to lessen the need for transracial adoption. First, foster families of color should be actively recruited for
kinship and non-kinship foster care and especially to participate in fost adoption programs, if such programs are to continue. Second, active and ongoing
efforts to recruit and retain adoptive families of color should be increased so
that the pool of available families equals or surpasses the numbers of children
of color who are available for non-kin adoption. Third, creative strategies
should continue to be developed to recruit adoptive families of color for
"hard to place" children or children with special needs. Such children should
continue to be placed according to their individual needs. Fourth, public policies and agency procedures should be established to require that children of
color receive equitable services in all areas of the child welfare system. Fifth,
statistics and outcome data relating to kinship foster care should be separated
from those pertaining to nonrelative foster care; the benefits of the former as
an acceptable permanent alternative to adoption should be evaluated. And
sixth, policymakers should address the larger issues involved in ensuring that
all children have access to the economic resources that can help them remain
out of the child welfare system.

Social work has a central role to play in carrying out these recommendations. This role may include advocating in agencies for equitable (bias-free) selection; recruiting foster and adoptive families; orienting agency administrators,
board members, and the general community regarding cultural definitions of
"family"; conducting research that can scientifically inform public policy; participating in practice oriented to strengthening and unifying families while protecting children; and educating students and new professionals in the
competent performance of such roles. A review of committee reports of the

most recent adoption legislation (H. Rep. No. 104-542, 104th Congress, 2nd Sess., 1996) demonstrates that statistical data, and the way they are collected and interpreted, play a primary role in the development of public policy. It is important, therefore, that social workers be actively involved in ensuring that complete and accurate research and numerical data are disseminated to public policymakers.

A limitation of this article is that in some instances the data were derived from studies of children in out-of-home care in a limited number of states. However, the consistency of the findings and the fact that research data on these topics are limited render available data useful in interpreting the state of the field and suggest directions for future research, policy, and practice.

Finally, seeking to solve the problems associated with the overrepresentation of children of color in the child welfare system by protecting transracial adoption is simplistic and fails to protect those who are most vulnerable in this society—the children dependent on that society. A more responsible approach is to understand and eliminate the circumstances that constitute the base cause of this situation. The most recent adoption legislation (Small Business Job Protection Act of 1996) only became effective on January 1, 1997, so it is too early to determine how adoption agencies will respond. However, this will be an important area for review.

References

Adoption Assistance and Child Welfare Act of 1980, P. L. No. 96–272, [section]473, 94 Stat. 500 (1981).

Adoption—Not just for Woody and Mia. (1992, September 23). *Wall Street Journal,* p. A16.

Barth, R. P., Courtney, M., Berrick, J., & Albert, V. (1994). *From child abuse to permanency planning: Child welfare services pathways and placements.* New York: Aldine de Gruyter.

Barth, R. P., Courtney, M., Berrick, J., Albert, V., & Needell, B. (1994). Kinship care: Rights and responsibilities, services and standards. In R. P. Barth, M. Courtney, J. Berrick, & V. Albert (Eds.), *From child abuse to permanency planning: Child welfare services pathways and placements* (pp. 195–219). New York: Aldine de Gruyter.

Bartholet, E. (1991). Where do black children belong? The politics of race matching in adoption. *University of Pennsylvania Law Review, 139,* 1163–1256.

Child Welfare League of America. (1988). *Child Welfare League of America standards for adoption service.* Washington, DC: Author.

Children's Defense Fund. (1995). *The state of America's children yearbook: 1995.* Washington, DC: Author.

Courtney, M. E., Barth, R. P., Berrick, J. D., Brooks, D., Needell, B., & Park, L. (1996). Race and child welfare services: Past research and future directions. *Child Welfare, 75,* 99–137.

Day, D. (1979). *The adoption of black children.* Lexington, MA: D.C. Heath.

Dubowitz, H., Feigelman, S., & Zuravin, S. (1993). A profile of kinship care. *Child Welfare, 72,* 153–169.

Elias, M. (1991, August 15). Black kids, white parents: Debating what's best for the kids. *USA Today,* p. 1D.

Flango, V. E., & Flango, C. (1994). *The flow of adoption information from the states* (Publication No. R-162). Williamsburg, VA: National Center for State Courts.

Folaron, G., & Hess, P. (1993). Placement considerations for children of mixed African American and Caucasian parentage. *Child Welfare, 72,* 113–125.

Foster care and adoption statistics: Adoption and foster care analysis and reporting system (1997, January 9). . . .

Fraser, M. W., Pecora, P. J., & Haapala, D. A. (1991). *Families in crisis: The impact of intensive family preservation services.* New York: Aldine de Gruyter.

Gant, L. M. (1984). *Black adoption programs: Pacesetters in practice.* Ann Arbor, MI: National Child Welfare Training Center.

Gilles, T., & Kroll, J. (1991). *Barriers to same race placement.* St. Paul, MN: North American Council on Adoptable Children.

Gould, K. H. (1991). Limiting damage is not enough: A minority perspective on child welfare issues. In J. E. Everett, S.S. Chipungu, & B. R. Leashore (Eds.), *Child welfare: An Africentric perspective* (pp. 58–77). New Brunswick, NJ: Rutgers University Press.

Hairston, C. F., & Williams, V. G. (1989). Black adoptive parents: How they view agency adoption practices. *Social Casework, 70,* 534–538.

Hermann, V. P. (1993). Transracial adoption: "Child-saving" or "child-snatching"? *National Black Law Journal, 13,* 147–164.

Herzog, E., Sudia, C., Harwood, J., & Newcomb, C. (1971). *Families for black children.* Washington, DC: U.S. Government Printing Office.

Homes for Black Children: Hearing of the Senate Subcommittee on Children, Family, Drugs, and Alcoholism, 103d Congress, 1st Sess. 26–68 (1993, July 15) (testimony of Sydney Duncan).

Indian Child Welfare Act of 1978, [section]1214, 95th Cong., 2d Sess. (1978).

Jackson-White, G., Dozier, C. D., Oliver, J. T., & Gardner, L. B. (1997). Why African American adoption agencies succeed: A new perspective on self-help. *Child Welfare, 76,* 239–254.

Kinney, J. M., Madsen, B., Fleming, T., & Haapala, D. A. (1977). Homebuilders: Keeping families together. *Journal of Consulting & Clinical Psychology, 45,* 667–673.

Mahoney, J. (1991). The black baby doll: Transracial adoption and cultural preservation. *University of Missouri-Kansas City Law Review, 59,* 487–501.

McRoy, R. G. (1989). An organizational dilemma: The case of transracial adoptions. *Journal of Applied Behavioral Science, 25,* 145–160.

McRoy, R. G. (1994). Attachment and racial identity issues: Implications for child placement decision making. *Journal of Multicultural Social Work, 3,* 59–74.

McRoy, R. G., Oglesby, Z., & Grape, H. (1997). Achieving same race adoptive placements for African-American children: Culturally sensitive practice approaches. *Child Welfare, 76,* 85–104.

Meezan, W., & Shireman, J. F. (1985). *Care and commitment: Foster parent adoption decisions.* Albany: State University of New York Press.

Multiethnic Placement Act of 1994, P.L. 103-382, [section]553, 108 Stat. 4057 (1995).

National Association of Black Social Workers. (1994). *Preserving African-American families: Position statement.* Detroit: Author.

National Association of Social Workers. (1997). *Social work speaks: NASW policy statements* (4th ed.). Washington, DC: NASW Press.

Omnibus Budget Reconciliation Act of 1993, P.L. 103-66, 107 Stat. 312.

Rezendes, M. (1994). Debate intensifies on adoptions across racial lines. *Boston Globe,* p. 1.

Richman, R. (1993, December 7). Transracial adoptions get vocal advocate. *Plain Dealer* (From the *Washington Post*), p. 6C.

Silverman, A. R. (1993). Outcomes of transracial adoption. *Future of Children, 3,* 104–118.

Simon, R. J., & Alstein, H. (1977). *Transracial adoption.* New York: John Wiley & Sons.

Simon, R. J., & Alstein, H. (1987). *Transracial adoptees and their families: A study of identity and commitment.* New York: Praeger.

Small Business Job Protection Act of 1996, P.L. 104–188, [sections] 1807 & 1808. . . .

Survey shows dramatic increase in child abuse and neglect, 1986–1993. [On-line]. . . .

Thornton, J. L. (1991). Permanency planning for children in kinship homes. *Child Welfare, 70,* 593–601.

VanDenBerg, J. E., & Grealish, M. (1996). Individualized services and supports through the wraparound process: Philosophy and procedures. *Journal of Child and Family Studies, 5,* 7–21.

Williams, C. C. (1991). Expanding the options in the quest for permanence. In J. E. Everett, S. S. Chipungu, & B. R. Leashore (Eds.), *Child welfare: An Africentric perspective* (pp. 266–289). New Brunswick, NJ: Rutgers University Press.

Ezra E. H. Griffith
and Rachel L. Bergeron

 **NO**

Cultural Stereotypes Die Hard: The Case of Transracial Adoption

The adoption of black children by white families, commonly referred to as transracial adoption in the lay and professional literature, is the subject of a debate that has persisted in American society for a long time.[1] On one side of the divide are those who believe that black children are best raised by black families. On the other are the supporters of the idea that race-matching in adoption does not necessarily serve the best interests of the child and that it promotes racial discrimination.[2]

Coming as it does in the midst of myriad other discussions in this country about black-white interactions, transracial adoption has occupied an important place in any debate about adoption policy. But in addition, as can be seen in language utilized by the Fifth Circuit Court in a 1977 case,[3] there is a long-held belief that since family members resemble one another, it follows that members of constructed families should also look like each other so as to facilitate successful adoption outcomes.

> [A]doption agencies quite frequently try to place a child where he can most easily become a normal family member. The duplication of his natural biological environment is part of that program. Such factors as age, hair color, eye color and facial features of parents and child are considered in reaching a decision. This flows from the belief that a child and adoptive parents can best adjust to a normal family relationship if the child is placed with adoptive parents who could have actually parented him. To permit consideration of physical characteristics necessarily carries with it permission to consider racial characteristics [Ref. 3, pp 1205-6].

In utilizing this language, the court acknowledged that transracial adoption ran counter to the cultural beliefs that many people held about the construction of families. Still, the court concluded that while the difficulties attending transracial adoption justified the consideration of race as a relevant factor in adoption proceedings, race could not be the sole factor considered. With a bow to both sides in the transracial adoption debate, the argument could only continue.

As the debate marches on, mental health professionals are being asked to provide expert opinions about whether it would be preferable for a particular

From *The Journal of the American Academy of Psychiatry and the Law*, vol. 34, no. 3, 2006, pp. 303–314.

black child to be raised by a black family or by a family or adult of a different ethnic or racial group. There are, of course, different scenarios that may lead to the unfolding of these adoption disputes. For example, the question may arise when a black child is put up for adoption after having spent a number of months or years in an out-of-home placement. The lengthy wait of black children for an adoptive black family may understandably increase the likelihood of a transracial adoption. In another situation, the death of a biracial child's parents, one of whom was white and the other black, may lead to competition between the white and black grandparents for the right to raise the child. In a third possible context, the divorce of an interracial couple may result in a legal struggle for custody of the biracial child, with race trumpeted at least as an important factor if not the crucial factor to be considered in the decision about who should raise the child. Mental health professionals should therefore make an effort to stay abreast of the latest developments around this national debate if they intend to provide an informed opinion about the merits or problems of a potential transracial adoption.

We have already alluded to two significant factors that have played a role in the evolution of adoption policy concerning black children, particularly with respect to the question of whether race-neutral approaches make sense and whether transracial adoption is good practice. One factor has been judicial decision-making. In a relatively recent review, Hollinger[4] reminded us that, in general, racial classifications are invalidated unless they can survive the "strict scrutiny" test, which requires meeting a compelling governmental interest. Hollinger suggested that the "best-interest-of-the-child" standard commonly used in adoption practice would serve a substantial governmental interest. Such argumentation would allow the consideration of race as one element in an adoption evaluation. Following this reasoning, while race-neutral adoption may be a lofty objective, the specific needs of a particular child could legally allow the consideration of race.

The second factor to influence the evolution of adoption policy in this arena has been the academic research on transracial adoption.[5-9] This work has cumulatively demonstrated that black children can thrive and develop strong racial identities when nurtured in families with white parents. Transracially adopted children also do well on standard measures of self-esteem, cognitive development, and educational achievement. However, neither judicial decision-making nor scholarly research has settled the debate on transracial adoption policy.

In this article, we focus on a third factor that emerged as another mechanism meant to deal with transracial adoptions and the influential race-matching principle. These statutory efforts started with the Multiethnic Placement Act, which Hollinger stated "was enacted in 1994 amid spirited and sometimes contentious debate about transracial adoption and same-race placement policies."[4] We will point out that even though the statutory attempts were meant to eliminate race as a controlling factor in the adoption process, their implementation has left room for ambiguity regarding the role that race should play in adoption proceedings. Consequently, even though the statutes were intended to eliminate adoption delays and denials because of race-matching, they may have allowed the continued existence of a cultural stereotype—that black children belong with black families—and may have facilitated its continued existence. This article is therefore principally about statutory attempts in the past decade to influence public policy concerning transracial adoption. Secondarily, we shall comment on potential implications of these developments for the practice of adoption evaluations.

We emphasize once again that in referring to transracial adoption, we mean the adoption of black children by white parents. This is the focus of the statutes we consider. The adoption by Americans of children from other countries (international adoptions) and other transcultural adoptions (such as the adoption of Native American children by Anglos) are explicitly outside the parameters of this article. We also do not wish to suggest that although transracial adoption has been the subject of a significant national debate it is a numerically common phenomenon. Later in this article, we review the available data on transracial adoption.

Brief Review of Race-Matching in Adoption

Feelings about who should raise a black child have run high in the United States for a long time. These feelings come from different groups for different reasons. Kennedy[1] presented a number of historical cases to illustrate this. Among the cases he described, Kennedy told the early 1900s story of a white girl who was found residing with a black family (Ref. 1, p 368). The authorities concluded that the child had been kidnapped and rescued her. They then placed her with a white family. When it was learned later that the child was black, she was returned to the black family because it was not proper for the black child to be living with a white family. This case, along with others described by Kennedy, is part of the fabric of American racism and racial separatist practices. Kennedy also pointed to the practice during slavery of considering "the human products of interracial sexual unions" as unambiguously black and the mandate that they be reared within the black slave community as an attempt to undermine any possibility of interracial parenting (Ref. 1, pp 367-8).

Whites have not been the only ones to support the stance of race-matching—the belief that black or white children belong with their own group. In 1972, the National Association of Black Social Workers (NABSW) stated unambiguously that white families should never be allowed to adopt black children.[10] The NABSW opposed transracial adoption for two main reasons: the Association claimed that transracial adoption prevents black children from forming a strong racial identity, and it prevents them from developing survival skills necessary to deal with a racist society.

Since its 1972 statement, the NABSW has remained steadfast in its opposition to transracial adoption. In testimony before the Senate Committee on Labor and Human Resources in 1985, the President of the NABSW reiterated the Association's position and stated that the NABSW viewed the placement of black children in white homes as a hostile act against the black community, considering it a blatant form of race and cultural genocide.[11]

In 1991, the NABSW reaffirmed its position that black children should not be placed with white parents under any circumstances, stating that even the most loving and skilled white parent could not avoid doing irreparable harm to an African-American child.[12] In its 1994 position paper on the preservation of African-American families, the NABSW indicated that, in placement decisions regarding a black child, priority should be given to adoption by biological relatives and then to black families.[13] Transracial adoption "should only be considered after documented evidence of unsuccessful same race placements has been reviewed and supported by appropriate representatives of the African American community" (Ref. 13, p 1).

The NABSW's position was reflected in the 1981 New York case of *Farmer v. Farmer*.[14] Mr. Farmer, a black man, sought custody of his six-year-old daughter after he and his white wife divorced. He argued that his daughter, who looked black, would do better being raised by him than by her white mother and that her best interests could be achieved only by awarding custody to him, the parent with whom she would be racially identified by a racially conscious society. Three experts testified on his behalf. Each addressed the importance of racial identity problems that the child would face and the importance of her identification with her black heritage, but none would state categorically that custody of the child should be determined by her dominant racial characteristic. The judge rejected Mr. Farmer's race-based argument, finding that "between two natural parents of different races who have opted to have a child, neither gains priority for custody by reason of race alone. Nor can race disqualify a natural parent for custody" (Ref. 14, pp 589–90). He awarded custody to the mother based on the determination of the best interests of the child. In this determination race was not a dominant, controlling, or crucial factor, but was weighed along with all other material elements of the lives of the family.

Race-matching has been and remains an influential and controversial concept regarding how best to construct adoptive families. Matching, in general, has been a classic principle of adoption practice, governing non-relative adoptions for much of the 20th century. Its goal was to create families in which the adoptive parents looked as though they could be the adopted child's biological parents. Matching potential adoptive parents and children on as many physical, emotional, and cultural characteristics as possible was seen as a way of insuring against adoptive failure.[5] It was not uncommon for potential adoptive parents to be denied the possibility of adoption if their hair and eye color did not match those of a child in need of adoption.[5] Differences among family members in constructed families were seen as threats to the integration of an adopted child and the child's identification with the adoptive parents. Race, along with religion, was considered the most important characteristic to be matched, and it continued to be important even as the matching concept regarding other characteristics began to shift.[5] For example, in 1959, in its *Standards for Adoption Service* (SAS), the Child Welfare League of America (CWLA) recommended that

> . . . similarities of background or characteristics should not be a major consideration in the selection of a family, except where integration of the

child into the family and his identification with them may be facilitated by likeness, as in the case of some older children or some children with distinctive physical traits, such as race [Ref. 5, pp 3–4].

The CWLA reiterated its view in its discussion of the role of physical characteristics: "Physical resemblances should not be a determining factor in the selection of a home, with the possible exception of such racial characteristics as color" (Ref. 5, p 4). It was not until 1968 that the CWLA omitted any reference to color as a criterion for adoption: "Physical resemblances of the adoptive parents, the child or his natural parents should not be a determining factor in the selection of a home" (Ref. 5, p 6). By 1971, the CWLA considered characteristics that had been encompassed in the matching concept to be broad guidelines rather than specific criteria and the weight afforded them depended on the potential adoptive parents (i.e., their desire for a child similar to them in particular ways should be taken into consideration).[5] While not identified as a strict criterion of adoption, matching continued to be a broad principle in adoption practices. For example, the CWLA's 1988 *Standards for Adoption Service* and its 1993 statement of its children's legislative agenda reflected its belief that the developmental needs of black adopted children could best be met by black adoptive parents.[5,6]

> Children in need of adoption have a right to be placed into a family that reflects their ethnicity or race. Children should not have their adoption denied or significantly delayed, however, when adoptive parents of other ethnic or racial groups are available. . . . In any adoption plan, however, the best interests of the child should be paramount. If aggressive, ongoing recruitment efforts are unsuccessful in finding families of the same ethnicity or culture, other families should be considered [Ref. 5, p 32].

Matching, of course, continued to influence child placement decisions outside of adoption agencies, as evidenced by the comments of the Drummond court. Following that court's decision, the general rule has been that trial courts may consider race as a factor in adoption proceedings as long as race is not the sole determinant.[15,16]

Statutory Attempts at Remedies

As we previously noted, in 1972 the National Association of Black Social Workers (NABSW) issued a position paper in which the Association vehemently opposed the adoption of black children by white families.[10] The Black Social Workers had a quick and striking effect on transracial adoption policy. Following the appearance of the paper, adoption agencies, both public and private, either implemented race-matching approaches or used the NABSW position to justify already existing race-matching policies. As a result, the number of transracial adoptions were estimated to drop significantly—39 percent within one year of the publication of the NABSW statement.[17] Although robust data were lacking, it was thought that the number and length of stay of black children in out-of-home placements increased as social workers and other foster care and adoption professionals, believing that same-race placements were in the best interest of the child, searched for same-race foster and adoptive parents. Agencies and their workers had considerable discretion in deciding the role race played in placement decisions. States, while generally requiring that foster care and adoption decisions be made in the best interest of the child, varied in their directions regarding the extent to which race, culture, and ethnicity should be taken into account in making the best-interest determination.[18]

While race-matching policies were not the sole determinant of increasing numbers of black children in institutions and out-of-home placements, there was growing concern that such policies, with their focus on same-race placement and their exclusion of consideration of loving, permanent interracial homes, kept black children from being adopted.[19] Because he was concerned that race had become the determining factor in adoption placements and that children were languishing in foster care homes and institutions, Senator Howard Metzenbaum introduced legislation to prohibit the use of race as the sole determinant of placement.[19] Senator Metzenbaum believed that same-race adoption was the preferable option for a child, but he also believed that transracial placement was far preferable to a child's remaining in foster care when an appropriate same-race placement was not available.[19]

Multiethnic Placement Act

Congress passed the Howard Metzenbaum Multiethnic Placement Act (MEPA) and President Clinton signed it into law on October 20, 1994.[20] MEPA's main goals were to decrease the length of time children had to wait to be adopted; to prevent discrimination based on race in the placement of children into adoptive or foster homes; and to recruit culturally diverse and minority adoptive and foster families who could meet the needs of children needing placement.[18] In passing MEPA, Congress was concerned that many children, especially those from minority groups, were spending lengthy periods in foster care awaiting adoption placements.[19] Congress found, within the parameters of available data, that nearly 500,000 children were in foster care in the United States; tens of thousands of these children were waiting for adoption; two years and eight months was the median length of time children waited to be adopted; and minority children often waited twice as long as other children to be adopted.[21]

Under MEPA, an agency or entity receiving federal funds could not use race as the sole factor in denying any person the opportunity to become an adoptive or foster parent. Furthermore, an agency could not use race as a single factor to delay or deny the placement of a child in an adoptive or foster care family or to otherwise discriminate in making a placement decision. However, an agency could consider a child's racial, cultural, and ethnic background as one of several factors—not the sole factor—used to determine the best interests of the child.[22] MEPA stated:

> An agency, or entity, that receives Federal assistance and is involved in adoption or foster care placements may not—(A) categorically deny to any person the opportunity to become an adoptive or a foster parent, solely on

the basis of the race, color or national origin of the adoptive or foster parent, or the child involved; or (B) delay or deny the placement of a child for adoption or into foster care, or otherwise discriminate in making a placement decision, solely on the basis of the race, color, or national origin of the adoptive or foster parent, or the child involved.[23]

However, MEPA also contained the following permissible consideration:

An agency or entity . . . may consider the cultural, ethnic, or racial background of the child and the capacity of the prospective foster or adoptive parents to meet the needs of a child of this background as one of a number of factors used to determine the best interests of a child.[24]

So, under MEPA, agencies could consider a child's race, ethnicity, or culture as one of a number of factors used to determine the best interests of the child, as long as it was not the sole factor considered, and they could consider the ability of prospective parents to meet the needs of a child of a given race, ethnicity, or culture.[22]

Following the passage of MEPA, the Department of Health and Human Services (DHHS), Office of Civil Rights, provided policy guidance to assist agencies receiving federal financial assistance in complying with MEPA.[25] The guidance permitted agencies receiving federal assistance to consider race, culture, or ethnicity as factors in making placement decisions to the extent allowed by MEPA, the U.S. Constitution and Title VI of the Civil Rights Act of 1964.[25]

Under the Equal Protection Clause of the Fourteenth Amendment, laws or practices drawing distinctions on the basis of race are inherently suspect and subject to strict scrutiny analysis.[26] To pass such analysis, classifications or practices based on race have to be narrowly tailored to meet a compelling state interest.[26] The Supreme Court has not specifically addressed the question of transracial adoption. It has considered race as a factor in a child placement decision in the context of a custody dispute between two white biological parents when the mother, who had custody of the child, began living with a black man, whom she later married. The Court found the goal of granting custody on the basis of the best interests of the child to be "indisputably a substantial government interest for purposes of the Equal Protection Clause" (Ref. 27, p 433). The DHHS guidance on the use of race, color or national origin as factors in adoption and foster care placements addressed the relevant constitutional issues and indicated that the only compelling state interest in the context of child placement decisions is protecting the best interests of the child who is to be placed.[25] So, under MEPA, consideration of race or ethnicity was permitted as long as it was narrowly tailored to advance a specific child's best interests.[25] Agencies receiving federal funds could consider race and ethnicity when making placement decisions only if the agency made a narrowly tailored, individualized determination that the facts and circumstances of a particular case required the contemplation of race or ethnicity to advance the best interests of the child in need of placement.[18,25] Agencies could not assume that race, ethnicity, or culture was at issue in every case and make general policies that applied to all children.[18] The guidance also specifically prohibited policies that established periods during which same-race searches were conducted, created placement preference hierarchies based on race, ethnicity, or culture, required social workers to justify transracial placement decisions or resulted in delayed placements to find a family of a particular race, ethnicity, or culture.[18]

The DHHS policy guidance did address MEPA's permissible consideration of the racial, cultural, or ethnic background of a child and the capacity of the prospective foster or adoptive parents to meet the needs of a child of this background as one of a number of factors in the best-interest-of-the-child determination. The guidance allowed agencies to assess the ability of a specific potential adoptive family to meet a specific child's needs related to his or her racial, ethnic, or cultural background, as long as the assessment was done in the context of an individualized assessment[18,25]:

> As part of this assessment, the agency may examine the attitudes of the prospective family that affect their ability to nurture a child of a particular background and consider the family's ability to promote development of the child's positive sense of self. The agency may assess the family's ability to nurture, support, and reinforce the racial, ethnic, or cultural identity of the child, the family's capacity to cope with the particular consequences of the child's developmental history, and the family's ability to help the child deal with any forms of discrimination the child may encounter [Ref. 18, pp 9–10].

However, agencies were not allowed to make decisions based on general assumptions regarding the needs of children of a specific race, ethnicity, or culture or about the ability of prospective parents of a specific race, ethnicity, or culture to care or nurture the identity of a child of a different race, ethnicity, or culture.[18]

To increase the pool of potential foster or adoptive parents, MEPA also required states to develop plans for the recruitment of potential foster and adoptive families that reflected the ethnic and racial diversity of the children needing placement.[28] The recruitment efforts had to be focused on providing all eligible children with the opportunity for placement and on providing all qualified members of the community with an opportunity to become an adoptive or foster parent.[18] As a result, while MEPA sought in a reasonable way to recruit a broad racial and cultural spectrum of adoptive families, the law was at the same time underlining the idea that there was something special about a black child's being raised by a black family.

Those who objected to the permissive consideration of race in MEPA asserted that it allowed agencies to continue to delay adoptions of minority children based on race concerns.[21] They also argued that race-matching policies could and did continue under MEPA. Social workers could, for example, use race as a factor to support a finding that a transracial adoption was not in a given child's best interest. Supporters of MEPA reached their own conclusion that it did not accomplish its goal of speeding up the adoption process and moving greater numbers of minority children into foster care or adoption placements and that the permissive consideration of race allowed agencies legitimately to continue race-matching to deny or delay the placement of minority children with white adoptive parents.[22] Senator Metzenbaum himself agreed with this conclusion about MEPA and worked for its repeal.[29] As we shall see later, the arguments and counterarguments about the effectiveness of MEPA were being made in the absence of robust data.

The Interethnic Adoption Provisions

MEPA was repealed when on August 20, 1996, President Clinton signed the Small Business Job Protection Act of 1996. Section 1808 of the Act was entitled "Removal of Barriers to Interethnic Adoption" (The Interethnic Adoption Provisions; IEP).[30] MEPA's permissible consideration provision was removed and its language changed. (The words in brackets were part of MEPA and do not appear in the IEP.)

> A person or government that is involved in adoption or foster care placements may not—(a) [categorically] deny to any individual the opportunity to become an adoptive or a foster parent, [solely] on the basis of race, color, or national origin of the individual, or the child involved; or (b) delay or deny the placement of a child for adoption or into foster care [or otherwise discriminate in making a placement decision, solely] on the basis of race, color, or national origin of the adoptive or foster parent, or the child, involved [Ref. 22, pp 1616–17].

Under the IEP, states were still required to "provide for the diligent recruitment of potential foster and adoptive families that reflect the ethnic and racial diversity of children in the State for whom foster and adoptive homes are needed."[28]

Failure to comply with MEPA was a violation of Title VI of the Civil Rights Act of 1964[17]; failure to comply with the IEP is also a violation of Title VI.[31] Under MEPA, an agency receiving federal assistance that discriminated in its child placement decisions on the basis of race and failed to comply with the Act could forfeit its federal assistance[17] and an aggrieved individual had the right to bring an action seeking equitable relief in federal court[32] or could file a complaint with the Office of Civil Rights. The IEP added enforcement provisions that specified graduated fiscal sanctions to be imposed by DHHS against states found to be in violation of the law and gave any individual aggrieved by a violation the right to bring an action against the state or other entity in federal court.[33]

The Department of Health and Human Services issued two documents to provide practical guidance for complying with the IEP: a memorandum[34] and a document in question-and-answer format.[35] According to the guidance, Congress, in passing the IEP, clarified its intent to eliminate delays in adoption or foster care placements when they were in any way avoidable. Race and ethnicity could not be used as the basis for any denial of placement nor used as a reason to delay a foster care or adoptive placement.[34] The repeal of MEPA's "permissible consideration" provision was seen as confirming that strict scrutiny was the appropriate standard for consideration of race or ethnicity in adoption and foster care placements.[34] DHHS argued that it had never taken the position that MEPA's permissible consideration language allowed agencies to take race into account routinely in making placement decisions because such a view would be inconsistent with a strict scrutiny standard.[34] It reaffirmed that any decision to consider race as a necessary element in a placement decision has to be based on concerns arising out of the circumstances of the particular situation:

> The primary message of the strict scrutiny standard in this context is that only the most compelling reasons may serve to justify consideration of race and ethnicity as part of a placement decision. Such reasons are likely to emerge only in unique and individual circumstances. Accordingly, occasions where race or ethnicity lawfully may be considered in a placement decision will be correspondingly rare [Ref. 34, p 4].

The guidance again made clear that the best interest of the child is the standard to be used in making placement decisions. So, according to the guidance, the IEP prohibits the routine practice of taking race and ethnicity into consideration ("Public agencies may not routinely consider race, national origin, and ethnicity in making placement decisions" (Ref. 35, p 2)), but it allows for the consideration of race, national origin, and ethnicity in certain specific situations ("Any consideration of these factors must be done on an individualized basis where special circumstances indicate that their consideration is warranted" (Ref. 35, p 2)). Once again, such language seems to suggest that, in certain contexts, the adoptive child may well benefit from placement in a same-race family.

The DHHS guidance seemed to frame the possibility for adoption agencies to continue the practice of race-matching.[22] For example, while warning that assessment of a prospective parent's ability to serve as a foster or adoptive parent must not act as a racial or ethnic screen and indicating that considerations of race must not be routine in the assessment function, the guidance conceded that an important aspect of good social work is an individualized assessment of a prospective parent's ability to be an adoptive or foster parent.

Table 1

Children Waiting to be Adopted From the Public Foster Care System, by Race, by Fiscal Year

	On Sept. 30, 2002*		On Sept. 30, 2003†	
	Number	%	Number	%
Black/non-Hispanic	54,832	43	47,630	40
White/non-Hispanic	58,975	46	43,820	37
Total	127,942	100	119,000	100

*Reference 37.
†Reference 38.

Thus, it allows for discussions with prospective adoptive or foster care parents about their feelings, preferences, and capacities regarding caring for a child of a particular race or ethnicity.[22,35]

Data Collection

Hansen and Simon[36] have pointed out that the Adoption and Safe Families Act (ASFA) of 1995 created an adoption incentive program that paid bonuses to states that increased the number of adoptions of children from foster care. The incentive program also provided an incentive for data collection, using a system known as the Adoption and Foster Care Analysis and Reporting System (AFCARS). States must submit data to AFCARS on each adoption in which a public child welfare agency was involved in any fashion. AFCARS issues periodic reports, and others (such as the Child Welfare League of America) use the AFCARS data to publish analytic reports from time to time. AFCARS reports may be preliminary, interim, or final as data continue to be submitted by states over many months.

Tables 1 and 2 show that in fiscal year (FY) 2002 and in FY 2003, more whites were adopted than blacks in the public foster care system. The two fiscal years show some difference between whites and blacks in terms of the comparative number of whites and blacks waiting for adoption. The data for FY 2003 show that more whites than blacks were in the foster care system. Of course, these numbers of children in the foster care system must be viewed in light of their representation in the general population. Data from the 2000 U.S. Census . . . show that of the total population under age 18 years, 68.6 percent (49,598,289) are white and 15.1 percent (10,885,696) are black. Consequently, a substantially greater proportion of blacks (.4%), in comparison to whites (.09%), were awaiting adoption in September 2003. Still, of the children awaiting adoption in September 2002, 30 percent of black children were adopted in FY 2003 in comparison to 36 percent of white children.

The AFCARS data from FY 2001 have been the subject of greater analysis, which has led to the following conclusions.[36,39] In FY 2001, mean time for adoption of black children was 18 months compared with 15 months for

Table 2

Children Adopted From the Public Foster Care System, by Race, by Fiscal Year

	Fiscal Year 2002*		Fiscal Year 2003†	
	Number	%	Number	%
Black/non-Hispanic	18,957	36	16,570	33
White/non-Hispanic	27,272	52	20,940	42
Total	52,138	100	50,000	100

*Reference 37.
†Reference 38.

white children. It was also estimated that about 17 percent of black children adopted in FY 2001 were adopted transracially by white, non-Hispanic parents. This figure of transracial adoptions (about 2,500) provided for the public foster care system is not significantly above estimates given for earlier years—about 2,574 in 1971. However, the FY 2001 data do not include private sector adoptions. This has led Hansen and Simon[36] to conclude that there has been no clear increase in transracial adoptions, at least in the arena of public child welfare agency adoptions. In 2003, McFarland[40] published a report pointing out that while AFCARS is now producing robust data about public sector adoptions, information about private sector adoptions is scant.

Nevertheless, it has been estimated that in 2001, about 127,000 children were adopted in the United States,[41] including public, private, and intercountry adoptions. These adoptions arise out of the estimated 500,000 children in out-of-home placements in the United States.

Discussion

The IEP addresses individual cultural elements such as race, color, or national origin and does not address the broad role of culture in placement decisions. The DHHS guidance notes:

> There are situations where cultural needs may be important in placement decisions, such as where a child has specific language needs. However, a public agency's consideration of culture would raise Section 1808 [IEP] issues if the agency used culture as a proxy for race, color or national origin. Thus, while nothing in Section 1808 directly prohibits a public agency from assessing the cultural needs of all children in foster care, Section 1808 would prohibit an agency from using routine cultural assessments in a manner that would circumvent the law's prohibition against the routine consideration of race, color, or national origin [Ref. 35, p 2].

This raises questions about the role of cultural capacity or cultural competence of parents in adoption and foster care decisions. In response to a question regarding whether public agencies may assess the cultural capacity of all foster parents, the DHHS responded in the negative, but seemed to open the door to such assessment, at least of particular parents:

> Race, color and national origin may not routinely be considered in assessing the capacity of particular prospective foster parents to care for specific children. However, assessment by an agency of the capacity of particular adults to serve as foster parents for specific children is the heart of the placement process, and essential to determining what would be in the best interests of a particular child [Ref. 35, p 2].

The DHHS guidance makes a similar statement regarding cultural competency:

> The term "cultural competency," as we understand it, is not one that would fit in a discussion of adoption and foster placement. However, agencies

should, as a matter of good social work practice, examine all the factors that may bear on determining whether a particular placement is in the best interest of a particular child. That may in rare instances involve the consideration of the abilities of prospective parents of one race or ethnicity to care for a child of another race or ethnicity [Ref. 35, p 5].

Such language is obviously far from being lucid and specific. It grants the potential importance of considering race and cultural competence, but cautions against general and routine use of these factors, while contemplating their utility in particular situations.

In considering the best interests of a child who is being placed for adoption, DHHS is suggesting that there could be special circumstances uniquely individualized to the child that require consideration of ethnicity and race of the potential adoptive parents. Presumably this should not be done routinely and should not be seen as serving as a proxy for a consistent and mundane contemplation of ethnicity or race in the adoption context. Undoubtedly, what constitutes special circumstances in the practices of any given adoption agency is likely to be a matter of interpretation. While agencies can readily assert what their routine practices are, much may turn on how vigorously supervised are the claims that special circumstances exist with respect to a particular black child that dictate consideration of ethnicity and race in that child's case. As a practical result, while it appears no one is now allowed to claim that every black child needs a black family, it may still be reasonable and practicable to claim that a black child requires adoption by a black family, as dictated by consideration of the best interests of that child. For example, Kennedy (Ref. 1, p 416) has raised the possibility that an older child might say he or she wanted to be adopted only by a black family. Such a context could indeed make it difficult for the child's wish to be refused outright, without any consideration whatsoever.

Such reasoning is articulated starting from the point of view of the child. Giving consideration to the interests of the potential adoptive parent is another matter. In other words, what should we consider about the adoptive parent's interest in raising black children and the parent's ability to do so? The opinions about this matter remain divided. Kennedy (Ref. 1, pp 416, 434) and Bartholet[42] have proposed that prospective adoptive parents be allowed to state a preference for adopting a child from a particular ethnic group. This is, in their view, permissible race-matching that ultimately serves the best interests of the child. After all, what would be the use of forcing a family to adopt a child they really did not want? In addition, both authors also have argued that state intervention in such racial selectivity in the formation of families would be akin to imposing race-based rules on the creation of married couples. However, Banks[43] has opposed this accommodationist stance, where in practice adoption agencies would simply show prospective adoptive parents only the class of ethnic children the adoptive parent was interested in adopting. Banks thought this merely perpetuated the status quo, as white adoptive parents had little interest in black children. This would result in black children's continuing to languish in out-of-home placements, and their time spent awaiting adoption would remain prolonged.

Kennedy and Bartholet were permissive in their attitude toward the racial selectivity of prospective adoptive parents, respecting parents' choice to construct families as they wish.

There has been and continues to be strong support for the belief that black children belong with black adoptive parents. It is not only the NABSW, which has called for the repeal of the IEP,[13] that has taken this position. For example, in a 1998 letter to the Secretary of the Department of Health and Human Services, a former executive director of the Child Welfare League of America strongly disagreed with the DHHS's interpretation of MEPA/IEP, stating that prohibiting any consideration of race in adoptive and foster care placement decisions contradicts best-practice standards in child welfare:

> CWLA standards for adoption and foster care services clearly state that the best practice requires consideration of race. . . .Children in need of adoption have a right to be placed into a family that reflects their ethnicity or race. . . . These standards—calling for the explicit consideration of race in adoption and foster care placement decisions—reflect the best thinking of child welfare experts from across the country [Ref. 44, p 2].

The CWLA, in its most recent *Standards of Excellence for Adoption Services* (2000), reiterated its belief that race is to be considered in all adoptions and that placement with parents of the same race is the first choice for any child. Other placements should be considered only after a vigorous search for parents of the same race has failed:

> All children deserve to be raised in a family that respects their cultural heritage. . . . If aggressive, ongoing recruitment efforts are unsuccessful in finding families of the same race or culture as the child, other families should be considered to ensure that the child's adoptive placement is not delayed [Ref. 45, p 68].

In its most recent policy statement on foster care and adoption (2003), the National Association of Social Workers also reiterated its position that consideration of race should play a central role in placement decisions:

> Placement decisions should reflect a child's need for continuity, safeguarding the child's right to consistent care and to service arrangements. Agencies must recognize each child's need to retain a significant engagement with his or her parents and extended family and respect the integrity of each child's ethnicity and cultural heritage [Ref. 46, p 147].
>
> The social work profession stresses the importance of ethnic and cultural sensitivity. An effort to maintain a child's identity and his or her ethnic heritage should prevail in all services and placement actions that involve children in foster care and adoption programs [Ref. 46, p 148].
>
> The placement of choice should be within the child's family of origin, among relatives (kinship placement) who can provide a more stable environment for the child during the period of family crisis. If no such relatives are available, every effort should be made to place a child in the home of foster parents who are similar in racial and ethnic background to the child's own family. The recruitment of foster parents from

each relevant racial and ethnic group should be pursued vigorously to
meet the needs of children who require placement [Ref. 46, p 150].

Others[47–49] have espoused the view that inracial adoption is the preferred option for a black child because black families inherently possess the
competence to raise children with strong black identities and the ability to
cope with racism. While questions of cultural competence to raise a black
child often arise about prospective white adoptive parents, no such questions
are posed about prospective black adoptive parents.[1] The competence of black
families to raise black children is regularly referred to as though black families are culturally identical or homogeneous and all are equally competent to
raise black children and equip them to live in our society.[1,50] We may all
think about black cultural competence as though it is a one-dimensional concept. Indeed, we may all be referring simply to stereotypical indicators of
what we think it means to be black. We may be referring to our own personal
preferences for the stereotypic activities of black people: involvement in a
black church; participation in a community center where black-focused programs are operating; viewing movies with a clearly black theme; reading literature authored by blacks. What is rarely considered is that some black families
are drawn to rap music, others to jazz greats, and still others to traditional
classical music. Indeed, some families obviously manage to exhibit an interest
in all these genres of music. With respect, therefore, to even these stereotyped
indicators of what it means to be black, black families vary in the degree of
their attachment to the indicators. This is to say that blacks differ in their level
of commitment to the salience of black-oriented culture in their individual
and family lives. As a result, there is considerable cultural heterogeneity
among black families. Such variability may well lead to differences in black
families' ways of coping with racism.[50]

To date, the statutory attempts to deal with trans-racial adoptions have
not been considered as spectacularly successful, especially in the case of
MEPA. Nevertheless, efforts have been made to limit the routine consideration
of race and ethnicity in adoption, with the result that black children may be
remaining for shorter periods in undesirable out-of-home placements.
(National data are not yet able to demonstrate clear trends.[36,40]) However,
DHHS guidance still permits consideration of race and ethnicity in specific
cases, with the apparent concession that some black children may need a
black family for the realization of the child's best interests.

The burden is on forensic psychiatrists and other mental health professionals who perform adoption evaluations to point out cogently and logically
two points: first, whether race is a factor that is relevant in the adoption evaluation; and second, whether there is something unique or particular about that
adoption context that requires race to be considered. It will require special
argumentation for the evaluator to claim that a particular black child could
benefit more from placement with a black family than with a non-black family. As stated earlier, the evidence is clear that black children can do well in
transracial placements. The pointed objective, therefore, in future evaluations
will be to show that a particular black child has such unique and special

needs that he or she deserves particular consideration for placement in a black family. It will be interesting to see whether our forensic colleagues, in striving for objectivity, will consider the factor of race in their evaluations only when something unique about that particular adoption context cries out for race to be considered so that the best-interest-of-the-child standard can be met. It seems clear that forensic professionals must be careful not to state that they routinely consider race in their adoption evaluations unless they intend to argue clinically that race is always relevant. And even then, they should be cautious about not articulating a general preference for inracial over transracial adoptions.

Despite federal statutory attempts to remove race as a controlling factor in adoption and foster care placement decisions, the debate over transracial adoption is not over. Indeed, strains of the debate are evidenced in the statutes and their implementation guidelines and the argument continues among our mental health colleagues. For example, following passage of MEPA and the IEP, a group of adoption experts from different disciplines was assembled by the Stuart Foundation to reconsider the controversies surrounding racial matching and transracial adoption. The Adoption and Race Work Group concluded that "race should not be ignored when making placement decisions and that children's best interests are served—all else being equal—when they are placed with families of the same racial, ethnic, and cultural background as their own" (Ref. 51, p 169). The Work Group decided that the research to date was insufficient, even though research has supported transracial adoption.

The ultimate outcome of the group's deliberations is perhaps the clearest indication of how difficult it is in this debate to meld passion and scholarship. The ongoing debate exemplifies Courtney's conclusion that "those with strongly held views are likely to maintain their convictions: advocates of TRA will continue to believe that the research supports their beliefs, while opponents will contend that TRA is harmful, or that the jury is still out" (Ref. 52, p 753). After two years of work analyzing racial matching and transracial adoption, the Stuart work group acknowledged that thinking about the debate in terms of those who oppose or support transracial or inracial adoptions may get us nowhere. "It may be more productive to regard the issue in terms of assessing, deciding, and documenting when the law allows us to place more or less emphasis on race and racial matching and when good social work practice calls for it" (Ref. 52, p 177). This may be a concession to the notion that, with respect to transracial adoption, cultural stereotypes die hard.

References

1. Kennedy R: Interracial Intimacies: Sex, Marriage, Identity and Adoption. New York: Pantheon Books, 2003
2. For further commentary on the debate, see: Griffith EEH, Duby JL: Recent developments in the transracial adoption debate. Bull Am Acad Psychiatry Law 19:339–50, 1991. Griffith EEH: Forensic and policy implications of the transracial adoption debate. Bull Am Acad Psychiatry Law 23:501–12, 1995

3. Drummond v. Fulton County Department of Family and Children's Services, 563 F.2d 1200 (5th Cir. 1977)

4. Hollinger JH: A Guide to the Multiethnic Placement Act of 1994 as Amended by the Interethnic Adoption Provisions of 1996. National Resource Center on Children and the Law. . . .

5. Simon RJ, Alstein H: Adoption, Race and Identity: From Infancy to Young Adulthood. New Brunswick, NJ: Transaction Publishers, 2002

6. Vroegh KS: Transracial adoptees: developmental status after 17 years. Am J Orthopsychiatry 67:568–75, 1997

7. Griffith EEH, Adams AK: Public policy and transracial adoptions of black children, in Family, Culture and Psychobiology. Edited by Sorel E. Ottawa, ON, Canada: Legas Press, 1990, pp 211–33

8. Griffith EEH, Silverman IL: Transracial adoptions and the continuing debate on the racial identity of families, in Racial and Ethnic Identity: Psychological Development and Creative Expression. Edited by Harris HW, Blue HC, Griffith EEH. New York: Routledge, 1995, pp 95–114

9. Burrow AL, Finley GE: Transracial, same-race adoptions, and the need for multiple measures of adolescent adjustment. Am J Orthopsychiatry 74:577–83, 2004

10. National Association of Black Social Workers: Position Statement on Transracial Adoptions. September 1972. . . .

11. Testimony of William T. Merritt, President of the National Association of Black Social Workers, Hearings Before the Committee on Labor and Human Resources, United States Senate, 99th Congress, June 25, 1985

12. Institute for Justice: Separate is not equal: striking down state-sanctioned barriers to interracial adoption. . . .

13. National Association of Black Social Workers: Preserving Families of African Ancestry. Washington, DC: NABSW, 2003

14. Farmer v. Farmer, 439 N.Y.S.2d 584 (N.Y. Sup. Ct. 1981)

15. Farrell T, Gregor R, Payne A, et al: Adoption § 138 Interethnic Adoption. Am Jur 2d:138, 2004

16. Zitter JM: Race as a factor in adoption proceedings. ALR 4th 34:167, 2004

17. Marby CR: "Love alone is not enough!" in transracial adoptions: scrutinizing recent statutes, agency policies, and prospective adoptive parents. Wayne Law Rev 42:1347–423, 1996

18. Bussiere A: A Guide to the Multiethnic Placement Act of 1994. ABA Center on Children and the Law. . . .

19. Metzenbaum HM: S. 1224—In Support of the Multiethnic Placement Act of 1993. Duke J Gender Law Policy 2:165–71, 1995

20. 42 U.S.C. § 5115a (1994)

21. Varan R: Desegregating the adoptive family: in support of the Adoption Anti-discrimination Act of 1995. J Marshall Law Rev 30:593–625, 1997

22. Campbell SB: Taking race out of the equation: transracial adoption in 2000. SMU Law Rev 53:1599–626, 2000

23. 42 U.S.C. § 5115a (a) (1)(A)-(B) (1994)

24. 42 U.S.C. § 5115a(a)(2) (1994)

25. Hayashi D: Policy Guidance on the Use of Race, Color or National Origin as Considerations in Adoption and Foster Care Placements. Washington, DC: Office of Civil Rights, Department of Health and Human Services. . . .

26. Adarand Constructors, Inc. v. Pena, 515 U.S. 200 (1995)

27. Palmore v. Sidoti, 466 U.S. 429 (1984)

28. 42 U.S.C. § 622(b)(9)

29. Statement of the Honorable Howard Metzenbaum: Testimony Before the Sub-committee on Human Resources of the House Committee on Ways and Means. Hearing on Interethnic Adoptions, September 15, 1998. . . .

30. 42 U.S.C.S. § 1996 b(1) (2003)

31. 42 U.S.C.S. § 1996 b(2) (2003)

32. 42 U.S.C.S. § 5115a(b) (1994)

33. 42 U.S.C.S. § 674(d) (2003)

34. Hayashi D: Interethnic Adoption Provisions of the Small Business Job Protection Act of 1996. Memorandum, Office for Civil Rights, Department of Health and Human Services. June 4, 1997. . . .

35. Questions and Answers Regarding the Multiethnic Placement Act of 1994 and Section 1808 of the Small Business and Job Protection Act of 1996. Office for Civil Rights, Department of Health and Human Services. . . .

36. Hansen ME, Simon RJ: Transracial Placement in Adoptions With Public Agency Involvement: What Can We Learn From the AFCARS Data? . . .

37. National Data Analysis System. . . .

38. U.S. Department of Health and Human Services, Administration for Children and Families: The AFCARS Report 10. . . .

39. The Multiethnic Placement Act. National Data Analysis System. . . .

40. McFarland MC: Adoption Trends in 2003: A deficiency of Information. National Center for State Courts, 2003. . . .

41. National Adoption Information Clearinghouse: How Many Children Were Adopted in 2000 and 2001? . . .

42. Bartholet E: Private race preferences in family formation. Yale Law J 107:2351-6, 1998

43. Banks RR: The color of desire: fulfilling adoptive parents' racial preferences through discriminatory state action. Yale Law J 107: 875-964, 1998

44. Letter from David Liederman, Former CWLA Executive Director to Donna Shalala, HHS Secretary, December 21, 1998. . . .

45. Child Welfare League of America: Standards of Excellence: Standards of Excellence for Adoption Services (Revised edition). Washington, DC: Child Welfare League of America, Inc., 2000

46. National Association of Social Workers: Foster care and adoption, in Social Work Speaks: National Association of Social Workers Policy Statements, 2003–2006 (ed 6). Washington, DC: NASW Press, 2003, pp 144–51

47. Chimezie A: Transracial adoption of black children. Social Work 20:296–301, 1975

48. Jones E: On transracial adoption of black children. Child Welfare 51:156–64, 1972

49. Bowen JS: Cultural convergences and divergences: the nexus between putative Afro-American family values and the best interests of the child. J Family Law 26:487–531, 1987–1988

50. Griffith EEH: Culture and the debate on adoption of black children by white families, in American Psychiatric Press Review of Psychiatry (vol 14). Edited by Oldham JM, Riba MB. Washington, DC: American Psychiatric Press, 1995, pp 543–64

51.   Brooks D, Barth RP, Bussiere A, *et al*: Adoption and race: implementing the Multiethnic Placement Act and the Interethnic Adoption Provisions. Social Work 44:167–78, 1999

52.   Courtney ME: The politics and realities of transracial adoption. Child Welfare 76:749–79, 1997

POSTSCRIPT

Should Adoptive Parents Adopt Only within Their Own Racial/Ethnic Group?

As with any discussion of race, culture, or ethnicity, presumptions, perceptions, and biases can all affect how a person forms her or his opinion about this sensitive topic.

Consider your reactions to the readings—would your views change at all if the discussion were not about two parents of the same racial or ethnic background adopting a child from a different background, but rather about a man and a woman of two different racial or ethnic background choosing to procreate together? Why or why not? In doing so, the couple is intentionally creating a child who will have a race or ethnicity that is different from—albeit, a combination of—their own. If adopting outside of one's own group is okay—or not okay—with you, what about planned procreation, done within the context of a long-term committed relationship?

Also, consider your own racial or ethnic makeup—how, do you think, does this come into play as you think about your position for or against transracial adoption? If your initial response is, "not at all," I encourage you to go back and think again. It is impossible for who we are not to play some kind of role, even a small one, in how we think about issues pertaining to social membership, whether it is race, ethnicity, or culture, religion, sexual orientation, gender, or anything else.

Later in this edition, we will discuss adoption by same-sex parents. Keep the thoughts you had in response to this topic in mind as you read the later issue, and see whether your arguments can be applied to a same-sex couple adopting a child who may be heterosexual.

Suggested Readings

H. M. Dalmadge, *Tripping on the Color Line: Black-White Multiracial Families in a Racially Divided World.* Piscataway, NJ: Rutgers University Press, 2000.

H. Fogg-Davis, *Ethics of Transracial Adoption.* Ithaca, NY: Cornell University Press, 2001.

J. Lang, *Transracial Adoptions: An Adoptive Mother's Documentary of Racism, Injustice & Joy.* iUniverse, Incorporated, 2002.

S. Patton, *Birthmarks: Transracial Adoption in Contemporary America.* New York: New York University Press, 2000.

R. J. Simon, and H. Altstein, *Adoption across Borders: Serving the Children in Transracial and Intercountry Adoptions*. Lanham, MD: Rowman & Littlefield Publishers, Inc., 2000.

R. J. Simon, and R. Roorda, *In Their Own Voices: Transracial Adoptees Tell Their Stories*. New York: Columbia University Press, 2000.

G. Steinberg, and B. Hallinan, *Inside Transracial Adoption: Strength Based, Culture Sensitizing Parenting Strategies for Inter Country or Domestic Adoptive Families That Don't Match*. Indianapolis: Perspectives Press, Inc., 2000.

J. J. J. Trenka, S. Y. Shin, J. C. Oparah, and S. Y. Shin, eds., *Outsiders Within: Writing on Transracial Adoption*. Cambridge, MA: South End Press, 2006.

ISSUE 3

Does Divorce Create Long-Term Negative Effects for Children?

YES: Elizabeth Marquardt, from "The Bad Divorce," *First Things* (February 2005)

NO: Constance Ahrons, from *We're Still Family: What Grown Children Have to Say About Their Parents' Divorce* (Harper Collins, 2004)

ISSUE SUMMARY

YES: In reviewing Constance Ahrons' book, *We're Still Family: What Grown Children Have to Say About Their Parents' Divorce*, Elizabeth Marquardt, director of the Center for Marriage and Families at the Institute for American Values, argues that the manner in which Ahrons's questions were asked in her study yielded comments from participants in which they minimized the negative effects that their parents' divorce had on them. Through a combination of her own personal experience as a child of divorce and her work in the field, she maintains that divorce is a "tragedy" that dramatically and negatively impacts children for the rest of their lives.

NO: Constance Ahrons, author of *What Grown Children Have to Say About Their Parents' Divorce* and founding co-chair of the Council on Contemporary Families, found in her research findings that the ideas that children of divorced families end up much more troubled and unable to form adult relationships themselves are myths, that many adults whose parents divorced emerged from the experience stronger, wiser, and with closer relationships with their fathers, remaining connected to their families of origin even when the parent with whom they lived created a new stepfamily.

Interestingly enough, divorce rates among heterosexual married couples in the United States, which skyrocketed during the 1970s, started to decrease shortly thereafter. More recently, we are seeing an increase. Some people may have heard the oft-quoted statistic that the divorce rate in the United States between heterosexual married couples is around 50 percent, meaning 1 out of 2 marriages will end in divorce. According to writer Dan Hurley, the rate is a bit lower than that, at around 41 percent (from "Divorce Rate: It's Not as High as You Think," *The New York Times*, April 19, 2005). Other researchers, however, stand by the calculations that yielded the 50 percent number.

The statistics aside, an ongoing concern of estranged couples is how their relationship challenges may affect their child or children, especially if the couple chooses to separate or divorce. Aside from the logistical considerations—custody, visitation, decision making for the child—couple and youth professionals alike are concerned about the effects that being a child of divorced parents or caregivers can have on a child's ongoing development, as well as the child's perspective on love and committed relationships. Historically, professionals have maintained that divorce has long-standing, deleterious effects on a child's self-image, ability to relate to others, and much more. While many professionals maintain these views, many others are much more centrist, arguing that, even though divorce can have negative effects on children, these effects can be mitigated by the manner in which the divorce is handled by the parents. Many other professionals are at the other end of the argument, citing research that demonstrates how children of divorce actually ended up with higher self-esteem and a great feeling of independence than children of parents who stayed in unhealthy or unsatisfying relationships.

As you read the following viewpoints, consider the people in your own life—do you have friends or contemporaries whose parents divorced or are divorcing? What about your own parents or family members? How do your personal experiences jibe with or contradict the arguments stated by the authors?

In the following selections, Elizabeth Marquardt offers extensive criticism of the conclusions Constance Ahrons draws from the data she collected and reported on in her book, *We're Still Family*. . . . Also an author of a book about the effects of divorce and the adult child of divorced parents, Marquardt asserts that even amicable divorces have negative effects on children. Constance Ahrons, however, maintains that the arguments of Marquardt and others who disagree with her findings can actually be grouped into several categories of misconceptions, to which she responds individually. Divorce, she says, is complicated—so the blanketed labeling of divorce as always problematic to children is as oversimplified as it is inaccurate.

YES

Elizabeth Marquardt

The Bad Divorce

It is often said that those who are concerned about the social and personal effects of divorce are nostalgic for the 1950s, yearning for a mythical time when men worked, women happily stayed home baking cookies for the kids, and marriages never dissolved. Yet often the same people who make the charge of mythology are caught in a bit of nostalgia of their own, pining for the sexual liberationism of the 1970s, when many experts began to embrace unfettered divorce, confident that children, no less than adults, would thrive once "unhappy" marriages were brought to a speedy end.

Constance Ahrons, who coined the term "the good divorce" in the title of an influential 1992 book that examined ninety-eight divorcing couples, is very much a member of the latter camp. In her new book, *We're Still Family: What Grown Children Have to Say About Their Parents' Divorce,* Ahrons returns to those ninety-eight couples to survey their now-grown children. The result is a study based on telephone interviews with 173 young adults from eighty-nine families that tries to advance the idea it is not divorce itself that burdens children but rather the way in which parents divorce. As in her earlier book, Ahrons argues that the vocabulary we use to discuss divorce and remarriage is negative; she would prefer that we regard divorced families as "changed" or "rearranged" rather than broken, damaged, or destroyed. She claims that upbeat language will, above all, help children feel less stigmatized by divorce. Both of her books offer many new terms, such as "binuclear" and "tribe," to describe divorced families. The specific novelty of the new book is Ahrons' claim that her interviewees view their parents' divorces in a positive light.

It is with delight, then, that Ahrons shares surprising new findings from her on-going study. According to Ahrons, over three quarters of the young people from divorced families who she interviewed do not wish their parents were still together. A similar proportion feel their parents' decision to divorce was a good one, that their parents are better off today, and that they themselves are either better off or not affected by the divorce. To general readers who have been following the debates about children of divorce in recent years, such findings might sound like big news. But there are problems.

According to Ahrons, over three-quarters of the young people whom she interviewed do not wish that their parents were still together. A similar proportion feel that their parents' decision to divorce was a good one, that their parents are better off today, and that they themselves are either better off because of the divorce or have not been affected by it. Statistically, that sounds overwhelmingly convincing. But an answer to a survey question tells us very little unless we have a context for interpreting it and some grasp of the actual experiences that gave rise to it.

Like those whom Ahrons interviewed, I grew up in a divorced family, my parents having split when I was two years old. Like Ahrons, I am a researcher in the field, having led, with Norval Glenn, a study of young adults from both divorced and intact families that included a nationally representative telephone survey of some 1,500 people. As someone who studies children of divorce and who is herself a grown child of divorce, I have noticed that the kinds of questions that get asked in such studies and the way the answers are interpreted often depend on whether the questioner views divorce from the standpoint of the child or the parent.

Take, for example, Ahrons' finding that the majority of people raised in divorced families do not wish that their parents were together. Ahrons did not ask whether as children these young people had hoped their parents would reunite. Instead, she asked if they wish today their parents were still together. She presents their negative answers as gratifying evidence that divorce is affirmed by children. But is that really the right conclusion to draw?

Imagine the following scenario. One day when you are a child your parents come to you and tell you they are splitting up. Your life suddenly changes in lots of ways. Dad leaves, or maybe Mom does. You may move or change schools or lose friendships, or all of the above. Money is suddenly very tight and stays that way for a long time. You may not see one set of grandparents, aunts, uncles, and cousins nearly as much as you used to. Then, Mom starts dating, or maybe Dad does. A boyfriend or girlfriend moves in, perhaps bringing along his or her own kids. You may see one or both of your parents marry again; you may see one or both of them get divorced a second time. You deal with the losses. You adjust as best you can. You grow up and try to figure out this "relationship" thing for yourself. Then, some interviewer on the telephone asks if you wish your parents were still together today. A lifetime of pain and anger and adjustment flashes before your eyes. Any memory of your parents together as a couple—if you can remember them together at all—is buried deep under all those feelings. Your divorced parents have always seemed like polar opposites to you. No one could be more different from your mother than your father, and vice versa. "No," you reply to the interviewer, "I don't wish my parents were still together." Of course, one cannot automatically attribute such a train of thought to all of Ahrons' interview subjects. Still, it is plausible, and it might explain at least some of the responses. But Ahrons does not even consider it.

Ahrons tells us that the vast majority of young people in her study feel that they are either better off or not affected by their parents' divorce. For a child of divorce there could hardly be a more loaded question than this one. The generation that Ahrons is interviewing grew up in a time of massive changes in family life, with experts assuring parents that if they became happier after divorce, their children would as well. There wasn't a lot of patience for people who felt otherwise—especially when those people were children, with their agg-ravating preference for conventional married life over the adventures of divorce, and their tendency to look askance at their parents' new love interests.

However, a child soon learns the natural lesson that complaining about a parent's choices is a surefire way to be ignored or worse, and that what parents want above all is praise for those choices. Few things inspire as much admira-tion among divorced parents and their friends as the words of a child reassur-ing them that the divorce was no big deal—or even better, that it gave the child something beneficial, like early independence, or a new brother or sister. Par-ents are proud of a resilient child. They are embarrassed and frustrated by a child who claims to be a victim. And who among us wants to be a victim? Who would not rather be a hero, or at least a well-adjusted and agreeable per-son? When the interviewer calls on the telephone, what will the young adult be more likely to say? Something like "I'm damaged goods"? Or "Yes, it was tough at times but I survived it, and I'm stronger for it today." It is the second reply that children of divorce have all their lives been encouraged to give; and the fact that they are willing to give it yet again is hardly, as Ahrons would have it, news.

Thus, Ahrons' statistics on their own hardly constitute three cheers for divorce. Far more meaningful and revealing are the extended quotations from interview subjects with which the book is liberally studded. She writes, for instance, that Andy, now thirty-two, sees "value" in his parents' divorce. Why? Because:

> "I learned a lot. I grew up a lot more quickly than a lot of my friends. Not that that's a good thing or a bad thing. People were always thinking I was older than I was because of the way I carried myself."

Treating a sad, unfortunate experience (like being forced to grow up more quickly than one's peers) as something neutral or even positive is merely one example of what can happen when a person attempts to conform to a culture that insists that divorce is no big deal. To take such an ambivalent response as clear evidence that divorce does no damage, as Ahrons does is inexcusable.

Ahrons cheerfully reports other "good" results of divorce. Here for example is Brian, whose parents split when he was five:

> "In general, I think [the divorce] has had very positive effects. I see what hap-pens in divorces, and I have promised myself that I would do anything to not get a divorce. I don't want my kids to go through what I went through."

Tracy, whose parents divorced when she was twelve, sees a similar upside to divorce:

> "I saw some of the things my parents did and know not to do that in my marriage and see the way they treated each other and know not to do that to my spouse and my children. I know [the divorce] has made me more committed to my husband and my children."

These are ringing endorsements of divorce as a positive life event? Like the testimony of a child who's learned a painful but useful lesson about the dangers of playing with fire, such accounts indicate that the primary benefit of divorce is to encourage young people to avoid it in their own lives if at all possible.

Then there are the significant problems with the structure of Ahrons' study itself. While the original families were recruited using a randomized method, the study lacks any control group. In other words, Ahrons interviewed plenty of young people from divorced families but spoke to no one of similar ages from intact families. So she really can't tell us anything at all about how these young people might differ from their peers.

Rather than acknowledging that her lack of a control group is a serious limitation, Ahrons sidesteps the issue. In several places she compares her subjects to generalized "social trends" or "their contemporaries" and decides, not surprisingly, that they are not all that different. Thus, Ahrons notes that many of the young people from divorced families told her they frequently struggled with issues of "commitment, trust, and dealing with conflict," but on this finding she comments, "These issues are precisely the ones that most adults in this stage of their development grapple with, whether they grow up in a nuclear family or not." Never mind that she has not interviewed any of those other young people, or cited any studies to back up her contention, or acknowledged the possibility that, while all young people do have to deal with these kinds of interpersonal issues, some have a much harder time doing it than others. Ahrons instead wholly dismisses the pain expressed by the children of divorce and assures us that they are simply passing through a normal development phase.

When it comes to her conclusions, Ahrons claims that "if you had a devitalized or high-conflict marriage, you can take heart that the decision to divorce may have been the very best thing you could have done for your children." While research does show that children, on average, do better after a high-conflict marriage ends (the same research, by Paul Amato and Alan Booth, also shows that only one-third of divorces end high-conflict marriages), no one—Ahrons included—has shown that children do better when an adult ends a marriage he or she perceives as "devitalized." Children don't much care whether their parents have a "vital" marriage. They care whether their mother and father live with them, take care of them, and don't fight a lot. . . .

Ahrons' also remains preoccupied with the concept of stigma. She writes, for instance, that we are seeing "progress" because a high divorce rate has the effect of reducing the stigma experienced by children of divorce. That's all well and good, but one wonders why Ahrons gives stigma so much attention while saying nothing about a far more damaging social problem for children of divorce—namely, silence. Consider my own experience. The type of family in which I grew up was radically different from the intact family model. Yet no one around me, not even therapists, ever once acknowledged that fact. Never mind that my beloved father lived hours away, or that the mother I adored was often stressed as she tried to earn a living while also acting as a single parent. I was left to assume, like many children of divorce, that whatever problems I struggled with were no one's fault but my own. The demand that children of divorce keep quiet and get with the program puts them in the position of protecting adults from guilt and further stress—effectively reversing the natural order of family life in which the adults are the protectors of children.

Ahrons is remarkably unsympathetic to the children on whom this burden is laid. What do children of divorce long for? According to Ahrons, they nurture unrealistic hopes for "tidy," "perfect" families. She uses these words so frequently—the first term appears at least six times in the book and the second at least four times—that she sometimes appears to be portraying children of divorce as weird obsessives. Speaking directly to children of divorce, Ahrons offers the following advice: "You may not have the idyllic family you dreamed of . . . [but] often the only thing within our control is how we perceive or interpret an event." "For example, you can choose to see your family as rearranged, or you can choose to see it as broken." Indeed, the curative powers of social constructivism are nothing short of miraculous. Encouraging readers to stop using the descriptive term "adult child of divorce," she asserts that "it's a stigmatizing label that presumes you are deficient or traumatized. . . . If you have fallen prey to using it to explain something about yourself, ask yourself if it is keeping you from making changes that might bring you more satisfaction in your life." Apparently, coming to grips with one's family history and the deepest sources of one's sadness and loneliness is the worst thing a child can do. . . .

Ahrons surely knows more about the tragedies of divorce than her thesis allows her to admit. She has studied divorced families for years. She has worked with them as a clinician. She has been through divorce herself. Yet she inevitably follows up heartbreaking observations of interviewees with the confident assertion that everyone involved would be so much happier if only they talked themselves out of—and even walked away from—their anguish. As she writes in one (unintentionally haunting) passage, "Over the years I have listened to many divorcing parents in my clinical practice talk about how much they look forward to the day when their children will be grown and they won't have to have anything more to do with their exes." Is it possible to image a sadder or more desperate desire than this one—the longing for one's children to grow up faster so that relations with one's ex-spouse can be more effectively severed? In such passages it becomes obvious that all of Ahrons' efforts to explain away the tragedy of divorce and its legacy are in vain. In the end, the theory collapses before reality.

Ahrons' poorly structured study and far too tendentious thesis are of no help to us in thinking through our approach to divorce and its consequences. Children of divorce are real, complex people who are deeply shaped by a new kind of fractured family life—one whose current prevalence is unprecedented in human history. These children are not nostalgic for "tidy," "perfect," "idyllic" families. They grieve the real losses that follow from their parents' divorce. They don't need new words to describe what they've been through. Ordinary words will serve quite well—provided that people are willing to listen to them.

No Easy Answers: Why the Popular View of Divorce Is Wrong

It was a sunny, unseasonably warm Sunday morning in October. In a quaint country inn in New Jersey, surrounded by a glorious autumn garden, my young grandchildren and I waited patiently for their Aunt Jennifer's wedding to begin. The white carpet was unrolled, the guests were assembled, and the harpist was playing Pachelbel's Canon.

A hush came over the guests. The first member of the bridal party appeared. Poised at the entry, she took a deep breath as she began her slow-paced walk down the white wedding path. Pauline, my grandchildren's stepgreat-grandmother, made her way down the aisle, pausing occasionally to greet family and friends. A round of applause spontaneously erupted. She had traveled fifteen hundred miles to be at her granddaughter's wedding, when only days before, a threatening illness made her presence doubtful.

Next in the grand parade came the best man, one of the groom's three brothers. Proudly, he made his way down the aisle and took his position, ready to be at his brother's side. Then the two maids of honor, looking lovely in their flowing black chiffon gowns, made their appearance. My grandchildren started to wiggle and whisper: "It's Aunt Amy [my younger daughter]! And Christine [the longtime girlfriend who cohabits with Uncle Craig, my daughters' half-brother]!" As they walked down the aisle and moved slowly past us, special smiles were exchanged with my grandchildren—their nieces and nephew.

Seconds later, my youngest granddaughter pointed excitedly, exclaiming, "Here comes Mommy!" They waved excitedly as the next member of the bridal party, the matron of honor—*their mother, my daughter*—made her way down the path. She paused briefly at our row to exchange a fleeting greeting with her children.

Next, the groom, soon officially to be their "Uncle Andrew," with his mother's arm linked on his left, and his father on his right. The happy three-some joined the processional. Divorced from each other when Andrew was a child, his parents beamed in anticipation of the marriage of their eldest son.

Silence. All heads now turned to catch their first glimpse of the bride. Greeted with oohs and aahs, Aunt Jennifer was radiant as she walked arm in arm with her proud and elegant mother, their stepgrandmother, Grandma Susan. Sadly missed at that moment was the father of the bride, my former husband, who had passed away a few years earlier.

When I told friends in California I was flying to the East Coast for a family wedding, I stumbled over how to explain my relationship to the bride. To some I explained: "She's my exhusband's daughter by his second wife." To others, perhaps to be provocative and draw attention to the lack of kinship terms, I said, "She's my daughters' sister." Of course, technically she's my daughters' halfsister, but many years ago my daughters told me firmly that that term "half-sister" was utterly ridiculous. Jennifer wasn't a half anything, she was their *real* sister. Some of my friends thought it strange that I would be invited; others thought it even stranger that I would travel cross-country to attend.

The wedding reception brought an awkward moment or two, when some of the groom's guests asked a common question, "How was I related to the bride?" With some guilt at violating my daughters' dictum, but not knowing how else to identify our kinship, I answered, "She is my daughters' halfsister." A puzzled look. It was not that they didn't understand the relationship, but it seemed strange to them that I was a wedding guest. As we talked, a few guests noted how nice it was that I was there, and then with great elaboration told me stories about their own complex families. Some told me sad stories of families torn apart by divorce and remarriage, and others related happy stories of how their complex families of divorce had come together at family celebrations.

At several points during this celebratory day, I happened to be standing next to the bride's mother when someone from the groom's side asked us how we were related. She or I pleasantly answered, "We used to be married to the same man." This response turned out to be a showstopper. The question asker was at a loss to respond. First and second wives aren't supposed to be amicable or even respectful toward one another. And certainly, first wives are not supposed to be included in their exhusband's new families. And last of all, first and second wives shouldn't be willing to comfortably share the information of having a husband in common.

Although it may appear strange, my exhusband's untimely death brought his second and first families closer together. I had mourned at his funeral and spent time with his family and friends for several days afterward. A different level of kinship formed, as we—his first and second families—shared our loss and sadness. Since then, we have chosen to join together at several family celebrations, which has added a deeper dimension to our feelings of family.

You may be thinking, "This is all so rational. There's no way my family could pull this off." Or perhaps, like the many people who have shared their stories with me over the years, you are nodding your head knowingly, remembering similar occasions in your own family. The truth is we are like many extended families rearranged by divorce. My ties to my exhusband's family are not close but we care about one another. We seldom have contact outside of family occasions, but we know we're family. We hear stories of each other's comings and goings, transmitted to us through our mutual ties to my daughters, and now, through grandchildren. But if many families, like my own, continue to have relationships years after divorce, why don't we hear more about them?

Quite simply, it's because this is not the way it's supposed to be. My family, and the many others like mine, don't fit the ideal images we have about families. They appear strange because they're not tidy. There are "extra" people and relationships that don't exist in nuclear families and are awkward to describe because we don't have familiar and socially defined kinship terms to do so. Although families rearranged and expanded by divorce are rapidly growing and increasingly common, our resistance to accepting them as normal makes them appear deviant.

Societal change is painfully slow, which results in the situation wherein the current realities of family life come into conflict with our valued images. Sociologists call this difference "cultural lag," the difference between what is real and what we hold as ideal. This lag occurs because of our powerful resistance to acknowledging changes that challenge our basic beliefs about what's good and what's bad in our society.

Why Good Divorces Are Invisible

Good divorces are those in which the divorce does not destroy meaningful family relationships. Parents maintain a sufficiently cooperative and supportive relationship that allows them to focus on the needs of their children. In good divorces children continue to have ties to both their mothers and their fathers, and each of their extended families, including those acquired when either parent remarries.

Good divorces have been well-kept secrets because to acknowledge them in mainstream life threatens our nostalgic images of family. If the secret got out that indeed many families that don't fit our "mom and pop" household ideal are healthy, we would have to question the basic societal premise that marriage and family are synonymous. And that reality upsets a lot of people, who then respond with familiar outcries that divorce is eroding our basic values and destroying society.

Although we view ourselves as a society in which nuclear families and lifelong monogamous marriages predominate, the reality is that 43 percent of first marriages will end in divorce. Over half of new marriages are actually remarriages for at least one of the partners. Not only have either the bride or groom (or both) been divorced but increasingly one of them also has parents who are divorced.

Families are the way we organize to raise children. Although we hold the ideal image that marriage is a precursor to establishing a family, modern parents are increasingly challenging this traditional ideal. Families today arrange—and rearrange—themselves in many responsible ways that meet the needs of children for nurturance, guidance and economic support. Family historian Stephanie Coontz, in her book *The Way We Never Were*, shows how the "tremendous variety of workable childrearing patterns in history suggests that, with little effort, we should be able to forge new institutions and values."

One way we resist these needed societal changes is by denying that divorce is no longer deviant. We demean divorced families by clinging to the belief that families can't exist outside of marriage. It follows then that stories of healthy families that don't fit the tidy nuclear family package are rare and stories that show how divorce destroys families and harms children are common.

In this way, bad divorces appear to represent the American way of divorce and good divorces become invisible.

Messages That Hinder Good Divorces

When the evils of divorce are all that families hear about, it makes coping with the normal transitions and changes that inevitably accompany divorce all the more difficult. Negative messages make children feel different and lesser, leading to feelings of shame and guilt. Parents who feel marginalized in this way are less likely to think about creative solutions to their problems. That all of this unnecessary anxiety is fueled by sensationalized reports of weak findings, half-truths and myths of devastation is deplorable. Only by sorting out the truths about divorce from the fiction can we be empowered to make better decisions, find healthy ways to maintain family relationships, and develop important family rituals after divorce. Let's take a close look at the most common misconceptions about divorce.

Misconception 1: Parents Should Stay Married for the Sake of the Kids

This is message that pervades our culture, and it rests on a false duality: Marriage is good for kids, divorce is bad. Underlying this premise is the belief that parents who divorce are immature and selfish because they put their personal needs ahead of the needs of their children, that because divorce is too easy to get, spouses give up on their marriages too easily and that if you're thinking about divorcing your spouse, you should "stick it out till the kids are grown." A popular joke takes this message to its extreme. A couple in their nineties, married for seventy years, appears before a judge in their petition for a divorce. The judge looks at them quizzically and asks, "Why now, why after all these years?" The couple responds: "We waited until the children were dead."

The research findings are now very clear that reality is nowhere near as simple and tidy. Unresolved, open interparental conflict between married spouses that pervades day-to-day family life has been shown again and again to have negative effects on children. Most experts agree that when this is the case it is better for the children if parents divorce rather than stay married. Ironically, prior to the initiation of no-fault legislation over twenty years ago, in most states this kind of open conflict in the home was considered "cruel and inhumane" treatment and it was one of the few grounds on which a divorce would be granted—if it could be proved.

But the majority of unsatisfying marriages are not such clearcut cases. When most parents ask themselves if they should stay married for the sake of their children, they have clearly reached the point where they are miserable in their marriages but wouldn't necessarily categorize them as "high-conflict." And here is where, in spite of the societal message, there is no agreement in the research findings or among clinical experts. That's because it's extremely complex and each individual situation is too different to allow for a "one-size-fits-all" answer.

A huge list of factors comes into play when assessing whether staying married would be better for your kids. For example,

- Is the unhappiness in your marriage making you so depressed or angry that your children's needs go unmet because you can't parent effectively?
- Do you and your spouse have a cold and distant relationship that makes the atmosphere at home unhealthy for your children?
- Do you and your spouse lack mutual respect, caring or interests, setting a poor model for your children?
- Would the financial hardships be so dire that your children will experience a severely reduced standard of living?

Add to this your child's temperament, resources and degree of resilience, and then the personal and family changes that take place in the years after the divorce, and you can see how the complexities mount.

It is a rare parent who divorces *too easily*. Most parents are responsible adults who spend years struggling with the extremely difficult and complex decision of whether to divorce or stay married "for the sake of the children." The bottom line is that divorce is an adult decision, usually made by one spouse, entered into in the face of many unknowns. Without a crystal ball, no one knows whether their decision will be better for their children. As you read further in this book, however, you may gain some perspective on what will be most helpful in your situation, with your children, by listening carefully to the reactions and feelings of various children of divorce *as they have changed over twenty years.*

Misconception 2: "Adult Children of Divorce" Are Doomed to Have Lifelong Problems

If your parents divorced when you were a child, you are often categorized as an ACOD, an "adult child of divorce," and we all know there's nothing good to be said about that. I dislike this label because it is stigmatizing. It casts dark shadows over divorcing parents and their children, results in feelings of shame and guilt, and is another way of pathologizing divorce.

Years ago I coined a term, "divorcism," to call attention to the stereotypes and stigma attached to divorce. To put children with divorced parents in a special category is divorcism in action. It stereotypes them as a group with problems, and like all stereotypes it ignores individual differences.

If your parents didn't divorce, are you then called an "adult child of marriage"? No, you're just "normal." Normal kids must have two parents of different genders who live in the same household; anything else is abnormal, and if you're abnormal then you must be dysfunctional. That's the way the American family story goes.

Perhaps the worst outcome of this labeling is that it makes parents and children feel that this one event has doomed them and they don't have the power to change anything. This pinpointing of divorce as the source of personal problems is pervasive. Parents worry that whatever problems their kids have, even when they are normal developmental issues, were caused by the divorce. Children are encouraged to blame the divorce for whatever unhappiness they may feel, which makes them feel helpless about improving their lives. Teachers are often too quick to identify divorce as the reason for a child's school behavior problem. The greater society points a finger at divorce as the reason for a wide range of greater social problems.

The truth is that, for the great majority of children who experience a parental divorce, the divorce becomes part of their history but it is not a defining factor. Like the rest of us, most of them reach adulthood to lead reasonably happy, successful lives. Although children who grew up with divorced parents certainly share an important common experience, their ability to form healthy relationships, be good parents, build careers, and so on, are far more determined by their individual temperaments, their sibling relationships, the dynamics within their parents' *marriages* and the climate of their *postdivorce* family lives.

Misconception 3: Divorce Means You Are no Longer a Family

There's this myth that as long as you stay married your family is good but as soon as you announce you're separating, your family is thrown into the bad zone. Your family goes from being "intact" to being "dissolved," form two-parent to single parent, from functional to dysfunctional. Even though we all know that people don't jump from happy marriages right into divorce, there is an assumption that the decision to separate is the critical marker. It doesn't seem to matter whether your marital relationship was terrible, whether you were miserable and your children troubled. Just as long as you are married and living together in one household, the sign over the front door clearly states to the world, "We're a normal family."

The inaccurate and misleading message that divorce destroys families is harmful to both parents and children because it hides and denies all the positive ways that families can be rearranged after divorce. It sends the destructive message to children that divorce means they only get to keep one parent and they will no longer be part of a family. Although two-parent first-married households now represent less than 25 percent of all households, and an increasing number of children each year are raised by unmarried adults, many people cling to the belief that healthy families can only be two-parent married families and social change is always bad and threatening to our very foundations.

ↄ⊕ↄ

When Julie, one of the participants in my study, married recently, she walked down the aisle with a father on either side. On her left was her biological father, on her right was her stepfather of eighteen years. Her mother was her matron of honor, who joined her former and present husbands, all standing together to witness the marriage. Two best men, the groom's eleven-year-old twin sons from his first marriage, stood next to him. Helen, the groom's former wife, sat close by, accompanied by Tony, her live-in partner.

While this wedding ceremony doesn't fit the traditional pattern, Don and Julie have joined the three-quarters of American households who have living arrangements other than that of the "traditional" family.

My older daughter thanked me for coming to Jennifer's wedding. She told me that my being there made it possible for her to share this happy occasion with *all* her family, instead of feeling the disconnections that some children feel in divorced families. This bonding spreads to the third generation so that my grandchildren know us all as family.

The truth is that although some divorces result in family breakdown, the vast majority do not. While divorce changes the form of the family from one household to two, from a nuclear family to a binuclear one, it does not need to change the way children think and feel about the significant relationships within their families. This does not mean that divorce is not painful or difficult, but over the years, as postdivorce families change and even expand, most remain capable of meeting children's needs for family.

Misconception 4: Divorce Leaves Children without Fathers

This message is linked closely with the preceding one because when we say that divorce destroys families we really mean that fathers disappear from the family. The myths that accompany this message are that fathers are "deadbeat dads" who abandon their kids and leave their families impoverished. The message strongly implies that fathers don't care and are unwilling or unable to make continuing commitments to their children. While this reflects the reality for a minority of divorced fathers, the majority of fathers continue to have loving relationships with their children and contribute financially to their upbringing.

The truth is that many fathers do spend less time with their children after divorce, but to stereotype them as parents who abandon their children only creates more difficulty for both fathers and their children. It establishes a myth that men are irresponsible parents who don't care about their children, when in reality most feel great pain that they are not able to see their children more frequently. In the vast majority of divorces, over 85 percent, mothers are awarded sole custody, or in the case of joint custody, primary residence. This means that most fathers become nonresidential parents after divorce. Being a nonresidential father is a difficult role with no preparation or guidelines.

Most of the research on dads after divorce focuses on absentee fathers, while involved fathers are frequently overlooked. Many fathers continue to be excellent parents after divorce and in fact some fathers and children report that their relationships actually improve after the divorce. In much the same way that good divorces are invisible in the public debate, so are involved fathers.

Misconception 5: Exspouses Are Incapable of Getting Along

When I first started to study divorce in the early 1970s, it was assumed in the literature that any continuing relationship between exspouses was a sign of serious pathology, an inability to adjust to the divorce, to let go and to move on with their lives.

In the late 1970s, when joint custody was first introduced, it was met with loud cries of skepticism from the opposition. How could two parents who couldn't get along well enough to stay married possibly get along well enough to continue to share parenting? Two decades ago I confronted the skeptics by writing several articles arguing that we needed to accept the reality of our divorce rates and needed to transform our values about parenting after divorce. The issue was no longer *whether* divorced parents should share parenting to meet their children's needs but *how*.

Although there have been many legal changes over the years, and some form of joint custody legislation exists now in all states, questions about its viability still prevail. These accusations, citing joint custody as a failed "social experiment," are not based on research findings, which are still very limited and inconclusive, but instead on the ill-founded stereotype that all divorcing spouses are bitter enemies, too lost in waging their own wars to consider their children. Certainly this is true for some divorcing spouses, the ones that make headlines in bitter custody disputes, but it is not true for the majority.

Although we have come to realize that parents who divorce still need to have some relationship with one another, the belief that it's not really possible still lingers. In fact, when exspouses remain friends they are viewed as a little strange and their relationship is suspect. Yet, the truth is that many divorced parents *are* cooperative and effective coparents. Like good divorces and involved fathers, they are mostly invisible in the media.

Despite much resistance, joint custody has become increasingly common, and new words, such as "coparents," have emerged in response to this reality. The newest edition of *Webster's College Dictionary* (2000) recognizes the term, defining it as separated or divorced parents who share custody and child rearing equally. While I don't agree that coparenting is limited only to those parents who share child rearing equally, or even that those who coparent need to share equally in time or responsibility, the inclusion of the word in the dictionary sanctions important new kinship language for divorced families, thereby advancing our ability to acknowledge complex family arrangements.

Misconception 6: Divorce Turns Everyone into Exfamily; In-Laws Become Outlaws

When it comes to the semantics of divorce-speak, all of the kinship ties that got established by marriage dissolve abruptly. On the day of the legal divorce, my husband and all of his relatives suddenly became exes. But even though the kinship is *legally* terminated, meaningful relationships often continue. My friend Jan, during her fifteen-year marriage, formed a very close relationship with her mother-in-law. Now, twenty years later, she still calls her eighty-two-year-old exmother-in-law "Mom," talks with her several times a week and has dinner with her weekly. Exmother-in-law is certainly not an adequate description of this ongoing relationship.

As a culture we continue to resist accepting divorce as a normal endpoint to marriage even though it is an option chosen by almost half of those who marry. It is this cultural lag, this denial of current realities that causes the inaccurate language, not only for the family ties that continue but also for the family we inherit when we, our former spouses, our parents or our children remarry. Kinship language is important because it provides a shorthand way for us to identify relationships without wading through tedious explanations.

We have terms like "cousin," "great-aunt" or uncle, and "sister-in-law" that help us quickly identify lineage in families. Even these kinship terms are sometimes inadequate and confusing. For example, "sister-in-law" can mean my brother's wife, or my husband's sister, or my husband's brother's wife. And even though you don't know exactly *how* she is related to me, you do at least know that she belongs in the family picture. The in-law suffix quickly tells you that we are not blood relatives but we are related through marriage lines.

Our failure to provide kinship language that recognizes some kind of viable relationship between parents who are no longer married to each other, as well as language that incorporates old and new family as kin, makes children feel that their identity is shattered by divorce. It is no wonder that we remain in the dark ages when it comes to normalizing complex families after divorce and remarriage.

Our language and models for divorce and remarriage are inadequate at best, and pejorative at worst. Relegating the relationship between divorced spouses who are parents to the term "exspouse" hurls children and their parents into the dark territory of "exfamily." The common terms of "broken home," "dissolved family," and "single-parent family" all imply that children are left with either no family or only one parent.

This lack of positive language is one more way that the invisibility of good divorces impacts postdivorce families.

Misconception 7: Stepparents Aren't Real Parents

One of the implications of the high divorce rate is that the shape and composition of families have changed dramatically in the last twenty years. All over the world, weddings no longer fit the traditional model: there are stepparents, half siblings, stepsiblings, stepchildren, intimate partners of parents, stepgrandparents and even, on rare occasions, exspouses of the bride or groom.

٭۞٭

To complicate the wedding picture even more, one or both of the bride and groom's parents may have been divorced. And given that well over half of those who divorce eventually remarry, we are likely to find that the majority of those who have divorced parents also have stepparents. Add the dramatic increase in cohabitation to that equation and it is not unusual for an "unmarried intimate partner" of one of the parents to be present as well. These complex families require photographers to quickly switch to their wide-angle lens and totally revamp their traditional formats for wedding photos.

Over half the children today have adults in their lives for whom they can't attach socially accepted kinship terms. They lack social rules that would help them know how they are supposed to relate and how to present these adults to the social world around them. I am reminded here of a *Herman* cartoon, showing a boy holding his report card and asking his teacher: "Which parent do you want to sign it: my natural father, my stepfather, my mother's third husband, my real mother or my natural father's fourth wife who lives with us?"

As the cartoon clearly suggests, there are real and natural parents, and then there are stepparents. Stepmothers are stereotyped in children's literature as mean, nasty and even abusive. The only time we hear about stepfathers is when the media highlights the sensationalized case of sexual abuse. Added to these negative images is the reality that stepparents have no legal rights to their stepchildren. The research on stepparents is still very limited and positive role models are lacking.

Children and their new stepparents start off their relationships with two strikes against them. They have to fight an uphill battle to overcome negative expectations, and they have to do so without much help from society. Since almost 85 percent of the children with divorced parents will have a stepparent at some time in their lives, it is shocking that we know so little about how these relationships work. Clearly, societal resistance to recognizing the broad spectrum of postdivorce families has hindered the development of good role models for stepchildren and their stepparents.

Painting a False Picture

Taken together, these negative messages paint a false picture of divorce, one that assumes family ties are irretrievably broken so that postdivorce family relationships appear to be nonexistent. Despite these destructive messages, many divorced parents meet the needs of their children by creating strong families after divorce. Without a doubt, divorce is painful and creates stress for families, but it is important to remember that most recover, maintaining some of their kinship relationships and adding new ones over time.

By making good divorces invisible we have accepted bad divorces as the norm. In so doing, children and their divorced parents are being given inaccurate messages that conflict with the realities they live and make them feel deviant and stigmatized. It is time we challenge these outdated, ill-founded messages and replace them with new ones that acknowledge and accurately reflect current realities.

The Distortions of Oversimplifying

Just a little over a decade ago, in January 1989, the *New York Times* Magazine ran a cover story called "Children after Divorce," which created a wave of panic in divorced parents and their children. Judith Wallerstein and her coauthor, Sandra Blakeslee, a staff writer for the *New York Times,* noted their newest unexpected finding. Calling it the "sleeper effect," they concluded that only ten years after divorce did it become apparent that girls experience "serious effects of divorce at the time they are entering young adulthood."

When one of the most prestigious newspapers in the world highlights the findings of a study, most readers take it seriously. "That 66 percent of young women in our study between the ages of nineteen and twenty-three will suffer debilitating effects of their parents' divorce years later" immediately became generalized to the millions of female children with divorced parents. The message—just when you think everything may be okay, the doom of divorce will rear its ugly head—is based on a *mere eighteen out of the grand total of twenty-seven women* interviewed in this age group. This detail wasn't mentioned in the fine print of the article but is buried in the appendix of the book that was scheduled for publication a month after the *New York Times* story appeared. And it is on this slim data that the seeds of a myth are planted. We are still living with the fallout.

In sharp contrast to Wallerstein's view that parental divorce has a powerful devastating impact on children well into adulthood, another psychologist made headlines with a completely opposite thesis. In her book, *The Nurture Assumption: Why Children Turn Out the Way They Do*, Judith Rich Harris proposes that what parents do makes little difference in how their children's lives turn out. Half of the variation in children's behavior and personality is due to genes, claims Harris, and the other half to environmental factors, mainly their peer relationships. For this reason, Harris asserts parental divorce is not responsible for all the ills it is blamed for.

These extreme positions—of divorce as disaster and divorce as inconsequential—oversimplify the realities of our complex lives. Genes and contemporary relationships notwithstanding, we have strong evidence that parents still make a significant difference in their children's development. Genetic inheritance and peer relationships are part of the story but certainly not the whole story.

Sorting Out the Research Findings

Drawing conclusions across the large body of research on divorce is difficult. Studies with different paradigms ask different questions that lead to different answers. A classic wisdom story shows the problem. Three blind men bumped into an elephant as they walked through the woods. They didn't know what it was, but each prided himself on his skill at "seeing." So one blind man reached out and carefully explored the elephant's leg. He described in great detail the rough, scratchy surface that was huge and round. "Aha, this is an ancient mighty tree. We're in a new forest." "No, no," said the blind man who had taken hold of the elephant's trunk. "We're in great danger—this is a writhing snake, bigger than any in our hometown. Run!" The third man laughed at them both. He'd been touching the elephant's tusk, noticing the smooth hard surface, the gentle curve, the rounded end. "Nonsense! We have discovered an exquisitely carved horn for announcing the emperor's arrival."

The blind men described what they "saw" accurately. Their mistake was to claim that what they saw was the whole. Much like the three blind men, researchers see different parts of the divorce elephant, which then frames their investigations.

It should come, then, as no surprise that reports of the findings about divorce are often contradictory and confusing. It is impossible for any study to take account of all the complexities of real life, or of the individual differences that allow one family to thrive in a situation that would create enormous stress, and frayed relationships, in another. But it is in these variations that we can begin to make sense of how divorce impacts the lives of individuals and families.

Facing Reality

Hallmark Cards recently launched a line of greeting cards called "Ties That Bind" aimed at various nontraditional unions—from stepfamilies to adopted child households to unmarried partnerships. "Our cards reflect the times," says Marita Wesely-Clough, trend group manager at Hallmark. "Relationships today are so nebulous that they are hard to pin down, but in creating products, we have to be aware that they are there. Companies need to respect and be sensitive to how people are truly living their lives now, and not how they might wish or hope for them to live."

Advertising agencies and marketing services make it their business to assess social realities. To sell their products, they have to evaluate the needs and desires of their potential consumers. They do not share the popular cultural anxiety about the changes in families. Instead they study them and alter their products to suit. Policy makers would do well to take some lessons from them and alter their preconceived notions about families to reflect current realities.

While the political focus today is on saving marriages and preserving traditional family values, Americans in large numbers are dancing to their own drummers. They're cohabiting in increasingly large numbers, having more children "out of wedlock" and engaging in serial marriages. While the rates of divorce have come down from their 1981 highs, they have leveled off at a high rate that is predicted to remain stable. To meet the needs of children and parents, we need to burst the balloon about idealized families and support families as they really live their lives. And that means we have to face the true complexities of *our* families and not search for simple answers.

As you read this book, keep in mind that we can all look back on our childhoods and note something about our mothers or fathers or sisters or brothers that has had lasting effects on our personalities. If you are looking to answer the question of whether a parental divorce results in children having more or less problems than children who grew up in other living situations, you will be disappointed. Nor will you find answers to whether the stresses of divorce are worse for children than other stresses in life. However, you will find answers here to questions about how and why individual children respond in different ways to the variations in their divorced families.

Divorce is a stressful life event that requires increased focus on parenting. The effort and care that parents put into establishing their postdivorce families are crucial and will pay off over the years in their many benefits to the children. But remember, families are complex, and if you find easy answers, they are likely to be wrong.

POSTSCRIPT

Does Divorce Create Long-Term Negative Effects For Children?

In considering the effects, negative, neutral, or even positive, of divorce, it is important to consider a number of questions—among them being:

- Did the child have individual relationships with each parent prior to the divorce, and is each parent determined to maintain that close bond moving forward?
- Did the divorce come as a result of active conflict—such as an infidelity, ongoing disagreements or arguing, or even violence?
- How old is the child at the time of the divorce?
- Does either or both parents end up in new, long-term committed relationships with new partners or spouses?

It is clear that even these simple questions do not have clear answers, particularly when it comes to their outcome on the children of the parents who divorced. For example, what if one of the divorced parents moves a significant distance away from the family of origin? This would, indeed, make maintaining the relationship with the child challenging, although advances in technology has begun to aid in this process. If there were a great deal of conflict in the home prior to the divorce, and a child is affected developmentally, can the effects be isolated to the conflict or attributed to the dissolution of the relationship? The younger a child is when parents separate, the less likely they are to understand it, although if there is much conflict in the home, a child may respond viscerally or behaviorally without even necessarily connecting it to what is going on with her or his parents. Finally, when a new partner or spouse comes into a divorced parent's life, a young person must deal with forming a new relationship with that person, who may very well become a parent-figure or caregiver to them.

Again, none of this is easy, but according to some researchers, it is possible. As with transracial adoption, there is still stigma attached to divorce, but it appears to be reducing as people come to understand divorce a bit better as well as the reasons behind it. And in reviewing the potential harms to a child of divorced parents, much more research is needed to determine the effects of an estranged couple who stay together for the sake of a child or children, but who model little or no affection for the child or argue consistently. Should a couple ever stay together for the sake of their children? Or divorce for the same sake? Under what circumstances?

Suggested Readings

C. Ahrons, *We're Still Family: What Grown Children Have to Say About Their Parents' Divorce.* New York: HarperCollins Publishers, 2005.

A. Clarke-Stewart, and C. Brentano, *Divorce: Causes and Consequences.* New Haven: Yale University Press, 2006.

C. Everett, ed. *Divorce and the Next Generation: Perspectives for Young Adults in the New Millennium.* Binghamton, NY: The Haworth Press, 2001.

J. Harvey, and M. A. Fine, *Children of Divorce Stories of Loss and Growth.* Mahwah, NJ: Lawrence Erlbaum Associates, Inc., 2004.

E. M. Hetherington, and J. Kelly, *For Better or for Worse: Divorce Reconsidered.* New York: W. W. Norton and Company, 2003.

E. Marquardt, *Between Two Worlds: The Inner Lives of Children of Divorce.* New York: Crown Publishing Group, 2006.

J. S. Wallerstein, J. Lewis, and S. Blakeslee, *The Unexpected Legacy of Divorce: The 25 Year Landmark Study.* New York: Hyperion Books, 2000.

J. Zimmerman, and E. Thayer, *Adult Children of Divorce.* Oakland: New Harbinger Publications, 2003.

ISSUE 4

Should Parents Homeschool Their Children?

YES: Chris Jeub, from "Homeschool" and "Reasons for Home-schooling." *Focus on the Family* (2006)

NO: Carole Moore, from "Why It's Not Right for Us," Scholastic.com (2006)

ISSUE SUMMARY

YES: Chris Jeub, writer and president of Training Minds Ministries, is a former public school teacher with 11 children, all of whom he and his wife have homeschooled. Naming several famous homeschooled individuals, such as Winston Churchill, Benjamin Franklin, and Florence Nightingale, he argues that the home is the best environment in which to teach children, for social, academic, family strengthening, and religious reasons. Homeschooling, he maintains, frees parents to impart their own values to their children without concern for how these beliefs might clash with what is presented in the public school system.

NO: Carole Moore, a freelance writer, discusses how she weighed the options of home vs. public schooling and argues that even though homeschooling might offer some benefits to children, in the end, children who are homeschooled provides a distorted view of the world at large. Children will, she writes, make good decisions and bad decisions as a part of growing up, and whether they are homeschooled or public schooled is not the determining factor in whether they grow up healthy and well-adjusted.

Education for children in the United States was not originally required; it was up to parents to decide whether and how to educate their children, including whether to send them to school. In 1850, however, Massachusetts became the first state to pass a law requiring "schooling" for children. Some of this took place in school buildings, and some was done by parents at home—but requiring that children be educated became more and more commonplace as time went on. And as early as the beginning of the twentieth century, there were proponents who believed that school-based education failed children, and that children were better off educated at home.

According to the Home School Association of California, the home-schooling that took place between then and the 1970s tended to be a bit more clandestine and to be found in rural areas. The early 1980s saw the emergence of homeschooling publications and groups that were associated specifically with conservative and religious (in particular, Christian) ideologies. Fearing the "godlessness" of public school, members of these groups received ongoing support for teaching their children at home. As we moved into the 1990s, homeschooled children in the United States increased, with a federal government survey in 1999 estimating that nearly 900,000 children are being homeschooled in this country, a number that can only have increased over the past eight years.

In your opinion, what are the benefits to children attending school with other children and being taught by a trained teacher that they can't receive being taught at home? What are some of the benefits, do you think, of teaching children at home, within the context of one's own family values, and without the distractions of other people, noise, and social pressures? There are clear arguments on each side, some of which are expressed in the following selections.

Chris Jeub's reasoning is outlined by topic areas, in which he describes his perceptions—having been a schoolteacher himself—of the ways in which homeschooling benefits children, as well as parents, more than traditional education in a shared classroom environment. Homeschooling, he argues, gives children much more freedom to pursue individual interests, and parents much more leeway to integrate religious messages into their teaching, something a public school is not allowed to do. Carole Moore considered homeschooling very carefully, and acknowledges some of the potential strengths, some of which center around safety issues for young people. In the end, however, she chose not to homeschool her own child, and argues that doing so creates a much more sheltered life for young people, which does not reflect the reality of the world at large.

YES ⬅

Chris Jeub

Homeschool

Introduction

She innocently asked, "So, where do your children go to school?"

Of all casual questions one teacher could ask another, this one always creates butterflies in my stomach.

"Well, uh, my wife and I tutor them," I say. Then I try to think of something to change the subject. But I never think of anything quick enough.

"Tutor them?" she might say, squinting her nose and ruffling her brows as if I had held a cockroach up to her face. "You mean, you home school them?"

These situations inevitably lead to an hour-long apologetic on why we educate our kids at home. This should not surprise me. Home schooling is still unusual and a bit radical. Teachers and others in education—or in any field, for that matter—naturally question new, innovative practices.

But home education is not so rare anymore. Twenty years ago there were roughly 15,000 home-schooled students in the United States. By 1991 the U.S. Department of Education figured there were 350,000 home schools in the U.S. and 40,000 in Canada. Today estimates stretch over 2 million home schools nationwide.

The world of education has had to adjust to this exploding movement. There are many magazines and newspapers for home schools, numerous home-school curriculum distributors and countless home-school network and contact groups. Why do parents choose to teach their children at home?

Social Reasons

Home-schooling parents believe that children can learn basic life skills—working together, sharing, showing respect for others—without formal classroom experience. The students can develop social graces by being involved in community and church activities.

Pat Farenga, publisher of Growing Without Schooling, a catalog of home-school resources, has written: "Group experiences are a big part of education, and home schoolers have plenty of them.

They write to us about how they form or join writing clubs, book discussion groups and local home-schooling groups. Home schoolers also take part in school sports teams and music groups [in nearby public schools], as well as in the many public and private group activities our communities provide. These young people can and do experience other people and cultures without going to school."

Our children have many church and neighborhood friends. Our community has a home-school contact group where they often get together for field trips and outings that give our kids more than enough socialization. We have gone on camping trips, facilitated soccer tournaments, traveled to speech and debate tournaments and coordinated educational classes.

But not all socialization is necessarily good for a child. Certain social plagues like drugs, alcohol, premarital sex, violence and gangs damage a child's growth and development. A home-school environment frees the child from the increasingly persuasive peer pressure prevalent in many schools.

The positive side of socialization—building respect and communication, getting along with and relating to others—is wonderfully fulfilled in a home-school setting. Behavioral psychologist Urie Bronfenbrenner concluded that "meaningful human contact" is best accomplished with few people.

Academic Reasons

While some parents choose to teach at home to promote positive socialization, others make the decision for academic reasons. Any teacher will agree that the smaller the class size, the more learning takes place. The one-on-one tutoring atmosphere is the healthiest, most productive and most progressive atmosphere for a student's academic success.

Take a look at some famous home-schooled students: Andrew Carnegie, Charlie Chaplin, Agatha Christie, Winston Churchill, Charles Dickens, Thomas Edison, Benjamin Franklin, Florence Nightingale, Woodrow Wilson and the Wright brothers.

People ask how parents—especially parents with little or no post-secondary education—can teach children every discipline available to public school students. Although I have my degree in English, am I qualified to teach math or science to my kids? My wife has a business administration degree; is she able to teach the language arts? With sufficient information and dedication to the task, we certainly are.

Even if parents do not have an abundance of academic training themselves, they can find solutions to fill the gaps. For example, many home schools will team up with other home schools to exchange skills. I traded skills with another home school family by going to their house once a week to teach English to three of their sons. In return, their mom taught algebra to my two oldest daughters.

Most communities today have enrichment classes students can sign up for much like college students sign up for electives. Here in Colorado Springs, the High Plains Christian Home Educators support group has hired a full-time administrator who coordinates 60 classes for over 200 students. Cooperatives such as this are becoming more popular as home schooling grows.

But education is more than individual academic courses—more than teaching what the teacher knows or training students in a particular skill. It is actually passing on a worldview. Separating the disciplines—as if English had nothing to do with math, and science was unrelated to civics—promotes a fragmented vision of true education.

A wise man once said, "A good teacher teaches himself out of a job." When I taught English in the public schools, I was not merely repeating what I learned in college; I was teaching students to love and passionately engage in the language arts. And when I taught, I integrated all disciplines—history, science, social studies, even math—into my lessons. Treating any learning discipline as separate from others misrepresents real life. Real life is interdisciplinary, and home-school instruction lends itself to a cross-disciplinary approach.

Students have the freedom to pursue their interests and strengths. They also receive the attention needed to improve skills in their more difficult learning areas. Pat Farenga explains the benefits of solitary reflection: "Children, like adults, need time to be alone to think, to muse, to read freely, to daydream, to be creative, to form a self independent of the barrage of mass culture." Granting such a time presents a struggle in traditional schools, but home schools allow such freedom.

Family Reasons

Home-school parents see their role as the single most important responsibility they carry. The family helps to build strong minds and healthy personalities.

Along with strengthening the family and setting firm foundations for kids, home-school parents discover some personal pluses. Wendy and I are now much closer to our kids, more in touch with their needs and feelings. Alicia and Alissa attended public school through first- and third-grade respectively until I completed college and Wendy returned home from full-time work (to unpaid full-time work).

While Alicia's grades were excellent, she needed to be home for security's sake. Alissa, on the other hand, loved the social contact at school but struggled in basic writing and reading skills. Wendy and I noticed positive changes immediately in Alicia's esteem and Alissa's academics. They both became more confident. I can only accredit this improvement to the loving and affirming atmosphere of the family.

Religious Reasons

It is no secret that public schools have not taken religion seriously. Fear of church and state laws keep some schools from even mentioning the influence of religion in American life. Instead of recognizing religion as part of our culture, civil liberties organizations have fought hard in the courts to make religion illegal in the classroom.

This has been too bad. With the exclusion of religion many parents have felt compelled to go elsewhere—even to their own homes—to teach their children basic moral and religious truths to provide a well-rounded and liberal education.

Teaching our kids at home frees us to handle religious questions and spiritual training without worrying about public school issues. While some districts restrict the discussion of religious influence in history, literature and science, home schools can incorporate the impact of spiritual beliefs into all curricula.

Mutual Respect

Home schooling is being recognized by professional educators and by society as a reasonable educational option for families. Some public schools and private schools have formed alliances with home education groups and have adopted programs that suit the home education lifestyle.

Home schooling is not so much a rebellion against public schools as it is a choice made on social, academic, family and religious grounds. As educators and home schoolers get to know one another, we will see that we share many of the same goals for our children.

Carole Moore

→ **NO**

Why It's Not Right for Us

I became interested in homeschooling a few years ago when a friend told me how much she loved it. A former cop turned writer, I approached the editor at the newspaper where I worked and convinced him to let me write a series on the topic. I interviewed dozens of homeschooling parents and students. All told, including the work on the series plus my own follow-up research, I spent over a year studying the possibility and debating whether learning at home would be best for my kids—a daughter, then age 10, and a son, age 8.

I learned that many families homeschooled because they didn't like the secular curriculum. Others complained that classes were dumbed down, which caused boredom and restlessness in bright students. A lot chose to remove their kids from what they perceived as an unhealthy social atmosphere. All were convinced they'd done the right thing.

They explained the differences in the types of homeschooling to me: Some followed rigorous religious-based curricula, while others used the same materials as their public schools. A few, called unschoolers, followed nothing but their hearts and let the kids themselves pick what they wanted to study. Many bartered with other parents on subjects requiring special expertise, such as trading French instruction for piano lessons.

The kids' education seemed balanced and academically sound, but most appealing was the bond they shared with their parents. My own daughter, anxious to grow up, nibbled at her ties to me, with her younger brother fast on her heels. I wondered if homeschooling could bring us closer.

Still, as I spoke with homeschooling families from one coast to the other, certain troubling questions bubbled to the surface—many of them familiar to me from my days in law enforcement.

Our community is nowhere near a major city. Still my children went to elementary school with a girl whose father committed suicide in her presence, kids with both parents in prison, and youngsters who couldn't read, yet knew all the words to filthy rap songs. As a police officer, I often dealt with adolescent drug dealers, pregnant teens, and runaways—kids whose lives were out of control. Certainly the largest majority of them were enrolled in public schools, but not all. Some of the most troubled kids I dealt with came from homes where they'd been very sheltered.

I remember one teenager in particular. After years of alternately being homeschooled and attending a very strict, small, church-based school, she moved to a public school—where she spiraled out of control. She drank. She took drugs. And she had sex. Her parents were appalled; that was not how they'd raised their daughter.

Some would blame the influence of the public school system. They'd say she made friends with bad kids. And they'd be right. But that wasn't the only reason she got into so much trouble. In my opinion, her problem went much deeper: she didn't know how to handle the sudden combination of freedom and exposure to a side of life she'd never personally confronted. Her parents had talked about these things. She'd heard about them in church. But talk alone isn't a substitute for reality, and the forbidden often looms sweet and tantalizing by virtue of its mystery.

Academics form only part of the equation when it comes to teaching life skills. Kids need to know how to write a persuasive essay, but they also should learn about real life and, in the process, develop the skills they need to cope with it.

My daughter, who now attends a public high school, has made good choices in both her academic and social lives so far. We've talked about sex, but nothing I've ever said to her has provided as strong a deterrent to casual, early sex as the girl in her class with the ever-expanding belly. Nothing makes my daughter more aware of the effects of drugs than seeing burnt-out kids. And nothing brings home the consequences of drinking and driving than the empty seat of a boy who did just that.

They're tough lessons, but ones she will never forget. Seeing the aftermath of negative behavior with her own eyes impresses her much more than simple words or even our own good examples.

Do I like that my children are exposed to life's underbelly? Of course not. I'd much prefer to bring them up in an atmosphere of innocence and trust. But we can't raise our children in carefully controlled environments and expect them to instinctively know how to handle evil. Pretending that it doesn't exist won't make it go away.

Homeschooling would have built a wall around my kids and kept them safe—for a little awhile. Ultimately, they would have had to go out into the real world. Public school has exposed them to bad influences as well as good ones. I believe they're stronger for having had to make tough choices. And going through it together has strengthened our relationship, making it easier for me to start letting go of their hands.

POSTSCRIPT

Should Parents Homeschool Their Children?

There is limited research available about how effective school-based education vs. homeschooling is, much of which cannot control for the myriad factors that come into play. In schools, factors include teacher experience, school and district leadership, the socioeconomic status of the community in which the school is located, and more. In homeschooling, issues include whether a parent can afford financially to stay home and devote the time and energy necessary to homeschool effectively, whether the parent(s) can facilitate a social life for their child(ren) that is comparable to their school-based peers, and whether the child(ren) can still access nonacademic activities such as organized sports, theater, and student clubs.

Ask young people who have been homeschooled whether they liked it, and you will receive a range of responses. A Web site, www.faqfarm.com, asked people to comment on what they felt the longer-term effects of homeschooling were; here is what several people had to say:

"I was homeschooled for 1st–9th grade. I attended 10th and part of 11th grade. I took my proficiency test and attended community college on and off for 6 years. My younger brother was homeschooled from 1st–8th grade and attended 9th–12th grade. He did not attend college. Almost all the kids I hung out w/ were homeschooled also. We were both socially impaired by it; our parents made a point to keep us in sports and try to keep us socializing w/ other kids. But it wasn't enough. Most of our friends were also homeschooled too. Some of us turned out OK, some didn't."

"I am 30 years old now, and was homeschooled through junior high and high school. . . . Part of the answer to [the] question is this: Socialization with adults is improved, while socialization with peers is hindered. . . . There are so many social do's and don'ts that are very arbitrary and are pounded home by peer pressure, teasing, cliques, etc."

"I homeschooled through junior high and high school. I agree that there are some social disadvantages to homeschooling, but I think that they can be avoided or changed. I realized when I was 15 that I was awkward around most of my peers and so I worked really hard at changing that. If parents are careful to involve their children in social groups the kids will be able to learn the necessary skills. I was lucky; there is a big homeschooling community where I live, with many children to interact with. . . . I am now in college and I don't have any qualms about participating in social groups with other students, whether homeschooled or not. If done right, I don't think homeschooling interferes a whole lot with social skills." (from http://www.faqfarm.com/Q/What_are_the_long-term_effects_of_homeschooling).

Do these quotes reinforce your beliefs, or change your mind?

Suggested Readings

R. Barfield, *Real-Life Homeschooling: The Stories of 21 Families Who Teach Their Children at Home.* New York: Simon & Schuster Adult Publishing Group, 2002.

S. Bielick, K. Chandler, and S. P. Broughman, *Homeschooling in the United States: 1999.* Accessible online at http://nces.ed.gov/programs/quarterly/Vol_3/3_3/q3-2.asp, 2001.

R. H. Davis, "Homeschooling a Personal Choice not a Movement." *Teachers College Record,* May 16, 2005. Accessible online at www.tcrecord.org/Content.asp?ContentID=11876.

P. T. Hill, "Home Schooling and the Future of Public Education." *Peabody Journal of Education* 75, no. 1&2 (2000): 20–31.

J. Kaufield, *Homeschooling for Dummies.* Hoboken, NJ: John Wiley & Sons, 2001.

C. Lubienski, "Whither the Common Good? A Critique of Home Schooling." *Peabody Journal of Education* 75, no. 1&2 (2000): 207–232.

C. Lubienski, "A Critical View of Home Education." *Evaluation and Research in Education* 17, no. 2/3 (2003): 167–178.

R. G. Medlin, "Home Schooling and the Question of Socialization." *Peabody Journal of Education* 75, no. 1&2 (2000): 107–123.

ISSUE 5

Do Mothers Who Work Outside of the Home Have a Negative Effect on Their Children?

YES: Jeanne Brooks-Gunn, Wen-Jui Han, and Jane Waldfogel, from "Maternal Employment and Child Cognitive Outcomes in the First Three Years of Life: The NICHD Study of Early Child Care," *Child Development* (July/August 2002)

NO: Thomas M. Vander Ven et al., from "Home Alone: The Impact of Maternal Employment on Delinquency," *Social Problems* (May 2001)

ISSUE SUMMARY

YES: Child developmentalists Jeanne Brooks-Gunn, Wen-Jui Han, and Jane Waldfogel assert that their findings show many types of negative effects from maternal employment on the later cognitive and educational outcomes of children.

NO: Professor of sociology and anthropology Thomas M. Vander Ven and his colleagues argue that their studies show that the qualities or quantities of a mother working have relatively little or no influence on the social, emotional, and behavioral functioning of her children.

O ver a decade ago, former First Lady Hillary Rodham Clinton made what became an often-quoted statement from an African saying: "It takes a village to raise a child." Although there are those who would agree with this sentiment, the role of the mother—and, in particular, the child's biological mother—has received and continues to receive intense scrutiny. Even with so many members of a family or a "village," a bias exists toward the effects a mother has on her child's development—good, bad, or indifferent.

Since the 1950s, this scrutiny has focused on working women—those who work professional jobs outside of the home in addition to parenting a child or children. As some know, during World War II, thousands of women in the United States felt it was their patriotic duty to fill in for their husbands and other men who were fighting overseas in the war by working in factories and doing other jobs that traditionally had been held by men. The good news is that doing this kept many industries alive in the 1940s. The bad news for many women is that when U.S. soldiers returned stateside, the women were expected to give up their jobs and return home—and many were resistant to doing so.

In the 1960s and 1970s, the women's rights movement gave women much more support for working outside the home—although this meant that many women who did *not* want to work outside of the home, who wanted to be stay-at-home mothers, were criticized for making this choice. Some people are very invested in keeping women at home, for a range of reasons—not the least of which, they say, is that it is vitally important for a woman to be with her child during the child's early years.

Over the past 20 years, the number of women who have become parents and then entered or returned to the workforce has risen from 31 percent to 59 percent. It is currently estimated that 70 percent of mothers with children who are their dependents are working today. Researchers have been curious about and explored what effects working mothers who place their children in some kind of care—whether in an organized daycare or with a nanny—have on children's early development. The results are inconclusive, although there are strong opinions on both sides of the argument—those who maintain that not having a mother at home with a child, particularly an infant, is harmful, and those who insist it is not. The "harms" range from impaired cognitive development (e.g., challenges in thought and learning processes) to delinquency (e.g., either illegal or antisocial behavior).

There are many claims that a woman who works outside of the home will not bond as effectively with her child, claims that those who disagree would say are simply a conservative viewpoint and unsubstantiated by research. They believe that the push to have women return home rather than remain in the workplace is an ongoing backlash against the feminism that paved the way for it to be acceptable for a woman to be a mother as well as a full-time professional.

What do you think? Is it enough for mothers to be home with their children in the evening and morning hours? What about the other folks in their lives—like their partners or spouses or other family members? Is it important for a child to bond with a significant adult, or must it be the biological mother?

In the following selections, Jeanne Brooks-Gunn, Wen-Jui Han, and Jane Waldfogel argue that the data show that there are significant long-term negative effects on cognitive development for children whose mothers work outside of the home during the child's earlier years. Conversely, Thomas M. Vander Ven and his colleagues maintain that a child who is born to a mother who works outside of the home is not more likely to exhibit delinquent behavior—unless, at the very basic level, supervision of the child is an issue.

YES ←

Jeanne Brooks-Gunn, Wen-Jui Han, and Jane Waldfogel

Maternal Employment and Child Cognitive Outcomes in the First Three Years of Life

The past few decades have seen an unprecedented increase in early maternal employment. The share of mothers who return to work before their child's first birthday doubled from 1976 to 1998, rising from 31% to 59% (Bachu & O'Connell, 1998). Women are now nearly as likely to be working when they have an infant as they are when they have an older preschooler (U.S. Department of Labor, Bureau of Labor Statistics, 2000). Yet, questions remain as to what the impact of this rapid shift toward early maternal employment might be. With increased attention being paid on the part of parents and policy makers to the importance of early experiences for children, establishing what links might exist between early maternal employment and child cognitive outcomes is more important than ever.

The potential impacts of early maternal employment and early child care on child development have been extensively studied (for reviews, see Belsky, 2001; Bornstein, Gist, Hahn, Haynes, & Voigt, 2001; Lamb, 1998; Shonkoff & Phillips, 2000; Weinraub & Jaeger, 1990). Most relevant to the present study are the results from (1) studies using the National Longitudinal Survey of Youth–Child Supplement (NLSY-CS) to examine the effects of early maternal employment on child outcomes, and (2) studies using the National Institute of Child Health and Human Development Study of Early Child Care (NICHD-SECC) to examine the effects of early child care on child development.

A large literature has studied the effects of early maternal employment on children's cognitive outcomes using data on children born to respondents of the NLSY-CS (for a helpful overview of this dataset, see Chase-Lansdale, Mott, Brooks-Gunn, & Phillips, 1991). Because these NLSY-CS studies are reviewed elsewhere (see, e.g., Han, Waldfogel, & Brooks-Gunn, 2001), only a brief overview is provided here. The studies that have examined the effects of first-year maternal employment separately from the effects of employment later in the preschool years have tended to find negative effects of first-year maternal employment on children's later cognitive outcomes (see, e.g., Baydar & Brooks-Gunn, 1991; Belsky & Eggebeen, 1991; Blau & Grossberg, 1992; Han et al., 2001;

Hill, Waldfogel, Brooks-Gunn, & Han, 2001; Ruhm, 2000; Waldfogel, Han, & Brooks-Gunn, 2002; but see also Harvey, 1999). An important limitation of these studies is that none have been able to control for the quality of the child-care settings in which the children of the working mothers are placed. Although the NLSY-CS contains retrospective data on the type of child care in which children are placed, it does not contain any assessment of the quality of that care. A further limitation is that none of the NLSY-CS studies have been able to control for the quality of the mothers' interactions with their children. The NLSY-CS contains no direct assessment of the sensitivity of the mother's care for the child. The NLSY-CS does contain data on one measure of the quality of the home environment, the Home Observation of the Measurement of the Environment (HOME) Scale, but it did not start administering the HOME until 1986, so for many children in the sample (children born in 1983 or earlier) this measure was not administered until they were age 3 or older and therefore no data on the earlier home environment are available.

Thus, when studies using the NLSY-CS have found that early maternal employment has negative effects on children's later cognitive outcomes, the extent to which these effects might be due to the poor quality of child care experienced by these children and/or the poor quality of their home environments has not been clear. Establishing the mechanism by which early maternal employment is linked to poorer cognitive outcomes, and the role played by child care or home environments, is critical to understanding the source of the links and also potential policy remedies.

For this reason, the present study turned to newly available data from the NICHD-SECC. This dataset is extremely well suited to address the limitations of the prior NLSY-CS studies and the questions they could not answer, because it contains data on child-care quality and the quality of children's home environment, as well as detailed data on maternal employment and child outcomes (for an excellent overview of this dataset, see NICHD Early Child Care Research Network, in press). It also contains a rich set of data on child and mother characteristics, including a measure of maternal depression, which is not available in the NLSY-CS. The NICHD-SECC dataset has not been used to study the effects of early maternal employment. It was designed as a study of the effects of early child care on child development and has been used extensively to study that topic (for results on the effects of early child care on children's development at age 54 months, see, e.g., NICHD Early Child Care Research Network, in press). . . .

Methods

Data for the present study were obtained from the NICHD-SECC, a unique longitudinal dataset that has followed 1,364 children from 10 sites around the nation since the time of their birth in 1991. (For a detailed description of the dataset, including how the sample was selected and interviewed, see NICHD Early Child Care Research Network, 2000, in press). It is important to note that some groups were excluded from the sample (e.g., mothers under 18, families who anticipated moving, infants who were multiple births or had health problems or disabilities, mothers who did not speak English, mothers with medical problems or substance-abuse problems, or families living in a dangerous neighborhood). A total of 1,525 families were deemed eligible for inclusion in the study and agreed to be interviewed; of these, 1,364 completed an interview and became participants in the study.

The NICHD-SECC conducted home visits to the children in the sample at 1, 6, 15, 24, and 36 months, supplemented by phone interviews every 3 months to track maternal employment and child-care use. The study also conducted visits to the children's child-care settings at 6, 15, 24, and 36 months (if children were in care more than 10 hr per week). In addition, the children were assessed at home and in the laboratory at ages 15, 24, and 36 months (later visits and assessments were also conducted, but those data have not yet been released for public use). . . .

Discussion

The present study took advantage of a newly available dataset, the NICHD-SECC, to examine the effects of early maternal employment on children's cognitive outcomes at ages 15, 24, and 36 months, controlling for child care (quality and type) and home environment (assessed with the HOME Scale and a rating of maternal sensitivity). The study analyzed three related sets of questions: (1) Is maternal employment in the first year of life associated with negative child cognitive outcomes in the first 3 years of life and, if so, are these effects more pronounced when mothers work full-time? (2) Are there subgroups for whom these effects are more likely to be found? and (3) To what extent are these effects mediated by quality of child care and home environment in the first 3 years of life? These analyses took as their point of departure the literature on the timing of early maternal employment, which has relied mainly on analyses of the NLSY-CS. Because this literature (with important input from developmentalists, economists, and sociologists) has been increasingly concerned with issues of selection bias and model specification, the present study included a large array of covariates that were not available in the NLSY-CS, such as measures of child care and the early home environment. It also drew extensively on the literature on the effects of early child care, in particular the recent work by the NICHD Early Child Care Research Network on the timing and intensity of early child care. The work of the NICHD Early Child Care Research Network was followed closely in terms of how the rich child-care and child-assessment data available in the NICHD-SECC dataset were utilized and also in how the factors that might mediate the effects of early maternal employment on later child outcomes were conceptualized. However, unlike the NICHD Early Child Care Research Network, the focus in the present research was on early maternal employment rather than early child care, reflecting our interest in extending and updating the prior work from the NLSY-CS as well as contributing to the literature regarding women and employment. Thus, we believe the results of the present study complement those of the NICHD Early Child Care Research Network, because it tackled essentially different questions than those addressed in that group's work.

To review the main findings, with regard to the first research question, this study found that children whose mothers worked at all by the ninth month of their life had lower scores on the Bracken [School Readiness Scale] at 36 months than did children whose mothers did not work by that time. The effects of any maternal employment by 1, 3, 6, or 12 months were also negative, although only the effect of maternal employment by 9 months was statistically significant (the effect of employment by 6 months was marginally significant at $p < .10$). This pattern of results suggests that there may be something particularly problematic about having a mother who went to work between 6 and 9 months and/or something unusual about the children whose mothers began employment at this time (which about 5% of the sample did), and the few prior studies that had examined timing effects of maternal employment within the first year (Baydar & Brooks-Gunn, 1991; Han et al., 2001) provided some support for this idea. However, it is also important to note that these results provided some evidence of negative effects of earlier employment as well. Moreover, once the intensity of employment was taken into account, larger negative effects were found, which were statistically significant for employment beginning by 6 months as well as 9 months. Specifically, the negative effect of having a mother who began employment by the ninth month was most pronounced for children whose mothers worked longer hours (30 hr or more per week) in the first year; the same was true for children whose mothers began employment by the sixth month.

The significant negative effects found on the Bracken at 36 months for any employment by the ninth month, and for employment of 30 hr or more per week by the sixth month or ninth month, were consistent with previous findings from the NLSY indicating that early maternal employment had significant negative effects on children's PPVT-R [Peabody Picture Vocabulary Test-Revised] at 36 months (see, e.g., Han et al., 2001; Waldfogel et al., 2002). The fact that these effects were strongest for European American non-Hispanic children was also consistent with prior findings from the NLSY-CS. No effects were found for early maternal employment on children's Bayley MDI [Mental Development Index] scores at 15 or 24 months. The fact that there were negative effects of early maternal employment on the Bracken at 36 months but not on the Bayley MDI in the first 2 years of life is most likely due to the different cognitive competencies tapped in the first 2 years compared with the later preschool years. The cognitive competencies tapped at 15 and 24 months may be less likely to be influenced by environmental events than those tapped later on. Studies that looked at the effects of poverty, for example, found few effects on cognition in the first 18 months of life using the Bayley MDI, but found effects when language and reasoning were assessed in the third year of life (see, e.g., Klebanov et al., 1998). In addition, competencies tapped in the first 2 years of life may not be as predictive of later functioning (McCall, 1983; McCall, Hogarty, & Hurlbut, 1972).

With regard to the second research question, the present results showed that some subgroups of children were more likely to be affected than were others. The effects of early and full-time maternal employment were larger for children whose mothers were rated as insensitive at 6 months (compared with those whose mothers were rated as sensitive), for boys (compared with girls), and for children with married parents (compared with single mothers). The finding on sensitivity was consistent with prior results from the NICHD-SECC (i.e., investigators found that children whose mothers were rated as not sensitive and were in early child care more than 10 hr per week were more vulnerable to attachment problems than were other children in care more than 10 hr per week; NICHD Early Child Care Research Network, 1997). The findings on differences by gender and by parents' marital status were consistent with prior results from the NLSY-CS (see Desai et al., 1989, on gender; Han et al., 2001, on marital status). With regard to the more negative impacts for boys, some analysts have observed that boys are more vulnerable to early stressors in general (see, e.g., Rutter, 1979; Zaslow & Hayes, 1986) and that boys may be more affected by nonmaternal child care as well (for an excellent discussion on this topic, see Bornstein et al., 2001). With regard to the more negative impacts for children of married parents, one possible explanation is that the extra income generated by the mothers' employment may be more valuable, on average, to families headed by unmarried mothers than it is to married-couple families. If so, to the extent that positive income effects offset otherwise negative effects of early maternal employment, this would explain why the observed effects of early maternal employment seemed to be more negative in married-couple families. These differences by subgroup are intriguing and warrant further research, which might shed more light on the mechanisms that underlie the effects of early maternal employment on child cognitive outcomes. In this regard, it would also be useful to conduct research on individual differences in children's vulnerability to early and full-time maternal employment.

With regard to the third research question, it was found that both child care (quality and type) and home environment (as measured by both maternal sensitivity and the HOME Scale) mattered for children's Bracken scores at 36 months. Also found was some evidence that early and full-time maternal employment was negatively associated with the quality of subsequent child care and home environments. Children whose mothers worked more than 30 hr per week by 9 months were in lower quality child-care settings at 36 months than children whose mothers worked fewer hours per week in the first year. Moreover, children whose mothers worked more than 30 hr per week by 9 months had mothers who were rated as providing less sensitive care at 36 months than children whose mothers did not work in the first year (this result is consistent with the finding of the NICHD Early Child Care Research Network, 1999, that children who spent more hours in early child care had mothers who provided less sensitive care at 36 months), although their home environments (as assessed by the HOME Scale) were not significantly different (this latter result may indicate that early and full-time maternal employment may have offsetting effects, reducing some resources due to the limitations on mothers' time available for activities with their children but increasing other resources due to the increased income available to the family through the mothers' employment). However, even after controlling for child care and home environment, a negative association was still found between full-time employment begun in the first 9 months of children's lives and the children's Bracken scores at 36 months.

Because the NICHD-SECC is an observational (rather than experimental) study, it is important to be cautious in interpreting these results. It is possible that mothers' entry into full-time work in the first 9 months did adversely affect their children's cognitive performance at age 3. If this is correct, then one could conclude that encouraging mothers who would otherwise be employed full-time to stay home or work part-time during the first year would produce children with higher Bracken School Readiness scores. However, the NICHD-SECC did not experimentally assign mothers to employment or non-employment, so it is not known from these estimates whether full-time maternal employment by 9 months was causing the lower Bracken School Readiness scores. It is possible that there were pre-existing differences between mothers who did and did not work full-time in the first 9 months of their children's lives that were not observed in the data and that mattered for children's cognitive outcomes. These differences may have had to do with characteristics of the mothers, or with the reasons that they were working. Although selection bias in the present study was controlled for to the extent possible by including a large set of covariates (several of which were not available in prior work with the NLSY-CS), clearly, further work on this topic is needed.

The results of the present study do have some implications for policy. One clear implication is the need to improve the quality of child care that children experience in the first 3 years of life. The results confirm that quality of care matters and also document that, all else equal, children whose mothers work full-time in the first year of life go on to experience poorer quality care in their first 3 years. This lower quality of care in part explains why cognitive outcomes are worse at 36 months for children whose mothers worked full-time rather than part-time in the first year of life. This suggests that improving the quality of child care used by the children of full-time working mothers might help to mitigate the observed negative effects of mothers' early and full-time employment on children's cognitive development. It is important to keep in mind that the present study examined a specific group of children who were infants and toddlers in the early 1990s, and was, therefore, situated in the context of the quality of child care available in the United States during those years. If the quality of that care was, on average, lower than the quality of care that the children's mothers would have offered had they not been working, then that "mismatch" could help to explain the negative relation between early and full-time maternal employment and cognitive development at age 36 months reported in this article. (It was not possible to control for this directly because we did not observe the care that the mother would have provided had she not been working; we only observed the care that she did provide, which may have been affected by the fact that she was employed.) Studies in other countries in which the quality of care is higher have reported different results (see, e.g., Andersson, 1989, 1992, who found that Swedish children who entered child care earlier in the first year of life had better cognitive outcomes than those who entered care later).

A second implication has to do with family leave policy. The United States currently has family leave provisions that guarantee less than 3 months of leave for new mothers as compared with an average of 10 months in the advanced industrialized nations who are members of the Organization for Economic and Community Development (OECD); the United States also differs from peer industrialized nations by not providing paid leave and by having a national law that covers less than half the private sector workforce (Kamerman, 2000; Waldfogel, 2001a). If any maternal employment by the ninth month (and maternal employment of 30 hr or more per week by the sixth or ninth month) has adverse effects on children's cognitive development, this is relevant to consideration of proposals to extend U.S. leave provisions to the 10-month OECD average, provide paid leave, and provide coverage for a larger portion of the U.S. workforce (see, e.g., Kamerman, 2000; Waldfogel, 2001a).

A third implication has to do with family-friendly policies that make it easier for mothers (and fathers) to combine work and family responsibilities. In addition to child care and family leave, such policies include flexible hours, part-time or job-sharing arrangements, and other workplace policies that might reduce the stress or fatigue experienced by working parents with young children. Although, as noted above, the United States lags behind other countries in its provision of family leave, it has at least made some progress in this area with the passage of the Family and Medical Leave Act (FMLA) in 1993. The same is not true of other family-friendly benefits for families with young children. The share of employers who provide such benefits is quite low and has not increased in recent years (Waldfogel, 2001b).

Taken together, the results of the present study illustrate the extent to which the effects of early maternal employment on children's cognitive outcomes depend crucially on both the quality of care that children receive at home and the quality of care that children receive in child care. Good-quality care at home, and good-quality child care, can go a long way toward buffering the negative links between early maternal employment and later child outcomes. Nevertheless, it is concerning that even after controlling for home-environment quality and child-care quality, full-time maternal employment by the ninth month was found to be associated with lower Bracken scores at 36 months. Until there is better understanding with regard to what causes this association and how to buffer it, it would be prudent for policy makers to go slow on measures (such as the recent Temporary Assistance to Needy Families reforms) that would require mothers to enter the labor force (full-time) early in the first year of life and to consider measures (such as proposed FMLA extensions) that would allow more mothers to choose to delay their return to the labor force and/or to work part-time until later in the first year of life. More generally, we concur with the conclusions of the recent National Academy of Sciences expert panel on the science of early development (Shonkoff & Phillips, 2000), that call for policies to improve the quality of child care, extend family leave provisions, and expand other family-friendly policies, to give parents more and better choices about how to balance their work and family responsibilities in the first year of their children's lives.

Thomas M. Vander Ven et al.   ➡ **NO**

Home Alone: The Impact of Maternal Employment on Delinquency

In recent decades, American family life has been transformed dramatically. Family scholars debate the causes and consequences of these major changes, routinely clashing over whether family forms are changing for the better (Stacey 1993) or whether our most important social institution is experiencing a moral and functional freefall (Gill 1993; Poponoe 1993).

One of the most profound changes is the unprecedented number of women who have entered the paid workforce since the 1950s. Census data show that female labor force participation rose from approximately 28 percent in 1940 to close to 60 percent in 1992 (U.S. Bureau of Census 1993). This wave of women entering the labor force was accompanied by a large increase in maternal employment. While only 16 percent of all children had working mothers in 1950, close to 70 percent of all mothers with dependent children work today (Coontz 1977). Recent estimates show that over half of those with children less than one year old are employed outside the home and over 60 percent of those with children younger than six are employed (Gerson 1996).

While the mass entrance of women and mothers into the labor market might be regarded as a sign of social progress, many Americans are worried about the trend and have been for some time (Greenberger, Goldberg, Crawford, and Granger 1988). And in what may be seen as part of the "backlash" to feminist political victories (Faludi 1991), politicians, social critics, and parenting "experts" have frequently pointed to the working mother as the cause of many of our social problems.

While supporting empirical evidence is scarce, the political Right charges that feminist philosophies damage the American family by encouraging women to choose work and self-fulfillment over family obligations (Cohen and Katzenstein 1988). Additionally, noted psychologists argue that the neglected child of the working mother may suffer from an attachment disorder, which is widely believed to be a major causal factor in the production of extreme child behavior problems. One pediatrician and TV personality warns that mothers should stay home to raise their infants or risk the disruption of the critical mother-child bonding period: "if he doesn't have that through infancy, it's hard to put it in later . . . and these kids that never get it . . . will become difficult in school,

From *Social Problems* by Thomas M. Vander Ven et al., pp. 236 257. Copyright © 2001 by University of California Press, Journals Division. Reprinted by permission.

they'll never succeed in school, they'll make everybody angry, they'll become delinquents later and eventually they'll become terrorists" (see Eyer 1996:6).

Although there is no shortage of claims that maternal employment causes negative child outcomes, there is little evidence that this is the case. Recent research shows that the children of working mothers are no less attached than other children (Chira 1998) and that they experience no deficits in social, emotional, or behavioral functioning (Harvey 1999; Hoffman 1989; Parcel and Menaghan 1994). While no work and family issue attracts more scholarly attention than the potential effects of maternal employment on children's development (Barling 1990), few researchers have investigated the possible link between working mothers and delinquency.

In this context, we analyze the impact of maternal employment—of kids being left "home alone"—on delinquency using models that include different characteristics of maternal employment (e.g., hours, workplace controls), variations in maternal non-employment (e.g., welfare reliance), and child care arrangements. Our analysis is influenced by the research program of Parcel and Meneghan (1994, 1994a), who investigated the impact of various dimensions of parental work on a range of social, cognitive, and behavioral outcomes. Similarly, we test models that consider the number of hours usually employed, working conditions, and the timing of work. This more comprehensive measurement of maternal work improves upon past research on maternal employment and delinquency, where mother's work was simply divided into "working mother" and "non-working mother" categories (e.g., Glueck and Glueck 1950; Hirschi 1969; Sampson and Laub 1993).

Furthermore, in an attempt to isolate the independent effects of maternal work, we simultaneously consider the impact of maternal resources (i.e., maternal cognitive skills, maternal education, family income), child care arrangements, and marital status. By controlling for maternal resources, we are better able to isolate the independent effects of maternal employment. . . .

꒰◉꒱

Although there is a tremendous body of literature on the effects of maternal employment on child outcomes, studies on the link between maternal work and delinquency are relatively scarce. Early researchers tended to find a small positive effect of maternal employment on delinquency, which they usually assumed was the consequence of low maternal supervision (Glueck and Glueck 1950; Hirschi 1969; Nye 1963; Roy 1963; see also, Sampson and Laub 1993). Most contemporary researchers found little or no connection between maternal work status and delinquency (Broidy 1995; Hillman and Sawilowsky 1991; Riege 1972; Wadsworth 1979). Other studies suggest that delinquency is less common among the children of regularly employed mothers (Farnworth 1984; West 1982; Zhao, Cao, and Cao 1997). In some cases, maternal work actually served as insulation against delinquent risks because working mothers effectively raised the family income, thus improving the living conditions of their children. Maternal employment, then, should be considered as an economic dimension of family life and may be most beneficial for children when the alternative is poverty or welfare dependency (Baca-Zinn 1989).

When examined closely, the extant literature on maternal employment and delinquency suggests that working conditions are an important factor that must be included in analytical models. Glueck and Glueck (1950), for example, found that delinquency was highest among the children of occasionally employed mothers. This finding is provocative because occasional or sporadic work may be indicative of secondary labor market employment. Employment in the secondary labor market is often erratic and coercive due to the vulnerability of the low-skilled, uneducated workers at this level (Edwards 1979). Such employment may be criminogenic if coercive workplace experiences negatively shape parenting techniques (Colvin and Pauly 1983).

In a related vein, Roy (1963) found that maternal work was related to delinquency in urban settings, but not in rural areas. This effect, also, may reflect important differences between working conditions in urban vs. rural communities. It may be that maternal work in urban centers and among minority populations is, on average, more likely to be coercive, secondary labor market work (see Haurin 1992). In light of these findings, better measures of maternal employment—including measures for workplace controls and regularity of employment (part-time vs. full-time) are needed. . . .

Methodology

Sample

In the 1960s, the United States Department of Labor hired the Center for Human Resource Research at the Ohio State University to gather longitudinal data on the labor market experiences of four representative target groups among the U.S. population (Fahey 1995). A fifth cohort of men and women between the ages of 14 and 22 was identified in 1979. Known as the National Longitudinal Survey of Youth (NLSY), this project involved a multistaged stratified random sampling that produced 12,686 subjects, 11,404 of whom were interviewed annually about their occupational, educational, familial, and childbearing experiences (see Chase-Landsdale, Mott, Brooks-Gunn, and Phillips 1991, Parcel and Menaghan 1994).

By 1994, 10,042 children of sample mothers were identified to report on their home environment, family relations, and school experiences in addition to taking a number of inventories designed to measure cognitive and socioemotional development. To investigate the relationship between maternal work and delinquency, we conduct our analysis on a sample of 707 adolescents who were between the ages of 12 and 14 in 1994. These children are the offspring of female respondents originally interviewed in 1979. Each of these respondents completed the Child Self-Administered Supplement (CSAS) in 1992 and in 1994. This self-report booklet collects information on a wide range of variables including child-parent interaction, peer relationships, and involvement in various delinquent activities. . . .

Dependent Variable: Delinquency

The 1994 CSAS includes nine highly correlated items that assess involvement in deviant and delinquent acts. Five of the items measure relatively minor to moderate acts of youth deviance: breaking parents' curfew, dishonesty (i.e., lying to a parent), school problems (i.e., parent came to school because of child behavior), truancy, and staying out all night. The other four items involve more serious acts of lawbreaking: alcohol abuse, vandalism (i.e., damaged school property on purpose), store theft, and violence (i.e., hurt someone badly enough to need bandages or a doctor). These nine items are summed to create our scale measuring youth deviance and delinquency (alpha = .78). . . .

Independent Variables

Maternal employment status. A continuous measure of hours usually worked is used in this analysis. In past studies, (e.g., Parcel and Menaghan 1994, 1994a) investigators assigned missing values to work-hour variables for non-employed mothers, who were then excluded from the analysis. Thus, these studies focused on the effects of paid maternal employment among a sub-group of working mothers only. Other studies include non-employed mothers but as a dummy category that is used in equations with other dummy variables capturing increasing levels of time commitment to paid employment (e.g., part-time, full-time, overtime) (Baydar and Brooks-Gunn 1991; Muller 1995; Parcel, Nickoll, and Dufur 1996). Measuring maternal work hours via a series of dummy variables is arguably a good strategy for organizing information and for detecting non-linear effects (see Harvey 1999). As Harvey points out, however, this method is problematic because the dummy categories are formed from continuous variables so there are infinite ways one could create categories and arbitrary boundaries between categories are often created. Moreover, using continuous variables does not prevent the detection of nonlinear effects (Harvey 1999). Based on this rationale, we use a continuous measure of hours worked in our primary analysis. . . .

Occupational class. We measure occupational class in two ways. First, following Parcel and Menaghan (1994), we construct a 19-item-based occupational complexity scale by matching occupational titles reported by NLSY respondents to job descriptions reported in the Dictionary of Occupational Titles. . . .

Our primary measure of workplace conditions is developed based on the work of Mark Colvin (Colvin 2000; Colvin and Pauly 1983). Drawing from Kohn (1977) and Edwards (1979), Colvin links the workplace controls experienced by parents to the patterns and styles of control parents exert upon children. Unskilled, non-unionized employees (Fraction I workers) are subjected to "simple control" in the workplace, which is coercive and alienating. . . .

Skilled laborers and craftspersons (Fraction II workers), who often belong to labor unions, experience greater job security and are controlled via "technical control"—the machine-paced atmosphere of manufacturing and industrial workplaces where workers are motivated to produce by wage increases and job security. . . .

Fraction III workers are those skilled workers, technicians, salaried professionals, and supervisory staff who experience greater self-direction, job complexity, and job security in the workplace. . . .

Family income.   Total family income is included in all models. By employing a family income measure, we are able to assess the impact of mother's employment experiences while controlling for the total standard of living of each family included in the analysis. Controlling for family income helps to isolate the independent effects of occupational variables in the analysis.

Child care.   Following Parcel and Menaghan (1994), we measure child care with a series of dummy variables. Dummy variables representing professional daycare settings, childcare provided by a relative (including fathers), and childcare provided by a non-relative are included. . . .

Discussion

Are the children of working mothers more likely to be delinquent than other children? According to past studies and to the results of our analysis, the answer is a qualified "No." The present study demonstrates that regardless of how this issue is examined, having a working mother has only a small and indirect effect on delinquency. This general pattern holds whether we considered maternal employment in a child's pre-school years or maternal work in adolescence. Furthermore, with the lone exception of maternal supervision, maternal employment has little influence on several known pathways to delinquency.

Like Parcel and Menaghan (1994, 1994a) and more recent findings by Harvey (1999), our research suggests that the widespread concern over the fates of working women and their children is largely unsupported. Rather than being a social problem whose untoward effects can be demonstrated empirically, the maternal employment-delinquency connection is better understood as a socially constructed problem. As a perceived social problem, the dark side of maternal employment has a long history in America. Fueled by scientific data on the link between early family processes and delinquency and by cherished popular beliefs in the sanctity of the "first relationship"—the coupling of mother and child—for decades politicians and social commentators have pointed to modern trends in female labor participation to explain social problems such as crime. But if the unprecedented entrance of mothers into the paid workforce is related to delinquency, it must be because working mothers fail their children by depriving them of the support and discipline they need. The current study adds to the growing literature that casts doubt on these assumptions.

Our findings suggest other notable conclusions. First, it is maternal and family resources, rather than the characteristics of maternal work, that most influence some well-known pathways to delinquency in our study. Maternal AFQT [Armed Forces Qualifications Test] score, a measure of intellectual resources, affects both parental support and mother-child bonds in early childhood and in adolescence: mothers who draw from greater cognitive resources are more supportive in parenting and raise more securely attached children.

Although the AFQT measures an individual's intellectual capacity, it reflects the subject's developed abilities rather than a biologically assigned aptitude (Menaghan and Parcel 1991). The AFQT score varies with family of origin, geographic region, and years of schooling, which implies that, like maternal education, an AFQT score reflects relative social advantage or disadvantage (Maume, Cancio, and Evans 1996; Menaghan and Parcel 1991). Our findings should be interpreted as further evidence that social disadvantage is reproduced partly through its effect on parent-child relations. Consistent with this theme, our analysis found that an important family resource, family income, exerts a positive influence on warm and responsive parenting in adolescence, while welfare reliance has the opposite effect. This relationship is consistent with past research that identified economic hardship as a strain on family functioning (McLoyd 1990; Siegal 1984).

The most powerful predictors of delinquency in our analysis are maternal supervision, delinquent peer association, and school attachment. Adolescents who are supervised more closely, those who have fewer delinquent peers, and those who are more attached to school show less involvement in delinquency. This result supports a large body of research that identifies these factors as important to the production of antisocial behavioral patterns. We reiterate, here, our discovery that maternal employment had relatively little negative impact on these important pathways to delinquency.

In one instance, however, workplace controls had a small indirect effect on delinquency. Specifically, bureaucratic work controls were negatively related to maternal supervision and, thus, had a slightly positive effect on delinquency. One interpretation of this result is that professional mothers may invest more time in their careers than the average mother does which may diminish their ability to monitor children. On the other hand, the negative effect of bureaucratic controls on supervision may not reflect a difference in time spent with children so much as a difference in parenting style. The freedom and autonomy experienced by the professional parent may translate into a parenting style characterized by less overt supervision and greater attempts to equip children with internal normative controls.

Conversely, we found that maternal work hours were indirectly related to lower involvement in delinquency, through their positive effect on supervision. Again, although the effect is small, maternal work hours is actually related to greater supervision in our sample. This may be due to the stabilizing influence of steady employment on family life. As Wilson (1996:73) has argued, a job "constitutes a framework for daily behavior and patterns of interaction because it imposes disciplines and regularities" upon a parent.

Furthermore, while no maternal employment variable is related to delinquent peer association, neighborhood disorder is. This finding is consistent with social disorganization theory (Shaw and Mckay 1942): the breakdown of informal neighborhood controls leaves children at a greater risk for being socialized in intimate delinquent peer groups. It is instructive that our analysis points to community breakdown, as it operates through delinquent peer influence, as a cause of delinquency rather than family breakdown related to the absence of a working mother.

Finally, if improving family life is a goal of crime control policy, it would make good sense to aim at addressing the structural factors that limit maternal and family resources and that contribute to community disorder. Our study suggests that policy debates should avoid ideological attacks on working mothers, which portray them as leaving their children "home alone," and concentrate instead on the economic and educational inequalities that weaken families and neighborhoods.

Note

1. Contrary to past work by Parcel and Menaghan (e.g., 1994), we did not find that mother's working conditions had a substantial impact on parenting or home environment. In their research, higher quality work was related to higher quality home environments. Whether we measured mother's working conditions with the occupational complexity scale favored by Parcel and Menaghan or our series of dummy variables representing the three fractions of the working class, we found no such effect. Our contradictory findings may be explained, in part, by the measurement of our pathway variables. As discussed earlier, many of our delinquency pathway variables are one-item measures that lack the sensitivity of the multi-item family and home variables used by Parcel and Menaghan.

POSTSCRIPT

Do Mothers Who Work Outside the Home Have a Negative Effect on Their Children?

In 2007, the cost of living has exploded to the highest levels seen to date. A family who wants more than one bedroom in a New York City apartment can expect to pay $3,000 or more per month in rent—not including gas, electricity, and other utilities. To even move into an apartment in this city, one must be able to put down an additional first and last month's rent, plus a broker's fee, which could be as high as 17% of a year's rent. So just to sign a lease, a person would need to have just over $10,000 in cash. This does not begin to cover the other expenses involved in raising a child.

This is just one possible scenario—but it demonstrates that in many family situations where there are two parents, both parents are working not because they think it is an important aspect of their identity or self-esteem, but because they need to in order to survive. The scenario above seems like no big deal to an investment banker on Wall Street, but it would be a huge deal to a sanitation worker and his partner, a city bus driver. For many parents, therefore, working is a necessity that is not up for discussion, not a luxury, a hobby, or part of some political agenda.

In the end, does it help to know the effects that mothers working outside of the home have on the development of their children if there is nothing a mother can do about it? What about the effects of fathers? It is interesting how biased so many cultures are toward mothers and against fathers. While there is research looking at the effects of a mother's working on her child's development, what about the effects of a father working? What about families in which there are two mothers? Families in which there is no mother, but another adult caregiver?

There is no easy answer to this question, and there are certainly arguments for and against parents working outside of the home if they even have the capacity to entertain that argument. Regardless of how one feels about this issue, however, it is important to avoid judging a parent's decision about whether to work or stay home; guaranteed, whatever decision was made was very likely a difficult one to make!

Suggested Readings

Barnett, W.S. (1995). Long-Term Effects of Early Childhood Programs on Cognitive and School Outcomes. *The Future of Children*, Vol. 5(3), Winter 1995.

Brooks-Gunn, J., Berlin, L. J., & Fuligni, A. S. (2000). Early childhood intervention programs: What about the family? In J. P. Shonkoff & S. J. Meisel (Eds.), *The handbook of early childhood intervention.* New York: Cambridge University Press.

Harvey, E. (1999). "Long-term effects of early parental employment on children of the National Longitudinal Survey of Youth." *Developmental Psychology* 35: 445–449.

Shonkoff, J.P. & Phillips, D.A., Eds. (2000). *From Neurons to Neighborhoods: The Science of Early Childhood Development.* Washington, DC: National Academies Press.

Internet References . . .

Sexuality Information and Education Council of the United States

The Sexuality Information and Education Council of the United States is a national organization advocating for comprehensive sexuality education, sexual health programs and services, and sexual rights.

http://www.siecus.org

For Health Freedom

For Health Freedom is a nonpartisan, nonprofit research center or "think tank" based in Washington, DC. It does not endorse any health care treatment, product, provider, or organization, but rather aims to present the ethical and economic case for strengthening personal health freedom.

http://www.forhealthfreedom.org

Intersex Society of North America

The Intersex Society of North America is devoted to systemic change to end shame, secrecy and unwanted genital surgeries for people born with an anatomy that someone decided is not standard for male or female.

http://www.isna.org/

The American Society for Human Genetics

The American Society of Human Genetics (ASHG), founded in 1948, is the primary professional membership organization for human geneticists in the Americas, including researchers, academicians, clinicians, laboratory practice professionals, genetic counselors, nurses, and others involved in or with special interest in human genetics.

http://www.ashg.org

National Right to Life Committee

The National Right to Life Committee (NRLC) was founded in 1973 in direct response to the United States Supreme Court's decision in the *Roe v. Wade* case, which guaranteed women the right to access abortion in the first trimester of their pregnancy, with some exceptions.

http://www.nrlc.org

Planned Parenthood Federation of America

Planned Parenthood Federation of America is the nation's oldest and largest reproductive health organization, believing in "the fundamental right of each individual, throughout the world, to manage his or her fertility, regardless of the individual's income, marital status, race, ethnicity, sexual orientation, age, national origin, or residence."

http://www.plannedparenthood.org

How Much Control Should Parents Have Over Their Children's Lives?

*M*ost *people can recall at one time or another being a child, and wanting to do something their parent didn't want them to do. When they asked their parent, "Why not?" the answer that came back was, "Because I said so." Parents have an enormous amount of social control over children, from a very young age. This power extends, however, beyond decisions about who a child can play with, how long she or he can stay up at night, or whether she or he can watch television for 10 more minutes. These decisions extend into areas that can affect a child for the rest of her or his life, including health and education. How much say should parents have in these types of decisions? How much say should a young child have? A teenager?*

This section examines six particularly challenging parental decisions:

- Should "Abstinence-Until-Marriage" Be the Only Message for Teens?

- Should Parents Routinely Vaccinate Their Children?

- Should Parents Be Able to Select the Biological Sex of Their Children?

- Should Parents Surgically Alter Their Intersex Infants?

- Should Minors Be Required to Get Their Parents' Permission in Order to Obtain an Abortion?

ISSUE 6

Should "Abstinence-Until-Marriage" Be the Only Message for Teens?

YES: Bridget E. Maher, from "Abstinence Until Marriage: The Best Message for Teens," *Family Research Council* (2004)

NO: Sue Alford, from "What's Wrong with Federal Abstinence-Only-Until-Marriage Requirements?" *Transitions* (March 2001)

ISSUE SUMMARY

YES: Bridget E. Maher, an analyst on marriage and family issues at the Family Research Council, argues that far too much funding has gone into programs that teach young people about sexuality and contraception—programs that she asserts are ineffective. She argues that most teens say they and their peers should receive strong messages about abstinence.

NO: Sue Alford, editor and director of public information services at Advocates for Youth, argues that young people are receiving sexuality information and messages from so many sources that it is irresponsible to restrict sexuality and other educators from discussing only abstinence. She maintains that the programs taught under the Abstinence Until Marriage funding often provide factually inaccurate information and hyperbolic assertions pertaining to the potential consequences of sexual relationships outside of marriage.

In 1996, President Clinton signed the welfare reform law. Attached to this law was a federal entitlement program allocating $50 million per year over a five-year period to abstinence-only-until-marriage educational programs. This Act specifies that a program is defined as "abstinence-only" education if it:

- has as its exclusive purpose teaching the social, psychological, and health gains to be realized by abstaining from sexual activity;
- teaches that abstinence from sexual activity outside of marriage is the expected standard for all school-age children;
- teaches that abstinence from sexual activity is the only certain way to avoid out-of-wedlock pregnancy, sexually transmitted diseases, and other associated health problems;

- teaches that a mutually faithful monogamous relationship in the context of marriage is the expected standard of sexual activity;
- teaches that sexual activity outside the context of marriage is likely to have harmful psychological and physical side effects;
- teaches that bearing children out-of-wedlock is likely to have harmful consequences for the child, the child's parents, and society;
- teaches young people how to reject sexual advances and how alcohol and drug use increase vulnerability to sexual advances; and,
- teaches the importance of attaining self-sufficiency before engaging in sexual activity. *(Section 510(b) of Title V of the Social Security Act, P.L. 104-193)*.

In order to access these funds, an entity must agree to teach all of these points, not just a few. Failure to do so would result in loss of the funding.

Those who support the teaching of comprehensive sexuality education disagree with the tenets that abstinence-only-until-marriage (AOUM) supports. They present research that demonstrates how comprehensive sexuality education programs help young people to delay the onset of risky sexual behaviors, and to use contraceptives more effectively once they do start engaging in these behaviors. Some argue that AOUM is exclusionary, excluding non-heterosexual youth; is fear- and shame-based, and is wildly out of touch with the reality in which young people are living. They are quick to point out that AOUM supports have yet to provide empirical evidence that their programs "work."

AOUM supporters believe that comprehensive sexuality education programs teach "too much, too soon." They believe strongly that providing information about abstinence, along with safer sex information, confuses teens, and gives them permission to become sexually active when the potential consequences for sexual activity are much more serious.

Take a look at the language of the legislation. The language refers to "sexual activity." What does that include to you? Would you be able to support this if it included some behaviors, but not others? Are there some messages you agree with and not others? If you were an educator, would you be able to teach all eight points?

As you read these selections, think about any sexuality education classes you may have had—do you think they should have taught you more? Less? Consider, too, young people who are already sexually active. Would abstinence messages work for them? Did a more comprehensive program "fail" them?

In the following selections, Bridget E. Maher outlines some of the negative consequences of teen sex, and why abstinence is the only 100 percent effective option for avoiding those negative consequences. She argues that more comprehensive sexuality education programs, while purporting to teach about abstinence, actually rarely, if ever, do. Sue Alford describes what she perceives to be flaws in the assertions made by AOUM proponents, such as the idea that if educators teach only abstinence, teens won't have sex. Highlighting some of the core values behind sexuality education, she asserts that teaching only about abstinence conflicts with these core values.

YES ↵

Bridget E. Maher

Abstinence Until Marriage: The Best Message for Teens

The federal government has provided some abstinence-until-marriage funding in recent years, but comprehensive sex education and contraception programs are vastly over-funded in comparison. In 2002, abstinence-until-marriage programs received $102 million, while teen-sex education and contraception programs received at least $427.7 million. In his last budget, President Bush proposed an increase of $33 million for abstinence-until-marriage programs, following upon his campaign promise to try to equalize funding between comprehensive sex education and abstinence programs. This is a good first step, but it still doesn't bring true parity between these programs. It's time for our government to get serious about fulfilling the president's promise to at least level the playing field with regard to funding of the positive and healthy message of abstinence-until-marriage versus that of promoting premarital sex and contraception.

Teens are greatly influenced by the messages they receive about sex in school. Unfortunately, the majority of schools teach "safe sex"—"comprehensive" or so-called "abstinence plus" programs—believing that it's best for kids to have all the information they need about sexuality and to make their own decisions about sex. Abstinence is downplayed while sexual activity and condom use are encouraged in these curriculums, because it's assumed that children are eventually going to have sex. A 2002 report by the Physicians Consortium, which investigated comprehensive sex programs promoted by the Centers for Disease Control, reveals that abstinence is barely mentioned and condom use is clearly advocated in these curriculums.

Abstinence-until-marriage programs, on the other hand, teach young people to save sex for marriage, and their message has been very effective in changing teens' behavior. Today, there are over one-thousand abstinence-until-marriage programs around the United States and one-third of public middle and high schools say that abstinence is "the main message in their sex education." Abstinence organizations do more than just tell teens to say no to unwed sex: they teach young people the skills they need to practice abstinence. Classes cover many topics including self-esteem building, self-control, decision-making, goal-setting, character education, and communication skills.

From *Family Research Council,* June 12, 2004. Copyright © 2004 by Family Research Council. Reprinted by permission.

Choosing the Best, Teen-Aid, Inc., and Operation Keepsake are just a few of the many effective abstinence programs in the U.S. . . .

Teens want to be taught abstinence. Nearly all (93 percent) of teenagers believe that teens should be given a strong message from society to abstain from sex until at least after high school. A 2000 poll found that 64 percent of teen girls surveyed said sexual activity is not acceptable for high-school age adolescents, even if precautions are taken to prevent pregnancy and sexually transmitted diseases.

Those who do not abstain from sex are likely to experience many negative consequences, both physical and emotional. Aside from the risk of pregnancy, teens have a high risk of contracting a sexually transmitted disease (STD). Each year 3 million teens—25 percent of sexually active teens—are infected with an STD. About 25 percent of all new cases of STDs occur in teenagers; two-thirds of new cases occur in young people age 15–24. Teens who engage in premarital sex are likely to experience fear about pregnancy and STDs, regret, guilt, lowered self-respect, fear of commitment, and depression. . . .

Public opinion polls show that teens value abstinence highly. Nearly all (93 percent) of teenagers believe that teens should be given a strong message from society to abstain from sex until at least after high school.[1] A 2000 poll found that 64 percent of teen girls surveyed said sexual activity is not acceptable for high-school age adolescents, even if precautions are taken to prevent pregnancy and sexually transmitted diseases.[2] Moreover, teens who have not abstained often regret being sexually active. In 2000, 63 percent of sexually active teens said they wish they had waited longer to become sexually active.[3]

Negative Consequences of Unwed Teen Sex

Teens need to be taught to save sex for marriage, because premarital sex has many negative consequences, both physical and emotional. One of the most obvious outcomes of engaging in premarital sex is having a child outside marriage; today, one-third of all births are out-of-wedlock.[4] Teen birthrates have declined since the early 1990s, but the highest unwed birthrates are among those age 20–24, followed by those 25–29.[5] This shows that many young girls abstain from sex while they are in high school, but not afterward.

Teen unwed childbearing has negative consequences for mothers, children, and society. Unwed teen mothers are likely to live in poverty and be dependent on welfare, and only about 50 percent of them are likely to finish high school while they are adolescents or young adults.[6] Children born to teen mothers are more likely than other children to have lower grades, to leave high school without graduating, to be abused or neglected, to have a child as an unmarried teenager, and to be delinquent.[7] Teen childbearing costs U.S. taxpayers an estimated $7 billion per year in social services and lost tax revenue due to government dependency.[8] The gross annual cost to society of unwed childbearing and its consequences is $29 billion, which includes the administration of welfare and foster care programs, building and maintaining additional prisons, as well as lower education and resultant lost productivity among unwed parents.[9]

Aside from the risk of pregnancy, teens have a high risk of contracting a sexually transmitted disease (STD). Each year 3 million teens—25 percent of sexually active teens—are infected with an STD.[10] About 25 percent of all new cases of STDs occur in teenagers; two-thirds of new cases occur in young people age 15-24.[11]

Chlamydia and gonorrhea are two of the most common curable STDs among sexually active teens. According to the Centers for Disease Control, gonorrhea rates are highest among 15- to 19-year-old females and 20- to 24-year-old males, and more than five to 10 percent of teen females are currently infected with chlamydia.[12] If these diseases are untreated, they can lead to pelvic inflammatory disease, infertility, and ectopic pregnancy.[13] Studies have found that up to 15 percent of sexually active teenage women are infected with the human papillomavirus (HPV), an incurable virus that is present in nearly all cervical cancers.[14]

In addition to being at risk for STDs, unwed sexually active teens are likely to experience negative emotional consequences and to become both more promiscuous and less interested in marriage. Teens who engage in premarital sex are likely to experience fear about pregnancy and STDs, regret, guilt, lowered self-respect, fear of commitment, and depression.[15] Also, adolescents who engage in unwed sex at a younger age are much more likely to have multiple sex partners. Among young people between the ages of 15–24 who have had sex before age 18, 75 percent had two or more partners and 45 percent had four or more partners. Among those who first had sex after age 19, just 20 percent had more than one partner and one percent had four or more partners.[16] Premarital sex can also cause teens to view marriage less favorably. A 1994 study of college freshmen found that non-virgins with multiple sex partners were more likely to view marriage as difficult and involving a loss of personal freedom and happiness. Virgins were more likely to view marriage as "enjoyable." . . .[17]

"Safe Sex" or "Comprehensive Sex Education" Programs

In addition to the influence of their parents, teens are also affected by the messages on sex and abstinence that they receive in school. Unfortunately, the majority of schools teach "safe sex," "comprehensive," or so-called "abstinence plus" programs, believing that it is best for children to have all the information they need about sexuality and to make their own decisions about sex.[18] Abstinence is downplayed and sexual activity and condom use are encouraged in these curriculums, because it is assumed that kids are eventually going to have sex. A 2002 report by the Physicians Consortium, which investigated comprehensive sex programs promoted by the Centers for Disease Control, reveals that abstinence is barely mentioned and condom use is clearly advocated in these curriculums. Not only do students learn how to obtain condoms, but they also practice putting them on cucumbers or penile models. Masturbation, body massages, bathing together, and fantasizing are listed as "ways to be close" in one curriculum. . . .[19]

The Effectiveness of Abstinence-Until-Marriage Programs

Abstinence-until-marriage programs, on the other hand, teach young people to save sex for marriage, and their message has been very effective in changing teens' behavior. According to the Physicians Resource Council, the drop in teen birth rates during the 1990s was due not to increased contraceptive use among teens, but to sexual abstinence.[20] This correlates with the decrease in sexual activity among unwed teens. In 1988, 51 percent of unwed girls between the ages of 15 and 19 had engaged in sexual intercourse compared to 49 percent in 1995. This decrease also occurred among unwed boys, declining from 60 percent to 55 percent between 1988 and 1995.[21]

Today, there are over one thousand abstinence-until-marriage programs around the United States, and one-third of public middle and high schools say both that abstinence is "the main message in their sex education" and that abstinence is taught as "the only option for young people."[22] Started by non-profit or faith-based groups, these programs teach young people to save sex for marriage. However, abstinence organizations do more than just tell teens to say no to unwed sex: They teach young people the skills they need to practice abstinence. Classes cover many topics including self-esteem building, self-control, decision making, goal setting, character education, and communication skills. Sexually transmitted diseases, the realities of parenthood and anatomy are also discussed.[23] The effectiveness of birth control may be discussed, but it is neither provided nor promoted in these programs.

Choosing the Best, an abstinence program based in Marietta, Georgia, and started in 1993, has developed curriculum and materials that are used in over two thousand school districts in 48 states. Students in public or private schools are taught abstinence by their teachers, who have been trained by Choosing the Best's staff. Appropriate for 6th through 12th graders, the curriculum teaches students the consequences of premarital sex, the benefits of abstaining until marriage, how to make a virginity pledge, refusal skills, and character education. Choosing the Best involves parents in their children's lessons and teaches them how to teach abstinence to their children. . . .

This abstinence program has contributed to lower teen-pregnancy rates in Georgia. In Columbus, Georgia, Choosing the Best's materials were used in all 8th grades for a period of four years. A study requested by the Georgia State Board of Education to examine the effectiveness of this curriculum found a 38-percent reduction in pregnancies among middle-school students in Muscogee County between 1997 and 1999. Other large school districts that did not implement Choosing the Best's program experienced only a 6-percent reduction in teen pregnancies during those same years.

Teen-Aid, Inc., based in Spokane, Washington, has been promoting abstinence until marriage and character education for over twenty years. This program seeks to teach young people the knowledge and skills they need to make good decisions and to achieve goals. Parent-child communication is a key component of the Teen-Aid curriculum, as parents are involved in every lesson. In 1999–2000, over 41,000 families in public schools, churches, and community organizations used these materials.

A 1999 study conducted by Whitworth College in Spokane, Washington found many positive results among teens in Edinburg, Texas who were taught the Teen-Aid curriculum. On the pretest administered to students after the course, 62 percent said "having sex as a teenager would make it harder for them to get a good job or be successful in a career," compared to 71 percent on the post test. When asked if they were less likely to have sexual intercourse before they got married, 47 percent responded yes on the pretest, compared to 54 percent after taking the course. . . .[24]

Operation Keepsake, a Cleveland, Ohio-based abstinence program started in 1988, has its "For Keeps" curriculum in 90 public and private schools in the greater Cleveland area. It is presently taught to over 25,000 students, including those in middle and high school, as well as college freshman. Along with a classroom component, this program also includes peer mentoring, guest speakers, opportunities to make an abstinence pledge, and parental involvement.

Case Western Reserve University evaluated Operation Keepsake's program in 2001, finding that it is having a positive impact on adolescents' beliefs and behavior regarding abstinence. Over nine hundred 7th and 8th graders completed the pretests and post tests. According to the study, the program had "a clear and sustainable impact on abstinence beliefs" because students in the program had "higher abstinence-until-marriage values" at the follow-up survey than did those in the control group, who did not attend the abstinence program. . . .[25]

Virginity pledges are also successful in encouraging sexual abstinence among unwed teens. A 2001 study based on the National Longitudinal Study of Adolescent Health . . . found that teens who take a virginity pledge are 34 percent less likely to have sex before marriage compared to those who do not pledge, even after controlling for factors such as family structure, race, self-esteem, and religiosity. . . .[26]

Conclusion

These are only some of the many abstinence-until-marriage programs in the United States. Their success in changing young people's views and behavior regarding abstinence is due to their telling the truth about sex to young people: that it is meant to be saved for marriage and that it is possible to live a chaste life. Along with this message, they give kids the encouragement and skills they need to save themselves for marriage. . . .

Notes

1. "The Cautious Generation? Teens Tell Us About Sex, Virginity, and 'The Talk,'" National Campaign to Prevent Teen Pregnancy, April 27, 2000.

2. Ibid.

3. "Not Just Another Thing to Do: Teens Talk About Sex, Regret and the Influence of Their Parents," National Campaign to Prevent Teen Pregnancy, June 30, 2000.

4. Joyce A. Martin et al., *Births: Final Data for 2001*, National Vital Statistics Reports 51, December 18, 2002, National Center for Health Statistics, Table C.

5. Bridget Maher, *The Family Portrait: A Compilation of Data, Research and Public Opinion on the Family*, Family Research Council, 2002, p. 73, 162.
6. Rebecca Maynard, *Kids Having Kids: Economic and Social Consequences of Teen Pregnancy*, The Urban Institute, 1997, p. 2–5.
7. Ibid, p. 205–229, 257–281, Judith Levine, Harold Pollack and Maureen E. Comfort, "Academic and Behavioral Outcomes Among the Children of Young Mothers," *Journal of Marriage and Family* 63 (May 2001): 355–369 and Amy Conseur et al., "Maternal and Perinatal Risk Factors for Later Delinquency," *Pediatrics* 99 (June 1997): 785–790.
8. Rebecca A. Maynard, ed., *Kids Having Kids: A Robin Hood Foundation Special Report on the Costs of Adolescent Childbearing*, The Robin Hood Foundation, 1996, p. 19.
9. Ibid, pp. 20, 88–91.
10. The Alan Guttmacher Institute, "Teen Sex and Pregnancy," *Facts in Brief*, 1999.
11. Linda L. Alexander, ed., et al., "Sexually Transmitted Diseases in America: How Many Cases and at What Cost?" The Kaiser Family Foundation, December 1998, 8.
12. Centers for Disease Control, *Tracking the Hidden Epidemics: Trends in the United States 2000*, 4.
13. The Alan Guttmacher Institute, "Teen Sex and Pregnancy."
14. Ibid. See also the Kaiser Family Foundation, "HPV (Human Papillomavirus) and Cervical Cancer," *Fact Sheet*, July 2001.
15. Tom and Judy Lickona, *Sex, Love and You*, (Notre Dame: Ave Maria Press, 1994), 62–77.
16. Centers for Disease Control, "Current Trends: Premarital Sexual Experience Among Adolescent Women—United States, 1970–1988," *Morbidity and Mortality Weekly Report* 39 (January 4, 1991): 929–932. . . .
17. Connie J. Salts et al., "Attitudes Toward Marriage and Premarital Sexual Activity of College Freshmen," *Adolescence* 29 (Winter 1994): 775–779.
18. Tina Hoff and Liberty Greene et al., "Sex Education in America: A Series of National Surveys of Students, Parents, Teachers, and Principals," Kaiser Family Foundation, September 2000, 16.
19. The Physicians Consortium, "Sexual Messages in Government-Promoted Programs and Today's Youth Culture," April 2002.
20. Cheryl Wetzstein, "Drop in Teen Birthrates Attributed to Abstinence," *The Washington Times*, February 11, 1999, A6.
21. Joyce C. Abma and Freya L. Sonenstein, *Sexual Activity and Contraceptive Practices Among Teenagers in the United States, 1988 and 1995*, Series 23: Data from the National Survey of Family Growth, National Center for Health Statistics, Washington, D.C., April 2001, Table 1.
22. Tina Hoff and Liberty Greene et al., "Sex Education in America: A Series of National Surveys of Students, Parents, Teachers, and Principals," 14.
23. Barbara Devaney et al., "The Evaluation of Abstinence Education Programs Funded Under Title V Section 510: Interim Report," Mathematica Policy Research, Inc., April 2002, 14.
24. Raja S. Tanas, "Report on the Teen-Aid Abstinence-Education Program Fifth-Year Evaluation 1998–1999, Whitworth College, Spokane, WA, July 1999.
25. Elaine Borawski et al., "Evaluation of the Teen Pregnancy Prevention Programs Funded Through the Wellness Block Grant (1999–2000), Case Western Reserve University, March 23, 2001.
26. Peter S. Bearman and Hannah Bruckner, "Promising the Future: Virginity Pledges and First Intercourse," *American Journal of Sociology* 106 (January 2001): 859–912.

Sue Alford

 **NO**

What's Wrong with Federal Abstinence-Only-Until-Marriage Requirements?

1. Federally mandated abstinence-only-until-marriage education jeopardizes the health and lives of young people by denying them information that can prevent unintended pregnancy and infection with sexually transmitted diseases (STDs), including HIV.

Youth need to know *how* to avoid the potential negative consequences of sexual intercourse. Every young person urgently needs accurate information about contraception and condoms. STDs and unintended pregnancy are extremely common. Consider the following:

- One-half of all new HIV infections occur among people ages 25 or less.[1]
- One-quarter of all new HIV infections occur among people under age 21.[1]
- The human papilloma virus—genital warts—is so common that experts believe three-quarters of *all* the sexually active people in the world have been infected with it.[2]
- In the 1995 National Survey of Family Growth, 28 percent of *all* women reported having had an unintended birth, and one-fifth of those women reported the birth as unwanted.[3]

2. Proponents of abstinence-only-until-marriage education assume that, if young people do not learn about contraception, they will not have sexual intercourse.

Throughout human history, people have had sexual intercourse. Often, people had to rely on contraceptive methods that were not very effective in preventing unwanted pregnancy because highly effective methods were not available. Today, highly effective methods are available to help people avoid unintended pregnancy, if they know about these methods and have access to them.

The fact that some U.S. teens report oral and/or anal intercourse while considering themselves 'virgins' underscores the fact that lacking information does not prevent young people from having sexual intercourse. It may, however, prevent them from making healthy choices about sexuality.

Research shows that teenagers who receive contraceptive education in the same year that they choose to become sexually active are about 70 percent more likely to use contraceptive methods (including condoms) and more than twice as likely to use oral contraceptives as those not exposed to contraceptive education. That is why the National Institutes of Health recommends that, although sexual abstinence is a desirable objective, programs must include instruction in safer sex behavior, including condom use.[3]

However, abstinence-only-until-marriage education goes further. It *discourages* young people from using contraception. It encourages young people to believe that condoms and modern methods of contraception—such as birth control pills, injectable contraception, implants, and the intra-uterine device (IUD)—are far less effective than they, in fact, are. Many abstinence-only-until-marriage programs discuss modern methods of contraception *only* in terms of failure rates (often exaggerated) and censor information about their correct use and effectiveness. Thus, many of these programs keep young people in ignorance of the very facts that would encourage them to protect themselves when they eventually become sexually active.

- By age 18, about 71 percent of U.S. youth have had sexual intercourse.[6]
- One recent study found that, by the age of 18, more than 75 percent of young people have engaged in various heavy petting behaviors.[7]
- Another study found that 25 to 50 percent of teens report having had oral sex.[8]
- A third study focusing exclusively on adolescent 'virgins' (defined in the study as teens who had not experienced vaginal intercourse) found that nearly one-third of respondents reported having participated in masturbation with a partner. In the same study, 10 percent of teens who defined themselves as virgins had participated in oral intercourse and one percent had participated in anal intercourse.[9]
- Data from a nationally representative survey indicate that, in 1999, 49.9 percent of all high school students have had sexual intercourse. The percentage rises by grade level—38.6 percent of ninth graders have had sexual intercourse compared with 64.9 percent of seniors.[10]
- By the time young people reach age 20, about 80 percent of males and 76 percent of females have had sexual intercourse.[6]

Federal legislation does not define sexual activity when it requires sexuality education classes to teach that *abstinence from sexual activity outside of marriage is the expected standard for all school-age children.*[5] Holding hands, kissing, deep kissing, petting—each of these may be included in the disapproved category of 'sexual activity' in individual abstinence-only-until-marriage curricula. At the same time, these curricula provide no guidance about very real behaviors that put youth at risk—oral and/or anal intercourse. Yet, the reality is that almost every American teenager today has had at least one romantic relationship by the time he/she is 18, and most young people have engaged in 'sexual activity.' In fact, most American parents would be likely to worry about the well-being of a teenager who went through his/her entire teenage years without even one romantic relationship.

If these young people have had abstinence-only-until-marriage sexuality education, they will not know how to protect themselves and their partners from STDs and unintended pregnancy. In the end, research demonstrates that, instead of keeping young people from having sexual intercourse, abstinence-only-until-marriage programs merely keep them from having *safer* sexual intercourse.

> 3. Federal requirements assume that young people will not learn about sexuality from any source other than sexuality education classes.

Legislators and congressional staff do not acknowledge the world in which young people live. If they did, they would hesitate to push, as an *ultimate value*, something that is actually a *norm*. Moreover, it is a norm that is contradicted by nearly every television show, movie, popular magazine, song, or music video that young people see, hear, or read. This legislatively mandated norm is contrary to the behaviors of many adults (including members of Congress and their staff) that young people hear or read about. Young people learn about sexual expression nearly everywhere they turn in society. They do not learn about responsible, mutually respectful, sexual expression in many places—and certainly not in abstinence-only-until-marriage programs. In such programs, they learn instead about a single congressionally mandated standard that is at odds with nearly every other sexuality message they receive from the society in which they live.

Federally funded abstinence-only-until-marriage programs must teach that *a mutually faithful monogamous relationship in the context of marriage is the expected standard of human sexual activity.*[5] By contrast, a recent nationally representative poll found that 56 percent of U.S. adults agreed that sexual intercourse should be reserved for a committed, monogamous relationship, *whether or not* people are married. Only 33 percent believed that sexual intercourse should occur only within marriage.[11] Moreover, 93 percent of men and 79 percent of women report having had sexual intercourse prior to marriage.[12]

The refusal of abstinence-only-until-marriage proponents to accept the reality of young people's lives also creates a vacuum for youth as to what constitutes 'sexual activity.' Indications are emerging that many youth engage in unprotected sexual activities, such as oral and anal intercourse, while avoiding coitus (vaginal-penile intercourse). Abstinence-only-until-marriage programs cannot even address these issues because they shrink from discussing specific sexual behaviors.

Comprehensive sexuality education rests upon certain core values, including

- Every individual has dignity and self-worth.
- Sexual relationships should never be coercive or exploitative.
- All sexual decisions have effects or consequences.
- Every person has the right and the obligation to make responsible sexual choices.[13]

Comprehensive sexuality education encourages young people to complement these values with the values of their parents, society, and culture and to define and clarify the values by which they can live fulfilling, satisfying lives. Comprehensive sexuality education does not supplant family values; rather it provides young people with the tools to integrate these values into their lives and daily decision-making.

When a teen identifies his/her own values and the norms that are consonant with those values, that teen is unlikely to fall back on doing something because 'everyone is doing it' or to engage in activities just to circumvent an arbitrarily imposed standard. A vital developmental component in comprehensive sexuality education is encouraging teens to think and teaching them *how* to think rather than *what* to think. It is a component that is missing in abstinence-only-until-marriage education, which prefers to tell teens *what* to think and distrusts their ability to think for themselves.

> 4. Federally funded abstinence-only-until-marriage education too often provides young people with medically inaccurate information.

Abstinence-only-until-marriage education provides no information about contraception and condoms other than failure rates. Moreover, it often provides inaccurate information, even about failure rates. In asserting that condoms are ineffective, abstinence-only-until-marriage education usually relies on studies that either pre-date today's highly effective latex condoms or that are not scientific in their research and analysis and, thus, are not published in peer-reviewed journals. Another tactic of proponents of abstinence-only-until-marriage education is to link condom failure with sexually transmitted infections that may occur in areas of the body that condoms do not cover and, thus, *could not* protect. For example, recent abstinence-only arguments against using the condom to prevent HIV infection have focused on the inability of condoms to protect one totally against human papillomavirus (genital warts).[14] What opponents fail to mention, however, is that genital warts may be transmitted across portions of the anatomy (such as the upper thighs, lower abdomen, the groin, testicles, labia majora, or anus) that condoms do not cover.[2]

Second, federal guidelines require abstinence-only-until-marriage programs to teach that *sexual activity outside of marriage is likely to have harmful psychological and physical effects.*[5] First, consider the assertion about harmful physical effects of sexual activity outside of marriage. Certainly, sexual intercourse can result in unplanned pregnancy, STDs, and/or HIV infection. But these results are not necessarily "likely." Moreover, these negative physical consequences are not linked to marital status and may occur inside or outside of marriage. It is precisely to protect against negative physical consequences that comprehensive sexuality education provides young people with information on contraception and condoms.

Next, consider the claim about negative psychological effects of sexual activity outside of marriage. There is simply no sound public health or medical data to support this assertion. Most people have had sexual relations prior to marriage with absolutely no negative psychological consequences. For example, one study reported that, when premarital sexual intercourse is satisfying, it positively affects the relationship for both males and females.[15] The largest study ever undertaken of adult sexual behavior found that more than 90 percent of men and more than 70 percent of women recall wanting their first sexual intercourse to happen when it did.[12]

Sexuality is a natural, normal, and positive component of life. Comprehensive sexuality education can address issues in a positive, helpful manner that encourages young people to make responsible and safe decisions that protect their sexual health.

Notes

1. Centers for Disease Control & Prevention. *Young People at Risk for HIV Infection*. Atlanta, GA: The Centers, 1999.

2. Marr L. *Sexually Transmitted Diseases: A Physician Tells You What You Need to Know*. Baltimore, MD: Johns Hopkins University Press, 1998.

3. National Center for Health Statistics. *Fertility, Family Planning, and Women's Health: New Data from the 1995 National Survey of Family Growth*. [Vital & Health Statistics, Series 23, no. 19]. Hyattsville, MD: U.S. Dept. of Health & Human Services, 1997.

4. National Institutes of Health. *Consensus Development Conference Statement*. Rockville, MD: The Institutes, 1997.

5. Welfare Reform Act of 1996 (P.L. 104-193).

6. Alan Guttmacher Institute. *Sex and America's Teenagers*. New York: The Institute, 1994.

7. Roper Starch Worldwide. *Teens Talk about Sex: Adolescent Sexuality in the '90s*. New York: SIECUS, 1994.

8. Newcomer S, Udry J. Oral sex in an adolescent population. *Archives of Sexual Behavior* 1985; 14:41–46.

9. Schuster MA, Bell RM, Kanouse DE. The sexual practices of adolescent virgins: genital sexual activities of high school students who have never had vaginal intercourse. *American Journal of Public Health* 1996; 86:1570–1576.

10. Centers for Disease Control & Prevention. Youth risk behavior survey, American high school students, 1999. *Morbidity & Mortality Weekly Report* 2000; 49(SS-5).

11. Hickman-Brown Public Opinion Research. *Overview of Research Results*. Report to Advocates for Youth and SIECUS. Washington, DC: Advocates for Youth, 1999.

12. Michael RT *et al. Sex in America: A Definitive Survey*. Boston: Little, Brown & Company, 1994.

13. National Guidelines Task Force. *Guidelines for Comprehensive Sexuality Education*. New York: SIECUS, 1994.

14. Wetzstein C. Unfamiliar sexual disease has no cure, spreads easily. *Washington Times*, Nov. 7, 2000.

15. Cate RM, et al. Sexual intercourse and relationship development. *Family Relations* 1993; (April):162.

POSTSCRIPT

Should "Abstinence-Until-Marriage" Be the Only Message for Teens?

In the United States, there are just under 900,000 teenage pregnancies every year. There are also as many as 4 million new cases of sexually transmitted infections (STIs) among the same age group annually in the United States.

Each side of the sexuality debate is working with what they consider to be a logical presumption. For AOUM proponents, the surest way to avoid an unintended pregnancy or STI is to not do anything sexually until a committed, monogamous relationship—which, to them, is only acceptable within the context of marriage. If people do not engage in the behaviors, they cannot be exposed to the negatives. Since AOUM supporters also believe that marriage is a commitment that is accompanied by a promise of monogamy, or sexual exclusivity, it is, for them, the only appropriate choice for teens.

For comprehensive sexuality education proponents, the logic is that sexual exploration is a normal part of adolescents' development. They believe that the "just say no" approach to sexual behaviors is as unrealistic as it is unhealthy. Rooted in education, social learning, and health belief theories, comprehensive sexuality education programs believe that youth can make wise decisions about their sexual health if given the proper information.

Society will likely never reach consensus on this issue. With AOUM program funding budgeted at an all-time high of $241.5 million for fiscal year 2007, and federal legislation supporting comprehensive sexuality sitting stagnant in the house for nearly 2 years, however, the debate will certainly continue.

ISSUE 7

Should Parents Routinely Vaccinate Their Children?

YES: Ferdinand D. Yates, Jr., from "Should Children Be Routinely Immunized?" Center for Bioethics and Human Dignity (April 16, 2004)

NO: Jini Patel Thompson, from "Should I Vaccinate My Child?" *Well Being Journal* (March/April 2003)

ISSUE SUMMARY

YES: Ferdinand Yates, Jr. supports routine childhood immunizations, and offers an array of research demonstrating their efficacy and relative low risk of harm. He argues that society needs to be able to think beyond its own family structure, and consider that not vaccinating a child puts that child at higher risk for several contagious diseases, which could then be transmitted to others.

NO: Jini Patel Thompson speaks from her position as a parent who had to decide whether to vaccinate her child, and, based on her own research, decided against it. She, too, cites a variety of research sources to demonstrate that the potential negative side effects of vaccinations, both long- and short-term, are not worth the potential positive outcomes for children.

Vaccines were created to strengthen the immune system so that diseases that previously resulted in serious physical and mental disabilities could be stopped before they affected the body. One of these diseases, smallpox, has not been a problem in the United States since the 1960s. Vaccines work by introducing a small amount of a bacterium or virus that is very weak. This causes the body to create antibodies that would attack the disease were it to be contracted. Antibodies can also be created by having a particular disease. This is why children who have chicken pox once will not get it again in their lives. With other infections, an individual may need a booster shot at different times in their lives. There are currently 11 vaccinations that children are given before they are two years old, which are delivered in as many as 16 doses. These immunizations protect against such potentially serious infections as measles, mumps, chicken pox, and hepatitis B.

The Centers for Disease Control and Prevention (CDC) estimate that between 37 and 56 percent of children in the United States have not been fully immunized by the time they are two years old. Parents are required to have their children vaccinated before the children can be enrolled in school or in day care. However, some babies and toddlers end up in day-care settings that are not licensed. Without the requirement, some children will not end up having the vaccinations. We see this, in particular, in low-income (particularly urban) areas where diseases that are uncommon in most parts of the United States today are more likely to occur in disproportionate numbers due to improper vaccination of the children living in the community.

Some parents do not feel that they should be required to have their children immunized. They believe that the risks of having such a young infant injected with an infection like hepatitis B are too great, especially if neither parent is in the high-risk population for the infection. Other people feel that the financial burden on parents to vaccinate their children against infections they believe their children are highly unlikely to contract is too great. Since only about half of health insurance plans cover childhood vaccines, the cost can add up for a low-income family. Others argue that the financial burden is not as great, since many public health departments offer vaccines for free or on a sliding fee scale. In addition, federal dollars are allocated in the hundreds of millions to provide free vaccinations to uninsured children and to educate parents about the need for childhood immunizations. They also maintain that spending money on vaccines today will save money down the line. According to the National Academy of Sciences' Institute of Medicine, every $1 spent on vaccinations saves $10 in healthcare-related costs later in the child's life.

As with any health-related procedure, there are risks involved in vaccinating an infant or child. Some children do suffer injuries or even die as a result of receiving a vaccination. In response to this, Congress passed the National Childhood Vaccine Injury Act in 1986. This act was designed to help ensure vaccine safety and availability and to provide financial recompense for the people or families of children injured or killed by vaccination. In addition, medical professionals are required to report significant adverse reactions they witness as a result of certain vaccines. In the first seven years after this act, the CDC received more than 20,000 reports.

In the following selections, Ferdinand Yates maintains that there is ongoing evidence demonstrating that childhood vaccinations are effective. By not vaccinating a child, he argues, parents are actually putting the health of the greater society at risk since their children are more likely to contract and be able to transmit infections to others. Jini Patel Thompson, writing as a parent of an infant she chose not to vaccinate, weighed the effectiveness, adverse effects, and long-term consequences, and asserts that the potential benefits of vaccinations do not outweigh the potential, possibly life-long negative effects of the vaccines. She enumerates both short- and long-term complications vaccinations can carry with them, and advises parents not to vaccinate, providing very conservative guidelines for what they can do to minimize potential harm should they change their minds and wish to vaccinate their children.

YES

Ferdinand D. Yates, Jr.

Should Children Be Routinely Immunized?

Parental concern regarding recommended vaccinations for the minor child is a very real issue that currently presents itself on a regular basis. Many parents are concerned about the risks of individual vaccination products, and moral and religious convictions also lead some parents to forego vaccination of their children. A generation ago most parents would have readily acknowledged that "the doctor knows best" and thus would have unquestioningly assented to his or her counsel. In today's autonomous society, however, such is not the case. Medical practitioners confronted with this issue must always be concerned with the beneficence, justice, and autonomy of those who seek our care. The following considerations are designed to assist parents and practitioners alike in making decisions regarding vaccination.

First, it is important to recognize that vaccinations have not always been offered. Older doctors may have a vivid recollection of the "Iron Lung" as the only available treatment for patients who had contracted the poliovirus. As a medical student, I took care of a child who was in one of these machines. The only contact that the child's mother had with this patient was to stroke her hair as she lay on her back, her body encased by the iron contraption. Many of the initial vaccination products became available during a time of limited medical care, and the vaccines actually saved thousands of lives. Prominent examples of childhood diseases that became preventable through vaccinations are measles, mumps, diphtheria, and even chickenpox. Due to the availability of vaccinations, it has become quite clear that these "normal childhood diseases" need not be routinely experienced. Such diseases are—to a large extent—preventable, and it is within our medical pervue to employ and encourage standard vaccination of our patients.

Second, it has been well documented that vaccinations work. The Centers for Disease Control and Prevention (CDC) have accumulated much data regarding the efficacy of vaccinations. We know that the frequency of illness decreases with increased success of community immunization programs. Waning immunity—through refusal to vaccinate and through the diminishing efficacy of a vaccination over time—leads to an increased reservoir of potential disease, often in adolescents and adults. In addition, there have been numerous

From *Center for Bioethics and Human Dignity*, April 16, 2004. Copyright © 2004 by Center for Bioethics and Human Dignity. Reprinted by permission. http://www.cbhd.org/resources/healthcare/yates_2004-04-16.htm

examples (at the international level) where an entire country has suspended vaccination requirements only to observe a notable increase in the frequency of reported cases of disease. It is reasonable to assume that latent viruses persist and may be spread (by close contact) to unprotected individuals.

Third, vaccinations are monitored. The Food and Drug Administration (FDA) and the CDC monitor both the use of and possible problems regarding vaccinations. For example, a vaccine approved for protection against Rotavirus (a viral disease causing severe diarrhea and dehydration, especially in young children) was discontinued after approximately one year of use. An increased frequency of intussusception (a condition where the bowel folds over itself) in patients who had received the vaccine was the reason for its discontinuation.

While vaccinations are often very beneficial and are subject to strict regulations, can their use nevertheless be problematic? Many people have alleged that certain vaccines may lead to very real harms. For example, links between the measles vaccine and autism, as well as inflammatory bowel disease, have been asserted. The vaccine for pertussis has also been associated with seizures, and a vaccine preservative (Thimerosal) has been said to negatively affect blood mercury levels. In many situations of this type, a relatively rare medical issue (e.g., seizure or autism) coexists with a very common medical practice (routine vaccination). In the quest to explain such rare phenomena, people are often quick to point out that the health problem is secondary to vaccination and, thus, vaccine-induced. Prolonged and detailed investigation has, however, disproved most of these allegations. It is nevertheless true that some vaccinations do carry a limited and specific (and exceedingly rare) complication—for example, the pertussis vaccine and the association with prolonged episodes of inconsolable crying and fussiness. In this situation, as in a few notable others, the risks and benefits of repeated vaccination need to be considered on an individual basis. In the case of Thimerosal, the Public Health Service and other organizations have recommended that the preservative be removed in an effort to decrease the total amount of mercury exposure that a child has—even though there has been no proof of harmful effect.

Many people are also concerned that vaccination of a child may carry with it moral guilt and wrongdoing. The issue of moral guilt (or moral complicity) arises because the initial source of some vaccination materials was a fetus who was electively aborted decades ago. Some individuals therefore feel that the administration of certain vaccines incriminates them in the promulgation of a wrongful act. It must be recognized, however, that medical science is simply extending the original cell line that was established from the aborted fetus, and that there is no ongoing abortive process to continue and maintain the cell line. Apart from concern about the method by which certain vaccines are derived, some communities of faith refuse vaccinations on the basis of their religious convictions. While we respect such positions, we must also take into account the evidence that clearly suggests an increased rate of disease in unvaccinated individuals. Because large pockets of unvaccinated individuals may contribute to the seriousness and prolongation of a community-wide outbreak, the decision not to vaccinate must be grappled with as well.

Finally, some parents express reluctance to vaccinate their child because they know that the risk of getting a particular disease is less than the admittedly minimal risk of the vaccination. They believe that it is their parental duty to protect their child from the minimal risk posed by the vaccine. This laudable desire must be balanced, however, against the societal obligation to maintain so-called "herd immunity" as a means of preventing epidemics. While it may be argued that parents' willingness to "ride on the coattails" of the rest of society is unjust, such a perspective may not trump their understanding of parental duty. Thus, it should also be pointed out that choices have consequences. A parent who refuses vaccination must be prepared to accept the risk of morbidity and mortality that may attend the occurrence of a vaccine-preventable illness. Not only would much guilt likely result in such instances, the child might suffer life-long complications or even loss of life— outcomes which could have been avoided.

In conclusion, vaccinations are important to both our individual and societal health. Whereas minimal distinct risks do exist for certain vaccination products and moral concerns may be raised, I believe that careful and thoughtful evaluation of such matters leads to the conclusion that vaccination programs are not only acceptable, but should be strongly encouraged.

Jini Patel Thompson

NO

Should I Vaccinate My Child?

- An unpublished study by the World Health Organization (WHO) on a "measles susceptible" (malnourished) group of children showed that the group who hadn't been vaccinated contracted measles at the normal contract rate of 2.4%. Of the group who *had* received the measles vaccine (MMR), 33.5% contracted measles.[1]
- In 1975 Japan raised the minimum age for infant vaccinations to two years. As a result, SIDS (Sudden Infant Death Syndrome, or crib death) and infant convulsions virtually disappeared. In the '80s, Japan lowered the minimum age back down to three months and the rate of SIDS returned to previous levels.[2]
- In an Australian study, a group of recruits were immunized for rubella, and all produced the expected antibodies. When later exposed to the disease, 80% of the recruits contracted it.[3]
- According to the U.S. National Childhood Vaccine Injury Act (est. 1986): To qualify for compensation, the adverse effects of vaccination must occur within *four hours* of receiving the vaccine. Despite this extremely severe limitation, as of February 28, 1998 compensatory payments have totalled $871,800,000. This figure is even more alarming when it is revealed that only one in four claimants were awarded compensation.[4]
- Some researchers postulate that the use of live viral vaccines introduces foreign genetic material into the human system, which has contributed to the unprecedented escalation of auto-immune disorders (like multiple sclerosis, rheumatoid arthritis, lupus, cancer, Crohn's disease, asthma, etc.) in recent decades.[5]

The above facts each highlight a different facet of the vaccination question: effectiveness, adverse effects and long-term consequences. The unspoken thread running through each of these is a pressing question: Why haven't more people been informed of this evidence, and indeed, why is vaccination presented carte blanche as a positive, imperative requisite for our children's health?

As the mother of a newborn, I knew it was important to find out what is really going on with infant and childhood vaccination and whether it is conclusively a beneficial or necessary procedure. Thus I embarked on four months of research into immunization—squeezed in between the demands of caring for and breastfeeding our new baby, Oscar!

Do Vaccines Actually Work?

As I researched the issue, I was amazed to discover that there is a large and growing body of clinical studies, fieldwork (in developing nations) and historical data refuting the safety and efficacy of vaccination. Unfortunately, the propaganda campaign for vaccination has been so successful that most of us automatically believe that vaccines are so effective they are responsible for the virtual eradication of serious childhood illnesses. In reality, this is not so, and if you examine the actual rates of incidence for each disease (from mainstream sources such as the *Lancet*, WHO and UNICEF), the graphs show a clearly different picture.

From the 1800s to the present, *in every case*, each disease had been virtually eliminated *decades* before the introduction of the relevant vaccine—through improved hygiene, better nutrition, clean drinking water and improved sanitation. Basically, as people's overall health and immune systems improved, they didn't get sick. As the physician W. J. McCormick summarized in 1950 (before vaccines for measles, mumps, scarlet fever and rheumatic fever were introduced):

". . . [T]he decline in diphtheria, whooping cough and typhoid fever began fully fifty years prior to the inception of artificial immunization and followed an almost even grade before and after the adoption of these control measures. In the case of scarlet fever, mumps, measles and rheumatic fever there has been no specific innovation in control measures, yet these also have followed the same general pattern in incidence decline."[6]

Furthermore, research reveals dozens of cases around the world where there was an outbreak of infectious disease (e.g., measles, polio, tetanus, smallpox, etc.) and contract rates were either similar among vaccinated and unvaccinated populations, or higher and more severe among the vaccinated. For example:

- Massachusetts in 1961 experienced a "type II" polio outbreak and "there were more paralytic cases in the triple vaccinates than in the unvaccinated."[7]
- In 1976, Dr. G. T. Stewart reported in the *British Medical Journal* that, "of 8,092 cases of whooping cough, 2,940 (36%) were fully immunized, while only 2,424 (30%) were definitely not immunized."[8]
- Professor George Dick, speaking at an environmental conference in Brussels in 1973, admitted that in recent decades, 75% of British people who contracted smallpox had been vaccinated. This, combined with the fact that only 40% of children (and a maximum of 10% of adults) had been vaccinated, clearly shows that vaccinated people have a much higher tendency to contract the disease.[9]

If vaccination is not responsible for the eradication of childhood illnesses, and vaccinated children are actually at a *greater* risk of contracting a disease than unvaccinated children, why is vaccination routinely presented as an effective safeguard for our children's health? When the historical data is referred to by pro-vaccine parties, it is often skewed and presented out of context. For example, in reference to a mass immunization campaign carried out in Thailand:

"... [T]he immunization coverage for measles has increased from 6% in 1984 to 63% in 1988, leading to a reduction in measles prevalence from 93.7/100,000 in 1984 to 37.1/100,000 in 1986."[10]

However, what the report doesn't indicate is that in 1987, the infection rate of measles was 87.1/100,000. And in 1988 it was 59.1/100,000, which is actually *higher* than the rate of infection in 1982 (57.1/100,000) when no one had been vaccinated. These statistics, however, are conveniently not included as they don't support the pro-vaccination stance of the report.

Aside from establishing that vaccines are not the reason infectious childhood illnesses have virtually disappeared, and that vaccinated children are actually at a greater risk of contracting disease, there are also the adverse effects and long-term consequences of vaccination to be considered.

Effects of Vaccination

Immediate Side Effects

Immediate or short-term effects of vaccination can include the following: encephalopathy (irreversible brain damage), ataxia (incoordination of voluntary muscle movements), mental retardation, aseptic meningitis (inflammation of the membranes of spinal cord or brain), seizure disorders, hemiparesis (half-body paralysis), retinopathy and blindness, hyperactivity, anaphylaxis, high pitched (encephalitic) screaming/prolonged crying, learning disorders, hay fever, asthma, sudden infant death (SIDS), brachial plexus neuropathy (disease affecting nerves that serve the arm, forearm and hand), and abdominal pain. Secondary complications can include juvenile-onset diabetes, Reye's syndrome and multiple sclerosis.

Unfortunately, it's virtually impossible to determine the real incidence of damaging adverse reactions. For example, a British government report claims the rate of permanent neurologic damage from the DPT vaccine to be 1 in 300,000.[11] However, other researchers indicate the permanent damage level to be anywhere from 1 in 62,000 to 1 in 300. Research by Coulter and Fisher on the 3.3 million children vaccinated yearly in the U.S. found there to be a total of 33,006 cases of acute neurological reactions (encephalitic screaming, convulsions, collapse) within 48 hours of receiving the DPT shot.

When the problems with vaccination are addressed in a serious manner by the pro-vaccination side, it usually involves a member of the bio-medical field qualifying that the dangers of vaccination, although real, are very rare, for example:

"Parents must be informed of the rare possibility of serious adverse effects, including seizure and allergic reaction. Every physician who administers vaccines therefore needs to become familiar with the reactions that may occur with each immunologic agent used. The best safeguard against litigation, when and if a serious reaction follows vaccination, is the indication that these considerations were discussed and that an informed choice was made."[12]

However, there is no scientific evidence as to the actual frequency or incidence of vaccine-induced injury, so in fact we have no idea whether reactions are indeed rare, or statistically significant. In articles such as the one above, no verifiable statistical evidence, reflecting reliable reporting or monitored study for this "rarity" is ever presented. As shown in the official minutes of the 15th session of the U.S. Panel of Review of Bacterial Vaccines and Toxoids with Standards and Potency:

"Many physicians are not cognizant of the importance of reporting untoward reactions, or may be unaware of their clinical features. Further, both physicians and manufacturers have been held liable for damage suits by patients who may suffer adverse effects from established vaccines. All of these factors undoubtedly discourage reporting; without some other form of surveillance, definition of the rates and significance of untoward reactions to current and future vaccines cannot be ascertained."[13]

For this reason, it is suspected that the number of adverse reactions and vaccine-damaged children is actually much, much higher than is currently presented by the medical/pharmaceutical community. Instead, there is a growing number of mothers and lay people, whose children have been irrevocably damaged, forming vaccine risk awareness groups. There continue to be incidents like the one in West Germany in 1967, where smallpox vaccination damaged the hearing of 3,296 children, and of these 71 were rendered completely deaf.[14] At the extreme end of the spectrum, we have occurrences like the one in Australia's Northern Territory where malnourished aboriginal children were vaccinated and in some areas 50% of them died.[15] According to Dr. B. Bloom at the Albert Einstein College of Medicine, there's even an emerging reluctance to further develop vaccines because financial losses due to the liability of established vaccines actually exceed the profits derived from them.

Whether these adverse reactions are caused by the vaccines themselves or the number of highly toxic additives contained in vaccines (e.g., formaldehyde, mercury, acetone, etc.), or a combination of the two, remains to be determined. As yet, no research has been carried out to resolve this question.

Long-Term Consequences

While these short-term consequences are alarming (especially if it happens to your child), the possible long-term consequences of vaccination are, in my opinion, even more of a worry. When you contract a disease naturally, the virus or bacteria normally enters via the body's natural filtration system—by being inhaled or swallowed or passing through the liver. With measles, for example, the airborne virus is carried first to the tonsils, then to the lymph nodes and then into the spleen, blood and other organs. This succession produces a variety of reactions: sneezing, coughing or the secretion of a local antibody within the respiratory tract, all designed to expel or weaken the virus at its port of entry. With vaccines, foreign antigens are usually injected directly into the body's tissues and carried throughout the circulatory system, giving them direct access to all of the body's vital organs and systems. To bypass the body's natural defense system, and at such a young age, is simply asking for trouble. In addition, because the vaccine contains an attenuated (or weakened) form of the virus, the body doesn't activate its major inflammatory response nor its non-specific immune defenses.

Another long-term complication of vaccination involves the "one cell-one antibody" rule. This means that once a B cell is committed to an antigen (disease-causing virus or bacteria), it becomes inert and incapable of responding to other antigens or attacks on the immune system. If a child contracts childhood diseases naturally, it is estimated that up to a total of 7% of his/her immune system is taken up with responding to these diseases. However, a child who undergoes the routine course of vaccinations risks having up to 70% of his/her immune system committed to these antigens and no longer available for other immune challenges. Current research suggests this reduced immune-response capacity is responsible for increased susceptibility to other infections, allergies and auto-immune diseases. Other researchers argue that these attenuated forms of the viruses remain in the body causing continual antigenic stimulation of the immune system—meaning the immune system is always in "attack" mode—which also weakens it and leads to auto-immune diseases.

A placebo-controlled trial of acellular pertussis vaccines in Sweden compared vaccinated children with un-vaccinated children of the same birth grouping. During the trial, an invasive bacterial infection occurred among the vaccinated group resulting in numerous deaths. A review of the trial data led researchers to conclude that "the hypothesis of an immunosuppressive effect of the vaccines, which would explain the deaths . . . could not be refuted by the data."[16]

As further evidence, one of the few double-blind trials that have ever been conducted on a vaccine shows the same immunosuppressive effect. In the trial, of the group who were vaccinated with the Salk polio vaccine, over 200 people went on to contract polio. Among the control group (unvaccinated), not one of them developed polio.[17]

Citing references from numerous valid sources, including four recognized textbooks on pediatrics and immunology, Harold Buttram, M.D., and John Hoffman, Ph.D., conclude that childhood vaccination "cannot help but have adverse effects on the immunologic system of the child, possibly leaving this system crippled in its ability to protect the child throughout life . . . opening the way for other diseases as a result of immunologic dysfunction."[18]

The other worrying aspect of live viral vaccines is they introduce foreign genetic material into the human body. Dr. Richard Moskowitz, M.D. and Harvard graduate, explains how this can lead to auto-immune disease susceptibility:

"Vaccinal attenuated viruses attach their own genetic 'episome' to the genome (half set of chromosomes and their genes) of the host cell, and are thus capable of surviving or remaining latent within the host cells for years. The presence of foreign antigenic material within the host cell sets the stage for their unpredictable provocation of various auto-immune phenomena such as herpes, shingles, warts, tumors—both benign and malignant—and diseases of the central nervous system, such as varied forms of paralysis and inflammation of the brain."[19]

Dr. Moskowitz states that in addition, vaccines do not just produce mild versions of the original disease, but all of them commonly produce a variety of their own symptoms. In some cases, "these illnesses may be considerably more serious than the original disease, involving deeper structures, more vital organs, and less of a tendency to resolve spontaneously. Even more worrisome is the fact that they are almost always more difficult to recognize."[20]

In addressing scientists at a conference sponsored by the American Cancer Society, Rutgers University professor R. Simpson warned:

"Immunization programs against flu, measles, mumps, polio and so forth may actually be seeding humans with RNA to form latent proviruses in cells throughout the body. These latent proviruses could be molecules in search of diseases, including rheumatoid arthritis, multiple sclerosis, systemic lupus erythematosus, Parkinson's disease and perhaps cancer."[21]

The bulk of the evidence gathered from numerous countries points out that not only is vaccination ineffective at preventing the spread of infectious disease, but vaccinated children are actually at a *higher* risk of contracting these illnesses. In addition, the adverse reactions to vaccination are much higher than presently documented in the medico-pharmaceutical literature and the long-term damaging effect of suppressing the immune system is rarely addressed.

In light of all the evidence to the contrary, why have vaccines been pressed upon the public as a necessary, beneficial way of preventing our children from getting sick? In the words of Dr. Raymond Obomsawin (who has held senior positions in UNICEF and CUSO), referring to mass vaccination, "It is reprehensible that such actions continue to be enforced by authorities, while parents and local health workers are not accorded any practical knowledge of the known dangers involved, and the extent to which there prevails a general ignorance of the longer term consequences."[22]

Combine this ignorance with the millions of dollars in profit generated by vaccination that goes straight into the pockets of manufacturing companies, governments and medical doctors, and it becomes clear that vaccination is more of a political and economic issue than a health issue. . . .

When you take into account the billions of dollars at stake in vaccination campaigns, it is not surprising that vaccination propaganda is foisted upon the public with almost religious fervour. The intense psychological pressure and fear that parents feel about vaccinating their children is no accident, but the result of well-planned, well-funded marketing campaigns. Needless to say, having completed my research, I have made sure Oscar remains completely un-vaccinated. As to whether you should vaccinate your child or not, only you can and should make that decision. It is very difficult to stand strong and resolute against the ubiquitous pressure to vaccinate. It's like having to keep insisting the Earth is round when authorities, your community, intellectuals, and the majority of scientists, etc., all insist it's flat. As with all matters of health, each of us has to go with what our gut tells us is right, or the best possible option for us at that time.

Vaccine Risk Awareness Websites
National Vaccine Information Center . . .
Concerned Parents for Vaccine Safety . . .
Immunisation Awareness Society . . .

Medical Information and Pro-Vaccine Websites
Immunization Action Coalition, www.immunize.org
WHO & Communicable Diseases Surveillance, www.who.int/emc/

Publications
Vaccination: 100 Years of Orthodox Research Shows That Vaccines Represent a Medical Assault on the Immune System, by Viera Scheibner, Ph.D.

Universal Immunization—Medical Miracle or Masterful Mirage? by Raymond Obomsawin, Ph.D. (available from Health Action Network, tel: 604-435-0512).

What Every Parent Should Know About Childhood Immunization, by Jamie Murphy.

How To Raise a Healthy Child in Spite of Your Doctor, by Robert Mendelsohn, M.D.

The Immunization Decision: A Guide For Parents, by Dr. Randall Neustaedter.

Vaccinations and Immunization: Dangers, Delusions and Alternatives, by Leon Chaitow, N.D., D.O.

Immunization: The Reality Behind The Myth, by Walene James.

Notes

1.   Robert Mendelsohn, M.D., *The Truth about Immunization.*
2.   Scheibner, Viera, *Vaccination.*
3.   Allen, B., *Australian Journal of Medical Technology,* Vol. 4, November 1973, pp. 26–27.
4.   Obomsawin, Raymond, *Universal Immunization: Medical Miracle or Masterful Mirage?*
5.   Buttram, H., "Live Virus Vaccines and Genetic Mutation," *Health Consciousness,* April 1990, pp. 44–45.
6.   McCormick, W. J., "Vitamin C in the Prophylaxis and Therapy of Infectious Diseases," *Archives of Pediatrics,* Vol. 68, No. 1, January 1951.
7.   U.S. House of Representatives, *Hearings on HR 10541,* p. 113.
8.   Stewart, G. T., *British Medical Journal,* January 31, 1976.
9.   Dettman, G., and Kalokerinos, A., "Viral Vaccines Vital or Vulnerable," *Australasian Nurses Journal,* August 1980, p. 29.
10. Obomsawin, Raymond, *Universal Immunization,* p. 12.
11. Alderslade, R., et al., "The National Childhood Encephalopathy Study," in *Whooping Cough: Reports from the Committee on Safety of Medicines and the Joint Committee on Vaccination and Immunization,* Department of Health and Social Security, Her Majesty's Stationery Office, London 1981, pp. 79–154.

12. Editor of *Postgraduate Medicine*, summarizing the following article: Zimmerman, B., and Stone, A. "Allergic Reactions Associated with Viral Vaccines," *Progress in Medical Virology*, Vol. 82, No. 5, October 1987, pp. 225–232.

13. Mendelsohn, R., *The Truth About Immunization*, p. 7.

14. James, W., *Immunization*, p. 18.

15. Dettman, G., and Kalokerinos, A., "Viral Vaccines Vital or Vulnerable," *Australasian Nurses Journal*, August 1980, p. 27.

16. Storsaeter, J., et al., "Mortality and Morbidity from Invasive Bacterial Infections During a Clinical Trial of Acellular Pertussis Vaccines in Sweden," *Pediatrics Infectious Disease Journal*, Vol. 78, 1988, pp. 637–645.

17. Mendelsohn, R., "The Medical Time Bomb of Immunization Against Disease," p. 52.

18. Buttram, H. E., and Hoffman, J. C., "Bringing Vaccines into Perspective," *Mothering*, Vol. 34, 1985, p. 42.

19. James, W., *Immunization*, p. 15.

20. Moskowitz, R., "The Case Against Immunizations," *Journal of the American Institute of Homeopathy*, Washington DC, 1983.

21. James, W., *Immunization*, p. 15.

22. Obomsawin, Raymond, *Universal Immunization*, p. 56.

23. Barbara Fisher in a talk before the International Chiropractic Pediatricians Association, Boston, MA, March 19, 1993.

24. The Burton Goldberg Group, *Alternative Medicine: The Definitive Guide*, p. 600.

POSTSCRIPT

Should Parents Routinely Vaccinate Their Children?

In 2002, the journal *Pediatrics* reported that newborn babies' immune systems are more than strong enough to handle receiving one or more vaccinations. The experts quoted in this study maintain that if a baby received all 11 available vaccines at one time, it would "use up" only about 0.1 percent of the immune system. This is, they say, because the B cells and T cells, which fight off infection and start being produced while the infant is still in utero, are constantly being regenerated.

For some people, this information adds fuel to the fire behind their argument that vaccination should be mandatory for all children, and that parents should not be able to keep their children from being vaccinated. However, this information does not necessarily mean anything to parents who either do not trust medicine, do not feel that even the smallest risk is worth taking when it comes to their own child, or whose cultural or religious beliefs do not support medical interventions of this kind. As a result, the debate on this issue continues to go back and forth.

Many of you who are readings this volume will not yet have children, although you may have children in your families. Think about how you feel about this issue. Were the children in your life vaccinated as babies? Were you? Do you plan on having your own children vaccinated? Why or why not?

There is a saying that goes, "Hindsight is 20/20." As you may know, this means that it is easier to look back on how we handled a particular situation or were treated in our own lives and base our values, beliefs, and decisions on the outcome of that situation. Quite simply, our vision is clear (or "20/20") when we have some personal experience with a topic or issue. For example, someone who was not vaccinated as a baby and ended up with whooping cough may have feelings about whether children should be vaccinated that come from personal experience. Someone who was not vaccinated and never had a disease growing up will base her or his opinions on that experience, as will someone who was vaccinated and remained healthy, without any adverse side effects to the vaccine. It is important to keep this hindsight perspective in mind when determining how we feel about any sensitive topic.

ISSUE 8

Should Parents Be Able to Select the Biological Sex of Their Children?

YES: John A. Robertson, from "Preconception Gender Selection,"
The American Journal of Bioethics (Winter 2001)

NO: Norman Daniels, from "It Isn't Just the Sex . . ."; **Carson Strong,**
from "Can't You Control Your Children?"; **Mary B. Mahowald,**
from "Reverse Sexism? Not to Worry"; and **Mark V. Sauer,** from
"Preconception Sex Selection: A Commentary," *The American Journal
of Bioethics* (Winter 2001)

ISSUE SUMMARY

YES: Professor John A. Robertson of the University of Texas at Austin's
School of Law argues that preconception gender selection of
infants in utero for medical purposes should be allowed, and that
insufficient data exist to demonstrate that any clear harm exists in
allowing parents to do so.

NO: Norman Daniels (Tufts University), Carson Strong (University
of Tennessee), Mary B. Mahowald (University of Chicago), and
Mark V. Sauer (Columbia University) each take one aspect of Professor Robertson's arguments to demonstrate why preconception
gender selection should not be allowed, including, for example, the
socioeconomic status inequity that allowing such a procedure, which
likely would not be covered by health insurance, would create.

Biological sex is determined by the male sperm cell, hundreds of millions
of which are present in semen after ejaculation. Among the chromosomes a
sperm cell will contain is a sex chromosome, typically either an "X" chromosome or a "Y" chromosome. A woman's egg will carry an "X" sex chromosome. When a sperm and egg meet, they create the chromosomal blueprint
for the sex of the offspring of any resulting pregnancy. If a man's sperm carries an "X" chromosome, the resulting "XX" baby will typically be a girl. If it
carries a "Y" chromosome, the baby will typically be a boy. A man can also
contain no sex chromosome, resulting in an "XO" baby, an extra "Y" chromosome, resulting in an "XYY" baby, and other chromosomal differences that

result in a range of biological sex variations, usually referred to as "intersex" conditions. These will be discussed more in Issue 9.

Many people believe that parents cannot currently select the biological sex of their children, yet preconception sex selection (PSS) has existed since the 1970s. Technology has been developed to determine whether a sperm carries either an X or a Y chromosome and implant it accordingly, although doing so is not always reliable, is an invasive medical procedure, and can be quite costly. It has been understood, therefore, that cases involving (PSS) have typically been done to avoid some kind of genetic disease that can be linked to either an X or a Y chromosome. Like with any medical procedure, however, there are those who may be able to access it for other reasons, and those who may not.

Why else would some people choose to select the sex of their children? For some families, having a first-born child who is either a boy or a girl is important to them. Others who know they plan to only have one child may have a strong preference for that child to be a boy or a girl. Still others may have a child of one sex, and wish to ensure gender variance within their family. Regardless of the reason, one concern that medical practitioners have is about parents who carry an erroneous preconceived notion that having a girl or boy will yield a particular type of child. What happens, for example, when a father who wants a son to teach him sports only to end up with a son who hates sports? When a mother who looks forward to taking her daughter shopping and for manicures ends up with a daughter who is an outstanding athlete? Adults, they say, connect sex (biology) to gender (how we express our biological sex), when the manners in which a child expresses her or his femaleness or maleness can be quite broad.

In the following selections, John Robertson outlines the arguments both for and against PSS, concluding that there is no ethical reason against it. He disagrees that a potential exists for the practice of PSS for gender variance in the family alone could potentially be sexist, and argues that, as long as parents keep the well-being of their child(ren) in mind, they should be able to have the family composition they wish. Norman Daniels, Carson Strong, Mary B. Mahowald, and Mark V. Sauer each address one aspect of Robertson's arguments to demonstrate why preconception gender selection should not be allowed unless there is a medically necessary reason to do so.

YES ↩

John A. Robertson

Preconception Gender Selection

Advances in genetics and reproductive technology present prospective parents with an increasing number of choices about the genetic makeup of their children. Those choices now involve the use of carrier and prenatal screening techniques to avoid the birth of children with serious genetic disease, but techniques to choose nonmedical characteristics will eventually be available. One nonmedical characteristic that may soon be within reach is the selection of offspring gender by preconception gender selection (PGS).

Gender selection through prenatal diagnosis and abortion has existed since the 1970s. More recently, preimplantation sexing of embryos for transfer has been developed (Tarin and Handyside 1993; The Ethics Committee of the American Society of Reproductive Medicine 1999). Yet prenatal or preimplantation methods of gender selection are unattractive because they require abortion or a costly, intrusive cycle of in vitro fertilization (IVF) and embryo discard. Attempts to separate X- and Y-bearing sperm for preconception gender selection by sperm swim-up or swim-through techniques have not shown consistent X- and Y-sperm cell separation or success in producing offspring of the desired gender.

The use of flow cytometry to separate X- and Y-bearing sperm may turn out to be a much more reliable method of enriching sperm populations for insemination. Laser beams passed across a flowing array of specially dyed sperm can separate most of the 2.8% heavier X- from Y-bearing sperm, thus producing an X-enriched sperm sample for insemination. Flow cytometry has been used successfully in over 400 sex selections in rabbit, swine, ovine, and bovine species, including successive generations in swine and rabbit (Fugger et al. 1998). A human pregnancy was reported in 1995 (Levinson, Keyvanfar, and Wu 1995).

The United States Department of Agriculture (USDA), which holds a patent on the flow cytometry separation process, has licensed the Genetics and IVF Institute in Fairfax, Virginia, to study the safety and efficacy of the technique for medical and "family balancing" reasons in an institutional review board–approved clinical trial. In 1998 researchers at the Institute reported a 92.9% success rate for selection of females in 27 patients, with most fertilizations occurring after intrauterine insemination (Fugger et al. 1998). A lower success rate (72%) was reported for male selection.

From *The American Journal of Bioethics,* Winter 2001, Vol. 1, No. 1, pp. 2–9. Copyright © 2001 by Taylor & Francis—Philadelphia. Reprinted by permission.

At this early stage of development much more research is needed to establish the high degree of safety and efficacy of flow cytometry methods of PGS that would justify widespread use. With only one published study of outcomes to date, it is too soon to say whether the 92% success rate in determining female gender will hold for other patients, much less that male selection will reach that level of efficacy. Animal safety data have shown no adverse effect of the dye or laser used in the technique on offspring, but that is no substitute for more extensive human studies (Vidal et al. 1999). In addition, if flow cytometry instruments are to be used for sperm separation purposes, they may be classified as medical devices that require U.S. Food and Drug Administration (FDA) approval. Finally, the holder of the process patent—the USDA—will have to agree to license the process for human uses.

If further research establishes that flow cytometry is a safe and effective technique for both male and female PGS, and regulatory and licensing barriers are overcome, then a couple wishing to choose the gender of their child would need only provide a sperm sample and undergo one or more cycles of intrauterine insemination with separated sperm. A clinic or physician that offers assisted reproductive technologies (ART) and invests in the flow cytometry equipment could run the separation and prepare the X- or Y-enriched sperm for insemination, or it could have the sperm processed by a clinic or firm that has made that investment. Flow cytometry separation would not be as cheap and easy as determining gender by taking a pill before intercourse, but it would be within reach of most couples who have gender preferences in offspring.

Demand for Preconception Gender Selection

Unknown at present is the number of people who have offspring gender preferences robust enough to incur the costs and inconvenience of PGS. Although polls have often shown a preference for firstborn males, they have not shown that a large number of couples would be willing to forego coital conception in order to select the gender of their children. If PGS proves to be safe and effective, however, it may be sought by two groups of persons with gender preferences.

One group would seek PGS in order to have a child of a gender different from that of a previous child or children. A preference for gender variety in offspring would be strongest in families that have already had several children of one gender. They may want an additional child only if they can be sure that it will be of the gender opposite to their existing children. Couples who wish to have only two children might use PGS for the second child to ensure that they have one child of each gender. If social preferences for two-child families remain strong, some families may use PGS to choose the gender of the second child.

A second group of PGS users would be those persons who have strong preferences for the gender of the first child. The most likely candidates here are persons with strong religious or cultural beliefs about the role or importance of children with a particular gender. Some Asian cultures have belief systems that strongly prefer that the firstborn child be a male. In some cases the preference reflects religious beliefs or traditions that require a firstborn son to perform funeral rituals to assure his parents' entrance into heaven (for a discussion of son preferences in India and China, see Macklin 1999, 148–151). In others it simply reflects a deeply embedded social preference for males over females. The first-child preference will be all the stronger if a one-child-per-family policy is in effect, as occurred for a while in China (Greenlagh and Li 1995, 627). While the demand for PGS for firstborn children is likely to be strongest in those countries, there has been a sizable migration of those groups to the United States, Canada, and Europe. Until they are more fully assimilated, immigrant groups in Western countries may retain the same gender preferences that they would have held in their homelands.

Other persons with strong gender preferences for firstborn children would be those who prize the different rearing or relational experiences they think they would have with children of a particular gender. They may place special value on having their firstborn be male or female because of personal experiences or beliefs. Numerous scenarios are likely here, from the father who very much wants a son because of a desire to provide his child with what he lacked growing up, to the woman who wants a girl because of the special closeness that she thinks she will have with a daughter (Belkin 1999).

The Ethical Dilemma of Preconception Gender Selection

The prospect of preconception gender selection appears to pose the conflict—long present in other bioethical issues—between individual desires and the larger common good. Acceding to individual desires about the makeup of children seems to be required by individual autonomy. Yet doing so leads to the risk that children will be treated as vehicles of parental satisfaction rather than as ends in themselves, and could accelerate the trend toward negative and even positive selection of offspring characteristics. The dilemma of reconciling procreative liberty with the welfare of offspring and families will only intensify as genetic technology is further integrated with assisted reproduction and couples seek greater control over the genes of offspring.

Arguments for Preconception Gender Selection

The strongest argument for preconception gender selection is that it serves the needs of couples who have strong preferences about the gender of their offspring and would not reproduce unless they could realize those preferences. Because of the importance of reproduction in an individual's life, the freedom to make reproductive decisions has long been recognized as a fundamental moral and legal right that should not be denied to a person unless exercise of that right would cause significant harm to others (Robertson 1994, 22–42). A corollary of this right, which is now reflected in carrier and prenatal screening practices to prevent the birth of children with genetic disease, is that prospective parents have the right to obtain preconception or prenatal information about the genetic characteristics of offspring, so that they may decide in a particular case whether or not to reproduce (Robertson 1996, 424–435).

Although offspring gender is not a genetic disease, a couple's willingness to reproduce might well depend on the gender of expected offspring. Some couples with one or more children of a particular gender might refuse to reproduce if they cannot use PGS to provide gender variety in their offspring or to have additional children of the same gender (E. F. Fugger, personal communication to author). In other cases they might have such strong rearing preferences for their firstborn child that they might choose not to reproduce at all if they cannot choose that child's gender. Few persons contemplating reproduction may fall into either group; but for persons who strongly hold those preferences, the ability to choose gender may determine whether they reproduce.

In cases where the gender of offspring is essential to a couple's decision to reproduce, the freedom to choose offspring gender would arguably be part of their procreative liberty (Robertson 1996, 434). Since respect for a right is not dependent on the number of persons asserting the right, they should be free to use a technique essential to their reproductive decision unless the technique would cause the serious harm to others that overcomes the strong presumption that exists against government interference in reproductive choice. Until there is a substantial basis for thinking that a particular use of PGS would cause such harms, couples should be free to use the technique in constituting their families. The right they claim is a right against government restriction or prohibition of PGS. It is not a claim that society or insurers are obligated to fund PGS or that particular physicians must provide it.

Arguments Against Preconception Gender Selection

There are several arguments against preconception gender selection. Although such methods do not harm embryos and fetuses or intrude on a woman's body as *prenatal* gender selection does, they do raise other important issues. One concern is the potential of such techniques to increase or reinforce sexism, either by allowing more males to be produced as first or later children, or by paying greater attention to gender itself. A second concern is the welfare of children born as a result of PGS whose parents may expect them to act in certain gender specific ways when the technique succeeds, but who may be disappointed if the technique fails. A third concern is societal. Widely practiced, PGS could lead to sex-ratio imbalances, as have occurred in some parts of India and China due to female infanticide, gender-driven abortions, and a one-child-per-family policy (Sen 1990). Finally, the spread of PGS would be another incremental step in the growing technologization of reproduction and genetic control of offspring. While each step alone may appear to be justified, together they could constitute a threat to the values of care and concern that have traditionally informed norms of parenting and the rearing of children.

Evaluation of Ethical and Social Issues

Concerns about sex-ratio imbalances, welfare of offspring, and technologizing reproduction may be less central to debates over PGS than whether such practices would be sexist or contribute to sexism. If the number of persons choosing PGS is small, or the technique is used solely for offspring gender variety, sex-ratio imbalances should not be a problem. If use patterns did produce drastic changes in sex ratios, self-correcting or regulatory mechanisms might come into play. For example, an over-abundance of males would mean fewer females to marry, which would make being male less desirable, and provide incentives to increase the number of female births. Alternatively, laws or policies that required providers of PGS to select for males and females in equal numbers would prevent such imbalances. A serious threat of a sex-ratio imbalance would surely constitute the compelling harm necessary to justify limits on reproductive choice.

It may also be difficult to show that children born after PGS were harmed by use of the technique. Parents who use PGS may indeed have specific gender role expectations of their children, but so will parents who have a child of a preferred gender through coitus. Children born with the desired gender after PGS will presumably be wanted and loved by the parents who sought this technique. Parents who choose PGS should be informed of the risk that the technique will not succeed, and counseled about what steps they will take if a child of the undesired gender is born. If they commit themselves in advance to the well-being of the child, whatever its gender, the risk to children should be slight. However, it is possible that some couples will abort if the fetus is of the undesired gender. PGS might thus inadvertently increase the number of gender-selection abortions.

Finally, technological assistance in reproduction is now so prevalent and entrenched that a ban on PGS would probably have little effect on the use of genetic and reproductive technologies in other situations. With some form of prenatal screening of fetuses occurring in over 80% of United States pregnancies, genetic selection by negative exclusion is already well-installed in contemporary reproductive practice. Although there are valid concerns about whether positive forms of selection, including nonmedical genetic alteration of offspring genes, should also occur, drawing the line at all uses of PGS will not stop the larger social and technological forces that lead parents to use genetic knowledge to have healthy, wanted offspring. If a particular technique can be justified on its own terms, it should not be barred because of speculation of a slippery slope toward genetic engineering of offspring traits (for an analysis of the slippery-slope problem with genetic selection, see Robertson 1994, 162–165).

Is Gender Selection Inherently Sexist?

A central ethical concern with PGS is the effect of such practices on women, who in most societies have been subject to disadvantage and discrimination because of their gender. Some ethicists have argued that any attention to gender, male or female, is per se sexist, and should be discouraged, regardless of whether one can show actual harmful consequences for women (see Grubb and Walsh 1994; and Wertz and Fletcher 1989). Others have argued that there are real differences between male and female children that affect parental rearing experiences and thus legitimate nonsexist reasons for some couples to prefer to rear a girl rather than a boy or vice versa, either as a single child or after they have had a child of the opposite gender.

To assess whether PGS is sexist we must first be clear about what we mean by sexism. *The Compact OED* (1991, 1727) defines sexism as "the assumption that one sex is superior to the other and the resultant discrimination practised against members of the supposed inferior sex, especially by men against women." By this definition, sexism is wrong because it denies the essential moral, legal, and political equality between men and women. Under this definition, if a practice is not motivated by judgments or evaluations that one gender is superior to the other, or does not lead to discrimination against one gender, it is not sexist.

Professor Mary Mahowald, an American bioethicist writing from an egalitarian feminist perspective, makes the same point with a consequentialist twist:

> Selection of either males or females is justifiable on medical grounds and *morally defensible in other situations* [emphasis added] so long as the intention and the consequences of the practice are not sexist. Sexist intentions are those based on the notion that one sex is inferior to the other; sexist consequences are those that disadvantage or advantage one sex vis-à-vis the other. (2000, 121)

In my view, the *OED* definition, modified by Mahowald's attention to consequences, is a persuasive account of the concept of sexism. If that account is correct, then not all attention to the biologic, social, cultural, or psychological differences between the sexes would necessarily be sexist or disadvantage females. That is, one could recognize that males and females have different experiences and identities because of their gender, and have a preference for rearing a child of one gender over another, without disadvantaging the dispreferred gender or denying it the equal rights, opportunities, or value as a person that constitutes sexism.

If this conjecture is correct, it would follow that some uses of PGS would clearly be sexist, while others would clearly not be. It would be sexist to use PGS to produce males because of a parental belief that males are superior to females. It would be nonsexist to use PGS to produce a girl because of a parental recognition that the experience of having and rearing a girl will be different than having a boy. In the latter case, PGS would not rest on a notion of the greater superiority of one gender over another, nor, if it occurred in countries that legally recognize the equal rights of women, would it likely contribute to sexism or further disadvantage women. As Christine Overall, a British feminist bioethicist, has put it, "sexual similarity or sexual complementarity are morally acceptable reasons for wanting a child of a certain sex" (1987, 27; quoted in Mahowald 2000, 117).

Psychological research seems to support this position. It has long been established that there are differences between boys and girls in a variety of domains, such as (but not limited to) aggression, activity, toy preference, psychopathology, and spatial ability (Maccoby and Jacklin 1974; Gilligan 1980; Kimura and Hampson 1994; Feingold 1994; Collaer and Hines 1995; and

Halpern 1997). Whether these differences are primarily inborn or learned, they are facts that might rationally lead people to prefer rearing a child of one gender rather than another, particularly if one has already had one or more children of a particular gender. Indeed, Supreme Court Justice Ruth Bader Ginsburg, a noted activist for women's rights before her appointment to the Supreme Court, in her opinion striking down a male-only admissions policy at the Virginia Military Institute (*United States v. Virginia,* 116 S. Ct. 2264 [1996]), noted that:

> Physical differences between men and women . . . are enduring: "[T]he two sexes are not fungible; a community made up exclusively of one [sex] is different from a community composed of both." . . . "Inherent differences" between men and women, we have come to appreciate, remain cause for celebration.

Some persons will strongly disagree with this account of sexism and argue that any attention to gender difference is inherently sexist because perceptions of gender difference are themselves rooted in sexist stereotypes. They would argue that any offspring gender preference is necessarily sexist because it values gender difference and thus reinforces sexism by accepting the gendered stereotypes that have systematically harmed women (Grubb and Walsh 1994; and Wertz and Fletcher 1989, 21). According to them, a couple with three boys who use PGS to have a girl are likely to be acting on the basis of deeply engrained stereotypes that harm women. Similarly, a couple's wish to have only a girl might contribute to unjustified gender discrimination against both men and women, even if the couple especially valued females and would insist that their daughter receive every benefit and opportunity accorded males.

Resolution of this controversy depends ultimately on one's view of what constitutes sexism and what actions are likely to harm women. Although any recognition of gender difference must be treated cautiously, I submit that recognizing and preferring one type of childrearing experience over the other can occur without disadvantaging women generally or denying them equal rights and respect. On this view, sexism arises not from the recognition or acceptance of difference, but from unjustified reactions to it. Given the biological and psychological differences between male and female children, parents with a child of one gender might without being sexist prefer that their next child be of the opposite gender. Similarly, some parents might also prefer that their firstborn or only child be of a particular gender because they desire a specific rearing and companionship experience.

If it is correct that using PGS for offspring diversity is sexist, then those who deny that biological gender differences exist, or who assume that any recognition of them always reinforces sexism or disadvantages women, will not have carried the burden of showing that a couple's use of PGS for offspring gender variety or other nonintentionally sexist uses is so harmful to women that it justifies restricting procreative choice. Until a clearer ethical argument emerges, or there is stronger empirical evidence that most choices to select the gender of offspring would be harmful, policies to prohibit or condemn as unethical all uses of nonmedically indicated PGS would not be justified.

The matter is further complicated by the need to respect a woman's autonomy in determining whether a practice is sexist. If a woman is freely choosing to engage in gender selection, even gender-selection abortion, she is exercising procreative autonomy. One might argue in response that the woman choosing PGS or abortion for gender selection is not freely choosing if her actions are influenced by strong cultural mores that prefer males over females. Others, however, would argue that the straighter path to equal rights is to respect female reproductive autonomy whenever it is exercised, even if particular exercises of autonomy are strongly influenced by the sexist norms of her community (Mahowald 2000, 188).

Public Policy and Preconception Gender Selection

Because of the newness of PGS and uncertainties about its effects, the best societal approach would, of course, be to proceed slowly, first requiring extensive studies of safety and efficacy, and then at first only permitting PGS for increasing the gender variety of offspring in particular families. Only after the demographic and other effects of PGS for gender variety have been found acceptable should PGS be available for firstborn children.

However, given the close connection between parental gender preferences for offspring and reproductive choice, public policies that bar all non-medical uses of PGS or that restrict it to choosing gender variety in offspring alone could be found unconstitutional or illegal. If there are physical, social, and cultural differences between girls and boys that affect the rearing or relational experiences of parents, individuals and couples would have the right to implement those preferences as part of their fundamental procreative liberty. The risk that exercising rights of procreative liberty would hurt offspring or women—or contribute to sexism generally—is too speculative and uncertain to justify infringement of those rights.

The claim of a right to choose offspring gender is clearest in the case of PGS for gender variety. If flow cytometry or other methods of PGS are found to be safe and effective, there would be no compelling reason to ban or restrict their nonmedical use by persons seeking gender variety in the children they rear. Couples with one child or several children of a particular gender might, without being sexist or disadvantaging a particular gender, prefer to have an additional child of the opposite gender. ART clinics should be free to proceed with PGS for offspring variety in cases where couples are aware of the risk of failure, and have undergone counseling that indicates that they will accept and love children of the dispreferred gender if PGS fails. Clinics providing PGS should also ask couples to participate in research to track and assess the effects of PGS on children and families.

The use of PGS to determine the gender of firstborn children is a more complicated question. The choice to have one's first or only child be female has the least risk of being sexist, because it is privileging or giving first place to females, who have traditionally been disfavored. The use of PGS to select firstborn males is more problematic because of the greater risk that this choice reflects sexist notions that males are more highly valued. It is also more likely to entrench male dominance. The danger of sexism is probably highest in those ethnic communities that place a high premium on male offspring, but it could exist independently of those settings.

Yet restricting PGS to offspring gender variety and firstborn females may be difficult to justify. Given that individuals could prefer to have a boy rather than a girl because of the relational and rearing experiences he will provide, just as they might prefer a girl for those reasons, it might be difficult to show that all preferences for firstborn males are sexist. Nor could one easily distinguish firstborn male preferences when the couple demanding them is of a particular ethnic origin. Although the risk that firstborn male preferences would be sexist is greatest if the PGS occurred in a country in which those beliefs prevailed, the chance that PGS would contribute to societal sexism lessens greatly if the child is reared in a country that legally protects the equal status of women and men.

If prohibitions on some or all nonmedical uses of PGS could not be justified and might even be unconstitutional, regulation would have to take different forms. One form would be to deny public or private insurance funding of PGS procedures, which would mean that only those willing to pay out-of-pocket would utilize them. Another form would be for the physicians who control access to PGS techniques to take steps to assure that it is used wisely. If they comply with laws banning discrimination, physician organizations or ART clinics could set guidelines concerning access to PGS. They might, for example, limit its use to offspring gender variety or firstborn female preferences only. As a condition of providing services, they might also require that any couple or individual seeking PGS receive counseling about the risks of failure and commit to rear a child even if its gender is other than that sought through PGS. Although such guidelines would not have the force of statutory law, they could affect the eligibility of ART clinics to list their ART success rates in national registries and could help define the standard of care in malpractice cases.

Conclusion

The successful development of flow cytometry separation of X- and Y-bearing sperm would make safe, effective, and relatively inexpensive means of nonmedical preconception gender selection available for selecting female, if not also for male, offspring. The nonmedical use of PGS raises important ethical, legal, and social issues, including the charge that any or most uses of PGS would be sexist and should therefore be banned or discouraged. Assessment of this charge, however, shows that the use of PGS to achieve offspring gender variety and (in some cases) even firstborn gender preference, may not be inherently sexist or disadvantaging of women. Although it would be desirable to have extensive experience using PGS to increase the variety of offspring gender before extending it to firstborn gender preferences, it may not be legally possible to restrict the technique in this way. However, practitioners offering PGS should restrict their PGS practice to offspring gender variety until further debate and analysis of the issues has occurred. In any event, physicians offering PGS should screen and counsel prospective users to assure that persons using PGS are committed to the well-being of their children, whatever their gender.

A policy solution that gives practitioners and patients primary control without direct legal or social oversight, although not ideal, may be the best way to deal with new reprogenetic techniques. Society should not prohibit or substantially burden reproductive decisions without stronger evidence of harm than PGS now appears to present. Ultimately, the use of PGS and other reprogenetic procedures will depend on whether they satisfy ethical norms of care and concern for children while meeting the needs of prospective parents.

**Norman Daniels, Carson Strong,
Mary B. Mahowald, and Mark V. Sauer**

 **NO**

It Isn't Just the Sex . . .

John Robertson argues that preconception sex selection (PSS) should remain a moral and legal prerogative of parental family planning, provided certain other conditions are met, including caveats about harms to others. If sound, his argument also applies to parental prerogatives to select offspring having any one of a family of traits that have properties and effects similar to sex (or sex selection). Bringing out this more general formulation will help us evaluate his argument.

Suppose, as Robertson does with regard to flow cytometry, that a specific sex-selection technology exists and has the following properties:

A. It is safe;
B. It imposes no harm on any fetus (because it is preconception);
C. It has quantifiably high reliability;
D. There is parental demand for using the technique (even though other techniques are much cheaper and more enjoyable); and
E. Some parents would not reproduce if they could not use it.

Now suppose that we also have techniques for preconception selection of traits other than sex, such as height, greater immune capacities, calmer temperament, or better memory, and that these techniques also have properties A E. Property E may now seem more problematic than when it was applied only to sex selection. Robertson imagines a family that has several children of one gender and would rather not reproduce again unless it could raise a child of a different gender. Similarly, we can imagine parents refusing to reproduce further unless they can have a much taller or much calmer child—one different from the ones they already have.

Exactly what role does property E play in Robertson's argument? Property E does clearly show the strength of the parental preference, but strength of preference seems irrelevant to establishing that we have a right to gender or other trait selection. For Robertson, the point of property E seems to be this: if the parents would not reproduce at all unless they could have a child with a particular gender or other trait, then state prohibitions on gender or other trait selection technologies interfere with their basic moral and legal liberty to make reproductive choices, unless, of course, there are harms to others that the prohibition is aimed at preventing. In contrast, if parents prefer to select for a

From *The American Journal of Bioethics*, Winter 2001, vol. 1, no. 1, pp. 10 13, 15 16, 28 29.
Copyright © 2001 by Taylor & Francis Journals. Reprinted by permission.

particular trait but would choose to reproduce even if they could not—that is, if property E is missing—then the state has not interfered with their liberty to make reproductive choices if it prohibits use of trait selection technologies.

Robertson's appeal to property E seems misguided. Consider Table 1:

Table 1

agents	First Choice	Second Choice	Third Choice
Ben and Lily	gender selection	take chances	no offspring
Max and Sophie	gender selection	no offspring	(take chances?)

Property E is present for Max and Sophie but not Ben and Lily. If gender selection is denied either couple, they get their second choice. The prohibition on sex selection affects both couple's reproductive choices in the same way. Perhaps it seems worse for Max and Sophie because they are then "driven" to have no children, whereas Ben and Lily still reproduce, but the result in both cases is determined by each couple's choice in the absence of their first choice. Property E thus seems to do no work in the argument, and I believe it should be dropped.

Perhaps what motivates Robertson's appeal to E is a narrow (perhaps legally constrained) interpretation of reproductive liberty: it is a negative right against government interference with the choice to reproduce or not. Given this narrow interpretation, we might still be able to derive a right against interference with some cases of gender selection if property E did the work that I have argued it fails to do. Since property E fails to do what this alternative requires, we have two options. We can adopt and justify a broader interpretation of reproductive liberties, one that provides a right against interference with reproductive choices about trait selection, provided there are no harms to others. Alternatively, we can retain the narrow interpretation of reproductive liberty but argue for an additional, broader (negative) right of parents to pursue what they think is best for their children (and their families) through the selection, shaping, and development of the traits of their offspring. This broader right will include means other than reproductive choices (Buchanan et al. 2000, 187 191).

Much of Robertson's paper focuses on the reasons for thinking that gender selection either poses no harm to others or poses harms that can be countered in ways that infringe less on liberty than would prohibitions on gender selection. The disjunction of conditions (F H) that Robertson's argument appeals to as constraints on gender selection constrains selection for other traits as well.

F. Neither individual cases of selection, nor the aggregate effect of many such selections, imposes (nonspeculative) harms on others;
G. Where there is a potential harm to others, it will correct itself in a reasonable time period (as in some cases of gender ratio imbalance); or
H. Any potential harm to others can be eliminated through regulation that does not directly infringe on basic reproductive liberties.

Robertson should have emphasized more the way in which the estimate of harms, and thus the justification of a liberty to select a trait, is sensitive to empirical facts about a society. He correctly argues that the case of family gender balancing does not by itself reinforce sexist beliefs or practices. When societies have a strong gender bias, permitting preconception sex selection beyond family balancing would reinforce existing biases and might lead to sex ratio imbalances. Under these conditions, permitting sex selection would require rigorous regulation of the grounds for selection. Robertson fails to emphasize the ways in which such regulations would appear to many as intrusions into basic parental liberties and how politically difficult it might be to sustain them.

One kind of harm Robertson does not mention, perhaps because it is not raised by gender selection, is the competitive or positional disadvantage that might result from allowing trait selection for certain traits, but financing them only through out-of-pocket payments. Advantages in wealth will then lead to the further transmission of advantage through access to trait selection. Fairness issues must be addressed in this case (for a discussion of these issues, see Buchanan et al. 2000, chs. 5-6).

Reference

Buchanan, A., D. Brock, N. Daniels, and D. Wikler. 2000. *From chance to choice: Genetics and justice.* New York: Cambridge University Press.

❧❦❧

Can't You Control Your Children?

In his paper "Preconception Gender Selection" (PGS), John Robertson (2001) discusses two issues: What limitations, if any, should the government impose on use of PGS? And what restrictions, if any, would it be justifiable for physicians to impose on prospective parents who request PGS? For both issues, the focus is on PGS for parental preference, as opposed to prevention of sex-linked diseases. The first issue requires the use of our constitutional law framework. According to that framework, procreative liberty is a *fundamental* right, which entails that government restrictions must be justified by compelling state interests. Meeting the test of being "compelling" requires especially strong reasons for infringing procreative liberty; according to Robertson, meeting the test typically requires showing that substantial harm to others would occur. The second issue does not require the constitutional framework. Here the question is whether some individuals—either individual physicians or groups of physicians—are justified in refusing to carry out patients' requests for PGS. In arguing that it is ethically justifiable for physicians to refuse such requests, it is not necessary to show that there are compelling reasons for the refusal. It is only necessary to show that the arguments for refusing are better than the arguments for carrying out the requests.

Unfortunately, this basic difference between constitutional and professional ethical argumentation is not clearly acknowledged in Robertson's article. Throughout the paper he appeals to the more demanding constitutional framework, even where the less demanding framework for professional ethical justifiability is all that is required. For example, he argues that PGS for offspring diversity is ethically permissible, despite the objection of some ethicists that it is sexist. He concludes his argument by stating:

> If this view is correct, then those who deny that biological gender differences exist, or who assume that any recognition of them always reinforces sexism or disadvantages women, will not have carried the burden of showing that a couple's use of PGS for offspring gender variety or other nonintentionally sexist uses is so harmful to women that it justifies restricting procreative choice. Until a stronger basis for finding harm to others from PGS exists, policies to prohibit or substantially restrict its use would not be justified.

Here Robertson appeals to the test of substantial harm. Later he advocates physician guidelines that permit PGS for gender diversity, but the only arguments for such guidelines that can be found in the paper appeal, like this one, to the test of substantial harm. This blurring of constitutional and professional ethics argumentation creates a problem in trying to justify physician guidelines. Robertson seems to approve of guidelines that permit PGS for gender diversity because objections to such guidelines do not meet the demanding "compelling reasons" test. But objections to physician guidelines simply do not have to meet this high standard.

This problem is significant because there are important arguments bearing on the issue of physician guidelines that Robertson does not address. In particular, in discussing concerns about the genetic control of offspring, he does not present those concerns in a particularly forceful form. As a result, his paper does not engage those issues very well. There are at least two concerns that should be discussed, and although they overlap, I believe it is useful to distinguish between them. First, there are concerns about the genetic enhancement of offspring. Second, there are concerns about parental genetic control of offspring characteristics irrespective of whether the purpose of the control is properly labeled "enhancement" (as in the case of control for offspring diversity, eye and hair color, or various other possibilities).

Let me begin with the first set of concerns, which is relevant to the issue of physician response to requests for PGS for firstborn male offspring. I want to emphasize that sex selection is not itself a form of enhancement. To claim otherwise is to imply that one gender is superior to the other. However, it is obvious that in our male-dominated society, being male confers advantages upon a person. Parents who seek genetically to enhance the ability of offspring to succeed in life could easily reason that being male would enhance that ability. When physicians allow PGS for firstborn male offspring, they are at least in some circumstances allowing parents who think this way to pursue their vision of genetic enhancement. Those who would want additional forms of genetic enhancement in the future could point to this as a precedent; we would *already* be a distance down the proverbial slippery slope. Let me mention two arguments that have been given to explain why we should be wary of the genetic enhancement of offspring. First, such technologies likely would not be available to all, but would be skewed among different socioeconomic and ethnic groups. The economically advantaged would be better able to afford the costs of the technology. Because enhancement can improve the offspring's opportunities, unequal access to it would exacerbate current social and economic inequities (for a similar argument in the context of germ-line genetic modification, see Zimmerman 1991). Second, allowing parents to choose enhancements might erode our opposition to state-sponsored programs that promote (or carry out) enhancements of offspring. There is wide concern that abuses might occur, as has happened in all previous eugenics programs, or that efforts would be made to redesign human nature, resulting in more harm than benefit (Wertz and Fletcher 1989; Anderson 1989).

It should be acknowledged that enhancement could have positive consequences, as well. In some cases, it might promote the happiness of parents and children and the quality of family life. Also, it has been pointed out that we do not have sufficient information to assess the risks and benefits of positive eugenics, and that we should not assume that it is automatically wrong (Munson and Davis 1992). Admittedly, it is difficult to predict the long-term consequences of enhancement. However, the arguments against enhancement of offspring raise concerns significant enough to suggest that we should not proceed with enhancement without a better understanding of where it might take us (Strong 1997, 143–144). These considerations, in addition to the argument from sexism, provide important reasons why, for now at least, physicians should not carry out requests for PGS for firstborn male offspring.

The concern about parental control of offspring characteristics applies to all uses of PGS, including its use for offspring diversity and for firstborn female offspring based on a parental desire for the rearing and companionship experiences that would be involved. There is a legitimate worry that genetic control of offspring characteristics, if it becomes common and is applied to many characteristics, would alter parent-child relationships and that children would become more like "products" (Botkin 1990; Strong 1997, 143–144) When offspring characteristics are under parental control (whether they are properly labeled "enhancement" or not), parents might be less willing to accept the shortcomings of their children. Such designing might undermine a child's ability to have self-esteem. Less parental tolerance of children's imperfections might result in less compassion for the handicapped. Also, there would be a greater tendency to blame parents for their children's imperfections. The question, "Can't you control your children?" might take on a darker meaning. Children themselves might blame their parents, and this could harm family relationships. These sorts of considerations suggest that we should be more wary about proceeding with PGS than Robertson would have us be. It is not necessary to have compelling reasons for physician refusal to carry out requests for PGS based on parental gender preferences. It is only necessary to have good reasons. Concerns about what we might be doing to our future seem to justify a cautionary approach. They support the view that, for now at least, physicians should not carry out any requests for PGS for parental preference.

References

Anderson, W. F. 1989. Human gene therapy: Why draw a line? *Journal of Medicine and Philosophy* 14:681–693.

Botkin, J. R. 1990. Prenatal screening: Professional standards and the limits of parental choice. *Obstetrics and Gynecology* 75:875–880.

Munson, R., and L. H. Davis. 1992. Germ-line gene therapy and the medical imperative. *Kennedy Institute of Ethics Journal* 2:137–158.

Robertson, J. A. 2001. Preconception gender selection. *American Journal of Bioethics,* 1(1) 2–9.

Strong, C. 1997. *Ethics in reproductive and perinatal medicine: A new framework.* New Haven: Yale University Press.

Wertz D. C., and J. Fletcher 1989. Fatal knowledge? Prenatal diagnosis and sex selection. *Hastings Center Report* 19:21–27.

Zimmerman, B. K. 1991. Human germ-line therapy: The case for its development and use. *Journal of Medicine and Philosophy* 16:593–612.

꒰◑꒱

Reverse Sexism? Not to Worry

I concur with John Robertson that preconception sex selection (PSS) would be morally objectionable if it were sexist, and that it is not necessarily sexist (anymore than post conception sex selection is necessarily sexist).[1] I disagree, however, that PSS is morally permissible on grounds of procreative liberty or the right to reproduce. Further, I believe that PSS is more likely than not to be sexist in its intent or in its consequences. Robertson appears to think otherwise.

According to Robertson, procreative liberty is the "freedom to reproduce or not to reproduce in the genetic sense." It also includes the freedom to gestate "whether or not there is a genetic connection to the resulting child" (Robertson 1996, 22–23). He deploys this definition in support of PSS by arguing that a couple who wish to have a biologically related child only if the child is of one sex rather than the other are deprived of their "fundamental right" to reproduce if PSS is not available to them. This argument erroneously assumes that the right to reproduce implies the right to reproduce a child of a specific kind. As Rebecca Dresser observes, "helping people to have children is different from helping them to have a particular kind of child" (Dresser 2001). It would be as wrong to say a couple have a fundamental right to reproduce a child who is a clone of one of them or to reproduce a child who has the same disabilities that they have. Although Robertson may affirm procreative liberty in these situations also, neither right is implied by the right to reproduce.

In *Children of Choice* Robertson (1996, 22) acknowledges that the right to reproduce is separable from the right to raise a child, but he does not fully examine the implications of that separability for sex selection. This leaves me wondering how he might respond to scenarios not addressed in his article. Would he defend the right to reproduce a child of the desired sex solely on grounds of that right even if the reproducing person had no intention of raising the child? Would a sperm "donor," for example, be entitled to flow cytometry so as to ensure, or to maximize the chance, that any embryo developed from his gametes is male?[2] Would a potential egg "donor" be entitled to require that embryos formed from her gametes be transferred to the recipient only if they are determined to be female? Or would a woman who desires to gestate the genetic offspring of another be entitled to exclude some embryos from that offer on grounds of their sex? In none of these cases is the rationale for sex selection necessarily sexist. But as Robertson defines it, the right to reproduce entails the right to sex selection in all of these cases, as well as those where the right to reproduce is exercised by those who intend to raise the child.

Neither does the right not to reproduce imply the right to terminate a pregnancy at any point during gestation for any reason. *Roe v. Wade* (410 U.S. 113 [1973]) allows the states to proscribe abortion after viability only if the pregnant woman's health is not threatened by continuation of the pregnancy. The rationale for this caveat is not simply procreative freedom but the woman's right to avoid harm to herself. Even those who, like me, do not agree with Robertson's claim that the right to reproduce includes the right to PSS, may support PSS on this basis. We may argue, for example, that the anticipation of social stigmatization or ostracization may provide moral justification for PSS by individuals in particular cultural milieux. However, this is not equivalent to justification of permissive policies for PSS.

In addition to his affirmation of procreative liberty, Robertson apparently supports permissive policies for PSS because such policies are unlikely to be sexist in their intent or consequences. In contrast, I think that sexist intent and sexist consequences are more likely than not to be associated with the social and legal permissibility of PSS. Neither Robertson nor I have empirical data to buttress our positions, in part because intent is difficult if not impossible to verify in most cases. The mere fact that individuals prefer to have a boy or girl as a first, only, or additional child does not count as evidence of sexism. But sexist consequences are evident in situations where sex selection is practiced, despite its illegality, because the preponderance of boys in such situations shows that in general male children are more valued than female children.

Even if male children are more valued for morally defensible reasons such as economic security or to avoid discriminatory or oppressive practices towards son-less women and their daughters, this constitutes complicity in sexism. Individuals themselves may not have sexist reasons for PSS, but their practice inevitably supports the view that one sex is inferior to the other. On an individual level, sexism may also be practiced by those who choose to have female children—if the intent or consequences of their choices are based on the notion that men are inferior to women. If and when a preponderance of female children in the general population shows them to be more valued than male children, we may then need to worry that the permissibility of PSS has led to "reverse sexism." Present circumstances lend little weight to that worry.

References

Dresser, R. 2001. Cosmetic reproductive services and professional integrity. *American Journal of Bioethics*, 1(1):11–12.

Mahowald, M. B. 2000. *Genes, women, equality.* New York: Oxford University Press.

Robertson, J. A. 1996. *Children of choice: Freedom and the new reproductive technologies.* Princeton: Princeton University Press.

Notes

1. My own views on sex selection, whether it is practiced prior to conception, prenatally or postnatally, are developed in Mahowald (2000, 115–121).

2. I put the term "donor" in quotation marks to call attention to the fact that the literal meaning of the term, i.e., one who gives a gift, is typically inapplicable in this context. In most cases, those who provide gametes to others are vendors rather than donors. Whether gamete providers are in fact donors or vendors, however, their right to reproduce does not imply a right to select the sex of their genetic offspring.

ᴄᴀ◉ᴀ

Preconception Sex Selection: A Commentary

Gender selection of offspring created through assisted reproductive technology (ART) has been hotly debated since the inception of the method of in vitro fertilization (IVF). Given the broad range of innovation enjoyed throughout the development of IVF it should not be surprising that couples would ask whether or not predetermination of gender is possible. Thus, early on, attempts at controlling outcomes began through the development of techniques that would preferentially select the desired sex of the embryo. What has never been universally agreed upon, however, is what, if any, situation should warrant attempts to manipulate the gender of the offspring.

The issue of sex selection through prenatal determination is one of the more difficult subjects facing clinicians. Ultimately physicians must decide whether or not to offer services; such decisions are based largely on the soundness of the medical and ethical practice. Today, couples choosing to select the gender of their children have essentially three options:

1. to terminate a pregnancy already established after the sex has been determined by chorionic villus sampling or amniocentesis;
2. to undergo preimplantation genetic diagnosis (PGD) by embryonic biopsy prior to embryo transfer; or
3. to alter the population of inseminated sperm so as to increase the likelihood of achieving a pregnancy of the desired sex.

Karyotyping a fetus or embryo is inherently invasive, expensive, and potentially dangerous to the mother and/or the pregnancy. However, it is the only way to guarantee that the sex of the embryo is the one desired by the mother.

Manipulating the insemination is appealing since the intervention occurs prior to conception, and avoids most issues involving abortion. From this perspective, sperm separation techniques would appear to have a decisive advantage over traditional methods. Unfortunately, to this date all techniques involving sperm separation are flawed since none guarantee success. As John Robertson points out, at best between 8% and 18% of pregnancies will result in the "wrong sex" even using flow cytometry to separate sperm of X and Y genotype. It is this fact of life that troubles most of us responsible for "assisting" in the creation of these lives. What happens to the pregnancies of the wrong sex? I would guess that many would choose to abort. As noted, "paying greater attention to gender" than to the importance of the life itself in many ways perverts the original intent of helping the infertile to conceive. Knowing that we live in a sexist world, there can be no doubt that many (mostly female) embryos would be terminated in the name of "procreative liberty."

All agree that the right of the individual to reproduce is fundamental. What isn't always clear is whether or not the pursuit of reproductive interventions requires regulation. Society and individuals speaking on behalf of the unborn have an equal right to object to gender selection when performed without clear medical justification. Physicians and patients with genetic diseases generally agree that the avoidance of X-linked illness is a valued reason for gender selection, whether through invasive or noninvasive means. However, "family balancing" is a politically correct euphemism that does little to diminish the valid concerns related to societal sexism.

The flow cytometry method has been neither clinically tested nor approved by the U.S. Food and Drug Administration. Yet, it has been discussed in the international press and news media and profiled as a treatment option in the medical literature. Naturally patients are inquiring as to its efficacy even though the procedure remains largely unavailable. Typically, the debate over whether or not it should be used is obscured by debate over the clinical success of the method.

Unfortunately, throughout the history of reproductive medicine, sensational press has often dictated medical practice. Many techniques in ART were introduced in this manner (e.g., intracytoplasmic sperm injection, cryopreservation, assisted hatching, and blastocyst culturing). Even IVF itself was equally unorthodox in its development and presentation. With respect to preconception sex selection, I agree with Robertson's assessment as to the need to "proceed slowly." In order for individuals to give informed consent, more needs to be known of the long-term effects, both medical and psychosocial, of flow cytometry. More importantly, I believe ethics committees at each institution should discuss how best to implement policy related to gender selection, and physicians should abide by these recommendations.

The Ethics Committee at Columbia University believes gender selection should not be performed except in instances in which a clear medical indication exists (e.g., a known genetic X-linked carrier status). Undoubtedly, many will disagree with that opinion. However, public debate is good for the field, and each physician should take a clear stand prior to introducing yet another untested procedure.

POSTSCRIPT

Should Parents Be Able to Select the Biological Sex of Their Children?

The idea of being able to select a child's biological sex is as fascinating as it is controversial. It is also nothing new. Throughout the late nineteenth and early twentieth century, people discussed and debated genetic engineering of children in order to eliminate so-called "undesirable" traits. Initially referring to disease, eugenicists (those who study or espouse the improvement of the human race through controlled selective breeding—www.dictionary.com) were often accused of racism, sexism, and other biases. What one person thinks would improve the human race others would see as tantamount to annihilation or extinction. Hitler's campaign to create a superior human race during World War II is a clear example of these concepts gone frighteningly awry.

For some the argument for PGS is about rights—people have the fundamental right to control their reproductive potential in all ways, including whether and when to have a child, and what sex their child will be. Others oppose PGS because if sex selection takes place for any other reason other than medical necessity, society is opening a Pandora's box of ethical issues that would be impossible to close.

Take, for example, any other traits that human beings possess. What if there were a test to determine eye color of a child, and prospective parents decided that they wanted their child's eyes to match theirs? Should they be able to genetically alter their child to reflect that? What about another physical characteristic like height?

What about something that is not physical, yet still in-born—our sexual orientation, or the gender(s) of the people to whom we are attracted physically or romantically? There is a fascinating fictional movie called *The Twilight of the Golds* in which a woman finds that she is pregnant, and takes a genetic test that determines within a certain percentage of certainty that the child that she will have will be gay. The movie centers around whether she will choose to carry the pregnancy to term or end it through having an abortion. Clearly, the different ways people might wish to affect their children can be endless, and endlessly controversial.

In 2001, the ethics committee of the American Society for Reproductive Medicine (ASRM) released a position statement in which they discussed PCG selection for medical and nonmedical reasons. The ASRM stresses that medical professionals must inform that the only current method of PCG selection available (separating X-bearing and Y-bearing sperm cells) is still an experimental procedure. If it were to become safer and eventually approved for PCG selection so that parents could select the gender of their children, the ASRM believes that PCG selection should only be offered:

- in clinic settings
- to couples who are seeking gender variety in their families
- provided that the couples are made fully aware of the risks of failure
- to couples who state that they would fully accept a child of a different sex should the PCG process fail
- to couples after counseling that their expectations of what it may be like to have a child of a particular gender may not match the eventual reality
- to couples who are given the opportunity to participate in a research study so that medical professionals can continue to track such issues as safety as effectively as possible

As the medical world continues to advance in leaps and bounds, this debate is far from over—in fact, we probably cannot even imagine how far it will reach in the years to come.

Suggested Readings

M. Darnovsky, "Revisiting Sex Selection: The Growing Popularity of New Sex Selection Methods Revives An Old Debate." *GeneWatch,* vol. 17, no. 1, January February 2004. Accessible online at http://www.gene-watch. org/genewatch/articles/17-1darnovsky.html

M. Darnovsky, "Sex Selection Moves to Consumer Culture—Ads For 'Family Balancing' In *The New York Times.*" *Genetic Crossroads: The Newsletter of the Center for Genetics and Society*, #33. August 20, 2003. Accessible online at http://www.genetics-and-society.org/newsletter/archive/33.html#II

D. King, "Eugenic Tendencies in Modern Genetics." In *Redesigning Life?,* edited by B. Tokar. New York: Zed Books, 2001.

R. Mallik, "A Less Valued Life: Population Policy and Sex Selection in India." The Center for Gender and Health Equity, 2002. Available online at www.genderhealth.org/pubs/MallikSexSelectionIndiaOct2002.pdf

R. McDougall, "Acting Parentally: An Argument Against Sex Selection." *Journal of Medical Ethics,* 2005, vol. 31, no. 10, pp. 601 605.

P. Moore, and L. Moore, *Baby Girl or Baby Boy: Choose the Sex of Your Child.* Tallahassee, FL: Washington Publishers, 2004.

Savulescu, J. and E. Dahl, "Sex Selection and Preimplantation Diagnosis: A Response to the Ethics Committee of the American Society of Reproductive Medicine." *Human Reproduction,* September 2000, vol. 15, no. 9, pp. 1879 1880.

R. Shettles, and D. M. Rorvik, *How to Choose the Sex of Your Baby.* New York: Broadway Books, 2006.

I. Simoncelli, "Preimplantation Genetic Diagnosis and Selection: From Disease Prevention to Customized Conception." *Different Takes: The Newsletter on Population and Development Program at Hampshire College,* no. 24, Spring 2003. Accessible online at http://www.genetics-and-society.org/resources/cgs/200303_difftakes_simoncelli.pdf

ISSUE 9

Should Parents Surgically Alter Their Intersex Infants?

YES: Amicur Farkas, B. Chertin, and Irith Hadas-Halpren, from "One-Stage Feminizing Genitoplasty: Eight Years of Experience With Forty-Nine Cases," *The Journal of Urology* (June 2001)

NO: Paul McHugh, from "Surgical Sex," *First Things* (November 2004)

ISSUE SUMMARY

YES: Amicur Farkas, B. Chertin, and Irith Hadas-Halpren, faculty of the Ben-Gurion University in Jerusalem, Israel, see ambiguous genitalia as a true emergency. They assert that feminizing surgery should be done on an infant with congenital adrenal hyperplasia to ensure that as an adult woman she will have sexual functioning and be able to give birth.

NO: Paul McHugh argues that a person's sense of gender identity is biologically based—that by changing an infant's or child's body before that child has a sense of who they are and risking being wrong about that sex assignment can do much more damage than good.

$\mathbf{T}$he term *intersex* is often more recognizable by its historical term, *hermaphrodite*, a term still used by many medical professionals. In Greek mythology, Hermaphroditus was the son of Hermes and Aphrodite. A nymph named Salmacis fell in love with Hermaphroditus, but he did not feel the same. Salmacis prayed that they would never be separated—so when Hermaphroditus swam in her stream, she combined with him to create a person with male and female characteristics in one body. Most individuals born with ambiguous or mixed genitalia and chromosomal structures prefer to be called intersex rather than hermaphrodite, the latter of which is considered by many intersex individuals to be negative. However, some intersex individuals have reclaimed the word *hermaphrodite* to describe themselves, just as members of other minority groups have reclaimed epithets as a way of asserting their power.

It is estimated that every year in the United States, approximately 65,000 babies are born with ambiguous genitalia. However, reliable statistics on the true incidence of intersexuality are limited. While attention to intersexuality and the medical, psychological, and social issues relating to intersexual individuals have increased dramatically over the last 10 years, disagreement still exists on how parents should respond when they are told that their infants have ambiguous genitalia.

Support for surgical sex assignment is rooted in the work of psychologist John Money. In 1967, Money conducted an experiment in gender identity involving an infant whose genitalia was not ambiguous at birth but deformed severely by a botched circumcision. In this now-notorious case, Money maintained that gender identity was fluid for the first few months of life. Money asserted that by completing the castration, providing the child with hormones, and raising the child as a girl, the child would "become" female. At the time, the case received a lot of attention and was declared a success when, at follow-up, Money noted that the then-nine-year-old girl was adjusting "normally."

About 30 years later, two other researchers, Milton Diamond and Keith Sigmundson, found that the child with whom Money had worked ended up depressed and confused by her strong feelings that she was actually male. Once the truth was revealed to her, she was extremely relieved. Her parents arranged for the surgeries and other treatments that would enable her to transition back to male. As an adult male, he lived with his wife and their children, whom he adopted.

As you read the selections, consider the reasoning behind each argument. There is the so-called locker room viewpoint—that adolescents have a tough enough time navigating through adolescence, why make it even harder by subjecting them to further torment in the locker room where their ambiguous genitalia would be revealed? There are also parents who believe that children should remain intact until they are older and can decide for themselves what, if anything, to do about their ambiguous genitalia.

In the following selections, Amitur Farkas, B. Chertin, and Irith Hadas-Halpren, provide a detailed description of what they call "feminizing" surgery. They believe that having this type of surgery is best for patients to ensure both cosmetic contentment and satisfactory intercourse. Paul McHugh argues that a person's sense of gender identity is biologically based—that by changing an infant's or child's body before that child has a sense of who they are and risking being wrong about that sex assignment can do much more damage than good.

**Amicur Farkas, B. Chertin,
and Irith Hadas-Halpren**

One-Stage Feminizing Genitoplasty: Eight Years of Experience With Forty-Nine Cases

The neonate with sexual ambiguity represents an enigmatic but true emergency in pediatric urology. In recent years several techniques of 1-stage feminizing genitoplasty have been described. Successful reconstruction depends on accurate preoperative recognition of the anatomy while the main area of interest is the location of the vaginal opening into the urogenital sinus and its relationship to the pelvic floor and external sphincter mechanism. Passerini-Glazel, and Gonzales and Fernandes described their techniques of 1-stage feminizing genitoplasty. The primary features of both techniques are the use of preputial skin in combination with the distal part of the urogenital sinus to construct a vaginal introitus and to avoid the frequent complications associated with previous types of operations, such as vaginal stenosis and injury of the urethral sphincter. We retrospectively analyzed the results of our modification of these techniques.

Materials and Methods

Between 1991 and 1998, 49 patients underwent 1-stage feminizing genitoplasty at our department. All patients were referred following complete evaluation of gender, and chromosomal and biochemical data by pediatric endocrinologists. Of the 49 patients 44 had congenital adrenal hyperplasia (CAH) due to 21-hydroxylase deficiency in 33 and 11-hydroxylase deficiency in 11, 3 were true hermaphrodites and 2 were adolescents with different degrees of the androgen insensitivity syndrome. All patients with CAH and the true hermaphrodites had 46 XX karyotype, and those with androgen insensitivity syndrome had 46 XY karyotype. The true hermaphrodites and androgen insensitivity syndrome patients were referred to us after surgical removal of the contradictory gonads and internal duct structure before the genitoplasty. Mean age was 0.9 ± 0.3 years, of the patients with CAH and 13 ± 2.3 of the remainder. Before surgical correction all patients underwent transabdominal pelvic ultrasound only to provide information for surgical decision making regarding status of the internal genitalia, length and anatomical position of the vagina, and whether the vaginal junction with the urogenital

From *Journal of Urology*, vol. 1 65, June 2001, pp. 2341–2346. Copyright © 2001 by Elsevier Inc.
Reprinted by permission.

sinus was distal or proximal to the pelvic floor. The ultrasound technique and results have been reported previously.

The patients with CAH underwent panendoscopy as an initial and integral step of the feminizing genitoplasty. The communication of the vagina and urogenital sinus was localized using a 10Fr pediatric cytoscope. In the majority of cases the cystocope was passed into the vaginal cavity. At that point the telescope was removed from the sheath and a 6Fr silicone Foley catheter was inserted into the vaginal cavity through the cytoscope sheath and its balloon was inflated to 2 cc. The cytoscope sheath was then pulled back and the catheter was clamped at the distal end of the urogenital sinus to avoid balloon deflation. The distal end of the catheter was cut off to enable complete removal of the cystoscope sheath. In some cases with a small vaginal opening a Fogarty catheter was used with the cytoscope inserted only as far as the opening and not into the vaginal cavity. After the cytoscope was removed an 8 to 10Fr silicone Foley was inserted into the bladder in the conventional manner. Of the 44 patients with CAH 41 had vaginal confluence at the level of the verumontanum and 3 had high vaginal confluence according to Powell types II and III classification. The patients were placed in an exaggerated lithotomy position and surgery was performed via the perineal approach by a senior urologist (A. F.) or under his personal supervision.

The operation begins with vertical incisions of the phallic skin on ventral and dorsal surfaces and degloving of the phallus circumferentially. The ventral incision is extended to the bottom of the labioscrotal folds in a Y shape and then terminates in an inverted U shaped perineal flap to provide good exposure of the urogenital sinus. The urogenital sinus including the vagina and urethra is then completely mobilized *en bloc* from the corporeal bodies. The dissection is done between the 2 crura of corpora cavernosa and mobilization continues below the lower rami of the pubis. Thereafter the dissection between the lateral and posterior walls of the sinus, including the vagina and the anterior rectal wall, is completed circumferentially so the posterior wall of the vagina can be brought to the perineum without tension.

At this point clitoroplasty is performed using the technique of Kogan et al. The plane of cleavage is developed between the corpora and dorsal neurovascular bundle via Buck's fascia, taking care to preserve the tunica of the corporeal body. Subsequently resection of the corpora is performed from the glans to the proximal part passing the bifurcation. The stumps of the corpora are placed and sutured by running 5-zero polyglactin sutures below the pubic bone. The proximal phallic skin sutured to the preputial skin and left around the glans clitoris corona creates a preputial hood. To avoid rectal injury and bleeding from the spongiosal tissue, traction 5-zero polyglactin sutures are placed on the urogenital sinus to bring the deeper structures to a more superficial level. All of this part of the procedure is done during meticulous palpation of the balloon of the Foley or Fogarty catheter, which is inserted into the vagina and serves as a guide during dissection.

The posterior vaginal wall is opened over the balloon between the traction sutures, and the connection between the vagina and urogenital sinus is closed from the internal surface of the vagina. The vagina is opened into an adequate caliber to prevent future stenosis. The previously dissected posterior inverted U is sutured to the dorsal vaginal wall. The redundant distal part of the urogenital sinus is partially opened on the dorsal surface leaving a long enough urethra. The inverted open strip of epithelium is sutured to the anterior and lateral vaginal walls enabling creation of a wet and wide introitus. The preputial and phallic skin is completely split down the midline, and sutured around the clitoris and to the lateral epithelial edges of the aforementioned urogenital strips to create the labia minora. The lateral labioscrotal skin can be brought down and sutured to the corners between the posterior U flap and lateral skin to form the labia majora. . . .

Results

Mean operating time was 145 minutes (range 120 to 180) and average hospitalization period was 4 to 5 days. Preoperative ultrasound provided the correct data regarding vaginal and internal genitalia anatomy in all of our cases, and the exact communication between the vagina and urogenital sinus was demonstrated in 41 of 44 (93%) with CAH. In 1 patient anterior rectal wall injury occurred intraoperatively and was immediately closed without further complications. The only immediate postoperative complication was mild wound infection of the buttock area in 3 cases. Mean followup was 4.7 ± 2.6 years. In 1 case total clitoris loss was later observed, and 2 patients presented with repeat clitoromegalia due to inadequate androgen suppression. All patients who underwent our modification of genitoplasty have had successful cosmetic and early functional results. In those cases with CAH who reached puberty repeat examinations showed normal menstruation, a wet and wide introitus and no evidence of fibrosis or scarring of the perineum. In the smaller girls we were able to calibrate the vaginal opening easily with a 20 to 22Fr bougie. No patient had urinary tract infection, and to date all patients are continent including those with a high vagina. None of the girls with CAH has yet achieved intercourse age and, therefore, we have no information regarding sexual satisfaction, possibility of vaginal delivery and psychosocial aspects of these forms of intersexuality. Both patients with partial AIS who presented initially with a small phallus and adequate vagina are now 18 and 22 years old, and report satisfactory sexual intercourse experiences.

Discussion

Existence of ambiguous genitalia is an emergency situation necessitating a team approach, which can provide quick identification of the genetic sex and biochemical profile. One of the most common causes of genital ambiguity is CAH, and today several surgical techniques are available for reconstruction. Feminizing genitoplasty should provide an adequate opening for the vagina into the perineum, create a normal-looking wet introitus, fully separate the urethral orifice from the vagina, remove phallic erectile tissue while preserving glandular innervation and blood supply, and prevent urinary tract complications.

Successful reconstruction depends on good knowledge of the anatomy of the urogenital sinus, particularly the location of the communication of the vagina to the urogenital sinus in relation to the pelvic floor and rectum. The surgeon must know whether the vagina is long enough to reach the perineum without any tension through a perineal approach and without compromising the pelvic floor and urethral continence mechanism. To provide the necessary information we perform only ultrasound in our patients.

The optimal time for genitoplasty is controversial. A few authors advise neonatal genitoplasty because of the presence of neonatal hypertrophy of the external and internal genitalia due to maternal and placental hyperstimulation with estrogens, and apparent easy vaginal mobilization.

In contrast, others suggest deferring definitive reconstruction of the intermediate and high vagina until after puberty. To spare our patients and parents the anxiety we endeavor to perform genitoplasty at around age 6 months when the child reaches 5 to 6 kg, as the risk of anesthesia at this age is negligible. Modern anesthesiology produces negligible risks in neonates and recently we started to operate on patients at age 3 months.

Historically, genital reconstruction in patients with CAH involved a 2-stage operation. At stage 1 simple amputation or reduction of the clitoris was performed in the neonatal period with the vaginoplasty being postponed until an older age. Currently, many authors recommend 1-stage genitoplasty, which can be done early in life using the perineal approach in the majority of cases even those with high vaginal confluence. We had no difficulty reaching the posterior wall of the vagina of those patients in the exaggerated lithotomy position via the perineal approach, especially as we made no effort to dissect and separate its communication with the urogenital sinus as described originally by Passerini-Glazel. Preservation of the megaloclitoris is advantageous once 1-stage genitoplasty is performed, as it enables easy dissection and *en bloc* mobilization of the urogenital sinus. The remaining redundant phallic and preputial skin after removal of the erectile tissue provides excellent material for reconstruction of the introitus and labia. Those cases referred to our hospital after clitorectomy or clitorous reduction were more challenging for reconstruction and are not included in this report.

Endoscopy is a crucial step in genitoplasty, which identifies the anatomy and enables insertion of a Foley or Fogarty catheter into the vagina through the communication to the urogenital sinus. We inserted the 10Fr cystoscope into the vagina so that a Foley catheter could be inserted into the vagina via the cystoscope sheath. The balloon of the Foley catheter that is used in the majority of our cases was bigger than that of the Fogarty catheter. This maneuver enables easier and safer localization of the posterior vaginal wall and prevents rectal injury.

Since 1989 different modifications of feminizing genitoplasty have become popular and replaced the classical Hendren and Crawford technique, decreased the percent of vaginal stenosis to negligible levels and improved the cosmetic appearance of the external genitalia. We have improved a few steps of the previously reported operations. Complete mobilization of the urogenital sinus *en bloc* including the vagina and urethra makes it possible to bring the sinus to the perineum and avoid the difficult step of dissection between the anterior vagina wall and overlying urethra and bladder neck. The connecting fistula between the urethra and vagina is closed from the internal surface of the vagina after opening the posterior vaginal wall. It is difficult to evaluate the failure and existence of a new fistula in small girls but to date no fistula has occurred in our adolescent and adult patients. Rink and Adams and Passerini-Glazel mention that fibrosis is the main reason for vaginal stenosis. The fact that we use the healthy posterior vaginal wall to create the vaginal opening instead of the distal fibrotic vaginal portion, which creates the fistula to the sinus, also prevents further stenosis. We use the inverted distal open strip of the urogenital sinus to create a wet introitus, which at the end of the operation has nearly a 320 degree circumference of epithelial tissue or preputial skin and, therefore, prevents vaginal stenosis.

One of the most important goals of feminizing genitoplasty is to provide sexual satisfaction and normal vaginal delivery. Our patients who have reached puberty have normal appearing external genitalia and clitoris. Only 2 patients had repeat clitomegalia due to inadequate androgen suppression necessitating reoperation to reduce the glandular part of the clitoris. Since none of our children has yet reached the age of sexual relations and childbearing, we cannot assess these results of our technique. However both XY patients with AIS who underwent identical feminizing genitoplasty are now 18 and 22 years old, and report normal and satisfactory intercourse.

Conclusions

Our modification of feminizing genitoplasty enables nearly all children presenting with ambiguous genitalia, 1-stage reconstruction early in life with good cosmetic and functional results. Undoubtedly the outcome of vaginoplasty should be reevaluated later.

Paul McHugh

 **NO**

Surgical Sex

When the practice of sex-change surgery first emerged back in the early 1970s, I would often remind its advocating psychiatrists that with other patients, alcoholics in particular, they would quote the Serenity Prayer, "God, give me the serenity to accept the things I cannot change, the courage to change the things I can, and the wisdom to know the difference." Where did they get the idea that our sexual identity ("gender" was the term they preferred) as men or women was in the category of things that could be changed?

Their regular response was to show me their patients. Men (and until recently they were all men) with whom I spoke before their surgery would tell me that their bodies and sexual identities were at variance. Those I met after surgery would tell me that the surgery and hormone treatments that had made them "women" had also made them happy and contented. None of these encounters were persuasive, however. The post-surgical subjects struck me as caricatures of women. They wore high heels, copious makeup, and flamboyant clothing; they spoke about how they found themselves able to give vent to their natural inclinations for peace, domesticity, and gentleness—but their large hands, prominent Adam's apples, and thick facial features were incongruous (and would become more so as they aged). Women psychiatrists whom I sent to talk with them would intuitively see through the disguise and the exaggerated postures. "Gals know gals," one said to me, "and that's a guy."

The subjects before the surgery struck me as even more strange, as they struggled to convince anyone who might influence the decision for their surgery. First, they spent an unusual amount of time thinking and talking about sex and their sexual experiences; their sexual hungers and adventures seemed to preoccupy them. Second, discussion of babies or children provoked little interest from them; indeed, they seemed indifferent to children. But third, and most remarkable, many of these men-who-claimed-to-be-women reported that they found women sexually attractive and that they saw themselves as "lesbians." When I noted to their champions that their psychological leanings seemed more like those of men than of women, I would get various replies, mostly to the effect that in making such judgments I was drawing on sexual stereotypes.

Until 1975, when I became psychiatrist-in-chief at Johns Hopkins Hospital, I could usually keep my own counsel on these matters. But once I was given authority over all the practices in the psychiatry department I realized that if I

From *First Things*, November 2004, pp. 34–38. Copyright © 2004 by Institute on Religion and Public Life. Reprinted by permission.

were passive I would be tacitly co-opted in encouraging sex-change surgery in the very department that had originally proposed and still defended it. I decided to challenge what I considered to be a misdirection of psychiatry and to demand more information both before and after their operations.

Two issues presented themselves as targets for study. First, I wanted to test the claim that men who had undergone sex-change surgery found resolution for their many general psychological problems. Second (and this was more ambitious), I wanted to see whether male infants with ambiguous genitalia who were being surgically transformed into females and raised as girls did, as the theory (again from Hopkins) claimed, settle easily into the sexual identity that was chosen for them. These claims had generated the opinion in psychiatric circles that one's "sex" and one's "gender" were distinct matters, sex being genetically and hormonally determined from conception, while gender was culturally shaped by the actions of family and others during childhood.

The first issue was easier and required only that I encourage the ongoing research of a member of the faculty who was an accomplished student of human sexual behavior. The psychiatrist and psychoanalyst Jon Meyer was already developing a means of following up with adults who received sex-change operations at Hopkins in order to see how much the surgery had helped them. He found that most of the patients he tracked down some years after their surgery were contented with what they had done and that only a few regretted it. But in every other respect, they were little changed in their psychological condition. They had much the same problems with relationships, work, and emotions as before. The hope that they would emerge now from their emotional difficulties to flourish psychologically had not been fulfilled.

We saw the results as demonstrating that just as these men enjoyed cross-dressing as women before the operation so they enjoyed cross-living after it. But they were no better in their psychological integration or any easier to live with. With these facts in hand I concluded that Hopkins was fundamentally cooperating with a mental illness. We psychiatrists, I thought, would do better to concentrate on trying to fix their minds and not their genitalia.

Thanks to this research, Dr. Meyer was able to make some sense of the mental disorders that were driving this request for unusual and radical treatment. Most of the cases fell into one of two quite different groups. One group consisted of conflicted and guilt-ridden homosexual men who saw a sex-change as a way to resolve their conflicts over homosexuality by allowing them to behave sexually as females with men. The other group, mostly older men, consisted of heterosexual (and some bisexual) males who found intense sexual arousal in cross-dressing as females. As they had grown older, they had become eager to add more verisimilitude to their costumes and either sought or had suggested to them a surgical transformation that would include breast implants, penile amputation, and pelvic reconstruction to resemble a woman.

Further study of similar subjects in the psychiatric services of the Clark Institute in Toronto identified these men by the auto-arousal they experienced in imitating sexually seductive females. Many of them imagined that their displays might be sexually arousing to onlookers, especially to females. This idea, a form of "sex in the head" (D. H. Lawrence), was what provoked their first adventure in dressing up in women's undergarments and had eventually led them toward the surgical option. Because most of them found women to be the objects of their interest they identified themselves to the psychiatrists as lesbians. The name eventually coined in Toronto to describe this form of sexual misdirection was "autogynephilia." Once again I concluded that to provide a surgical alteration to the body of these unfortunate people was to collaborate with a mental disorder rather than to treat it.

This information and the improved understanding of what we had been doing led us to stop prescribing sex-change operations for adults at Hopkins— much, I'm glad to say, to the relief of several of our plastic surgeons who had previously been commandeered to carry out the procedures. And with this solution to the first issue I could turn to the second—namely, the practice of surgically assigning femaleness to male newborns who at birth had mal-formed, sexually ambiguous genitalia and severe phallic defects. This prac-tice, more the province of the pediatric department than of my own, was nonetheless of concern to psychiatrists because the opinions generated around these cases helped to form the view that sexual identity was a matter of cultural conditioning rather than something fundamental to the human constitution.

Several conditions, fortunately rare, can lead to the misconstruction of the genito-urinary tract during embryonic life. When such a condition occurs in a male, the easiest form of plastic surgery by far, with a view to correcting the abnormality and gaining a cosmetically satisfactory appearance, is to remove all the male parts, including the testes, and to construct from the tis-sues available a labial and vaginal configuration. This action provides these malformed babies with female-looking genital anatomy regardless of their genetic sex. Given the claim that the sexual identity of the child would easily follow the genital appearance if backed up by familial and cultural support, the pediatric surgeons took to constructing female-like genitalia for both females with an XX chromosome constitution and males with an XY so as to make them all look like little girls, and they were to be raised as girls by their parents.

All this was done of course with consent of the parents who, distressed by these grievous malformations in their newborns, were persuaded by the pediatric endocrinologists and consulting psychologists to accept transforma-tional surgery for their sons. They were told that their child's sexual identity (again his "gender") would simply conform to environmental conditioning. If the parents consistently responded to the child as a girl now that his genital structure resembled a girl's, he would accept that role without much travail.

This proposal presented the parents with a critical decision. The doctors increased the pressure behind the proposal by noting to the parents that a decision had to be made promptly because a child's sexual identity settles in by about age two or three. The process of inducing the child into the female role should start immediately, with name, birth certificate, baby paraphernalia, etc. With the surgeons ready and the physicians confident, the parents were faced with an offer difficult to refuse (although, interestingly, a few parents did refuse this advice and decided to let nature take its course).

I thought these professional opinions and the choices being pressed on the parents rested upon anecdotal evidence that was hard to verify and even harder to replicate. Despite the confidence of their advocates, they lacked substantial empirical support. I encouraged one of our resident psychiatrists, "William G. Reiner (already interested in the subject because prior to his psychiatric training he had been a pediatric urologist and had witnessed the problem from the other side), to set about doing a systematic follow-up of these children—particularly the males transformed into females in infancy—so as to determine just how sexually integrated they became as adults.

The results here were even more startling than in Meyer's work. Reiner picked out for intensive study cloacal exstrophy, because it would best test the idea that cultural influence plays the foremost role in producing sexual identity. Cloacal exstrophy is an embryonic misdirection that produces a gross abnormality of pelvic anatomy such that the bladder and the genitalia are badly deformed at birth. The male penis fails to form and the bladder and urinary tract are not separated distinctly from the gastrointestinal tract. But crucial to Reiner's study is the fact that the embryonic development of these unfortunate males is not hormonally different from that of normal males. They develop within a male-typical prenatal hormonal milieu provided by their Y chromosome and by their normal testicular function. This exposes these growing embryos/fetuses to the male hormone testosterone—just like all males in their mother's womb.

Although animal research had long since shown that male sexual behavior was directly derived from this exposure to testosterone during embryonic life, this fact did not deter the pediatric practice of surgically treating male infants with this grievous anomaly by castration (amputating their testes and any vestigial male genital structures) and vaginal construction, so that they could be raised as girls. This practice had become almost universal by the mid-1970s. Such cases offered Reiner the best test of the two aspects of the doctrine underlying such treatment: (1) that humans at birth are neutral as to their sexual identity, and (2) that for humans it is the postnatal, cultural, nonhormonal influences, especially those of early childhood, that most influence their ultimate sexual identity. Males with cloacal exstrophy were regularly altered surgically to resemble females, and their parents were instructed to raise them as girls. But would the fact that they had had the full testosterone exposure in utero defeat the attempt to raise them as girls? Answers might become evident with the careful follow-up that Reiner was launching.

Before describing his results, I should note that the doctors proposing this treatment for the males with cloacal exstrophy understood and acknowledged that they were introducing a number of new and severe physical problems for these males. These infants, of course, had no ovaries, and their testes were surgically amputated, which meant that they had to receive exogenous hormones for life. They would also be denied by the same surgery any opportunity for fertility later on. One could not ask the little patient about his willingness to pay this price. These were considered by the physicians advising the parents to be acceptable burdens to bear in order to avoid distress in childhood about malformed genital structures, and it was hoped that they could follow a conflict-free direction in their maturation as girls and women.

Reiner, however, discovered that such re-engineered males were almost never comfortable as females once they became aware of themselves and the world. From the start of their active play life, they behaved spontaneously like boys and were obviously different from their sisters and other girls, enjoying rough-and-tumble games but not dolls and "playing house." Later on, most of those individuals who learned that they were actually genetic males wished to reconstitute their lives as males (some even asked for surgical reconstruction and male hormone replacement)—and all this despite the earnest efforts by their parents to treat them as girls.

Reiner's results, reported in the January 22, 2004, issue of the *New England Journal of Medicine,* are worth recounting. He followed up sixteen genetic males with cloacal exstrophy seen at Hopkins, of whom fourteen underwent neonatal assignment to femaleness socially, legally, and surgically. The other two parents refused the advice of the pediatricians and raised their sons as boys. Eight of the fourteen subjects assigned to be females had since declared themselves to be male. Five were living as females, and one lived with unclear sexual identity.

The two raised as males had remained male. All sixteen of these people had interests that were typical of males, such as hunting, ice hockey, karate, and bobsledding. Reiner concluded from this work that the sexual identity followed the genetic constitution. Male-type tendencies (vigorous play, sexual arousal by females, and physical aggressiveness) followed the testosterone-rich intrauterine fetal development of the people he studied, regardless of efforts to socialize them as females after birth.

Having looked at the Reiner and Meyer studies, we in the Johns Hopkins Psychiatry Department eventually concluded that human sexual identity is mostly built into our constitution by the genes we inherit and the embryo-genesis we undergo. Male hormones sexualize the brain and the mind. Sexual dysphoria—a sense of disquiet in one's sexual role—naturally occurs amongst those rare males who are raised as females in an effort to correct an infantile genital structural problem. A seemingly similar disquiet can be socially induced in apparently constitutionally normal males, in association with (and presumably prompted by) serious behavioral aberrations, amongst which are conflicted homosexual orientations and the remarkable male deviation now called autogynephilia.

Quite clearly, then, we psychiatrists should work to discourage those adults who seek surgical sex reassignment. When Hopkins announced that it would stop doing these procedures in adults with sexual dysphoria, many other hospitals followed suit, but some medical centers still carry out this surgery. Thailand has several centers that do the surgery "no questions asked" for any-one with the money to pay for it and the means to travel to Thailand. I am dis-appointed but not surprised by this, given that some surgeons and medical centers can be persuaded to carry out almost any kind of surgery when pressed by patients with sexual deviations, especially if those patients find a psychiatrist to vouch for them. The most astonishing example is the surgeon in England who is prepared to amputate the legs of patients who claim to find sexual excitement in gazing at and exhibiting stumps of amputated legs. At any rate, we at Hopkins hold that official psychiatry has good evidence to argue against this kind of treatment and should begin to close down the practice everywhere.

For children with birth defects the most rational approach at this moment is to correct promptly any of the major urological defects they face, but to postpone any decision about sexual identity until much later, while raising the child according to its genetic sex. Medical caretakers and parents can strive to make the child aware that aspects of sexual identity will emerge as he or she grows. Settling on what to do about it should await maturation and the child's appreciation of his or her own identity.

Proper care, including good parenting, means helping the child through the medical and social difficulties presented by the genital anatomy but in the process protecting what tissues can be retained, in particular the gonads. This effort must continue to the point where the child can see the problem of a life role more clearly as a sexually differentiated individual emerges from within. Then as the young person gains a sense of responsibility for the result, he or she can be helped through any surgical constructions that are desired. Genuine informed consent derives only from the person who is going to live with the outcome and cannot rest upon the decisions of others who believe they "know best." . . .

Much of the enthusiasm for the quick-fix approach to birth defects expired when the anecdotal evidence about the much-publicized case of a male twin raised as a girl proved to be bogus. The psychologist in charge hid, by actually misreporting, the news that the boy, despite the efforts of his parents to treat him and raise him as a girl, had constantly challenged their treatment of him, ultimately found out about the deception, and restored himself as a male. Sadly, he carried an additional diagnosis of major depression and ultimately committed suicide.

I think the issue of sex-change for males is no longer one in which much can be said for the other side. But I have learned from the experience that the toughest challenge is trying to gain agreement to seek empirical evidence for opinions about sex and sexual behavior, even when the opinions seem on their face unreasonable. One might expect that those who claim that sexual identity has no biological or physical basis would bring forth more evidence to persuade others. But as I've learned, there is a deep prejudice in favor of the idea that nature is totally malleable.

Without any fixed position on what is given in human nature, any manipulation of it can be defended as legitimate. A practice that appears to give people what they want—and what some of them are prepared to clamor for—turns out to be difficult to combat with ordinary professional experience and wisdom. Even controlled trials or careful follow-up studies to ensure that the practice itself is not damaging are often resisted and the results rejected.

I have witnessed a great deal of damage from sex-reassignment. The children transformed from their male constitution into female roles suffered prolonged distress and misery as they sensed their natural attitudes. Their parents usually lived with guilt over their decisions—second-guessing themselves and somewhat ashamed of the fabrication, both surgical and social, they had imposed on their sons. As for the adults who came to us claiming to have discovered their "true" sexual identity and to have heard about sex-change operations, we psychiatrists have been distracted from studying the causes and natures of their mental misdirections by preparing them for surgery and for a life in the other sex. We have wasted scientific and technical resources and damaged our professional credibility by collaborating with madness rather than trying to study, cure, and ultimately prevent it.

POSTSCRIPT

Should Parents Surgically Alter Their Intersex Infants?

Regardless of whether parents choose to alter their child's ambiguous genitalia or whether they choose to let their child decide later in life whether or not to have surgery, the experience of having an infant with ambiguous genitalia usually takes parents by surprise. For many parents, especially those who have little or no information about ambiguous genitalia, the experience can be quite alarming to them. Other parents struggle with the decisions but in the end feel good about the choices they make.

The support for assigning a sex surgically seems to be based in a portion of society's strong viewpoints on the role penis size plays in not just being able to define a child as male but also in a male child's sense of his own "maleness." In fact, nearly all infants born with ambiguous genitalia whose biological sex is determined surgically are made female because, quite simply, the surgery is better and easier. Moreover, parents and medical professionals alike struggle with the implications of a male child born with a micropenis. It is clear that some adults are motivated strongly by trying to avoid embarrassment for their male child. It would be better, they feel, to create a girl rather than leave an intact boy with an "inferior" penis.

Thirty years ago, the standard operating procedure was to select a biological sex at birth based on genital appearance alone. Today, with greater capacity for chromosomal and other types of testing, many medical professionals and associations are taking a much more conservative approach to dealing with a child born with ambiguous genitalia. Diamond and Sigmundson suggest the following guidelines for working with infants with ambiguous genitalia:

- **A complete physical is necessary.** This includes, they suggest, taking a thorough history of the patient's family. The physical should look not just at the external genitalia but also at the internal systems as they exist, at genetic structures, and at the endocrine system. They argue that many cases of intersexuality go undetected. This can avoid surprises and additional challenges later in the child's life.
- **Parents should be given full information on intersexuality and start being counseled immediately.** Intersexuality is among many conditions where medical professionals often withhold information until the final outcome and conclusions are drawn. Diamond and Sigmundson recommend full disclosure from the onset and immediate and ongoing counseling to help parents understand what intersexuality is, that they are not alone, and that many people with ambiguous genitalia grow up to live happy lives.

- **Medical professionals need to respect confidentiality, even within the hospital setting.** While giving the family the clear message that having an intersex child is nothing to be embarrassed about, medical professionals must be careful about not treating the family as a novelty.
- **Assign sex based on the most likely outcome.** This is an important distinction to make for parents who may have felt ambivalent about having a child of one sex versus the other. If they are disappointed with a child of one sex and would prefer to have the other, they must understand clearly that having an intersex child is not an opportunity for sex selection and that there is a potentially disastrous outcome if the assignment is based on desire for a son or daughter rather than the child's true nature.

Above all Diamond and Sigmundson discourage medical professionals and parents from opting for genital surgery for cosmetic rather than medical reasons.

Suggested Readings

Lenore Abramsky, Sue Hall, Judith Levitan, and Theresa M. Marteau, "What Parents Are Told After Prenatal Diagnosis of a Sex Chromosome Abnormality: Interview and Questionnaire Study," Available online at http://www.bmj.com/cgi/content/full/322/7284/463.

John Colapinto, *As Nature Made Him: The Boy Who Was Raised as a Girl* (HarperCollins Publishing, 2000).

M. Diamond and K. Sigmundson, "Management of Intersexuality: Guidelines for Dealing With Individuals With Ambiguous Genitalia," *Archives of Pediatrics and Adolescent Medicine* (June 10, 2002).

Alice Domurat Dreger, ed., *Intersex in the Age of Ethics* (University Publishing Group, 1999).

Anne Fausto-Sterling, "The Five Sexes, Revisited," *Sciences* (July 2000).

Anne Fausto-Sterling, *Sexing the Body: Gender Politics and the Construction of Sexuality* (Basic Books, 2000).

Melissa Hendricks, "Into the Hands of Babes," *Johns Hopkins Magazine* (September 2000).

Katherine A. Mason, "The Unkindest Cut: Intersexuals Launch a Movement to Stop Doctors From 'Assigning' Sex With a Scalpel," *New Haven Advocate* (March 29, 2001).

John Money, "Ablatio Penis: Normal Male Infant Sex-Reassigned as a Girl," *Archives of Sexual Behavior* (1975).

E. Nussbaum, "A Question of Gender," *Discover* (January 2000).

ISSUE 10

Should Minors Be Required to Get Their Parents' Permission in Order to Obtain an Abortion?

YES: Teresa Stanton Collett, from Testimony Before the Subcommittee on the Constitution, Committee on the Judiciary, U.S. House of Representatives (September 6, 2001)

NO: Planned Parenthood Federation of America, Inc., from "Fact Sheet: Teenagers, Abortion, and Government Intrusion Laws," Planned Parenthood Federation of America, Inc. (August 1999)

ISSUE SUMMARY

YES: Teresa Stanton Collett, former professor at South Texas College of Law, testifies in front of the U.S. House of Representatives in support of the federal Child Custody Protection Act. She advocates parental involvement in a minor's pregnancy, regardless of the girl's intention to carry or terminate the pregnancy. Parental involvement, Collett maintains, is not punitive; rather, it offers the girl herself additional protection against injury and sexual assault. Minors tend to have less access to information and education than adults; without this information and education, they are not able to provide truly "informed" consent, concludes Collett.

NO: Planned Parenthood Federation of America, Inc., the oldest and largest reproductive health organization in the United States, argues that parental notification and consent laws keep girls from exercising their legal right to access abortion. Notifying parents of their daughter's intent to terminate a pregnancy puts many girls at risk for severe punishment, expulsion from the home, or even physical violence. Planned Parenthood contends that, just as minors have the power to give their consent for other surgical procedures, they should be able to give their own consent to terminate a pregnancy.

In 1973 the United States Supreme Court decision *Roe v. Wade* guaranteed a woman's right to access abortion without restriction during the first trimester. The decision did not mention, however, the age of the woman seeking the abortion. A number of individual states, therefore, have statutes that require a girl under the age of 18 to either receive one or both parents' or legal guardians' consent in order to obtain an abortion, or to notify one or both parents.

A later Supreme Court decision, *Belotti v. Baird*, upheld the rights of states to place these restrictions on girls—provided there is an option for a "judicial bypass." This means that a girl can appear before a judge and either demonstrate that she is mature enough to make the decision to have an abortion or explain why notifying her parents would be detrimental to her. As the *Belotti* decision says, "[if] the court decides the minor is not mature enough to give informed consent, she must be given the opportunity to show that the abortion is in her best interest. If she makes this showing, the court must grant her bypass petition." Confidentiality is guaranteed, so that a girl's parents do not know that she has gone to court. Currently, 35 states have laws on their books about obtaining consent from or notifying at least one parent. Of these, 9 are currently not enforced. Twenty-eight states provide for a judicial bypass.

Any discussions around abortion rights are rooted in the fundamental support or opposition to abortion itself. It can be challenging, therefore, to separate out the question of abortion from the question of whether or not minors can make an informed decision. Even adults who consider themselves to be pro-choice may support an adult woman's right to choose whether to carry or terminate a pregnancy, while feeling differently about girls under the age of 18 being able to make this decision for themselves. Others are clear on their belief that abortion is wrong regardless of the circumstance or age of the girl or woman involved. And still others believe that any girl or woman, regardless of age, is able and has the right to make this personal decision for herself. Many encourage girls considering abortion to talk with their parent(s) or another trusted adult. However, the reality is that many girls know that doing so would create a significant conflict in their family setting.

Specific to the debate around parental notification is the issue of someone other than a parent facilitating an abortion for a girl under the age of 18. Supporters of parental notification laws believe that such legislation would prevent this from happening. Opponents agree that it would, and that it would be wrong to prosecute a family member for helping a niece or granddaughter under the age of 18 obtain an abortion.

In the following selections, Teresa Stanton Collett uses her knowledge of laws in different states to demonstrate what she feels is widespread support for parental involvement laws, focusing in particular on the Child Custody Protection Act. Planned Parenthood Federation of America, Inc., believes that since minors are able to access other medical care without parental consent, an abortion procedure should be no exception.

YES

Teresa Stanton Collett

Prepared Testimony of
Teresa Stanton Collett

UNITED STATES HOUSE OF REPRESENTATIVES
Committee on the Judiciary
Subcommittee on the Constitution
Congressman Steve Chabot, Subcommittee Chair
September 6, 2001

. . . I am honored to have been invited to testify on H.R. 476, the "Child Custody Protection Act." . . . My testimony represents my professional knowledge and opinion as a law professor who writes on the topic of family law, and specifically on the topic of parental involvement laws. It also represents my experience in assisting the legislative sponsors of the Texas Parental Notification Act during the legislative debates prior to passage of the act, and as a member of the Texas Supreme Court Subadvisory Committee charged with proposing court rules implementing the judicial bypass created by the Texas act. . . .

It is my opinion that the Child Custody Protection Act will significantly advance the legitimate health and safety interests of young girls experiencing an unplanned pregnancy. It will also safeguard the ability of states to protect their minor citizens through the adoption of effective parental involvement statutes. . . .

Parental Rights to Control
Medical Care of Minors

Just this past year, in a case involving the competing claims of parents and grandparents to decisionmaking authority over a child, the United States Supreme Court described parents' right to control the care of their children as "perhaps the oldest of the fundamental liberty interests recognized by this Court." In addressing the right of parents to direct the medical care of their children, the Court has stated:

> Our jurisprudence historically has reflected Western civilization concepts of the family as a unit with broad parental authority over minor children. Our cases have consistently followed that course; our constitutional system

From *U.N. Convention on the Rights of the Child* by Teresa Stanton Collett, 2001.

long ago rejected any notion that a child is "the mere creature of the State" and, on the contrary, asserted that parents generally "have the right, coupled with the high duty, to recognize and prepare [their children] for additional obligations." *Surely, this includes a "high duty" to recognize symptoms of illness and to seek and follow medical advice. The law's concept of the family rests on a presumption that parents possess what a child lacks in maturity, experience, and capacity for judgment required for making life's difficult decisions.*

It is this need to insure the availability of parental guidance and support that underlies the laws requiring a parent be notified or give consent prior to the performance of an abortion on his or her minor daughter. The national consensus in favor of this position is illustrated by the fact that there are parental involvement laws on the books in forty-three of the fifty states. Of the statutes in these forty-three states, eight have been determined to have state or federal constitutional infirmities. Therefore the laws of thirty-five states are in effect today. Nine of these states have laws that empower abortion providers to decide whether to involve parents or allow notice to or consent from people other than parents or legal guardians. These laws are substantially ineffectual in assuring parental involvement in a minor's decision to obtain an abortion. However, parents in the remaining twenty-six states are effectively guaranteed the right to parental notification or consent in most cases.

Widespread Public Support

There is widespread agreement that as a general rule, parents should be involved in their minor daughter's decision to terminate an unplanned pregnancy. This agreement even extends to young people, ages 18 to 24. To my knowledge, no organizations or individuals, whether abortion rights activists or pro-life advocates, dispute this point. On an issue as contentious and divisive as abortion, it is both remarkable and instructive that there is such firm and long-standing support for laws requiring parental involvement.

Various reasons underlie this broad and consistent support. As Justices O'Connor, Kennedy, and Souter observed in *Planned Parenthood v. Casey,* parental consent and notification laws related to abortions "are based on the quite reasonable assumption that minors will benefit from consultation with their parents and that children will often not realize that their parents have their best interests at heart." This reasoning led the Court to conclude that the Pennsylvania parental consent law was constitutional. Two of the benefits achieved by parental involvement laws include improved medical care for young girls seeking abortions and increased protection against sexual exploitation by adult men.

Improved Medical Care of Minors Seeking Abortions

Medical care for minors seeking abortions is improved by parental involvement in three ways. First, parental involvement laws allow parents to assist their daughter in the selection of a healthcare provider. As with all medical procedures, one of the most important guarantees of patient safety is the professional competence of those who perform the medical procedure or administer the medical treatment. In *Bellotti v. Baird,* the United States Supreme Court acknowledged the superior ability of parents to evaluate and select appropriate abortion providers.

For example, the National Abortion Federation recommends that patients seeking an abortion confirm that the abortion will be performed by a licensed physician in good standing with the state Board of Medical Examiners, and that he or she have admitting privileges at a local hospital not more than twenty minutes away from the location where the abortion is to occur. A well-informed parent seeking to guide her child is more likely to inquire regarding these matters than a panicky teen who just wants to no longer be pregnant.

Parental involvement laws also insure that parents have the opportunity to provide additional medical history and information to abortion providers prior to performance of the abortion.

> The medical, emotional, and psychological consequences of an abortion are serious and can be lasting; this is particularly so when the patient is immature. An adequate medical and psychological case history is important to the physician. Parents can provide medical and psychological data, refer the physician to other sources of medical history, such as family physicians, and authorize family physicians to give relevant data.

Abortion providers, in turn, will have the opportunity to disclose the medical risks of the various procedures to an adult who can advise the girl in giving her informed consent to the procedure ultimately selected. Parental notification or consent laws insure that the abortion providers inform a mature adult of the risks and benefits of the proposed treatment, after having received a more complete and thus more accurate medical history of the patient.

The third way in which parental involvement improves medical treatment of pregnant minors is by insuring that parents have adequate knowledge to recognize and respond to any post-abortion complication that may develop. In a recent ruling by a Florida intermediate appellate court upholding that state's parental involvement law, the court observed:

> The State proved that appropriate aftercare is critical in avoiding or responding to post-abortion complications. Abortion is ordinarily an invasive surgical procedure attended by many of the risks accompanying surgical procedures generally. If post-abortion nausea, tenderness, swelling, bleeding, or cramping persists or suddenly worsens, a minor (like an adult) may need medical attention. A guardian unaware that her ward or a parent unaware that his minor daughter has undergone an abortion will be at a serious disadvantage in caring for her if complications develop. An adult who has been kept in the dark cannot, moreover, assist the minor in following the abortion provider's instructions for post-surgical care. Failure to follow such instructions can increase the risk of complications. As the plaintiffs' medical experts conceded, the risks are significant in the best of circumstances. While abortion is less risky than some surgical procedures, abortion complications can result in serious injury, infertility, and even death.

Abortion proponents often claim that abortion is one of the safest surgical procedures performed today. However, the actual rate of many complications is simply unknown. At least one American court has held that a perforated uterus is a "normal risk" associated with abortion. Untreated, a perforated uterus may result in an infection, complicated by fever, endometritis, and parametritis. "The risk of death from postabortion sepsis [infection] is highest for young women, those who are unmarried, and those who undergo procedures that do not directly evacuate the contents of the uterus. . . . A delay in treatment allows the infection to progress to bacteremia, pelvic abscess, septic pelvic thrombophlebitis, disseminated intravascular coagulophy, septic shock, renal failure, and death."

Without the knowledge that their daughter has had an abortion, parents are incapable of insuring that the minor obtain routine post-operative care or of providing an adequate medical history to physicians called upon to treat any complications the girl might experience.

Increased Protection From Sexual Assault

In addition to improving the medical care received by young girls dealing with an unplanned pregnancy, parental involvement laws are intended to afford increased protection against sexual exploitation of minors by adult men. National studies reveal that "[a]lmost two thirds of adolescent mothers have partners older than 20 years of age." In a study of over 46,000 pregnancies by school-age girls in California, researchers found that "71%, or over 33,000, were fathered by adult post-high-school men whose mean age was 22.6 years, an average of 5 years older than the mothers. . . . Even among junior high school mothers aged 15 or younger, most births are fathered by adult men 6–7 years their senior. *Men aged 25 or older father more births among California school-age girls than do boys under age 18.*" Other studies have found that most teenage pregnancies are the result of predatory practices by men who are substantially older.

Abortion providers have resisted any reporting obligation to insure that men who unlawfully impregnate minors are identified and prosecuted. Just [recently] a lawsuit was filed in Arizona alleging that Planned Parenthood failed to report the sexual molestation of a twelve-year-old leading to her continued molestation and impregnation. If true, this conduct is consistent with the position of many abortion providers who argue that encouraging medical care through insuring confidentiality is more important than insuring legal intervention to stop the sexual abuse. While seemingly well intentioned, this reasoning fails since the ultimate result of this approach is to merely address a symptom of the sexual abuse (the pregnancy) while leaving the cause unaffected. The minor, no longer pregnant, then returns to the abusive relationship, with no continuing contact with an adult (other than the abuser) knowing of her plight. The clinic won't tell, the police and parents don't know, and the girl, still under the abuser's influence, is too confused or afraid to tell. . . .

States adopting parental involvement laws have come to the reasonable conclusion that secret abortions do not advance the best interests of most minor girls. This is particularly reasonable in light of the fact that most teen pregnancies are the result of sexual relations with adult men, and many of these relationships involve criminal conduct. Parental involvement laws insure that parents have the opportunity to protect their daughters from those who would victimize their daughters again and again and again. The Child Custody Protection Act would insure that men cannot deprive these minors of this protection by merely crossing state lines.

Effectiveness of Judicial Bypass

In those few cases where it is not in the girl's best interest to disclose her pregnancy to her parents, state laws generally provide the pregnant minor the option of seeking a court determination that either involvement of the girl's parent is not in her best interest, or that she is sufficiently mature to make decisions regarding the continuation of her pregnancy. This is a requirement for parental consent laws under existing United States Supreme Court cases, and courts have been quick to overturn laws omitting adequate bypass.

Opponents of the Child Custody Protection Act have argued that its passage would endanger teens since parents may be abusive and many teens would seek illegal abortions. This is a phantom fear. Parental involvement laws are on the books in over two-thirds of the states, some for over twenty-years, and there is no case where it has been established that these laws led to parental abuse or to self-inflicted injury. Similarly, there is no evidence that these laws have led to an increase in illegal abortions.

It [is] often asserted that parental involvement laws do not increase the number of parents notified of their daughters' intentions to obtain abortions, since minors will commonly seek judicial bypass of the parental involvement requirement. Assessing the accuracy of this claim is difficult since parental notification or consent laws rarely impose reporting requirements regarding the use of judicial bypass. The Idaho parental consent law enacted in 2000 is one of the few exceptions to this general rule. Based upon the reporting required under that law, no abortions obtained by minors were pursuant to a judicial bypass. From September 1, 2000 through April 3, 2001, thirty-three minors have been reported as obtaining an abortion in Idaho. Thirty-one of these abortions were performed after obtaining parental consent. One minor was legally emancipated and did not need parental consent, and one report did not indicate the nature of the consent obtained prior to performance of the abortion.

Obtaining comparable information in states having parental involvement laws with no mandatory reporting requirement is difficult. State agencies will not accumulate such information absent a legislative mandate. Nonetheless, it is safe to say that the use of judicial bypass to avoid parental involvement varies significantly among the states. While commonly used in Massachusetts, judicial bypass is seldom used in many states. In 1999, 1,015 girls got abortions in Alabama with a parent's approval and 12 with a judge's approval, according to state health department records. Indiana also has few bypass proceedings according to an informal study. In Pennsylvania, approximately 13,700 minors obtained abortions from 1994 through 1999. Of these only about seven percent or 1,000 girls bypassed parental involvement via court order. Texas implemented its Parental Notification Act in 2000. During the state legislative hearings, the Texas Family Planning Council submitted a study indicating that a parent accompanied 69% of minors seeking abortions in Texas. After passage of the Texas Parental Notification Act, 96% of all minors seeking an abortion in Texas involved a parent.

Conclusion

By passage of the Child Custody Protection Act, Congress will protect the ability of the citizens in each state to determine the proper level of parental involvement in the lives of young girls facing an unplanned pregnancy.

Experience in states having parental involvement laws has shown that, when notified, parents and their daughters unite in a desire to resolve issues surrounding an unplanned pregnancy. If the minor chooses to terminate the pregnancy, parents can assist their daughters in selecting competent abortion providers, and abortion providers may receive more comprehensive medical histories of their parents. In these cases, the minors will more likely be encouraged to obtain post-operative check-ups, and parents will be prepared to respond to any complications that arise.

If the minor chooses to continue her pregnancy, involvement of her parents serves many of the same goals. Parents can provide or help obtain the necessary resources for early and comprehensive prenatal care. They can assist their daughters in evaluating the options of single parenthood, adoption, or early marriage. Perhaps most importantly, they can provide the love and support that is found in the many healthy families of the United States.

Regardless of whether the girl chooses to continue or terminate her pregnancy, parental involvement laws have proven desirable because they afford greater protection for the many girls who are pregnant due to sexual assault. By insuring that parents know of the pregnancy, it becomes much more likely that they will intervene to insure the protection of their daughters from future assaults.

In balancing the minor's right to privacy and her need for parental involvement, the majority of states have determined that parents should know before abortions are performed on minors. This is a reasonable conclusion and well within the states' police powers. However, the political authority of each state stops at its geographic boundaries. States need the assistance of the federal government to insure that the protection they wish to afford their children is not easily circumvented by strangers taking minors across state lines.

The Child Custody Protection Act has the unique virtue of building upon two of the few points of agreement in the national debate over abortion: the desirability of parental involvement in a minor's decisions about an unplanned pregnancy, and the need to protect the physical health and safety of the pregnant girl. I urge members of this committee to vote for its passage.

⮕ **NO**

Fact Sheet: Teenagers, Abortion, and Government Intrusion Laws

Of all the abortion-related policy issues facing decision-makers in this country today, parental consent or notification before a minor may obtain an abortion is one of the most difficult. Few would deny that most teenagers, especially younger ones, would benefit from adult guidance when faced with an unwanted pregnancy. Few would deny that such guidance ideally should come from the teenager's parents. Unfortunately, we do not live in an ideal world. For a variety of reasons, including fear of parental maltreatment or abuse, teenagers frequently cannot tell their parents about their pregnancies or planned abortions.

In the 34 states with laws in effect that mandate the involvement of at least one parent in the abortion decision, teenagers who cannot tell their parents must either travel out of state or obtain approval from a judge—known as a "judicial bypass" procedure—to obtain an abortion. The result is almost always a delay that can increase both the cost of the abortion and the physical and emotional health risk to the teenager, since an earlier abortion is a safer one (Paul et al., 1999).

Currently, anti-choice members of Congress are seeking to make it even more difficult for minors living in states with mandatory parental involvement laws to obtain an abortion with the so-called "Child Custody Protection Act" (CCPA). The bill would make it a federal crime to transport a minor across state lines for an abortion unless the parental involvement requirements of her home state had been met. If the bill were enacted, persons convicted would be subject to imprisonment, fines, and civil suits (H. R. 1755, 2003; S. 851, 2003).

Requiring Parental Consent for Abortion Is Not Consistent with State Laws Regulating a Range of Medical Services for Minors

Proponents of mandated parental involvement contend that parents have a right to decide what medical services their minor children receive. However, states have long recognized that many minors have the capacity to consent to their own medical care and that, in certain critical areas such as mental health, drug and/or alcohol addiction, treatment for sexually transmitted infections (STIs), and pregnancy, entitlement to confidential care is a public health necessity (Donovan, 1998).

- Twenty-one states and the District of Columbia grant all minors the authority to consent to contraceptive services. Approximately eleven other states grant most minors this authority (AGI, 2004a).
- Thirty-four states and the District of Columbia authorize a pregnant minor to obtain prenatal care and delivery services without parental consent or notification (AGI, 2004b).
- All 50 states and the District of Columbia give minors the authority to consent to the diagnosis and treatment of sexually transmitted infections (AGI, 2004c).

Many of these laws allow minors to give consent to treatments that involve greater medical risk than a first-trimester abortion, such as surgical interventions during pregnancy and cesarean sections. Nevertheless, many of these same states require parental consent for abortion.

Most Teenagers Having Abortions Already Involve Their Parents, Even When Not Required To Do So By Law, and Many have Compelling Reasons to Seek Confidential Services

A minority of teenagers do not involve their parents. Overwhelmingly, they make this decision for compelling reasons. A 1991 study of unmarried minors having abortions in states without parental involvement laws found that

- Sixty-one percent of the respondents reported that at least one of their parents knew about their abortion.
- Of those minors who did not inform their parents of their abortions, 30 percent had histories of violence in their families, feared the occurrence of violence, or were afraid of being forced to leave their homes.
- Minors who did not tell their parents were also disproportionately older (aged 16 or 17) and employed.
- Among the respondents who did not inform their parents of their pregnancies, all consulted someone in addition to clinic staff about their abortions, such as their boyfriend (89 percent), an adult (52 percent), or a professional (22 percent) (Henshaw & Kost, 1992)

Lack of Confidential Reproductive Health Care Harms Teenagers

Evidence suggests that lack of confidentiality in accessing sexual health care services severely delays or even curtails minors' use of those services. A survey of abortion patients around the U.S., conducted by the Alan Guttmacher Institute (AGI), found that 63% of minors who were having later abortions (after 16 weeks' gestation) cited fear of telling their parents as reason for the delay (Torres & Forrest, 1988). In August 2002, the *Journal of the American Medical Association* published a study of minors seeking sexual health care services at

Planned Parenthood health centers in Wisconsin. Nearly half (47%) of the respondents reported that they would discontinue use of all Planned Parenthood services if their parents were notified that they were seeking prescription contraceptives. An additional 12% would delay or discontinue using specific sexual health care services if parental notification were required. But only one percent said they would stop having vaginal intercourse (Reddy et al., 2002).

Experience shows that teenagers who cannot involve their parents in their abortion services suffer harm in states with mandatory parental consent and notice laws. Whether they travel to other states or obtain judicial approval, the results are the same: delays that can greatly increase both the physical and emotional health risks as well as the costs.

- While nationwide most minors seeking judicial approval receive it, the process is unwieldy and, most importantly, time-consuming. Court proceedings in Minnesota routinely delayed abortions by more than one week, and sometimes up to three weeks (ACLU, 1986). . . .
- Studies conducted in Pennsylvania and Alabama found that the vast majority of courts in those states were unprepared to implement the judicial bypass. Some court officials had not even heard of the laws, despite the fact that they had been in effect for several years (Silverstein, 1999; Silverstein and Speitzel, 2002).
- The manner in which each state enforces its judicial bypass laws is erratic. In Minnesota, the federal district court found that the state courts "denied only an infinitesimal proportion of the petitions brought since 1981" (ACLU, 1986). A study in Massachusetts found that only nine of the 477 abortion requests studied had been denied (Yates & Pliner, 1988). However, an Ohio report found that the percentage of waivers denied ranged from 100 percent to 2 percent, depending on the county in which the petition was filed (Rollenhagen, 1992).

Some states go as far as to require the involvement of both parents. These statutes ignore the realities of teenagers' lives.

- In 2000, approximately 19 million children under the age of 18 lived with only one parent. Nearly three million more lived with neither parent (U.S. Census Bureau, 2001a). . . .
- Millions of children live with a single parent subsequent to divorce. In 2000, 54 percent of single parents with children under the age of 18 were divorced or separated (U.S. Census Bureau, 2001b). A study found that one-third of divorced fathers had no contact with their children during the previous year (Doherty et al., 1998).
- In Minnesota, more than one-quarter of the teenagers who sought judicial bypass were accompanied by one parent, who was most often divorced or separated. According to the federal district court that reviewed Minnesota's law, many of the custodial parents feared that notification would "bring the absent parent back into the family in an intrusive and abusive way" (*Hodgson v. Minnesota,* 1986).

Moreover, even if a teenager is able and willing to involve one or both parents, the procedures required by some state parental consent or notification laws make compliance impossible or difficult.

- Requiring that teenagers either obtain notarized evidence that parents have been notified or present a death certificate for a deceased parent may present impossible logistical barriers, lead to breaches of confidentiality for parents and teenagers, or cause serious delay.
- A requirement that the physician personally locate and notify the parents could easily both delay the procedure and increase the cost.

The Child Custody Protection Act Harms Minors

In April 2003, the CCPA was reintroduced in the House of Representatives and the Senate. The bill would make it a federal crime to transport a minor across state lines to obtain abortion services without fulfilling the parental consent or notice requirements of her home state. In 1998, the House of Representatives passed the bill by a vote of 276 to 150, but President Clinton threatened to veto it, and the Senate never took it up for consideration (Eilperin, 1999). In 1999, the House Judiciary Committee passed the CCPA, defeating five proposed amendments, including those that would create exceptions for grandparents, siblings, aunts and uncles, and clergy who assist minors in obtaining abortions (Superville, 1999). That year, the legislation passed in the full House of Representatives again, this time by a vote of 270 to 159. However, the Senate again failed to take it up for consideration. Although, if passed, the Act would only affect a small percentage of women seeking abortion services—minors account for fewer than one in 10 abortions performed—the impact of the Act would be dramatic.

- The CCPA would subject criminal penalties to anyone—a grandparent, adult sibling, member of the clergy, or medical professional—who assists a minor in traveling across state lines to receive an abortion without the parental consent or notification required by her home state.
- CCPA makes such assistance a crime even if confidential abortions are legal in the state where the abortion is to be performed and even if that state allows the accompanying grandparent or adult sibling to give lawful consent for the minor's abortion.
- CCPA thus isolates young women from the trusted friends and relatives who can assist them in time of crisis.
- The CCPA makes criminals out of family members and friends even in emergency situations when the minor needs an immediate abortion to protect her health.
- The CCPA potentially requires a minor to satisfy differing legal requirements in two states: the state she comes from and the state where she is to have the abortion. If those two states both have parental consent or notice requirements, the minor may have to seek waivers from judges in two states, further delaying her abortion and raising its costs and health risks.
- Because 87% of U.S. counties lack an abortion provider (Finer & Henshaw, 2003), CCPA will increase the burdens on the many young women who must cross state lines simply to access the *nearest* abortion provider.
- The CCPA also raises a number of other constitutional and legal questions, particularly those related to issues of federalism. The legislation effectively nullifies the laws of those states that allow physicians to provide confidential services to minors who enter the states for abortion

and deprives individuals of their right to cross state lines to obtain lawful services. Such intervention by the federal government would be unprecedented, and raises serious implications for states, and individuals' rights (Saul, 1998).

Cited References

ACLU–American Civil Liberties Union Foundation Reproductive Freedom Project. (1986). *Parental Consent Laws: Their Catastrophic Impact on Teenagers Right to Abortion.* New York: ACLU.

AGI–Alan Guttmacher Institute. (2003a, accessed May 28). *Minors Access to Contraceptive Services* [Online]. . . .

_____. (2004b, accessed July 29). *Minors' Access to Prenatal Care. State Policies in Brief.* [Online]. . . .

_____. (2004c, accessed July 29). *Minors' Access to STD Services* [Online]. . . .

CDC–Centers for Disease Control and Prevention. (2003, accessed May 28). *Unmarried Childbearing* [Online]. . . . *Child Custody Protection Act*, H. R. 1755, 108th Cong., 1st Sess. (2003).

_____, S.851, 108th Cong., 1st Sess. (2003).

Doherty, William J., et al. (1998). "Responsible Fathering: An Overview and Conceptual Framework." *Journal of Marriage and the Family*, 60(2), 277–292.

Donovan, Patricia. (1998). "Teenagers' Right to Consent to Reproductive Health Care." *Issues in Brief*. Washington, DC: Alan Guttmacher Institute.

Eilperin, Juliet. (1999, July 1). "House Acts to Bar Interstate Transport of Teens to Evade Abortion Laws." *Washington Post*, p. A06.

Henshaw, Stanley K. (1998). "Abortion Incidence and Services in the United States, 1995–1996." *Family Planning Perspectives*, 30(6), 263–270 & 287.

Henshaw, Stanley K. & Kathryn Kost. (1992). "Parental Involvement in Minors' Abortion Decisions." *Family Planning Perspectives*, 24(5), 196–207 & 213.

Hodgson v. Minnesota, 648 F. Supp. 756 (D. Minn. 1986).

Paul, Maureen, *et al.* (1999). *A Clinician's Guide to Medical and Surgical Abortion.* New York: Churchill Livingstone.

Reddy, Diane M., *et al.* (2002). "Effect of Mandatory Parental Notification on Adolescent Girls' Use of Sexual Health Care Services." *Journal of the American Medical Association*, 288(6), 710–14.

Rollenhagen, Mark. (1992, June 18). "Clinics Fight Notification Rule By Filing Suit." *Plain Dealer*, p. 1C.

Saul, Rebekah. (1998). "The Child Custody Protection Act: A 'Minor' Issue at the Top of the Anti-abortion Agenda." *Guttmacher Report on Public Policy*, 1(4), 1–2 & 7.

Silverstein, Helena. (1999). "Road Closed: Evaluating the Judicial Bypass Provision of the Pennsylvania Abortion Control Act." *Law & Social Inquiry*, 24(Winter), 73–96.

Silverstein, Helena & Leanne Speitel. (2002). "'Honey, I Have No Idea': Court Readiness to Handle Petitions to Waive Parental Consent for Abortion." *Iowa Law Review*, 88(1), 75–120.

Superville, Darlene. (1999, June 23, accessed 1999, July 1). "Teen Abortion Bill Clears House Committee." [Online]. *Associated Press*.

U.S. Census Bureau. (2001a, accessed 2003, May 28). *Household Relationship and Living Arrangements of Children under 18 Years: March 2000* [Online]. . . .

_____. (2001b, accessed 2003, May 28). *One-Parent Family Groups with Own Children Under 18: March 2000* [Online]. . . .

Yates, Suzanne & Anita J. Pliner. (1988). "Judging Maturity in the Courts: The Massachusetts Consent Statute." *American Journal of Public Health*, 78(6), 646–649.

POSTSCRIPT

Should Minors Be Required to Get Their Parents' Permission in Order to Obtain an Abortion?

The abortion debate, like many other controversies, is often viewed in extremes. One is pro-choice, or one is antichoice. There is no gray area in between. At the same time, however, introducing a minor into the discussion often alters the discussion—particularly the younger the girl is who is seeking the abortion. In some cases, the younger a girl is, the more protection adults may feel she needs. In other cases, the younger she is, the more likely some abortion opponents might be to make an exception, citing a preference for the "necessary evil" of abortion over letting a 14-year-old girl become a parent.

An important factor to keep in mind is the fact that not everyone has sexual intercourse by choice. While many abortion opponents will make an exception for pregnancies that are caused by rape or incest, others maintain that a pregnancy is a pregnancy and that no potential life should be punished even if it were conceived in a violent manner. If a state law requires that a parent be notified, and the parent who is notified is the one who caused the pregnancy, then parental notification may have stopped an abortion only to put a girl's safety or life in jeopardy. On the other hand, in cases of incest, parental notification could help to bring rape or incest—which are all too frequently hidden or kept private—out into the open so that it will not happen again, and the perpetrator, if known, can be arrested and the abuse stopped.

Legislating personal decisions is, as always, a slippery slope. How far do we go? How do laws legislating one behavior or type of procedure affect others? For example, parental consent is currently not required in order for a minor to obtain birth control. Controversy remains around one particular type of birth control, Emergency Contraception, formerly known as the "morning-after" pill. Emergency Contraception is not an abortion; it prevents pregnancy from happening. In fact, if a woman is pregnant without knowing it, has unprotected intercourse, and then takes Emergency Contraception, her pregnancy should not be affected by the Emergency Contraception. At the same time, however, since one of the ways in which Emergency Contraception works is by preventing a fertilized egg from implanting, those who believe that life begins at conception argue that Emergency Contraception is the same thing as abortion. Therefore, the door that is open to parental notification and consent laws remains open to support for parental notification or consent before Emergency Contraception can be dispensed. This in turn could lead to legislation requiring parental notification or consent for birth control pills and condoms.

In an ideal world, people would not have sex before they are old enough and established enough in their lives to be able to manage the potential consequences of being in a sexual relationship. In an ideal world, abortion would not be necessary because no pregnancy would be unplanned or come as the result of rape or incest. However, we do not live in an ideal world. People, regardless of age, have unprotected sex or use contraception incorrectly. People, regardless of age, are raped and sexually abused. Women, regardless of age, have pregnancies that may need to be terminated for medical reasons. In some households, the revelation of an unplanned pregnancy can result in violence against the pregnant teen and/or her partner.

Is there a solution between these two extremes that could enable parents to show their care and support of their adolescents while at the same time letting them make their own decisions? Where do your feelings about abortion in general come into play in your thoughts on this matter?

Suggested Readings

American Civil Liberties Union, *Parental Involvement Laws*. Fact sheet available online at http://www.aclu.org/issues/reproduct/parent_ inv.html.

Focus on the Family, "Talking Points for Laws Requiring Parental Involvement in Minor Abortions," *Citizen Link* (2000). Available online at http://www.family.org/cforum/research/papers/a0012619. html.

David J. Garrow, *Liberty and Sexuality: The Right to Privacy and the Making of Roe v. Wade* (University of California Press, 1998).

Deborah Haas-Wilson, "The Impact of State Abortion Restrictions on Minors' Demand for Abortions," *Journal of Human Resources* (vol. 31, no. 1, January 1999).

N. E. H. Hull and Peter Charles Hoffer, *Roe v. Wade: The Abortion Rights Controversy in American History* (University Press of Kansas, 2001).

NARAL, *Government-Mandated Parental Involvement in Family Planning Services Threatens Young People's Health*. Fact sheet available online at http://www.naral.org/mediaresources/fact/parental.html.

Annette Tomal, "Parental Involvement Laws and Minor and Non-Minor Teen Abortion and Birth Rates," *Journal of Family and Economic Issues* (vol. 20, no. 2, Summer 1999).

Internet References . . .

Child Rights Information Network

The Child Rights Information Network (CRIN) is a global network that disseminates information about the Convention on the Rights of the Child and child rights among non-governmental organizations, United Nations agencies, intergovernmental organizations, educational institutions, and other child rights experts.

http://www.crin.org/

Planned Parenthood Federation of America

Planned Parenthood Federation of America is the oldest and largest voluntary reproductive health organization in the United States.

http://www.plannedparenthood.org

Eagle Forum's Mission

Eagle Forum's Mission enables conservative and pro-family men and women to participate in the process of self-government and public policy making.

http://www.eagleforum.org/

UNICEF

UNICEF is mandated by the United Nations General Assembly to advocate for the protection of children's rights, to help meet their basic needs, and to expand their opportunities to reach their full potential.

http://www.unicef.org/

Revisiting Ozzie and Harriet: Where Do Same-Sex Couples and Their Families Fit In?

*N*ot too long ago, the words "lesbian and gay" appearing in front of the word "marriage" and "families" would have been considered an oxymoron. For some people, they still do. Others see diverse family structures as social progress. There are a number of issues that remain in the news today relating specifically to the rights of lesbian and gay individuals to have legal and social recognition in the context of family and relationships. This section examines three of these questions:

- Should Same-Sex Couples Be Allowed to Legally Marry?

- Should the U.S. Constitution Be Amended to Define "Marriage"?

- Should Lesbian and Gay Individuals Be Allowed to Adopt Children?

ISSUE 11

Should Same-Sex Couples
Be Allowed to Legally Marry?

YES: Human Rights Campaign, from *Answers to Questions about Marriage Equality* (HRC's FamilyNet Project, 2004)

NO: Peter Sprigg, from *Questions and Answers: What's Wrong with Letting Same-Sex Couples 'Marry'?* (Family Research Council, 2004)

ISSUE SUMMARY

YES: The Human Rights Campaign (HRC), America's largest lesbian and gay organization, outlines the current disparities American lesbian and gay couples experience because they are not allowed to marry legally, as well as the logistical considerations involved in granting same-sex couples the right to marry.

NO: Peter Sprigg, director of the Center for Marriage and Family Studies at the Family Research Council, outlines why non-heterosexual relationships do not carry with them the same validity as heterosexual relationships, and therefore should not be allowed to marry legally.

$\mathbf{T}$he past few years have seen the topic of same-sex marriage rush into the forefront of the news and other media. As of October 2004, the only state in the United States allowing same-sex marriage is Massachusetts, although this is being challenged by those opposed to same-sex marriage by changing the state's Constitution. Same-sex couples in other states are challenging current laws by suing for the right to marry legally. As of 2006, New Jersey's State Supreme Court ruled that same-sex couples have a constitutional right to receive the same state benefits, protections, and obligations as different-sex married couples, leaving the naming of same-sex committed relationships to the state legislature, which voted at the end of that year to call them "civil unions." This, too, is being contested by proponents who believe that calling same-sex marriage anything other than marriage perpetuates the same principles of "separate but equal" that was all-too-familiar to Black and African American individuals until the civil rights movement in the 1960s.

On the other side of the debate, eight additional states in 2006 voted to amend their state's constitutions to define marriage as being exclusively between a man and a woman: Idaho, Colorado, South Dakota, Virginia, Tennessee, South Carolina, Wisconsin, and Alabama.

As of the writing of this piece, New Jersey, Connecticut, and Vermont are the only three states that offer civil union-type benefits to same-sex couples. Vermont became the first state to make civil unions legal between two people of the same sex. Although a same-sex couple cannot have a marriage license or refer to their union as a marriage, the benefits are the same as they would be for a heterosexual marriage. These unions are not, however, recognized in any other state. This is due in great part to the Defense of Marriage Act, which was signed into law in 1996 by President Bill Clinton. This Act says that no state is required to recognize a same-sex union, and defines marriage as being between a man and a woman only. Therefore, same-sex unions that are legal in one state do not have to be recognized as legal in another. Over 30 states have passed legislation saying they would not recognize a same-sex union that took place in another state.

Those who oppose same-sex marriage believe that marriage is, and always has been, between a man and a woman. They believe that a key part of marriage for many heterosexual couples is reproduction or another type of parenting arrangement, such as adoption. In those cases, they believe that any child should have two parents, one male and one female. Many do not oppose granting domestic partner benefits to same-sex partners, or even, in some cases, civil unions. They do, however, believe that if lesbian and gay couples were allowed to marry and to receive the legal and social benefits thereof, it would serve only to further erode the institution of marriage as it is currently defined, which, in the United States, boasts one divorce for every two marriages.

Supporters of same-sex marriage believe that if lesbian and gay couples wish to make a lifetime commitment, they should be afforded the same rights, privileges, and vocabulary as heterosexual couples. While some would be as happy with the term "civil union," accompanied by equal rights, others believe that making marriage available to all is the only way to go. Some lesbian and gay couples who are in committed, loving relationships resent that they have fewer rights than a heterosexual couple in which there is alcohol or drug abuse or domestic violence.

An argument that is raised in this debate is that granting same-sex couples the right to marry would open the door for adult pedophiles to petition to marry the children with whom they engage in their sexual relationships. Most lesbian and gay individuals and their supporters find this offensive, as well as an invalid comparison. What do you think?

In the following selections, both the Human Rights Campaign and Peter Sprigg raise the most common questions pertaining to same-sex marriage. The Human Rights Campaign enumerates the rights that are not currently available to same-sex couples in long-term committed relationships, and maintains that granting equal rights to these couples is good not only for them, but also for society as a whole. Among the concerns Peter Sprigg raises pertains to the expectation of heterosexual marriage to raise children, and that a same-sex couple is a harmful setting in which to do that.

YES ⬅

Answers to Questions About Marriage Equality

Why Same-Sex Couples Want to Marry

Many same-sex couples want the right to legally marry because they are in love—either they just met the love of their lives, or more likely, they have spent the last 10, 20 or 50 years with that person—and they want to honor their relationship in the greatest way our society has to offer, by making a public commitment to stand together in good times and bad, through all the joys and challenges family life brings.

Many parents want the right to marry because they know it offers children a vital safety net and guarantees protections that unmarried parents cannot provide.

And still other people—both gay and straight—are fighting for the right of same-sex couples to marry because they recognize that it is simply not fair to deny some families the protections all other families are eligible to enjoy.

Currently in the United States, same-sex couples in long-term, committed relationships pay higher taxes and are denied basic protections and rights granted to married heterosexual couples. Among them:

- **Hospital visitation.** Married couples have the automatic right to visit each other in the hospital and make medical decisions. Same-sex couples can be denied the right to visit a sick or injured loved one in the hospital.
- **Social Security benefits.** Married people receive Social Security payments upon the death of a spouse. Despite paying payroll taxes, gay and lesbian partners receive no Social Security survivor benefits—resulting in an average annual income loss of $5,528 upon the death of a partner.
- **Immigration.** Americans in binational relationships are not permitted to petition for their same-sex partners to immigrate. As a result, they are often forced to separate or move to another country.
- **Health insurance.** Many public and private employers provide medical coverage to the spouses of their employees, but most employers do not provide coverage to the life partners of gay and lesbian employees. Gay employees who do receive health coverage for their partners must pay federal income taxes on the value of the insurance.

- **Estate taxes.** A married person automatically inherits all the property of his or her deceased spouse without paying estate taxes. A gay or lesbian taxpayer is forced to pay estate taxes on property inherited from a deceased partner.
- **Retirement savings.** While a married person can roll a deceased spouse's 401(k) funds into an IRA without paying taxes, a gay or lesbian American who inherits a 401(k) can end up paying up to 70 percent of it in taxes and penalties.
- **Family leave.** Married workers are legally entitled to unpaid leave from their jobs to care for an ill spouse. Gay and lesbian workers are not entitled to family leave to care for their partners.
- **Nursing homes.** Married couples have a legal right to live together in nursing homes. Because they are not legal spouses, elderly gay or lesbian couples do not have the right to spend their last days living together in nursing homes.
- **Home protection.** Laws protect married seniors from being forced to sell their homes to pay high nursing home bills; gay and lesbian seniors have no such protection.
- **Pensions.** After the death of a worker, most pension plans pay survivor benefits only to a legal spouse of the participant. Gay and lesbian partners are excluded from such pension benefits.

Why Civil Unions Aren't Enough

Comparing marriage to civil unions is a bit like comparing diamonds to rhinestones. One is, quite simply, the real deal; the other is not. Consider:

- Couples eligible to marry may have their marriage performed in any state and have it recognized in every other state in the nation and every country in the world.
- Couples who are joined in a civil union in Vermont (the only state that offers civil unions) have no guarantee that its protections will even travel with them to neighboring New York or New Hampshire—let alone California or any other state.

Moreover, even couples who have a civil union and remain in Vermont receive only second-class protections in comparison to their married friends and neighbors. While they receive state-level protections, they do not receive any of the *more than 1,100 federal benefits and protections of marriage.*

In short, civil unions are not separate but equal—they are separate *and* unequal. And our society has tried separate before. It just doesn't work. . . .

Answers to Questions People Are Asking

I Believe God Meant Marriage for Men and Women.
How Can I Support Marriage for Same-Sex Couples?
Many people who believe in God—and fairness and justice for all—ask this question. They feel a tension between religious beliefs and democratic values that has been experienced in many different ways throughout our nation's history. That is why the farmers of our Constitution established the principle

of separation of church and state. That principle applies no less to the marriage issue than it does to any other.

Indeed, the answer to the apparent dilemma between religious beliefs and support for equal protections for all families lies in recognizing that marriage has a significant religious meaning for many people, but that it is also a legal contract. And it is strictly the legal—not the religious—dimension of marriage that is being debated now.

Granting marriage rights to same-sex couples would *not* require Christianity, Judaism, Islam or any other religion to perform these marriages. It would not require religious institutions to permit these ceremonies to be held on their grounds. It would not even require that religious communities discuss the issue. People of faith would remain free to make their own judgments about what makes a marriage in the eyes of God—just as they are today.

Consider, for example, the difference in how the Catholic Church and the U.S. government view couples who have divorced and remarried. Because church tenets do not sanction divorce, the second marriage is not valid in the church's view. The government, however, recognizes the marriage by extending to the remarried couple the same rights and protections as those granted to every other married couple in America. In this situation—as would be the case in marriage for same-sex couples—the church remains free to establish its own teachings on the religious dimension of marriage while the government upholds equality under law.

It should also be noted that there are a growing number of religious communities that have decided to bless same-sex unions. Among them are Reform Judaism, the Unitarian Universalist Association and the Metropolitan Community Church. The Presbyterian Church (USA) also allows ceremonies to be performed, although they are not considered the same as marriage. The Episcopal Church and United Church of Christ allow individual churches to set their own policies on same-sex unions.

"This Is Different From Interracial Marriage. Sexual Orientation Is a Choice."

. . . Decades of research all point to the fact that sexual orientation is not a choice, and that a person's sexual orientation cannot be changed. Who one is drawn to is a fundamental aspect of who we are.

In this way, the struggle for marriage equality for same-sex couples is just as basic as the fight for interracial marriage was. It recognizes that Americans should not be coerced into false and unhappy marriages but should be free to marry the person they love—thereby building marriage on a true and stable foundation.

"Won't This Create a Free-For-All and Make the Whole Idea of Marriage Meaningless?"

Many people share this concern because opponents of gay and lesbian people have used this argument as a scare tactic. But it is not true. Granting same-sex couples the right to marry would in no way change the number of people who could enter into a marriage (or eliminate restrictions on the age or familial relationships of those who may marry). Marriage would continue to recognize the highest possible commitment that can be made between two adults, plain and simple. . . .

"I Strongly Believe Children Need a Mother and a Father."
Many of us grew up believing that everyone needs a mother and father, regardless of whether we ourselves happened to have two parents, or two *good* parents.

But as families have grown more diverse in recent decades, the researchers have studied how these different family relationships affect children, it has become clear that the *quality* of a family's relationship is more important than the particular *structure* of families that exist today. In other words, the qualities that help children grow into good and responsible adults—learning how to learn, to have compassion for others, to contribute to society and be respectful of others and their differences—do not depend on the sexual orientation of their parents but on their parents' ability to provide a loving, stable and happy home, something no class of Americans has an exclusive hold on.

That is why research studies have consistently shown that children raised by gay and lesbian parents do just as well on all conventional measure of child development, such as academic achievement, psychological well-being and social abilities, as children raised by heterosexual parents.

That is also why the nation's leading child welfare organizations, including the American Academy of Pediatrics, the American Academy of Family Physicians and others, have issued statements that dismiss assertions that only heterosexual couples can be good parents—and declare that the focus should now be on providing greater protections for the 1 million to 9 million children being raised by gay and lesbian parents in the United States today. . . .

"How Could Marriage for Same-Sex Couples Possibly Be Good for the American Family—or Our Country?"
. . . The prospect of a significant change in our laws and customs has often caused people to worry more about dire consequences that could result than about the potential positive outcomes. In fact, precisely the same anxiety arose when some people fought to overturn the laws prohibiting marriage between people of different races in the 1950s and 1960s. (One Virginia judge even declared that "God intended to separate the races.")

But in reality, opening marriage to couples who are so willing to fight for it could only strengthen the institution for all. It would open the doors to more supporters, not opponents. And it would help keep the age-old institution alive.

As history has repeatedly proven, institutions that fail to take account of the changing needs of the population are those that grow weak; those that recognize and accommodate changing needs grow strong. For example, the U.S. military, like American colleges and universities, grew stronger after permitting African Americans and women to join its ranks.

Similarly, granting same-sex couples the right to marry would strengthen the institution of marriage by allowing it to better meet the needs of the true diversity of family structures in America today. . . .

"Can't Same-Sex Couples Go to a Lawyer to Secure All the Rights They Need?"

Not by a long shot. When a gay or lesbian person gets seriously ill, there is no legal document that can make their partner eligible to take leave from work under the federal Family and Medical Leave Act to provide care—because that law applies only to married couples.

When gay or lesbian people grow old and in need of nursing home care, there is no legal document that can give them the right to Medicaid coverage without potentially causing their partner to be forced from their home—because the federal Medicaid law only permits married spouses to keep their home without becoming ineligible for benefits.

And when a gay or lesbian person dies, there is no legal document that can extend Social Security survivor benefits or the right to inherit a retirement plan without severe tax burdens that stem from being "unmarried" in the eyes of the law.

These are only a few examples of the critical protections that are granted through more than 1,100 federal laws that protect only married couples. In the absence of the right to marry, same-sex couples can only put in place a handful of the most basic arrangements, such as naming each other in a will or a power of attorney. And even these documents remain vulnerable to challenges in court by disgruntled family members.

"Won't This Cost Taxpayers Too Much Money?"

No, it wouldn't necessarily cost much at all. In fact, treating same-sex couples as families under law could even save taxpayers money because marriage would require them to assume legal responsibility for their joint living expenses and reduce their dependence on public assistance programs, such as Medicaid, Temporary Assistance to Needy Families, Supplemental Security Income disability payments and food stamps.

Put another way, the money it would cost to extend benefits to same-sex couples could be outweighed by the money that would be saved as these families rely more fully on each other instead of state or federal government assistance.

For example, two studies conducted in 2003 by professors at the University of Massachusetts, Amherst, and the University of California, Los Angeles, found that extending domestic partner benefits to same-sex couples in California and New Jersey would save taxpayers millions of dollars a year.

Specifically, the studies projected that the California state budget would save an estimated $8.1 million to $10.6 million each year by enacting the most comprehensive domestic partner law in the nation. In New Jersey, which passed a new domestic partner law in 2004, the savings were projected to be even higher—more than $61 million each year.

(Sources: "Equal Rights, Fiscal Responsibility: The Impact of A.B. 205 on California's Budget," by M. V. Lee Badgett, Ph.D., IGLSS, Department of Economics, University of Massachusetts, and R. Bradley Sears, J.D., Williams Project, UCLA School of Law, University of California, Los Angeles, May 2003, and "Supporting Families, Saving Funds: A Fiscal Analysis of New Jersey's Domestic

Partnership Act," by Badgett and Sears with Suzanne Goldberg, J.D., Rutgers School of Law-Newark, December 2003.)

"Where Can Same-Sex Couples Marry Today?"

In 2001, the Netherlands became the first country to extend marriage rights to same-sex couples. Belgium passed a similar law two years later. The laws in both of these countries, however, have strict citizenship or residency requirements that do not permit American couples to take advantage of the protections provided.

In June 2003, Ontario became the first Canadian province to grant marriage to same-sex couples, and in July 2003, British Columbia followed suit—becoming the first places that American same-sex couples could go to get married.

In November 2003, the Massachusetts Supreme Judicial Court recognized the right of same-sex couples to marry—giving the state six months to begin issuing marriage licenses to same-sex couples. It began issuing licenses May 17, 2004.

In February 2004, the city of San Francisco began issuing marriage licenses to same-sex couples after the mayor declared that the state constitution forbade him to discriminate. The issue is being addressed by California courts, and a number of other cities have either taken or are considering taking steps in the same direction.

Follow the latest developments in California, Oregon, New Jersey, New Mexico, New York and in other communities across the country. . . .

Other nations have also taken steps toward extending equal protections to all couples, though the protections they provide are more limited than marriage. Canada, Denmark, Finland, France, Germany, Iceland, Norway, Portugal and Sweden all have nationwide laws that grant same-sex partners a range of important rights, protections and obligations.

For example, in France, registered same-sex (and opposite-sex) couples can be joined in a civil "solidarity pact" that grants them the right to file joint tax returns, extend social security coverage to each other and receive the same health, employment and welfare benefits as legal spouses. It also commits the couple to assume joint responsibility for household debts.

Other countries, including Switzerland, Scotland and the Czech Republic, also have considered legislation that would legally recognize same-sex unions.

"What Protections Other Than Marriage Are Available to Same-Sex Couples?"

At the federal level, there are no protections at all available to same-sex couples. In fact, a federal law called the "Defense of Marriage Act" says that the federal government will discriminate against same-sex couples who marry by refusing to recognize their marriages or providing them with the federal protections of marriage. Some members of Congress are trying to go even further by attempting to pass a Federal Marriage Amendment that would write discrimination against same-sex couples into the U.S. Constitution.

10 FACTS

1. Same-sex couples live in 99.3 percent of all counties nationwide.
2. There are an estimated 3.1 million people living together in same-sex relationships in the United States.
3. Fifteen percent of these same-sex couples live in rural settings.
4. One out of three lesbian couples is raising children. One out of five gay male couples is raising children.
5. Between 1 million and 9 million children are being raised by gay, lesbian and bisexual parents in the United States today.
6. At least one same-sex couple is raising children in 96 percent of all counties nationwide.
7. The highest percentages of same-sex couples raising children live in the South.
8. Nearly one in four same-sex couples includes a partner 55 years old or older, and nearly one in five same-sex couples is composed of two people 55 or older.
9. More than one in 10 same-sex couples include a partner 65 years old or older, and nearly one in 10 same-sex couples is composed of two people 65 or older.
10. The states with the highest numbers of same-sex senior couples are also the most popular for heterosexual senior couples: California, New York and Florida.

These facts are based on analyses of the 2000 Census conducted by the Urban Institute and the Human Rights Campaign. The estimated number of people in same-sex relationships has been adjusted by 62 percent to compensate for the widely-reported undercount in the Census. . . .

At the state level, only Vermont offers civil unions, which provide important state benefits but no federal protections, such as Social Security survivor benefits. There is also no guarantee that civil unions will be recognized outside Vermont. Thirty-nine states also have "defense of marriage" laws explicitly prohibiting the recognition of marriages between same-sex partners.

Domestic partner laws have been enacted in California, Connecticut, New Jersey, Hawaii and the District of Columbia. The benefits conferred by these laws vary; some offer access to family health insurance, others confer co-parenting rights. These benefits are limited to residents of the state. A family that moves out of these states immediately loses the protections.

Peter Sprigg   → **NO**

Questions and Answers: What's Wrong With Letting Same-Sex Couples "Marry?"

What's Wrong With Letting Same-Sex Couples Legally "Marry?"
There are two key reasons why the legal rights, benefits, and responsibilities of civil marriage should not be extended to same-sex couples.

The first is that homosexual relationships are not marriage. That is, they simply do not fit the minimum necessary condition for a marriage to exist—namely, the union of a man and a woman.

The second is that homosexual relationships are harmful. Not only do they not provide the same benefits to society as heterosexual marriages, but their consequences are far more negative than positive.

Either argument, standing alone, is sufficient to reject the claim that same-sex unions should be granted the legal status of marriage.

Let's Look at the First Argument.
Isn't Marriage Whatever the Law Says It Is?
No. Marriage is not a creation of the law. Marriage is a fundamental human institution that predates the law and the Constitution. At its heart, it is an anthropological and sociological reality, not a legal one. Laws relating to marriage merely recognize and regulate an institution that already exists.

But Isn't Marriage Just a Way of Recognizing People
Who Love Each Other and Want to Spend Their Lives Together?
If love and companionship were sufficient to define marriage, then there would be no reason to deny "marriage" to unions of a child and an adult, or an adult child and his or her aging parent, or to roommates who have no sexual relationship, or to groups rather than couples. Love and companionship are usually considered integral to marriage in our culture, but they are not sufficient to define it as an institution. . . .

Why Should Homosexuals Be Denied the Right to Marry Like Anyone Else?
The fundamental "right to marry" is a right that rests with *individuals,* not with *couples.* Homosexual *individuals* already have exactly the same "right" to

marry as anyone else. Marriage license applications do not inquire as to a person's "sexual orientation.". . .

However, while every individual person is free to get married, *no* person, whether heterosexual or homosexual, has ever had a legal right to marry simply any willing partner. Every person, whether heterosexual or homosexual, is subject to legal restrictions as to whom they may marry. To be specific, every person, regardless of sexual preference, is legally barred from marrying a child, a close blood relative, a person who is already married, or a person of the same sex. There is no discrimination here, nor does such a policy deny anyone the "equal protection of the laws" (as guaranteed by the Constitution), since these restrictions apply equally to every individual.

Some people may wish to do away with one or more of these longstanding restrictions upon one's choice of marital partner. However, the fact that a tiny but vocal minority of Americans desire to have someone of the same sex as a partner does not mean that they have a "right" to do so, any more than the desires of other tiny (but less vocal) minorities of Americans give them a "right" to choose a child, their own brother or sister, or a group of two or more as their marital partners.

Isn't Prohibiting Homosexual "Marriage" Just as Discriminatory as Prohibiting Interracial Marriage, Like Some States Used to Do?

This analogy is not valid at all. Bridging the divide of the sexes by uniting men and women is both a worthy goal and a part of the fundamental purpose of marriage, common to all human civilizations.

Laws against interracial marriage, on the other hand, served only the purpose of preserving a social system of racial segregation. This was both an unworthy goal and one utterly irrelevant to the fundamental nature of marriage.

Allowing a black woman to marry a white man does not change the definition of marriage, which requires one man and one woman. Allowing two men or two women to marry would change that fundamental definition. Banning the "marriage" of same-sex couples is therefore essential to preserve the nature and purpose of marriage itself. . . .

How Would Allowing Same-Sex Couples to Marry Change Society's Concept of Marriage?

As an example, marriage will open wide the door to homosexual adoption, which will simply lead to more children suffering the negative consequences of growing up without both a mother and a father.

Among homosexual men in particular, casual sex, rather than committed relationships, is the rule and not the exception. And even when they do enter into a more committed relationship, it is usually of relatively short duration. For example, a study of homosexual men in the Netherlands (the first country in the world to legalize "marriage" for same-sex couples), published in the journal *AIDS* in 2003, found that the average length of "steady partnerships" was not more than 2 < years (Maria Xiridou et al., in *AIDS* 2003, 17:1029–1038).

In addition, studies have shown that even homosexual men who are in "committed" relationships are not sexually faithful to each other. While infidelity among heterosexuals is much too common, it does not begin to compare to the rates among homosexual men. The 1994 National Health and Social Life Survey, which remains the most comprehensive study of Americans' sexual practices ever undertaken, found that 75 percent of married men and 90 percent of married women had been sexually faithful to their spouse. On the other hand, a major study of homosexual men in "committed" relationships found that only seven out of 156 had been sexually faithful, or 4.5 percent. The Dutch study cited above found that even homosexual men in "steady partnerships" had an average of eight "casual" sex partners per year.

So if same-sex relationships are legally recognized as "marriage," the idea of marriage as a sexually exclusive and faithful relationship will be dealt a serious blow. Adding monogamy and faithfulness to the other pillars of marriage that have already fallen will have overwhelmingly negative consequences for Americans' physical and mental health. . . .

Don't Homosexuals Need Marriage Rights So That They Will Be Able to Visit Their Partners in the Hospital?

The idea that homosexuals are routinely denied the right to visit their partners in the hospital is nonsense. When this issue was raised during debate over the Defense of Marriage Act in 1996, the Family Research Council did an informal survey of nine hospitals in four states and the District of Columbia. None of the administrators surveyed could recall a single case in which a visitor was barred because of their homosexuality, and they were incredulous that this would even be considered an issue.

Except when a doctor limits visitation for medical reasons, final authority over who may visit an adult patient rests with that patient. This is and should be the case regardless of the sexual orientation or marital status of the patient or the visitor.

The only situation in which there would be a possibility that the blood relatives of a patient might attempt to exclude the patient's homosexual partner is if the patient is unable to express his or her wishes due to unconsciousness or mental incapacity. Homosexual partners concerned about this (remote) possibility can effectively preclude it by granting to one another a health care proxy (the legal right to make medical decisions for the patient) and a power of attorney (the right to make all legal decisions for another person). Marriage is not necessary for this. It is inconceivable that a hospital would exclude someone who holds the health care proxy and power of attorney for a patient from visiting that patient, except for medical reasons.

The hypothetical "hospital visitation hardship" is nothing but an emotional smokescreen to distract people from the more serious implications of radically redefining marriage.

Don't Homosexuals Need the Right to Marry Each Other in Order to Ensure That They Will Be Able to Leave Their Estates to Their Partner When They Die?

As with the hospital visitation issue, the concern over inheritance rights is something that simply does not require marriage to resolve it. Nothing in current law prevents homosexual partners from being joint owners of property such as a home or a car, in which case the survivor would automatically become the owner if the partner dies.

An individual may leave the remainder of his estate to whomever he wishes—again, without regard to sexual orientation or marital status—simply by writing a will. As with the hospital visitation issue, blood relatives would only be able to overrule the surviving homosexual partner in the event that the deceased had failed to record his wishes in a common, inexpensive legal document. Changing the definition of a fundamental social institution like marriage is a rather extreme way of addressing this issue. Preparing a will is a much simpler solution.

Don't Homosexuals Need Marriage Rights So That They Can Get Social Security Survivor Benefits When a Partner Dies?

... Social Security survivor benefits were designed to recognize the non-monetary contribution made to a family by the homemaking and child-rearing activities of a wife and mother, and to ensure that a woman and her children would not become destitute if the husband and father were to die.

The Supreme Court ruled in the 1970s that such benefits must be gender-neutral. However, they still are largely based on the premise of a division of roles within a couple between a breadwinner who works to raise money and a homemaker who stays home to raise children.

Very few homosexual couples organize their lives along the lines of such a "traditional" division of labor and roles. They are far more likely to consist of two earners, each of whom can be supported in old age by their own personal Social Security pension.

Furthermore, far fewer homosexual couples than heterosexual ones are raising children at all, for the obvious reason that they are incapable of natural reproduction with each other. This, too, reduces the likelihood of a traditional division of labor among them.

Survivor benefits for the legal (biological or adopted) *children* of homosexual parents (as opposed to their partners) are already available under current law, so "marriage" rights for homosexual couples are unnecessary to protect the interests of these children themselves. . . .

Even If "Marriage" Itself Is Uniquely Heterosexual, Doesn't Fairness Require That the Legal and Financial Benefits of Marriage Be Granted to Same-Sex Couples—Perhaps Through "Civil Unions" or "Domestic Partnerships?"

No. The legal and financial benefits of marriage are not an entitlement to be distributed equally to all (if they were, single people would have as much reason to consider them "discriminatory" as same-sex couples). Society grants benefits to marriage because marriage has benefits for society—including, but not limited to, the reproduction of the species in households with the optimal household structure (i.e., the presence of both a mother and a father).

Homosexual relationships, on the other hand, have no comparable benefit for society, and in fact impose substantial costs on society. The fact that AIDS is at least ten times more common among men who have sex with men than among the general population is but one example. . . .

Isn't It Possible That Allowing Homosexuals to "Marry" Each Other Would Allow Them to Participate in Those Benefits as Well?

Opening the gates of "marriage" to homosexuals is far more likely to change the attitudes and behavior of heterosexuals for the worse than it is to change the lifestyles of homosexuals for the better. . . .

What About the Argument That Homosexual Relations Are Harmful? What Do You Mean by That?

Homosexual men experience higher rates of many diseases, including:

- Human Papillomavirus (HPV), which causes most cases of cervical cancer in women and anal cancer in men
- Hepatitis A, B, and C
- Gonorrhea
- Syphilis
- "Gay Bowel Syndrome," a set of sexually transmitted gastrointestinal problems such as proctitis, proctocolitis, and enteritis
- HIV/AIDS (One Canadian study found that as a result of HIV alone, "life expectancy for gay and bisexual men is eight to twenty years less than for all men.")

Lesbian women, meanwhile, have a higher prevalence of:

- Bacterial vaginosis
- Hepatitis C
- HIV risk behaviors
- Cancer risk factors such as smoking, alcohol use, poor diet, and being overweight . . .

Do Homosexuals Have More Mental Health Problems as Well?

Yes. Various research studies have found that homosexuals have higher rates of:

- Alcohol abuse
- Drug abuse
- Nicotine dependence
- Depression
- Suicide

Isn't It Possible That These Problems Result From Society's "Discrimination" Against Homosexuals?

This is the argument usually put forward by pro-homosexual activists. However, there is a simple way to test this hypothesis. If "discrimination" were the cause of homosexuals' mental health problems, then one would expect those problems to be much less common in cities or countries, like San Francisco or the Netherlands, where homosexuality has achieved the highest levels of acceptance.

In fact, the opposite is the case. In places where homosexuality is widely accepted, the physical and mental health problems of homosexuals are greater, not less. This suggests that the real problem lies in the homosexual lifestyle itself, not in society's response to it. In fact, it suggests that increasing the level of social support *for* homosexual behavior (by, for instance, allowing same-sex couples to "marry") would only increase these problems, not reduce them. . . .

Haven't Studies Shown That Children Raised by Homosexual Parents Are No Different From Other Children?

No. This claim is often put forward, even by professional organizations. The truth is that most research on "homosexual parents" thus far has been marred by serious methodological problems. However, even pro-homosexual sociologists Judith Stacey and Timothy Biblarz report that the actual data from key studies show the "no differences" claim to be false.

Surveying the research (primarily regarding lesbians) in an *American Sociological Review* article in 2001, they found that:

- Children of lesbians are less likely to conform to traditional gender norms.
- Children of lesbians are more likely to engage in homosexual behavior.
- Daughters of lesbians are "more sexually adventurous and less chaste."
- Lesbian "co-parent relationships" are more likely to end than heterosexual ones.

A 1996 study by an Australian sociologist compared children raised by heterosexual married couples, heterosexual cohabiting couples, and homosexual cohabiting couples. It found that the children of heterosexual married couples did the best, and children of homosexual couples the worst, in nine of the thirteen academic and social categories measured. . . .

Do the American People Want to See "Marriages" Between Same-Sex Couples Recognized by Law?

No—and in the wake of the June 2003 court decisions to legalize such "marriages" in the Canadian province of Ontario and to legalize homosexual sodomy in the United States, the nation's opposition to such a radical social experiment has actually grown.

Five separate national opinion polls taken between June 24 and July 27, 2003 showed opponents of civil "marriage" for same-sex couples outnumbering supporters by not less than fifteen percentage points in every poll. The wording of poll questions can make a significant difference, and in this case, the poll with the most straightforward language (a Harris/CNN/Time poll asking "Do you think marriages between homosexual men or homosexual women should be recognized as legal by the law?") resulted in the strongest opposition, with 60 percent saying "No" and only 33 percent saying "Yes."

Even where pollsters drop the word "marriage" itself and use one of the euphemisms to describe a counterfeit institution parallel to marriage, we see a decline in public support for the homosexual agenda. The Gallup Poll, for instance, has asked, "Would you favor or oppose a law that would allow homosexual couples to legally form civil unions, giving them some of the legal rights of married couples?"

This question itself is misleading, in that it downplays the legal impact of "civil unions." Vermont, the only U.S. state to adopt "civil unions" (under coercion of a state court), actually gives all "of the legal rights of married couples" available under state law to people in a same-sex "civil union"—not just "some." But despite this distortion, a 49-percent-to-49-percent split on this question in May 2003 had changed to opposition by a margin of 58 percent to 37 percent when the *Washington Post* asked the identical question in August 2003.

Even the percentage of Americans willing to declare that "homosexual relations between consenting adults" (never mind homosexual civil "marriage") "should be legal" dropped from 60 percent to only 48 percent between May and July of 2003. The biggest drop in support, a stunning 23 percentage points (from 58 percent to 35 percent), came among African Americans—despite the rhetoric of pro-homosexual activists who seek to frame the issues of "gay rights" and same-sex unions as a matter of "civil rights." . . .

POSTSCRIPT

Should Same-Sex Couples Be Allowed to Legally Marry?

Part of this discussion is that marriage is a civil right, not an inherent or moral one. Those supporting marriage rights for lesbian and gay couples cite the struggles of the civil rights movement of the 1960s in their current quest for equality for all couples. Among the points they make is that up until 1967, it was still illegal in some states for people of different races to marry. Many opponents find the idea of comparing same-sex marriage to the civil rights struggles of the 1960s and earlier is offensive, that it is like comparing apples and oranges. Many of these individuals believe that sexual orientation is chosen, rather than an inherent part of who one is—unlike race, which is pre-determined. Most sexuality experts, however, agree that while we do not know for sure what "causes" a person to be heterosexual, bisexual, or homosexual, it is clear that it is determined very early in life, perhaps even before we are born. Regardless, is marriage a civil right? A legal right? An inherent right?

ISSUE 12

Should the U.S. Constitution Be Amended to Protect the "Sanctity of Marriage"?

YES: *National Review*, from "The Right Amendment—Marriage," *National Review* (January 26, 2004)

NO: **Jonah Goldberg**, from "Federal Marriage Amendment a Bad Idea," Townhall.com (2003)

ISSUE SUMMARY

YES: The *National Review*, a conservative news magazine, believes that a constitutional amendment is needed to reserve the word "marriage" for a man and a woman. It would also keep any state from allowing same-sex unions and any judge from making a decision inconsistent with federal law.

NO: Jonah Goldberg, editor of *National Review Online*, does not support same-sex marriage, but he does not think that a constitutional amendment is the way to go, either. He argues that many supporters of the Federal Marriage Amendment believe that this amendment protects and strengthens heterosexual marriage, and that this reasoning is flawed.

The U.S. Constitution is the basis of federal law. While states make their own individual laws, they must be consistent with federal law.

The Constitution, as it was drawn up in 1787, was designed to provide a framework for the U.S. government and determine how it would work now that it was independent of Great Britain. Within a few years, the Constitution was amended ten times, a document called the Bill of Rights. In total, the Constitution has been amended 27 times, addressing such things as the rights of women to vote (Nineteenth Amendment), the number of terms a president can hold office (Twenty-Second Amendment), and determining the secession should a president die before his term in office were complete (Twenty-Fifth Amendment), to name a few. Proposing an amendment to the Constitution requires a two-thirds vote in both houses in Congress. For the amendment to become effective, it must be approved (or "ratified") by three-fourths of the states. Clearly, it is not an endeavor that our government has taken, or should take, lightly. A Constitutional amendment is designed to stay—even though the Eighteenth Amendment, prohibiting alcohol production and sale, was repealed later by the Twenty-First Amendment.

In May 2003, Senator Marilyn Musgrave (R-CO) introduced the Federal Marriage Amendment. Endorsed enthusiastically by President George W. Bush, the language of the amendment reads, "Marriage in the United States shall consist only of the union of a man and a woman. Neither this Constitution or the constitution of any State, nor state or federal law, shall be construed to require that marital status or the legal incidents thereof be conferred upon unmarried couples or groups." In July 2004, the amendment was rejected by a procedural vote. In order for an amendment to move forward and be voted on, the debate on the issue must be closed (called "cloture"). This did not happen, but the amendment's supporters did not give up. In 2006, the proposed amendment was voted on again in the Senate, where it failed to receive the 60 required votes to move it to cloture and an actual vote.

Supporters of the amendment believe that marriage is a moral institution—and that at the heart of this morality is heterosexuality. They argue that among the goals of marriage is procreation; therefore, it should be entered into by two reproductively compatible individuals. Others believe that homosexuality is wrong, and that recognizing same-sex marriage validates homosexuality. Still other supporters of the amendment may believe that same-sex couples should be able to unite, but not call it "marriage."

Opponents to the amendment believe that this amendment violates the human rights of lesbian, gay, and bisexual individuals. If same-sex couples work, pay taxes, enter into lifetime commitments, and raise children, why should they not be afforded the same social and legal benefits and status as heterosexual couples? Many same-sex couples have had commitment ceremonies that have provided themselves, their friends, and their families the same ceremonial, public recognition that many heterosexual couples choose to have when they get married. Yet the recognition stops socially—and is not acknowledged by some at all.

Do you think that the government has a right to determine who we can and cannot marry? Under what circumstances? Should lesbian and gay couples be grateful for what they do have in many states—domestic partner benefits at work, anti-discrimination laws relating to housing and hiring, and more—and let the marriage argument go? Would having this type of amendment open the door for other marriage restrictions, such as marriage between two people of very different ages, religions, or races?

In the following selections, the *National Review* maintains that a Constitutional amendment is the only way to go. Otherwise, other states could do the same thing Massachusetts did. Conversely, Jonah Goldberg supports the view that the federal government should not have so much power in the ways in which states govern themselves. Although he opposes same-sex marriage, he does not think that a Constitutional amendment is the most effective way of bringing about its demise.

YES ↩   *National Review*

The Right Amendment—Marriage

In 1998, Hawaii's Supreme Court attempted to foist gay marriage on that state. The voters amended the state constitution to preserve the definition of marriage as the union of a man and a woman. In 2001, gay activists found a more hospitable venue. Vermont's constitution is very hard for voters to amend. So the state courts could force civil unions on the state with little real danger of reversal. At the time, this magazine suggested that it was pretty clear where things were headed. The courts, both state and federal, were going to keep pushing gay marriage and gay marriage lite until they succeeded some-where. Further legal actions would force the recognition of one state's gay marriages by all the other states. Or federal courts would, at some point, find the ground prepared for the national imposition of gay marriage. Whatever the precise methods, the courts would go as far in the direction of gay mar-riage as they could get away with. Each discrete step would be something that the public did not favor (and hence could not be enacted democratically) but also did not oppose so vehemently that it would be overturned.

We thought that the proper response to this campaign by legal activists and their judicial accomplices was a constitutional amendment. The Massachusetts high court's decision in favor of gay marriage in November 2003 has reinforced our view.

The public is beginning to see the danger that gay marriage will be brought to them without a vote. A New York Times poll in December found that 55 percent of Americans favor a constitutional amendment to define marriage in the traditional way. That is not a large enough number to ensure passage, but it is a strong one given how new the amendment is in the political debate.

Even among supporters of an amendment, however, there has been con-siderable disagreement about what precise form it should take. We have defended an amendment that would accomplish three things. First, it would reserve the word "marriage" for the union of one man and one woman: No court or legislature would be able to create "gay marriage."

Second, it would ban the federal or state governments—again, whether directed by a court or a legislature—from granting benefits that are conditioned on non-marital sexual relationships. Legislatures would be free to make a bene-fit, or civil-union status, available to unmarried persons. But availability must not be limited only to homosexual couples or to cohabiting heterosexuals. Siblings, friends, and roommates who are not in sexual relationships would also

From *National Review Online*, January 26, 2004, pp. 22–24. Copyright © 2004 by National Review, Inc. Reprinted by permission.

have to be eligible. A person's homosexuality would, in other words, not be of interest to the government when distributing any benefit.

Third, the amendment would block the courts, at both the federal and state levels, from second-guessing a legislature's decision to reserve a benefit for married couples. If the legislature has said that only married couples have joint adoption rights, for example, no court may grant that benefit to unmarried couples.

Some supporters of an amendment have wanted it to do more, and others less. The maximalists have wanted to ban all civil unions and other forms of marriage lite, and to deny certain benefits to homosexual couples. To accomplish these goals, however, would require the amendment to list in detail what benefits must be reserved to marriage. That would be unwise. The precise set of benefits that should attend marriage is not something that can be deduced from first principles. Different state legislatures may legitimately decide on different packages, as they always have. A maximalist amendment would be unwieldy, would delve into minutiae unsuitable for the Constitution, and would unduly limit the power of state legislatures. It would also be next to impossible to pass.

Most of the maximalists have now come around. The greater danger now comes from the minimalists. They want the amendment only to reserve the word "marriage" for the union of a man and a woman. State legislatures would be able to do anything else, including create civil unions for gays only that are legally identical to marriage in everything but name. The courts would be free to impose such policies, as well.

The minimalists have the ear of senior Republicans, and they are lobbying the White House to come out for their version of the amendment. That would be a mistake. As important as it is to prevent gay marriage, it is not the most important goal that an amendment should have. That goal is the end of judicial meddling with the institution. The campaign for an amendment should be as much for democratic self-government (and against judicial usurpation) as for traditional marriage (and against gay marriage). The minimalists' amendment, however, would allow the courts to impose Vermont-style civil unions on every state in the country.

We believe that it would be difficult, but possible, to pass the three-part amendment discussed above. Its proponents could say, truthfully, that the amendment would not keep gay couples from getting any particular benefit at all, except for governmental recognition of their sexual relationships. That should be defensible political ground for President Bush to hold.

If the amendment must be scaled back, however, the first and second parts of it are each more expendable than the third. It would be better, that is, to leave state legislatures free to create civil unions, any type of civil union, and even gay marriage at their own discretion—while banning judges from imposing either. It is not as though the public at large is clamoring for gay marriage in any state. If the public comes to do so of its own accord, and not under the tutelage of judges, then traditional marriage will be dead, and past the power of constitutions to save. The present danger is that the courts will push the country in a dangerous direction in which it would not otherwise go. It is that danger that a constitutional amendment should address.

Jonah Goldberg **NO**

Federal Marriage Amendment a Bad Idea

I guess I'm against the Federal Marriage Amendment.

I know that's not the sort of forthright lead columnists are supposed to start out with.

My wishy-washiness stems in part from the fact that I'm against gay marriage, but I'm also against this "solution." Moreover, I really don't like most of the arguments for *or* against gay marriage.

Both sides seem to suffer from a nasty case of consequentialism. That's the branch of thinking—of which utilitarianism is a subset—that says that a decision should be judged entirely on the consequences that result from that choice. So, what's wrong with that? Isn't that what politics is about?

Well, yes and no. There are two problems with consequentialism. The first is that, like utilitarianism, it dismisses principle or, worse, it pretends something is a principle when it isn't. So often we hear one political party or another cloak its positions in rhetoric about democracy or justice when really they're talking about personal enrichment or partisan advantage.

The second problem with consequentialism is that it often works on the false assumption that we can know what the consequences will be. The last great constitutional disaster was Prohibition. The 18th Amendment was supposed to get Americans to stop drinking booze. People made straight-line predictions that if you made hooch illegal, people would stop drinking it. Some did. Many didn't. . . .

Proponents of the FMA believe that it will have the straight-line effects they desire: no gay marriage, stronger traditional marriage, no more debate about gay marriage. The opponents of FMA make similar arguments about gay marriage itself, saying that the consequences will be obvious, beneficial and predictable.

I really don't buy any of it.

I think gay marriage is probably a bad idea. But, I admit, my feelings stem partly from a conservative view that holds that all radical new ideas are probably bad ones.

I like "muddling through," as the British say.

If I had my druthers, we'd take this issue very slowly, over a generation or two. It was only in 1973 and 1975 that the American Psychiatric Association and the American Psychological Association, respectively, removed homosexuality from their lists of mental disorders. That was the right decision, but it does illustrate how profoundly young a "mainstream" gay culture is.

If it is inevitable that civil marriage be redefined to include same-sex couples, I think that inevitability shouldn't be rushed. Why not first solve the practical, easier problems stable gay couples face—partnership benefits, hospital visitation, etc.—through some form of civil contracts?

And if eventually the stability and monogamy of homosexual relationships are so self-evident that it becomes obvious to a wide majority of Americans that gay marriage is a worthwhile next step, we can deal with that. As Edmund Burke, the father of modern conservatism, noted, "Example is the school of mankind, and they will learn at no other."

If, in the meantime, justice delayed equals justice denied to a handful of couples who want marriage now, well, I'm sorry. That's the way life works sometimes. As Burke also said, sometimes we "must bear with infirmities until they fester into crimes."

But no one's taking my advice. So, we have the FMA barreling down the tracks. The FMA would ban gay marriage "or the legal incidents thereof"—which many take to mean civil unions as well—in all 50 states for all time.

That may sound like a good idea if you're against gay marriage, civil unions and all the rest. But to me it sounds an awful lot like a replay of Prohibition. I can't tell you what the unforeseeable consequences of such an amendment are because, duh, they're unforeseeable. But what I can predict with almost mathematical certitude is that the FMA will not make this issue go away. Rather, it will more likely serve to radicalize the anti-FMA forces in much the same way Roe vs. Wade radicalized anti-abortion forces.

Historically, the way we cut these knots is by throwing the issue to the lowest, most local level possible. If South Carolina wants to ban alcohol, fine. But don't tell New York they have to, too. This way we get a multiplicity of examples to follow and debate, rather than a monarchal decree from above.

If Massachusetts really wants something called "gay marriage," I may disagree with the decision, but it's their decision. . . . And, while I'd probably be in favor of an amendment codifying the principle of the Defense of Marriage Act—which allows states to refuse to recognize the gay marriages of other states—the FMA goes much further than that.

You can't favor federalism for only good ideas or ideas you like. Experimentation means allowing local communities to make mistakes.

So, I guess I'm against the Federal Marriage Amendment.

POSTSCRIPT

Should the U.S. Constitution Be Amended to Protect the "Sanctity of Marriage"?

Some people think that whenever a group of people wants new rights, someone—usually someone in the power majority—needs to give up some power in order to make that happen. Fear of change is often rooted in the fear of loss. We saw this fear quite clearly during the civil rights and women's and gay rights movements of the 1960s and 1970s. Many believe that one cannot progress without someone falling behind. Others believe that one person's or group's progress serves only the greater good of society.

It is important to know that opinions and beliefs on this issue are not necessarily formed by a person's own sexual orientation. Not all lesbian, gay, and bisexual people support legal marriage. Some feel very strongly that it is a heterosexual institution, and that same-sex couples are imitating heterosexual ones when they have union or commitment ceremonies. Many heterosexual individuals believe that same-sex couples should be able to marry if they wish. Calling the union anything other than a marriage, they believe, would make it a separate, unequal arrangement.

There have been nearly 10,000 proposed Constitutional amendments since 1789. Among these were an amendment in 1912 that would have made marriage between races illegal, and another in 1914 that would have made it illegal to get divorced. How do you think our country would look today if either of these amendments had been ratified? How do you think the discussion of an amendment prohibiting same-sex marriage is similar to or different from either of these proposed amendments?

When you think about how you feel about this issue, on what are you basing your beliefs? If you know someone who is lesbian, gay, or bisexual, or are lesbian, gay, or bisexual yourself, how does this affect your opinion? If you are a member of a particular faith group, what kinds of messages have you received about homosexuality and same-sex marriage? Have these messages helped you to form your opinion?

ISSUE 13

Should Lesbian and Gay Individuals Be Allowed to Adopt Children?

YES: Joan Biskupic, from "Same-Sex Couples Redefining Family Life in USA," USATODAY.com (February 17, 2003)

NO: Timothy J. Dailey, from "State of the States: Update on Homosexual Adoption in the U.S." *Family Research Council* (no. 243, 2004)

ISSUE SUMMARY

YES: Joan Biskupic, legal affairs correspondent for *USA Today*, discusses both the personal challenges for same-gender couples attempting to adopt in states that are not friendly to them, and provides an update of legal issues and options available to lesbian and gay couples, indicating a changing tide of acceptance toward couples of the same gender, as well as lesbian and gay individuals, adopting children.

NO: Timothy J. Dailey, senior research fellow at the Center for Marriage and Family Studies, provides an overview of state laws pertaining to adoption by lesbian or gay parents. He points to studies showing that children do much better in family settings that include both a mother and a father, and that the sexual behaviors same-sex parents engage in make them, by definition, inappropriate role models for children.

Currently, there are thousands of children awaiting adoption. In many cases, there are strict requirements as to who can and cannot adopt. In one country, for example, a heterosexual couple must be married for at least four years—and if they already have one child, they can only adopt a child of a different gender. Most countries do not allow same-sex couples or openly lesbian or gay individuals to adopt children.

In the United States, same-sex couples can adopt in a number of ways. Some will adopt as single parents, even though they are in a long-term, committed relationship with another person, because the state or agency does not permit same-sex couples to adopt together. Others will do what is called "second parent" adoption—where one partner is the biological parent of the child, and the other can become the other legal parent by going through the court system. In other cases, the biological parent must terminate her or his own rights so that there can be a "joint adoption." Both parents jointly adopt the child and become equal, legal parents. This applies to unmarried different-sex couples, too.

There are a range of feelings about who should or should not parent children. Some individuals feel that children should be raised by a man and a woman who are married, not by a gay or lesbian individual or couple. Starting with the premise that homosexuality is wrong, they feel that such a relationship is an inappropriate context in which to raise children. For some of these opponents of lesbian and gay parenting, homosexuality is defined by behaviors. Because they fear that sexual orientation and behaviors can be learned, they also fear that a child raised by a lesbian or gay couple will be more likely to come out as lesbian or gay her or himself.

Other people do not believe that a person's sexual orientation determines her or his ability to parent. Whether a person is raised by one parent, two men, two women, or a man and a woman is less important than any individual's or couple's ability to love, support, and care for a child. They oppose the concept that a heterosexual couple in which there is abuse or where there are inappropriate sexual boundaries would be considered preferable to a lesbian or gay couple in a long-term, committed relationship who care for each other and their children. They point to the fact that most lesbian, gay, and bisexual adults were raised by heterosexual parents. Therefore, they believe, being raised by a lesbian or gay couple will not create lesbian, gay, or bisexual children, any more than being raised by a heterosexual, married couple would guarantee heterosexuality.

Some state laws support same-sex couples' right to adopt children, and some do not. In nine states, (New Jersey, California, Connecticut, Massachusetts, New York, Washington, D.C., Illinois, Pennsylvania, and Vermont), for example, joint or second parent adoption is currently available. In Utah, married heterosexual couples are given priority for foster or adoptive children, and in Mississippi, there is a law that outright bans a same-sex couple from being able to adopt children.

As you read this issue, think about what you think the characteristics of a good parent are. Can these characteristics be found only in heterosexual relationships, or can they be fulfilled by a same-sex relationship? Does the gender of a same-sex relationship affect your feelings on the subject? For example, do you find two women raising a child more or less threatening than two men?

In the following selections, Joan Biskupic discusses the assertive steps that lesbian, gay, and bisexual individuals have made to gain footage in the legal arena when it comes to adoption rights. She provides an overview of individual state statutes pertaining to adoption by same-gender couples, citing an increased focus on creating "functional" parents—regardless of the gender(s) of the parents involved. Timothy J. Dailey asserts that gay men are sexually promiscuous, and are therefore poor role models and parents for children. Lesbians, he believes, are ineffective parents because they are raising a child without the presence and influence of a father figure, which theorists, he maintains, argue is vital to the psychosocial development of children, male and female.

YES ⬅

Joan Biskupic

Same-Sex Couples Redefining Family Law in USA

Donna Colley and Margaux Towne-Colley, a lesbian couple bringing up a son in Omaha, face an ongoing dilemma.

They could stay in Nebraska, where Colley has a satisfying job as a lawyer, the couple own a home and are close to their neighbors. It's also where state law does not allow both women to be legal parents to Grayson, a blond, blue-eyed toddler who was delivered by Towne-Colley after she was artificially inseminated with sperm from an anonymous donor.

That leaves the couple with another option: Leave Nebraska and build a new life in one of about a dozen states that recognize same-sex couples as parents.

Such legal status isn't just symbolic. Because Colley can't be a legal parent to 16-month-old Grayson under Nebraska law, the child would not be entitled to government benefits if Colley were to become disabled or die. The boy would not be guaranteed support payments from Colley if the two women were to split up. And if Towne-Colley were to die, Colley wouldn't automatically receive custody of the boy.

Legal analysts say the choice they face is typical of the forces that are transforming family law across America. Gay and lesbian couples increasingly are going to court seeking to adopt children, acquire rights as parents, take on shared last names and secure a range of benefits similar to those enjoyed by heterosexual couples.

Nearly three years after Vermont approved civil unions for homosexual couples, the evolving acceptance of such couples nationwide is reflected in recent court decisions in which judges have looked not only at biology when determining who is a "parent," but at the roles people play in households. Many judges are saying sexual orientation shouldn't matter in deciding what makes a family. A few conservative groups are fighting the tide, without much success.

Recent cases in Pennsylvania and Delaware symbolize the new age in family law, and judges' increasing flexibility in defining parental roles. Courts in those states ordered lesbians to pay child support for children they had been rearing with their partners before the couples split up.

"People are recognizing that these non-traditional families are here to stay, and courts are finding ways to support the children," says Susan Becker, professor at the Cleveland-Marshall College of Law at Cleveland State University.

But as Colley and Towne-Colley's situation suggests, the rules aren't the same for everyone.

State laws—and local attitudes—vary widely when it comes to adoption, child support, domestic partnerships and other issues that affect same-sex couples. Courts, laws and government policies in conservative states in America's heartland and in the South generally are less tolerant of efforts to give gay and lesbian couples the same rights as heterosexuals:

- Nebraska's Supreme Court last year refused to allow a lesbian to formally adopt the boy whom she and her partner (the birth mother) are rearing. Such "second parent" adoptions, which allow a second adult to assume responsibility for a child without the biological parent losing any rights, are legal for gay and lesbian couples in California, Connecticut, Delaware, Illinois, Massachusetts, New Jersey, New York, Pennsylvania, Vermont and the District of Columbia. In a dozen other states, some local courts have backed such arrangements.
- Four states—Texas, Oklahoma, Kansas and Missouri—still ban sex between consenting homosexual adults, although the laws are rarely enforced. The U.S. Supreme Court on March 26 will consider a challenge to Texas' law.
- Eight states and about three dozen cities and counties—mostly on the East and West coasts—now provide benefits for the partners of their gay and lesbian public employees, gay-rights advocates say.

No group tracks all cases involving gay and lesbian family issues. But those on both sides of the debate over whether gay and lesbian parents should be granted more rights agree that homosexuals' increasing aggressiveness on family issues has won them gains in courts and beyond.

"In the past, when gay and lesbian couples tried to adopt, they really couldn't identify themselves as gay," says Michele Zavos, a Washington, D.C., lawyer who specializes in gay family law. "Now, they can, either when going through a second-parent adoption or with an agency." . . .

Gay-rights advocates say it's all a reflection of the rising profile of gay men and lesbians in politics, the workplace and everyday life. "People know now that gay and lesbian relationships are not exceptional," says Patricia Logue, a lawyer in Chicago for the Lambda Legal Defense and Education Fund. "Now, we're seeing what the political winds will bear in each state."

'I Am a Stranger to My Child'

Same-sex couples and their families have become hot topics for TV shows, movies and media reports in recent years. The increasing openness of same-sex couples, fueled by the successes of the gay-rights movement, has made it seem as though there has been an explosion of such families.

But firm numbers are difficult to come by. The U.S. Census Bureau did not collect figures on same-sex couples until 2000, so there are no reliable statistics on the growth in such households. The 2000 Census found 1.2 million people living in households with unrelated adults of the same sex, but analysts say that figure is low because it was derived from a part of the Census form that some people ignored.

Similarly, estimates of children of gay or lesbian parents vary widely. Judges have cited various reports that put the number of children living with at least one gay or lesbian parent at 6 million to 12 million.

"The sheer number of support groups, magazines and Web sites for gay and lesbian parents suggests that the number is significant," says Denver lawyer Kim Willoughby, who specializes in issues regarding same-sex couples.

Advances in reproductive technology, including artificial insemination, egg donation and in-vitro fertilization, have given gay men and lesbians ways to become parents beyond adoption.

Although it has become easier for same-sex couples to work with private adoption agencies, they sometimes do not disclose their sexual orientation, making reliable statistics about such adoptions difficult. Gay men or lesbians who adopt foreign children typically have one partner adopt as an individual, and the other partner initiate a second-parent adoption later.

After Towne-Colley, 38, got pregnant two years ago, she and Colley, 43, planned to return briefly to Vermont, where they had a civil union ceremony in 2000. (Towne added Colley's name to hers that year.) They wanted Grayson to be born there because the state would allow both women to be listed as parents on his birth certificate. But they were still in Nebraska in October 2001, when Grayson was born nine weeks early.

Working around Nebraska law, the couple drafted wills, a parenting agreement and other papers that spell out their responsibilities for Grayson. "We are trying to do everything we can to tie ourselves together legally and bind me to our son," says Colley, whose salary and benefits provide for the family.

Still, Colley says, "under the law, I am a stranger to my child." For now, she and Towne-Colley are staying in Nebraska and not challenging its parenting laws. They are mindful of last year's state Supreme Court decision against a lesbian couple and say they don't want to risk an adverse ruling.

Amy Miller, a lawyer for the ACLU of Nebraska, represented the lesbian couple whose case went to Nebraska's high court. The court said state law forbids a second adult from adopting a child unless the birth mother (in this case, one of the partners) gives up her rights to the child.

Miller says her unidentified clients wanted to make sure that if the birth mother died, their 3-year-old son, Luke, could receive Social Security and other benefits tied to her partner. After they lost in court, they moved to Portland, Ore. Thanks to a second-parent adoption there, Miller said, they both are Luke's legal parents.

In Cincinnati, Cheryl, 41, and Jennifer, 36, are rearing a 2-year-old boy who is the product of an egg harvested from Cheryl, fertilized by sperm from an anonymous donor, and implanted in Jennifer.

The couple, who agreed to be interviewed if only their first names were used, say they might seek shared parental rights. But they know that Ohio courts often reject such efforts. They say moving out of state is not an option. "This is just as much our state as anyone else's," Cheryl says.

Focusing on 'Functional' Parents

Ohio has been a battleground for the new generation of family law cases. The state Supreme Court has handed victories to those on both sides of the issue.

During the past year, the court endorsed shared last names for gay and lesbian couples but rejected second-parent adoptions for homosexuals. In Cleveland Heights, voters gave health benefits to gay and lesbian partners of city employees. An effort to reverse the move through a referendum failed. . . .

But Duke University law dean Katharine Bartlett says judges have struggled with nontraditional families since divorce rates jumped three decades ago. "Courts aren't trying to contribute to the demise of traditional families. But they recognize the reality of families today and 'functional' parents."

That was evident in a Pennsylvania case in December. The state Superior Court affirmed a trial judge's order that a lesbian should pay support for five children she had been bringing up with her ex-partner. That case followed one in Delaware in which a judge ordered a woman to pay support for a son that her former partner had through in-vitro fertilization.

But providing for children isn't always the overriding factor in such cases. Last year in Idaho, a local magistrate denied a gay man, Theron McGriff, custody of his two children from a marriage to a woman. The magistrate said McGriff, 38, couldn't visit them if he continued to live with another man. Idaho's Supreme Court agreed to hear McGriff's appeal.

"Sexual orientation should be irrelevant," says Shannon Minter, McGriff's attorney. . . .

Timothy J. Dailey

 **NO**

State of the States: Update on Homosexual Adoption in the U.S.

The legal status of homosexual adoption varies from state to state, and is constantly changing due to court decisions and new state laws addressing the issue. Further complicating the issue are gay activist organizations that present misleading accounts of court rulings and laws reflecting unfavorably on homosexual parenting.

States that Specifically Prohibit Gay Adoption

Three states, Florida, Mississippi, and Utah, have passed statutes specifically prohibiting homosexual adoption. The advocates of gay adoption downplay the Utah statute, asserting that it was not intended to prevent adoption by homosexuals. Liz Winfeld, writing in the *Denver Post,* discusses claims that the Utah law was aimed squarely at homosexuals: "Not true. Utah disallows any unmarried person from adopting regardless of gender or orientation."[1] . . .

In fact, the Utah law was enacted specifically to close loopholes in Utah adoption laws that were being taken advantage of by homosexual couples seeking to adopt children. . . .

The ensuing fight led to the legislature passing a statute barring homosexual adoptions. . . .

States that Specifically Permit Gay Adoption

USA Today reports that seven states, including California, Connecticut, Illinois, Massachusetts, New Jersey, New York, Vermont, and the District of Columbia permit homosexuals to adopt.[2] However, at present the inclusion of California on this list is inaccurate.

States that Permit Second-Parent Adoption

Homosexual couples have adopted children through "second-parent" adoption policies in at least twenty states. There is no evidence that homosexuals in the remaining states are permitted to adopt children, a fact admitted by the gay activist Human Rights Campaign (HRC): "In the remaining 24 states, our research has not revealed any second-parent adoptions."[3]

From *Family Research Council,* Issue 243, 2004. Copyright © 2004 by Family Research Council. Reprinted by permission.

At least one state has reversed its policy of permitting second-parent adoptions. In November 2000, the Superior Court of Pennsylvania ruled that same-sex couples cannot adopt children.[4] In addition, a court decision in California has reversed that state's policy of permitting homosexuals to adopt children. On October 25, 2001, the 4th District Court of Appeal (San Diego) ruled that there was no legal authority under California law permitting second-parent adoptions.[5] . . .

Homosexual Households in the United States

There are widely varying and unsubstantiated claims about the numbers of children being raised in gay and lesbian households. . . .

- The U.S. Census Bureau reports that there are 601,209 (304,148 male homosexual and 297,061 lesbian) same-sex unmarried partner households, for a total of 1,202,418 individuals, in the United States.[6] If one million children were living in households headed by homosexual couples, this would mean that, on average, *every* homosexual household has at least one child.
- However, a survey in *Demography* indicates that 95 percent of partnered male homosexual and 78 percent of partnered lesbian households do *not* have children.[7] This would mean that the one million children presumed to be living in homosexual households would be divided among the 15,000 (five percent of 304,148) male homosexual and 65,000 (22 percent of 297,061) lesbian households that actually have children. This would result in an astounding 12.5 children per gay and lesbian family.

The cases highlighted by the media to generate sympathy for homosexual adoption typically feature "two-parent" homosexual households. Of course, some children are also being raised by a natural parent who identifies himself or herself as homosexual and live alone. Nevertheless, the hypothetical calculations above give some indication of how absurdly inflated most of the estimates are concerning the number of children being raised by homosexuals. Far from being the proven success that some claim, homosexual parenting remains a relatively rare phenomenon.

Implications for Homosexual Parenting

Demands that homosexuals be accorded the right to . . . adopt children fit into the gay agenda by minimizing the differences between homosexual and heterosexual behavior in order to make homosexuality look as normal as possible. However, as already shown, only a small minority of gay and lesbian households have children. Beyond that, the evidence also indicates that comparatively few homosexuals choose to establish households together—the type of setting that is a prerequisite for the rearing of children. Consider the following:

- HRC claims that the U.S. population of gays and lesbians is 10,456,405, or 5 percent of the total U.S. population over 18 years of age.[8] The best available data supports a much lower estimate for those who engage in same-sex sexual relations.[9] However, assuming the higher estimate for the purposes of argument, this would indicate that *only 8.6 percent* of homosexuals (1,202,418 out of 10,456,405) choose to live in a household with a person of the same sex.

- HRC asserts that "30 percent of gay and lesbian people are living in a committed relationship in the same residence."[10] Assuming HRC's own figures, that would mean over three million gays and lesbians are living in such households, which, as shown above, is a wildly inflated estimate over the census figures. It is worth noting that the HRC claim amounts to a tacit admission that 70 percent of gays and lesbians choose not to live in committed relationships and establish households together.
- HRC claims that the numbers of gay and lesbian households were "undercounted" by the census. However, if true, it would represent an unprecedented, massive undercount of 260 percent on the part of the U.S. Census Bureau.

The census figures indicate that only a small minority of gays and lesbians have made the lifestyle choice that is considered a fundamental requisite in any consideration regarding adoption, and only a small percentage of those households actually have children. The evidence thus does not support the claim that significant numbers of homosexuals desire to provide a stable family setting for children.

The Nature of Homosexual "Committed Relationships"

Gay activists admit that the ultimate goal of the drive to legitimize homosexual marriage and adoption is to change the essential character of marriage, removing precisely the aspects of fidelity and chastity that promote stability in the home. They pursue their goal heedless of the fact that such households are unsuitable for the raising of children:

- Paula Ettelbrick, former legal director of the Lambda Legal Defense and Education Fund, has stated, "Being queer is more than setting up house, sleeping with a person of the same gender, and seeking state approval for doing so. . . . Being queer means pushing the parameters of sex, sexuality, and family, and in the process transforming the very fabric of society."[11]
- According to homosexual writer and activist Michelangelo Signorile, the goal of homosexuals is to redefine the term *monogamy*.

For these men the term 'monogamy' simply doesn't necessarily mean sexual exclusivity. . . . The term 'open relationship' has for a great many gay men come to have one specific definition: A relationship in which the partners have sex on the outside often, put away their resentment and jealousy, and discuss their outside sex with each other, or share sex partners.[12]

- The views of Signorile and Ettelbrick regarding marriage are widespread in the homosexual community. According to the *Mendola Report,* a mere

26 percent of homosexuals believe that commitment is most important in a marriage relationship.[13] . . .

Even those who support the concept of homosexual "families" admit to their unsuitability for children:

- In their study in *Family Relations,* L. Koepke et al. observed, "Even individuals who believe that same-sex relationships are a legitimate choice for adults may feel that children will suffer from being reared in such families."[14]
- Pro-homosexual researchers, J. J. Bigner and R. B. Jacobson describe the homosexual father as "socioculturally unique," trying to take on "two apparently opposing roles: that of a father (with all its usual connotations) and that of a homosexual man." They describe the homosexual father as "both structurally and psychologically at social odds with his interest in keeping one foot in both worlds: parenting and homosexuality."[15]

In truth, the two roles are fundamentally incompatible. The instability, susceptibility to disease, and domestic violence that is disproportionate in homosexual relationships would normally render such households unfit to be granted custody of children. However, in the current social imperative to grant legitimacy to the practice of homosexuality in every conceivable area of life, such considerations are often ignored.

But children are not guinea pigs to be used in social experiments in redefining the institutions of marriage and family. They are vulnerable individuals with vital emotional and developmental needs. The great harm done by denying them both a mother and a father in a committed marriage will not easily be reversed, and society will pay a grievous price for its ill-advised adventurism.

Notes

1. Liz Winfeld, "In a Family Way," *Denver Post,* November 28, 2001.
2. Marilyn Elias, "Doctor's Back Gay "Co-Parents," *USA Today,* February 3, 2002.
3. "Chapter 4: Second-Parent Adoption," in *The Family* (Human Rights Campaign, 2002). . . .
4. Ibid.
5. Bob Egelko, "Court Clarifies Decision on Adoptions," *San Francisco Chronicle,* November 22, 2001. The decision is under review by the California Supreme Court.
6. "PCT 14: Unmarried-Partner Households by Sex of Partners" (U.S. Census Bureau: Census 2000 Summary File 1).
7. Dan Black et al., "Demographics of the Gay and Lesbian Population in the United States: Evidence from Available Systematic Data Sources," *Demography* 37 (May 2000): 150.
8. David M. Smith and Gary J. Gates, "Gay and Lesbian Families in the United States: Same-Sex Unmarried Partner Households," *Human Rights Campaign* (August 22, 2001): 2.

9. Dan Black et al., "Demographics of the Gay and Lesbian Population," "4.7 percent of men in the combined samples have had at least one same-sex experience since age 18, but only 2.5 percent of men have engaged in exclusively same-sex sex over the year preceding the survey. Similarly, 3.5 percent of women have had at least one same-sex sexual experience, but only 1.4 percent have had exclusively same-sex sex over the year preceding the survey." (p. 141.)

10. Ibid.

11. Paula Ettelbrick, quoted in William B. Rubenstein, "Since When Is Marriage a Path to Liberation?" *Lesbians, Gay Men, and the Law,* (New York: The New Press, 1993), pp. 398, 400.

12. Michelangelo Signorile, *Life Outside* (New York: HarperCollins, 1997), p. 213.

13. Mary Mendola, *The Mendola Report* (New York: Crown, 1980), p. 53.

14. L. Koepke et al., "Relationship Quality in a Sample of Lesbian Couples with Children and Child-free Lesbian Couples," *Family Relations* 41 (1992): 228.

15. Bigner and Jacobson, "Adult Responses to Child Behavior and Attitudes Toward Fathering," Frederick W. Bozett, ed., *Homosexuality and the Family* (New York: Harrington Park Press, 1989), pp. 174, 175.

POSTSCRIPT

Should Lesbian and Gay Individuals Be Allowed to Adopt Children?

Parenting is an area that has so many unknown factors, influences, and outcomes. Two-parent, high-income families sometimes have children who grow up with emotional and/or behavioral problems. Single parents can raise healthy, well-adjusted children. Some heterosexual couples raise children effectively and some do not; some lesbian or gay couples raise children effectively, and some do not.

While there is much research exploring correlations between economic health, number of parents, and other factors, literature reviewing the connections between a parent's sexual orientation and her or his ability to parent remains inconclusive. There are studies maintaining that children need to be raised by a married, heterosexual couple, and there are studies asserting that a same-sex couple can do just as effective a job.

There is also insufficient information about homosexuality itself, and the effects that having a lesbian, gay, or bisexual parent may or may not have on a child. The lack of information and plethora of misinformation breed fear. In at least two countries, depending on the official(s) involved in screening for the adoption, the prospective parents may be required to provide proof that they are heterosexual. When people are afraid, they want to protect—in this case, people who do not understand the bases of sexual orientation feel they need to protect children. In doing so, they sometimes make decisions that are not always in the best interest of the child. For example, in 1996, a divorced heterosexual couple living in Florida was battling over custody of their 11-year-old daughter. The male partner had recently completed an eight-year prison sentence for the murder of his first wife, and had married his third. His ex-wife, however, had since met and partnered with a woman. A judge determined that the man and his new wife would provide a more appropriate home for the child than the child's mother because she was in a relationship with another woman. In the end, the judge believed that the child would do best in a home with a mother and a father, even though the father was convicted of second-degree murder and accused of sexually molesting his daughter from his first marriage.

How do you feel about this? If you feel that heterosexual couples are more appropriate parents than same-sex couples, how would the fact that one of the heterosexual partners had committed a capital crime affect your opinion?

Sometimes, we argue for what we think "should be" in a given situation. A challenge arises when comparing the "should be" to the "is"—what we think is best as opposed to the reality. If you feel that heterosexual married couples make the best parents, what should be done with those same-sex

219

couples who are providing a loving, stable home for their children? Would it be best to leave the child where she or he is, or do you think the child would be better off removed from her or his existing family structure and placed with a heterosexual couple? Clearly, this is a discussion and debate that will continue as more and more same-sex couples not only adopt, but also have biological children of their own.

Internet References . . .

American Association of Sex Educators, Counselors, and Therapists

The American Association of Sex Educators, Counselors, and Therapists is a not-for-profit, interdisciplinary professional organization whose members share an interest in promoting understanding of human sexuality and healthy sexual behavior.

http://www.aasect.org

American Association for Marriage and Family Therapy

The American Association for Marriage and Family Therapy (AAMFT) is the professional association for the field of marriage and family therapy. The AAMFT facilitates research, theory development and education, and develops standards for graduate education and training, clinical supervision, professional ethics and the clinical practice of marriage and family therapy. Their Web site also features a search engine for finding a licensed marriage/family therapist.

http://www.aamft.org

The Rape, Abuse, and Incest National Network

The Rape, Abuse, and Incest National Network is the nation's largest anti-sexual assault organization, operating the National Sexual Assault Hotline, offering educational information and resources, and advocating for effective policies to reduce the incidence of sexual assault.

http://www.rainn.org

Men Can Stop Rape

Men Can Stop Rape (formerly Men's Rape Prevention Project) works to empower male youth and the institutions that serve them to work as allies with women in preventing rape and other forms of "men's violence." Through awareness-to-action education and community organizing, the organization seeks to promote gender equity and build men's capacity to be strong without being violent.

http://www.mencanstoprape.org

The American Red Cross

The American Red Cross, founded in 1881 by Clara Barton, is the nation's "premier emergency response organization." In addition to domestic disaster relief, the Red Cross also offers services in the following areas: community services that help the needy; support and comfort for military members and their families; the collection, processing, and distribution of lifesaving blood and blood products; educational programs that promote health and safety; and international relief and development programs.

http://www.redcross.org

Twenty-First Century
Sexuality Issues

As times change, cultural beliefs about many things change. Nowhere is this more prevalent than in the discussion about romantic and sexual relationships. Technology, in particular the Internet, has added new dimensions to intimate relationships that were unimaginable even 15 short years ago. The media continue to depict images of what "idea" relationships should look like. The discussions and debates surrounding how we conduct ourselves in relationships are rooted deeply in how we were raised, our spiritual and cultural values and beliefs, and our past experiences with relationships. They are also dramatically affected by current messages that we are bombarded with from all factions of society. This section offers a look at three questions that are asked primarily within the context of heterosexual relationships:

- Is Cybersex "Cheating"?

- Are Open Relationships Healthy?

- Does Pornography Reduce the Incidence of Rape?

- Should Men Who Have Sex with Men Be Allowed to Donate Blood?

- Are Statutory Rape Laws Effective at Protecting Minors?

ISSUE 14

Is Cybersex "Cheating"?

YES: Stephen O. Watters, from *Real Solutions for Overcoming Internet Addictions* (Servant Publications, 2001)

NO: CBSNEWS.com, from "A Look at Internet Infidelity" (August 4, 2003)

ISSUE SUMMARY

YES: Stephen O. Watters shares personal experiences of several women whose marriages have been unsatisfying and who have sought connection with men online. He argues that the type of connection people can establish via the Internet can be extremely powerful, and that the significance of these relationships can be just as damaging to a marriage as a live affair—perhaps even more so, since these online sexual relationships can, he says, lead to an addiction.

NO: CBSNEWS.com reports that while Internet relationships may not be healthy for a relationship, they are not the same thing as, and should not be equated with, an actual affair. A sexual relationship maintained only in print is nowhere near as intense as a relationship that is consummated in person.

Since the dawn of the Internet, human beings have been using it as a source of information, improved communication, and in some cases, romantic or sexual partners. Web sites like match.com and planetout.com are among the many where people can, for a fee, peruse the ads of people whose photographs and descriptions sound intriguing to them. A visual version of newspaper and magazine personal ads, Internet dating has provided wonderful opportunities for many people to connect.

Some people, however, are not seeking a life partner or spouse, because they already have one at home. As some relationships mature, there may be any number of reasons one or both partners may have for seeking sexual pleasure outside of their primary relationship: feelings of love may be there, but feelings of attraction may have changed; one partner may have experienced some kind of disability that makes it no longer possible for her or him to perform sexually; the relationship may be flawed, but neither is willing to discuss the problem; the couple may decide, together, that they want to enhance their sexual relationship by opening it up to other partners, and then comparing notes at home, and so on. Regardless of the reasons why people open up their relationships, when it is done by one partner without the partner knowing—without an implicit or explicit agreement that this is acceptable—it can create problems in, and even end, the relationship.

If you were to do a Google search on the word "cybersex," over one million hits would be returned. Cybersex is the twenty-first-century's version of phone sex. It involves two (or more) people using instant-messaging capabilities to write erotic messages to each other online, leading to arousal and orgasm in some way. While committed couples may use cybersex when one partner is traveling, or when the couple is in a long-distance relationship, cybersex is most often used as an exchange between strangers—where both people can create and seek out what they see as ideal persona online, and have intimate experiences with no strings attached.

For some, cybersex is a wonderful way of expressing fantasies and experiencing sexual pleasure without obligation—no relationship, and no chance of an infection or pregnancy. Others find cybersex to be threatening, particularly if it is done by their partner or spouse behind their backs. What do you think?

As you read this issue, consider what you think are characteristics of a romantic relationship that you value. What do you expect from your partner when it comes to sexual behaviors? How would you feel if you found out that she or he were having cybersex online with someone? Do you think it's cheating, or as private as someone who chooses to masturbate in private?

In the following selections, Stephen O. Watters describes cybersex as a symptom of a much larger problem in a relationship. He argues that cybersex encounters that become regular appointments is "adultery," and that they can only lead to heartbreak for all the people involved—including the person whose partner or spouse is involved in the online relationship. CBSNEWS.com presents an alternate view—that cybersex does not carry the same risks as an in-person affair does, both emotionally and physically.

YES ⤶

Stephen O. Watters

Affairs

Question and Answer

Is Cybersex "Cheating"?

For a woman, the allure of a "knight in shining armor" online pushes her over the line and into adultery. She may arrange to meet several online lovers at hotels for sex. Yet when exactly did she cross the line? Does her relationship become adulterous when she has sex with another man, or does it begin as soon as she starts flirting?

"Women often justify their online relationships because they see them as virtual, not adulterous," says Marnie Ferree, "especially if the relationship is only emotional, not sexual yet."[1] Women cross the line, however, as soon they begin to sneak around behind their husband's backs to share intimate thoughts with another man." Stay-at-home moms in chat rooms are sharing all this personal stuff they are hiding from their partners," says Peggy Vaughan, America Online expert on problems caused by infidelity. She adds that such experiences can "quickly escalate into their thinking they have found a soul mate. It's so predictable, it is like a script."[2]

"[Online relationships] can threaten marriages, even if there is no sex involved," says Dr. Shirley Glass, a Baltimore-based psychologist who has been studying infidelity for over twenty years. "Such online liaisons involve the three elements of an emotional affair: secrecy, intimacy, and sexual chemistry."[3]

Understandably, many participants in online communities never intended for their innocent conversations to lead to fullblown affairs. Take Beth and Bob, for example. Both wandered into Christian chat rooms not knowing that the emotional connections made there could lead to adultery. Or take Julie, whose online affair led to a divorce. "I really wasn't wanting affairs from these men online," she says. "I really just wanted someone that would talk to me . . . and I could talk about everyday things and I thought they cared."

Not only did Julie have an unintended affair, she failed to find someone who could meet her deeper needs. "These people don't care," she says now. "They are just using each other. It truly is a meat market, and I don't think there are a lot of real feelings involved. Oh, in some crazy way they think there is, but there's also the fear that if you aren't online then they will find someone else. I guess that is why the people that are into that stay online so much. They are afraid of losing that partner—whoever they have been talking to. But it's inevitable, because no one can be on all the time, and sooner or later . . . they find someone that is more interesting or seems to say all the right things all over again."[4]

Debbie, a 36-year-old attorney from Los Angeles, wasn't looking for an affair; she just wanted someone to help her learn how to play a multiplayer game called DarknessFalls. One guy offered to help, but soon he started flirting with her. "I appreciated his help so much and wanted to continue getting it, so I innocently began flirting back," she said. "The flirtations grew, and soon enough we were having cybersex while we were in character. I grew less and less attracted to my husband, and the male character became my fantasy online husband in the game.

"I felt as though I had fallen in love with this character. My online husband and I began corresponding through email and expressed that love for each other and began talking on the phone. I started spending less time with my [real] husband and more time . . . online. Pretty soon I was missing court appearances because I couldn't get off the game. Luckily for me, my online husband [dumped me] after a year and a half. . . . My God, it was the worst feeling in the world. I felt like I had lost everything in the world that mattered to me. I left the game because I hurt so much."[5]

Both Debbie and Julie experienced a pattern that occurs frequently in relationships and has carried over to the Internet: the sex/intimacy exchange. "Women often give sex to get intimacy," says psychologist Dr. James Dobson, "and men give intimacy to get sex."[6] Internet chat rooms, newsgroups, and even online games have a way of bringing those tendencies together.

At first, a man may seem truly interested in discussing a favorite author with a woman in a literary newsgroup. As their conversation grows in intimacy, however, he may begin to pry about exotic interests. The woman who has invested in that relationship and has allowed it to meet a need for her may decide to respond in kind. "Having a meaningful relationship seems impossible for me," says the woman who is looking for a knight in shining armor. "I start to get attached emotionally and it scares men off; they just want free sex."[7]

A clandestine Internet relationship can seem fun for a season—swapping faceless messages can create the exhilaration of a masquerade ball. It's tempting to stay in an environment where your strengths can outweigh your weaknesses. Yet after that season is over what most people want is someone who will love them for who they really are. Especially when they're not at their best—when they're throwing up, when they have morning breath, or when they've just tripped up a flight of stairs. They desire the kind of intimacy where they are known for who they are—warts and all—and are still loved.[8]

Regrettably, that realization may not come until after they have developed a cybersex addiction or damaged their marriage with an online affair. What is your situation? Do you anxiously look forward to your next opportunity to connect with someone online? Do you prefer your online persona to who you are in real life? Have you developed an emotional relationship with someone online behind your spouse's back?

If you have had an adulterous online affair or show signs of cybersex addiction, you really need the help of a professional counselor. Few people are able to work their way back toward healthy sexuality and intimacy without the help of a professional who can guide them through unresolved emotional conflicts.

Notes

1. Telephone interview with Marnie Ferree, August 2000.

2. Karen S. Peterson, "Spouses Browse Infidelity Online," USA Today, July 6, 1999. . . .

3. Ibid.

4. Email posting on Cyber Windows newsgroup. Used by permission.

5. Jennifer P. Schneider, "A Qualitative Study of Cybersex Participants: Gender Differences, Recovery Issues, and Implications for Therapists." . . . Also published in Sexual Addiction and Compulsivity 7 (2000): 249–78.

6. James C. Dobson, Love for a Lifetime (Sisters, Ore.: Multnomah, 1996), 88.

7. Schneider, "A Qualitative Study . . ."

8. Steve Watters, "Strange Love," July 22, 1999. . . .

A Look at Internet Infidelity

The Internet has made it easy to view pornography and even have Internet affairs or "cyber-sex." In fact, 8 to 10 percent of Internet users actually become addicted to cyber-sex and one-third of divorce litigation is actually sparked by online affairs.

The big questions are: Is cyber-sex considered cheating? Is it actually adultery and what should you do if you suspect that your spouse is having an online affair? How close is a cyber-affair to a real affair? How easy is it to cross that line?

To help sort this all out, Dr. Joy Browne, radio talk-show host, author and clinical psychologist and relationship expert, and a woman named Christine who used spy software and caught her husband contacting women over the Internet, offer their views on the matter on *The Early Show*.

Christine suspected that her husband was having online affairs. She says what tipped her off was, "Long hours on the computer in his office. And when I'd walk in, he'd be switching so I couldn't see what he was doing. He'd say he was working. And then I had gotten a picture sent to me from my sister and I'm not very computer literate, and I was checking the computer to find out where I put the picture when I downloaded it. I started finding pictures that he had—some very interesting photos."

So Christine installed a software package called eBlaster by Spectorsoft on the computer that she and her husband shared.

The program kept track of all activity on the computer including all e-mails, instant messages, Web sites visited and even every keystroke made from that computer. Reports were e-mailed to her, and that's how she caught him.

She says, "And that's when I found out all the different sites he was going to, what he was looking for. He put out an ad with his picture. He was looking for women in our area. I think his words were, 'loose women in our area'; and also foursomes. And then that kind of triggered me. I started paying a little more attention and made copies of everything that was going on and then I set him up and I pretended I was somebody with a different name and so I was able to have a conversation with him for quite a while that I found out exactly what he was doing, what he was saying."

She's now in the middle of a divorce.

It is important to note, it is legal to put this spy software on a computer as long as you own the computer—which Christine did. But she would not have been legally allowed to put it on her husband's computer at work or any other computer that she did not own.

With the surge in cyber-affairs, a new market for electronic spying has developed. Web sites . . . describe an array of surveillance products capable of tracking a cheating spouse's e-mails and online chats, including some that can monitor each keystroke in real time.

But radio talk-show host Dr. Joy Browne says cyber-sex is really not cheating.

She says, "I'm one of those people who says no body fluids exchanged is not an affair. This is certainly tacky behavior." About Christine's situation, she notes before using the special software, Christine was already suspicious.

To Christine, Dr. Browne says, "You were having problems in your marriage, you probably weren't having sex. Whether you know the details about what he was doing, you have enough evidence. I feel like the software and computers is like looking in your kid's diary. You can find out by doing that, you can find out by object serving and you've got a much stronger case to say, 'look, I notice you're spending a lot of time at work.' I guess having the evidence may be helpful."

Christine says though she was aware of the problems in her marriage, she needed the extra proof. She says, "I still needed more. I was curious of what was going on because he would deny a lot of things and say it was nothing. Then he finally said, 'well, I'm just looking.' And this is a man who has always been very religious, very reputable."

When asked if there is any way cyber-affairs can be harmless, Dr. Browne says, "It's the same argument that people who use pot go on to use hard drugs. It seems to be circular reasoning. What we know is that men tend to talk to women when they're talking about emotional issues. If our men knew what we talked about with each other, they would go ballistic. But it's so expected and it's so understood.

"Do I think sort of talking in chat rooms when you're married is OK? I really don't. I think it's getting close to the edge. But it's not the same as an affair. If we make it the same as an affair then men will say, why not talk to them, why not date them, why not have sex with them? You're put at a different risk with sex involved doing anything other than typing. Typing is typing—sticky keyboard, but still typing," Dr. Browne says.

POSTSCRIPT

Is Cybersex "Cheating"?

We receive very clear messages from the time we are children about what a relationship is supposed to be—who should be involved, when and under what circumstances sexual behaviors are okay, and which behaviors are acceptable. As we get older, we analyze these messages and decide which are consistent and which are inconsistent with our own values and beliefs.

Relationships come in all different incarnations. When people get married, there is an expectation that they will stay together "'til death do we part." If a person is married at age 22, they may be talking about more than 60 years with the same person. Is it realistic to expect two people to be sexual only with each other for two-thirds of their adult life? Even if it's not realistic, does a couple just need to accept that mutual monogamy is an eternal part of their lifetime relationship? If not, what are the alternatives? Opening up a relationship can feel threatening to either or both partners. They may be concerned about comparisons between sexual performance and appearance, or that what was agreed upon as a sexual encounter actually blossomed into a love relationship.

For some, cybersex has provided this alternative. They do not believe that it is possible to fall in love with someone over the Internet—and that, since they have not come into physical contact with the other person, it's not the same as cheating. Others disagree, believing that cheating in one's head is the same as actually doing the act.

Regardless of how you feel about cybersex and open vs. monogamous relationships, this issue makes a clear point any way you slice it: Communicating about expectations within a relationship is key, and something that should be revisited throughout the duration of the relationship.

ISSUE 15

Are Open Relationships Healthy?

YES: Kathy Labriola, from "Models of Open Relationships," *Cat and Dragon Communications* (2006)

NO: Stanley Kurtz, from "Here Come the Brides: Plural Marriage Is Waiting in the Wings," *The Weekly Standard* (December 26, 2005)

ISSUE SUMMARY

YES: Counselor and nurse Kathy Labriola argues that our society has a very limited view of what can be seen as "healthy" when it comes to relationship structures by offering several possible models of nontraditional relationships involving various relationship compositions. If society did not exclusively sanction the heterosexual monogamous marriage as the ideal relationship structure, more people would realize that they have other options and potentially have more fulfilling relationships.

NO: Stanley Kurtz, a writer and senior fellow at the Ethics and Public Policy Center, argues against what he sees as some people's passivity to the reality of open relationships by discussing the Netherlands in which plural marriage is allowed. He believes that same-sex marriage is wrong, will lead to the acceptance of plural marriage, and that the institution of marriage as a whole will disintegrate.

Traditionally, the only type of respected long-term, committed relationship in most societies is marriage between a man and a woman. As different types of relationships continue to emerge, and people are more open about these relationships (for example, same-sex couples or different-sex couples who choose not to marry), cultures have been forced to look at their definitions of relationships and marriage. In some cases, cultures have made adjustments; in others, they've stood firm on their beliefs of what a long-term, committed relationship should be, and how it should be recognized. And in still other cases, the debate about how people should conduct themselves in relationships is and will continue to be ongoing.

One assumption that many people make when becoming spouses or life partners with someone else is that, along with other commitments, they will remain sexually faithful to each other for the duration of the relationship—or, as some people put it, "until death do us part." Doing so, they say, signals an ongoing dedication to one's partner or spouse, setting an example of self-control and devotion to the family structure.

Others feel differently. As early as the 1950s in the United States, people began the practice of "wife swapping," a practice that allegedly has its roots within wealthier suburbs. This term later became replaced by "swinging" and, more recently, as "the lifestyle." The first open swinger organization was seen in the 1960s in California; today there are swinger associations in countries throughout the world. Swinging is, technically, when two couples get together and exchange partners. The couples can be of any sexual orientation composition (heterosexual, lesbian or gay, bisexual), and the sex play can be same- or different-sex, but the implication is that a couple swings together, or not at all.

Different from swinging is something called an "open relationship," in which one or both partners remain committed to the primary relationship with a partner or spouse, but are then free to pursue sexual relationships with other people. For people who have always been taught and believe strongly in the one-partner-monogamy rule, these types of relationship feel very foreign, outlandish, and even unhealthy. For those who embrace having many sex partners but one primary partner or spouse, the idea of being sexual with one person for the rest of their lives feels equally as foreign, outlandish, and unhealthy. Still others support the idea of having more than one sexual and romantic partner, and develop polyamorous relationship structures. In some of these cases, three or more partners will set up household together and the partners have different types of relationships with each other, all of which is openly recognized and negotiated.

Do you think that people should be committed to only one person? Should that commitment be made for the remainder of one's life? Can healthy sexual expression only take place within the context of a committed relationship, or is it possible to have sex at home as well as with other people without it negatively affecting the primary relationship?

In the following selections, Kathy Labriola describes several models of open relationships to demonstrate that, although a great deal of work, these relationships can work. The key, she writes, is open communication about boundaries, desires, safer sex, and jealousy. Stanley Kurtz believes the only type of acceptable long-term committed relationship is heterosexual marriage, and denounces open relationships as outside of the purviews of the institution of marriage. Against anything other than heterosexual marriage, he argues that supporting same-sex marriage will lead to an endorsement of polamory, which will bring about the demise of the institution of marriage itself.

YES ⤶

Kathy Labriola

Models of Open Relationships

Introduction

The model of heterosexual, monogamous marriage is sanctioned by society, religion, and the law as the only acceptable type of sexual relationship. As a result, most people have not been exposed to other ways of life. In fact, we are so heavily socialized to believe in the ideals of monogamy and marriage, that many people cannot even imagine any other option. Frequent responses to the idea of open relationships are: "But I've never seen one"; "No one I know has ever tried that"; and "There's no way it could possibly work out." People always ask, "But how does it work? What's it like?" In fact, many successful models do exist. This pamphlet will give you an overview of the three main types of non-monogamous relationships which currently exist and the numerous variations on those models. To begin thinking about new ways of living, it can help to see some examples and to understand the advantages and drawbacks of each model. By examining each model, you may be able to discern whether an open relationship is right for you and, if so, which model may best fit your individual lifestyle. The possibilities are limitless and you can "customize" any of these models to accommodate your needs.

1. The Primary/Secondary Model

This is by far the most commonly practiced form of open relationship and it is the most similar to monogamous marriage. In this model, the "couple relationship" is considered primary, and any other relationships revolve around the couple. It is most frequently practiced by married people or other couples in long-term relationships. The couple decides that their relationship will have precedence over any outside relationships. The couple lives together and forms the primary family unit, while other relationships receive less time and priority. No outside relationship is allowed to become equal in importance to the primary relationship. The couple makes the rules; secondary lovers have little power over decisions and are not allowed to negotiate for what they want.

There are several distinct variations of this mode, including:

a. Heterosexual couples who are "swingers." They attend sex parties or meet sexual partners through personals ads or through various activities

From www.cat-and-dragon.com, 2006. Copyright © 2006 by Kathy Labriola. Reprinted by permission.

234

and networks. Some couples only have sex with other couples, others engage in three-way sex by locating another man for the woman or another woman for the man, and only have sexual adventures with their spouse present. Other straight couples allow either spouse to have recreational sex with other partners without the spouse present, but this is strictly sex and no emotional involvement or commitment is allowed.

For example,
Jane and Jim are a straight, married couple. They answer personals ads and have sex only with other couples, together as a foursome.

b. Gay male couples who go to the baths, the bars, sex clubs, or adult bookstores for recreational and/or anonymous sex. Many gay couples engage in this activity together, or have only "three-ways," but many couples have an agreement that either partner can go out alone and have sex with other men, but the goal is sex rather than relationships.

For example,
Joe and Jim are a Gay male couple who enjoy going to the baths together and meeting younger guys for three-way sex. Joe also likes to go to the park and have anonymous sex with other men, and occasionally answers personals ads to meet casual sex partners.

c. Couples of any and all sexual orientations who allow each spouse to have outside sexual relationships, either casual or long-term. These outside relationships are still considered secondary, and if any conflict develops, the primary couple relationship will take precedence. Usually the couple lives together, shares finances, spends weekends, holidays, and vacations together. The outside lovers usually do not live with them, spend much less time together, have very little voice in decisions and rule-making, and must arrange scheduling around the demands of the primary relationship. Some couples have rules that each spouse has veto power over any new lovers that his or her spouse may choose. In other words, if a woman is interested in a relationship with a new man, her husband has the power to veto that relationship before it starts, for any reason. Other couples allow each person to sleep with whomever they choose, but make rules about how much time they can spend with their other lovers, whether they can spend the night away from home, whether they can spend any weekend time with them, and other restrictions on these relationships.

For example,
Clare and Tom live together. Clare has a long-term sexual relationship with her neighbor, Melissa, who spends afternoons with Clare while Tom is at work. Tom has a series of short-term relationships with women he meets "on line" through polyamorous chat rooms. However, Tom falls in love with one of his outside lovers, so Clare insists that he break off the relationship because it threatens the primary couple relationship.

Pros and Cons of the Primary/ Secondary Model

This model is popular because it is the model most similar to traditional marriage and does not threaten the primacy of the couple. For most married or cohabiting couples, it is not such a stretch to have a few outside relationships as long as they know that the primary commitment is to the marriage. They can still be married, have children, live together, be socially acceptable, and "live a normal life," keeping their outside relationships secret from friends and family. It doesn't require making any radical changes in your lifestyle or your world view. One major benefit for many couples is that they feel secure that they won't be abandoned, because their spouse has agreed that outside relationships will be secondary. This is simpler and easier to organize logistically than other forms of open relationships. If there is any conflict over time, loyalty or commitment, the spouse always gets priority.

However, a major drawback of this model is that outside relationships are not so simple or easy to predict or control. Having a sexual relationship with someone else often leads to becoming emotionally involved and even falling in love, frequently causing a crisis in the primary relationship and even divorce. Initiating a sexual relationship is opening a door to many possibilities, and often secondary relationships grow into something else which does not fit neatly into the confines of this model. Many people who become "secondary" lovers become angry at being subjugated to the couple, and demand equality or end the relationship. For this model to be successful, couples must be very convinced that their relationship is strong enough to weather these ups and downs. Conversely, some couples who start with this model decide eventually to shift to some form of the Multiple Primary Partners model to allow secondary relationships to become equal to the primary couple relationship.

2. Multiple Primary Partners Model

While there are many variations on this theme, the key factor is that all primary partner models include three or more people in a primary relationship in which all members are equal partners. Instead of a couple having priority and control in the relationship, all relationships are considered primary, or have the potential of becoming primary. Each partner has equal power to negotiate for what they want in the relationship, in terms of time, commitment, living situation, financial arrangements, sex, and other issues.

Some examples of variations on this model:

a. Polyfidelity Model—Closed Multi-Adult Families

This is a "group marriage" model, essentially the same as being married—except you're married to more than one person. Usually consisting of three to six adults, all partners live together, share finances, children, and household responsibilities. Depending on the sexual orientation of the members, all adults in the family are sexual partners. For instance, if all members are heterosexual, all the women have sexual relationships with all the men. If the women are bisexual, they may have sexual relationships with the women as well as the men. And so on. However, this is a closed system, and sex is only allowed between family members—no outside sexual relationships are allowed. Some families are open to taking on new partners, but only if all members of the family agree to accept the new person as a partner. The new person then moves into the household and becomes an equal member of the family. The polyfidelity model was made famous during the 1970's and 80's by the Kerista commune in San Francisco, which had several households living this model for many years. Currently, the most common form of this model is a triad of two women and one man, or two men and one woman. However, recently there have been a number of polyfidelitous families formed by two heterosexual couples who become a four-some and live together as a family.

> For example,
> Jane and Tom and Mary and Bill all live together as a polyfidelitous family, and they have three children. They pool their incomes and make house payments, buy food, and provide for the children collectively, sharing child rearing and household responsibilities. They are heterosexual, so each of the women has sexual relations with both men; Jane falls in love with Joaquin, an outside friend. After much consideration, all partners agree that Joaquin can move into the household and join the family. He becomes an equal partner in the household and has sexual relations with Jane and Mary.

Pros and Cons of Polyfidelity

Polyfidelity can be a richly rewarding experience, creating an extended family and intentional community. Pooling resources is economical and ecological, and can reduce the stress of child rearing by spreading the work and the responsibility among several adults rather than just one or two parents. However, polyfidelity requires a very high level of compatibility and affinity between all partners. Everyone must agree on where to live, what to cook for dinner, how clean the house should be, how much money to spend and on what, whether to have children and how to raise them. Most people find it difficult enough to locate one partner they can successfully live with for the "long haul", much less two, three, four or more. And living together as a group decreases privacy and autonomy, often leading to interpersonal conflicts and stress. Living in a group requires excellent interpersonal skills, clear communication, assertiveness, co-operation, and flexibility in order to accommodate everyone's needs. Picking compatible partners and being accommodating are both key to successful polyfidelity.

b. Multiple Primary Partners—Open Model

This model is very different from polyfidelity in that all partners are given much more autonomy and flexibility in developing any relationships they choose and defining those relationships on their own terms. In the Primary/Secondary model the couple is the center of power, and in the polyfidelity model the entire family group makes decisions together and all must agree. In the Multiple Primary Partners Open Model, the individual is the basic unit of the family and is empowered to make his or her own rules and decisions. Partners may choose to live together, or they may choose to live with one or more partners, or live alone if that better suits their needs. This model is open, in that each partner has the right to choose other lovers at any time without the approval of any other partner. Each relationship evolves independently of partners' other relationships, with rules and level of commitment to be negotiated by each individual. No one can veto a potential partner or "pull rank" and insist on being the number one priority.

An example of this model is:

> Jennifer and Andrea are a lesbian couple who live together. Andrea also has another primary partner, Julia, who does not live with them, but receives equal time and priority. Andrea spends one-half of the week with each woman.

Pros and Cons of the Open Model

There is much more fluidity in this approach as relationships are allowed to evolve over time with very few rules to direct or restrict their direction or level of commitment. However, it is also much less predictable and may cause anxiety for people who like more structure and prefer a clear hierarchy.

Because all partners are considered equal, each partner can negotiate for what they want. However, all this "processing" requires time, effort, and excellent communication skills. And some people find the potential for conflicting loyalties to be too threatening. For instance, which partner will spend holidays or vacations with you? Will they both go, will they alternate each year, will you spend part of each holiday or vacation with each one? If one partner is going through a crisis, can they demand more of your time and commitment? If you are experiencing problems in one relationship or feel more drawn toward another partner, what behavior is appropriate? Weighing your own needs and the desires of each partner can be very stressful and confusing. Some people find this model requires too much thinking, problem-solving and "going with the flow," and prefer a more rigid structure such as the primary-secondary model or the polyfidelity model.

3. Multiple Non-Primary Relationships

While the first two models stress commitment and primary relationships, some people prefer to remain essentially single but participate in more than one relationship. They are not looking for a committed relationship. For them, non-monogamy offers the intimacy, love, and sexual satisfaction of involvement in relationships without the constraints of a primary relationship. This model works best for people who have a serious, all-consuming commitment to something other than relationships; people who are very busy with their work, their art, raising children alone, or political involvements. Usually they prefer relationships with people who, like themselves, want less commitment, or people who already have a primary relationship and are looking for a "secondary" relationship. People involved in this model usually don't make a lot of rules about their relationships, and retain a very high degree of personal freedom and autonomy. They usually live alone and make relationships a relatively low priority in their lives.

An example is:

> Jessica is a single mother with three kids and a full time job. She doesn't have time for a primary relationship, and has two long-term but casual sexual relationships with Jacob and Anthony. Jacob is a business executive who travels a lot for his job, so he is only free to see Jessica about once a week. Anthony is married to a nurse, but sees Jessica one evening a week when his wife works till 11:00 PM at the hospital.

Pros and Cons on Non-Primary Model

For this model to be successful, it is crucial to carefully choose partners who will be satisfied with a less committed relationship, and to communicate that clearly to potential partners. This model often works great as long as all parties are too busy or too committed elsewhere to want a primary relationship. However, conflict can arise when circumstances change and one person has more time or develop a desire for a primary relationship. For instance, when Jacob gets a promotion and no longer has to travel for his job, or a married lover gets divorced—they may suddenly demand more time and commitment or even demand a monogamous relationship. Such a change often proves fatal to the existing relationship. However, sometimes people see such a challenge as an opportunity for growth and are able to change their relationship to accommodate everyone's needs.

A Few Words of Parting Advice

There are many different types of open relationships. Some models will fit your needs much better than others. To identify your preferred model, ask yourself some tough questions: How much security do you need to feel safe in a relationship? Do you need to feel that you're "Number One," or can you share that priority with other lovers? How much privacy and personal freedom do you need to feel comfortable? Have you been happiest living alone, living with one person, or with a group? What pushes your buttons? How much time and energy do you have to devote to relationships? What are your expectations of love relationships?

For you to be happy in open relationships of any kind, you must first know what you want and which model will be most likely to work for you. Secondly, you must be able to articulately communicate what you want to potential partners in an honest and clear way. And last, but certainly not least, it is crucial to pick partners who want the same type of relationship and are comfortable with your chosen model. Excellent interpersonal and communications skills go a long way towards achieving these goals, along with a willingness to negotiate to satisfy everyone's needs. Following these steps will maximize your chances of developing satisfying and successful open relationships.

Stanley Kurtz

NO

Here Come the Brides: Plural Marriage Is Waiting in the Wings

On September 23, 2005, the 46-year-old Victor de Bruijn and his 31-year-old wife of eight years, Bianca, presented themselves to a notary public in the small Dutch border town of Roosendaal. And they brought a friend. Dressed in wedding clothes, Victor and Bianca de Bruijn were formally united with a bridally bedecked Mirjam Geven, a recently divorced 35-year-old whom they'd met several years previously through an Internet chatroom. As the notary validated a *samenlevingscontract*, or "cohabitation contract," the three exchanged rings, held a wedding feast, and departed for their honeymoon.

When Mirjam Geven first met Victor and Bianca de Bruijn, she was married. Yet after several meetings between Mirjam, her then-husband, and the De Bruijns, Mirjam left her spouse and moved in with Victor and Bianca. The threesome bought a bigger bed, while Mirjam and her husband divorced. Although neither Mirjam nor Bianca had had a prior relationship with a woman, each had believed for years that she was bisexual. Victor, who describes himself as "100 percent heterosexual," attributes the trio's success to his wives' bisexuality, which he says has the effect of preventing jealousy.

The De Bruijns' triple union caused a sensation in the Netherlands, drawing coverage from television, radio, and the press. With TV cameras and reporters crowding in, the wedding celebration turned into something of a media circus. Halfway through the festivities, the trio had to appoint one of their guests as a press liaison. The local paper ran several stories on the triple marriage, one devoted entirely to the media madhouse.

News of the Dutch three-way wedding filtered into the United States through a September 26 report by Paul Belien, on his Brussels Journal website. The story spread through the conservative side of the Internet like wildfire, raising a chorus of "I told you so's" from bloggers who'd long warned of a slippery slope from gay marriage to polygamy.

Meanwhile, gay marriage advocates scrambled to put out the fire. M.V. Lee Badgett, an economist at the University of Massachusetts, Amherst, and research director of the Institute for Gay and Lesbian Strategic Studies, told a sympathetic website, "This [Brussels Journal] article is ridiculous. Don't be fooled—Dutch law does not allow polygamy." Badgett suggested that Paul

Belien had deliberately mistranslated the Dutch word for "cohabitation contract" as "civil union," or even "marriage," so as to leave the false impression that the triple union had more legal weight than it did. Prominent gay-marriage advocate Evan Wolfson, executive director of Freedom to Marry, offered up a detailed legal account of Dutch cohabitation contracts, treating them as a matter of minor significance, in no way comparable to state-recognized registered partnerships.

In short, while the Dutch triple wedding set the conservative blogosphere ablaze with warnings, same-sex marriage advocates dismissed the story as a silly stunt with absolutely no implications for the gay marriage debate. And how did America's mainstream media adjudicate the radically different responses of same-sex marriage advocates and opponents to events in the Netherlands? By ignoring the entire affair.

Yet there is a story here. And it's bigger than even those chortling conservative websites claim. While Victor, Bianca, and Mirjam are joined by a private cohabitation contract rather than a state-registered partnership or a full-fledged marriage, their union has already made serious legal, political, and cultural waves in the Netherlands. To observers on both sides of the Dutch gay marriage debate, the De Bruijns' triple wedding is an unmistakable step down the road to legalized group marriage.

More important, the De Bruijn wedding reveals a heretofore hidden dimension of the gay marriage phenomenon. The De Bruijns' triple marriage is a bisexual marriage. And, increasingly, bisexuality is emerging as a reason why legalized gay marriage is likely to result in legalized group marriage. If every sexual orientation has a right to construct its own form of marriage, then more changes are surely due. For what gay marriage is to homosexuality, group marriage is to bisexuality. The De Bruijn trio is the tip-off to the fact that a connection between bisexuality and the drive for multipartner marriage has been developing for some time.

As American gay-marriage advocates   were quick to point out, the cohabitation contract that joined Victor, Bianca, and Mirjam carries fewer legal implications and less status than either a registered partnership or a marriage—and Dutch trios are still barred from the latter two forms of union. Yet the use of a cohabitation contract for a triple wedding is a step in the direction of group marriage. The conservative and religious Dutch paper *Reformatorisch Dagblad* reports that this was the first known occurrence in the Netherlands of a cohabitation contract between a married couple and their common girlfriend. . . .

So the use of cohabitation contracts was an important step along the road to same-sex marriage in the Netherlands. And the link between gay marriage and the De Bruijns' triple contract was immediately recognized by the Dutch. The story in *Reformatorisch Dagblad* quoted J.W.A. van Dommelen, an attorney opposed to the De Bruijn union, who warned that the path from same-sex cohabitation contracts to same-sex marriage was about to be retraced in the matter of group marriage.

Van Dommelen also noted that legal complications would flow from the overlap between a two-party marriage and a three-party cohabitation contract.

The rights and obligations that exist in Dutch marriages and Dutch cohabitation contracts are not identical, and it's unclear which arrangement would take precedence in case of a conflict. "The structure is completely gone," said Van Dommelen, as he called on the Dutch minister of justice to set up a working group to reconcile the conflicting claims of dual marriages and multipartner cohabitation contracts. Of course, simply by harmonizing the conflicting claims of dual marriages and triple cohabitation contracts, that working group would be taking yet another "small step" along the road to legal recognition for group marriage in the Netherlands.

The slippery-slope implications of the triple cohabitation contract were immediately evident to the SGP, a small religious party that played a leading role in the failed battle to preserve the traditional definition of marriage in the Netherlands. SGP member of parliament Kees van der Staaij noted the substantial overlap between marriage rights and the rights embodied in cohabitation contracts. Calling the triple cohabitation contract a back-door route to legalized polygamy, Van der Staaij sent a series of formal queries to Justice Minister Piet Hein Donner, asking him to dissolve the De Bruijn contract and to bar more than two persons from entering into cohabitation contracts in the future.

The justice minister's answers to these queries represent yet another small step—actually several small steps—toward legal and cultural recognition for group marriage in the Netherlands. To begin with, Donner reaffirmed the legality of multipartner cohabitation contracts and pointedly refused to consider any attempt to ban such contracts in the future. Donner also went so far as to assert that contracts regulating multipartner cohabitation can fulfill "a useful regulating function" (also translatable as "a useful structuring role"). In other words, Donner has articulated the rudiments of a "conservative case for group marriage."

The SGP responded angrily to Donner's declarations. In the eyes of this small religious party, Donner had effectively introduced a form of legal group marriage to the Netherlands. A party spokesman warned of an impending legal mess—especially if the De Bruijn trio, or others like them, have children. The SGP plans to raise its objections again when parliament considers the justice department's budget.

It's not surprising that the first English language report was a bit unclear as to the precise legal status and significance of the triple Dutch union. The Dutch themselves are confused about it. One of the articles from which Paul Belien drew his original report is careful to distinguish between formal marriage and the cohabitation contract actually signed by Victor, Bianca, and Mirjam. Yet the very same article says that Victor now "officially" has "two wives."

Even Dutch liberals acknowledge the implications of the De Bruijn wedding. Jan Martens, a reporter and opinion columnist for *BN/DeStem*, the local paper in Roosendaal, wrote an opinion piece mocking opposition to group marriage by religious parties like the SGP. Noting the substantial overlap between cohabitation contracts and marriage, Martens said he agreed with the SGP that the De Bruijn triple union amounts to a "short-cut to polygamy." Yet Martens emphasized that he "couldn't care less if you have two, three, four, or sixty-nine wives or husbands."

Minority religious parties and their newspapers excepted, this mixture of approval and indifference seems to be the mainstream Dutch reaction so far. Not only has Justice Minister Donner articulated the beginnings of a conservative case for group marriage, but Green party spokesman Femke Halsema, a key backer of gay marriage, has affirmed her party's support for the recognition of multipartner unions. The public has not been inclined to protest these developments, and the De Bruijn trio have been welcomed by their neighbors. . . .

When it comes to marriage, culture shapes law. (It's a two-way street, of course. Law also influences culture.) After all, Dutch same-sex marriage advocates still celebrate the foundational role of symbolic gay marriage registries in the early 1990s. Although these had absolutely no legal status, the publicity and sympathy they generated are now widely recognized as keys to the success of the Dutch campaign for legal same-sex unions and ultimately marriage. How odd, then, that American gay-marriage advocates should respond to the triple Dutch wedding with hair-splitting legal discourses, while ignoring the Dutch media frenzy and subsequent signs of cultural acceptance—for a union with far more legal substance than Holland's first symbolic gay marriages. Despite the denials of gay-marriage advocates, in both legal and cultural terms, Victor, Bianca, and Mirjam's triple union is a serious move toward legalized group marriage in the Netherlands.

Given the stir in Holland   it's remarkable that not a single American mainstream media outlet carried a story on the triple Dutch wedding. Of course the media were all over the Dutch gay marriage story when they thought the experiment had been a success. In late 2003 and early 2004, in the wake of the Supreme Court's *Lawrence v. Texas* decision, which ruled sodomy laws unconstitutional, and looming gay marriage in Massachusetts, several American papers carried reports from the Netherlands. The common theme was that Holland had experienced no ill effects from gay marriage, and that the issue was no longer contentious. . . .

Although the triple   Dutch union has been loosely styled "polygamy," it's actually a sterling example of polyamory. Polyamorists practice "responsible nonmonogamy"—open, loving, and stable relationships among more than two people (see "Beyond Gay Marriage: The Road to Polyamory," *The Weekly Standard,* August 4/August 11, 2003). Polygamous marriages among fundamentalist Mormons or Muslims don't depend on a blending of heterosexuality and bisexuality. Yet that combination perfectly embodies the spirit of polyamory. And polyamorists don't limit themselves to unions of one man and several women. One woman and two men, full-fledged group marriage, a stable couple openly engaging in additional shifting or stable relationships—indeed, almost any combination of partner-number and sexual orientation is possible in a polyamorous sexual grouping.

Polyamorists would call the De Bruijn union a "triad." In a polyamorous triad, all three partners are sexually connected. This contrasts with a three-person "V," in which only one of the partners (called the "hinge" or "pivot") has a sexual relationship with the other two. So the bisexuality of Bianca and Mirjam classifies the De Bruijn union as a polyamorous bisexual triad. In another sense, the De Bruijn marriage is also a gay marriage. The Bianca-Mirjam component of the union is gay, and legalized gay marriage in Holland has clearly helped make the idea of a legally recognized bisexual triad thinkable. . . .

The germ of an organized effort   to legalize polyamory in the United States can be found in the Unitarian Church. Although few realize it, the Unitarian Church, headquartered in Boston, played a critical role in the legalization of same-sex marriage in Massachusetts. Julie and Hillary Goodridge, lead plaintiffs in *Goodridge v. Department of Public Health*, were married at the headquarters of the Unitarian Universalists in a ceremony presided over by the Reverend William G. Sinkford, president of the Unitarian Universalist Association. Hillary Goodridge is program director of the Unitarian Universalist Funding Program. And Unitarian churches in Massachusetts played a key role in the struggle over gay marriage, with sermons, activism, and eventually with marriage ceremonies for same-sex couples. Choosing a strongly church-affiliated couple like the Goodridges as lead plaintiffs was an important part of the winning strategy in the *Goodridge* case.

It's a matter of interest, therefore, that an organization to promote public acceptance of polyamory has been formed in association with the Unitarian Church. Unitarian Universalists for Polyamory Awareness (UUPA) was established in the summer of 1999. At the time, the news media in Boston carried reports from neighboring Vermont, where the soon-to-be-famous civil unions case was about to be decided. And the echo effect of the gay marriage battle on the polyamory movement goes back even further. The first informal Unitarian polyamory discussion group gathered in Hawaii in 1994, in the wake of the first state supreme court decision favorable to same-sex marriage in the United States.

"Our vision," says UUPA's website, "is for Unitarian Universalism to become the first poly-welcoming mainstream religious denomination." Those familiar with Unitarianism's role in the legalization of gay marriage understand the legal-political strategy implicit in that statement. UUPA's political goals are spelled out by Harlan White, a physician and leading UUPA activist, on the society's website. Invoking the trial of April Divilbiss, the first American polyamorist to confront the courts, White says, "We are concerned that we may become the center of the next great social justice firestorm in America."

White maintains that American polyamorists are growing in number. An exact count is impossible, since polyamory is still surrounded by secrecy. Polyamorists depend on the Internet to connect. Even so, says White, "attendance at conferences is up, email lists and websites are proliferating, and poly support groups are growing in number and size." As for the Unitarian polyamorists, their email list has several hundred subscribers, and the group has put on well-attended workshops at Unitarian General Assemblies since 2002. And although the number of open polyamorists is limited, some Unitarian ministers already perform "joining ceremonies" for polyamorous families. . . .

Shortly after the second article appeared, UUA president Sinkford circulated a statement among Unitarians acknowledging that press interest in

Unitarian polyamory had "generated a great deal of anxiety" among the church's leadership. "Many of us are concerned that such press coverage might impair our ability to witness effectively for our core justice commitments." Sinkford appeared to be expressing a concern that had been stated more baldly in the original *Chronicle* article. According to the *Chronicle*, many of the students and faculty at the Unitarians' key west-coast seminary, Starr King School for the Ministry, in Berkeley, see the polyamory movement as a threat to the struggle for same-sex marriage.

In other words, Unitarians understand that moving too swiftly or openly to legitimize polyamory could validate the slippery-slope argument against same-sex marriage. So with news coverage prematurely blowing the cover off the Unitarians' long-term plan to legalize polyamory, President Sinkford took steps to hold UUPA at arm's length. Sinkford issued a public "clarification" that distanced the church from any formal endorsement of polyamory, yet also left room for the UUPA to remain a "related organization." . . .

The other fascinating angle in the *San Francisco Chronicle*'s coverage of the Unitarian polyamorists was the prominence of bisexuality. Most members of UUPA are either bisexual or heterosexual. One polyamorist minister who had recently come out to his congregation as a bisexual treated polyamory and bisexuality synonymously. "Our denomination has been welcoming to gays and lesbians and transgendered people," he said. "Bisexuals have not received the recognition they deserve." In other words, anything less than formal church recognition of polyamory is discrimination against bisexuals.

Two developing lines   of legal argument may someday bring about state recognition for polyamorous marriage: the argument from polyamory, and the argument from bisexuality. In a 2004 law review article, Elizabeth F. Emens, of the University of Chicago Law School, offers the argument from polyamory (see "Monogamy's Law: Compulsory Monogamy and Polyamorous Existence," *New York University Review of Law & Social Change*). Polyamory is more than the mere practice of multiple sexual partnership, says Emens. Polyamory is also a disposition, broadly analogous to the disposition toward homosexuality. Insofar as laws of marriage, partnership, or housing discriminate against polyamorous partnerships, maintains Emens, they place unfair burdens on people with "poly" dispositions. Emens takes her cue here from the polyamorists themselves, who talk about their "poly" inclinations the way gays talk about homosexuality. For example, polyamorists debate whether to keep their poly dispositions "in the closet" or to "come out."

Emens's case for a poly disposition was inspired by the radical lesbian thinker Adrienne Rich, who famously put forward a "continuum model" of lesbianism. Rich argued that all women, lesbian-identified or not, are in some sense lesbians. If women could just discover where they fall on the "lesbian continuum," then even those women who remain heterosexually identified would abandon any prejudice against homosexuality.

Following Rich, Emens argues that all of us have a bit of "poly" inside. By discovering and accepting our own desires for multiple sexual partners, then even those who remain monogamous would abandon their prejudice against polyamorists. Of course some people fall at the extreme ends of these continuums. Some folks are intensely monogamous, for example. But by the same token, others are intensely polyamorous. Whether for biological or cultural reasons, says Emens, some folks simply cannot live happily without multiple simultaneous sexual partners. And for those people, Emens argues, our current system of marriage is every bit as unjust as it is for homosexuals. . . .

The second legal strategy available to the polyamorists is the argument from bisexuality. No need here to validate anything as novel-sounding as a "polyamorous disposition." A case for polyamory can easily be built on the more venerable orientation of bisexuality. While no legal scholar has offered such a case, the groundwork is being laid by Kenji Yoshino, a professor at Yale Law School and deputy dean for intellectual life.

Yoshino's 2000 *Stanford Law Review* article "The Epistemic Contract of Bisexual Erasure" has a bewildering title but a fascinating thesis. Yoshino argues that bisexuality is far more prevalent than is usually recognized. The relative invisibility of bisexuality, says Yoshino, can be attributed to the mutual interest of heterosexuals and homosexuals in minimizing its significance. But according to Yoshino, the bisexuality movement is on the rise, and bound to become more visible, with potentially major consequences for the law and politics of sexual orientation.

Defining bisexuality as a "more than incidental desire" for partners of both sexes, Yoshino examines the best available academic studies on sexual orientation and finds that each of them estimates the number of bisexuals as equivalent to, or greater than, the number of homosexuals. Up to now, the number of people who actively think of themselves as bisexuals has been much smaller than the number who've shown a "more than incidental" desire for partners of both sexes. But that, argues Yoshino, is because both heterosexuals and homosexuals have an interest in convincing bisexuals that they've got to make an all-or-nothing choice between heterosexuality and homosexuality.

Heterosexuals, for example, have an interest in preserving norms of monogamy, and bisexuality "destabilizes" norms of monogamy. Homosexuals, notes Yoshino, have an interest in defending the notion of an immutable homosexual orientation, since that is often the key to persuading a court that they have suffered discrimination. And homosexuals, adds Yoshino, have an interest in maximizing the number of people in their movement. For all these reasons and more, Yoshino argues, the cultural space in which bisexuals might embrace and acknowledge their own sexual identity has been minimized. Yoshino goes on to highlight the considerable evidence for the recent emergence of bisexuality as a movement, and predicts that in our current cultural climate—and given the numerical potential—bisexuality activism will continue to grow.

In addition to establishing the numerical and political significance of bisexuality, Yoshino lays down an argument that could easily be deployed to legalize polyamory: "To the extent that bisexuals are not permitted to express their dual desires, they might fairly characterize themselves as harmed." Yet Yoshino does not lay out a bisexual defense of polyamory. Instead Yoshino attacks—rightly—the stereotype that treats all bisexuals as nonmonogamous.

Yet the same research that establishes the monogamous preferences of many bisexuals also confirms that bisexuals tend toward nonmonogamy at substantially higher rates than homosexuals. (See Paula C. Rust, "Monogamy and Polyamory: Relationship Issues for Bisexuals" in Firestein, ed., *Bisexuality: The Psychology and Politics of an Invisible Minority.*) That fact could easily be turned by a bisexuality rights movement into an argument for legalized polyamory. . . .

In 2004, the *Journal of Bisexuality* published a special double issue on polyamory, also released as the book *Plural Loves: Designs for Bi and Poly Living.* It's clear from *Plural Loves* that the polyamory movement now serves as the de facto political arm of the bisexual liberation struggle. As one contributor notes, "the large number of bi people in the poly movement provides evidence that bisexuality is one of the major driving forces behind polyamory. In other words, polyamory was created and spread partly to satisfy the need for bisexual relationship structures. . . . [T]he majority of poly activists are also bisexual. . . . Poly activism is bi activism. . . . The bi/poly dynamic has the potential to move both communities towards a point of culture-wide visibility, which is a necessary step on the road to acceptance."

Clearly, visibility and acceptance are on the rise. This past summer, the *Baltimore Sun* featured a long, friendly article on the polyamorists' national conference, held in Maryland. In September, the *New York Times* ran a long personal account of (heterosexual) polyamory in the Sunday Styles section. But the real uptick in public bisexuality/polyamory began with the October 2005 release in New York of the documentary *Three of Hearts: A Postmodern Family.*

Three of Hearts is the story of the real-life 13-year relationship of two men and a woman. Together for several years in a gay relationship, two bisexual-leaning men meet a woman and create a threesome that produces two children, one by each man. Although the woman marries one of the men, the entire threesome has a commitment ceremony. The movie records the trio's eventual breakup, yet the film's website notes their ongoing commitment to the view that "family is anything we want to create." . . .

Of course, many argue that true bisexuality does not exist. In this view—held by a variety of people, from some psychiatrists to certain pro-gay-marriage activists—everyone is either heterosexual or homosexual. From this perspective, so-called bisexuals are either in confused transition from heterosexuality to homosexuality, or simply lying about their supposedly dual sexual inclinations. Alternatively, it's sometimes said that while female bisexuality does exist, male bisexuality does not. A recent and controversial study reported on by the *New York Times* in July 2005 claimed to show that truly bisexual attraction in men might not exist.

Whatever view we take of these medical/psychiatric/philosophical controversies, it is a fact that a bi/poly rights movement exists and is growing. Whether Koen Brand and Bianca and Mirjam de Bruijn are "authentic" bisexuals or "just fooling themselves," they are clearly capable of sustaining polyamorous bisexual V's and triads for long enough to make serious political demands. *Three of Hearts* raises questions about whether the two men in the triangle are bisexual, or simply confused gays. But with two children, a 13-year relationship, and at one time at least a clear desire for legal-ceremonial confirmation, the *Three of Hearts* trio is a harbinger of demands for legal group marriage. Public interest in the De Bruijn triangle has already raised the visibility and acceptance of polyamorous bisexuality in the Netherlands. For legal-political purposes, acceptance is what matters. And given Yoshino's numerical analysis, the growth potential for self-identifying bisexuals is substantial.

Americans today respond to gay and bisexual friends and family members in a variety of ways. Despite stereotypical accusations of "homophobia," the traditionally religious generally offer a mixture of compassion and concern. Many other Americans, conservative and liberal alike, are happy to extend friendship, understanding, and acceptance to gay and bisexual relatives and acquaintances. This heightened social tolerance is a good thing. Yet somehow the idea has taken hold that tolerance for sexual minorities requires a radical remake of the institution of marriage. That is a mistake.

The fundamental purpose of marriage is to encourage mothers and fathers to stay bound as a family for the sake of their children. Our liberalized modern marriage system is far from perfect, and certainly doesn't always succeed in keeping parents together while their children are young. Yet often it does. Unfortunately, once we radically redefine marriage in an effort to solve the problems of adults, the institution is destined to be shattered by a cacophony of grown-up demands.

The De Bruijn trio, Koen Brand, the Unitarian Universalists for Polyamory Awareness, the legal arguments of Elizabeth Emens and Kenji Yoshino, and the bisexual/polyamory movement in general have been launched into action by the successes of the campaign for gay marriage. In a sense, though, these innovators have jumped too soon. They've shown us today—well before same-sex marriage has triumphed nationwide—what would emerge in its aftermath.

Liberals may now put behind-the-scenes pressure on the Dutch government to keep the lid on legalized polyamory for as long as the matter of gay marriage is still unsettled. The Unitarian polyamorists, already conflicted about how much recognition to demand while the gay marriage battle is unresolved, may be driven further underground. But let there be no mistake about what will happen should same-sex marriage be fully legalized in the United States. At that point, if bisexual activists haven't already launched a serious campaign for legalized polyamory, they will go public. It took four years after the full legalization of gay marriage in the Netherlands for the first polyamory test case to emerge. With a far larger and more organized polyamory movement in America, it might not take even that long after the nationalization of gay marriage in the United States.

It's easy to imagine that, in a world where gay marriage was common and fully accepted, a serious campaign to legalize polyamorous unions would succeed—especially a campaign spearheaded by an organized bisexual-rights movement. Yet win or lose, the culture of marriage will be battered for years by the debate. Just as we're now continually reminded that not all married couples have children, we'll someday be endlessly told that not all marriages are monogamous (nor all monogamists married). For a second time, the fuzziness and imperfection found in every real-world social institution will be contorted into a rationale for reforming marriage out of existence.

POSTSCRIPT

Are Open Relationships Healthy?

The language of relationships is quite interesting, and varies depending upon our age and the nature of the relationship(s) in which we are involved. For example, when a person is not in a committed relationship with or married to someone, that person is "dating" other people. This might involve a sexual relationship of some kind, and include short- as well as longer-term relationships. There is no expectation of monogamy, whether sexual or social, unless it is discussed between that person and her or his various partners. The younger a person is, the more being in different relationships is encouraged—our cultures use expressions like "sow your wild oats" before "settling down" into a long-term, committed relationship. As a person gets older, she or he is more likely to be asked, "When are you going to settle down and start a family?"

As a single person, one is expected to exhaust one's desire for multiple sex partners in order to prepare for a lifetime of sexual fidelity to one person. When a person chooses to be with someone for the rest of their lives, yet has sex with someone outside of that primary relationship, she or he is seen as having a "momentary indiscretion," as "straying," or even "cheating." Depending on the value that is placed on sexual expressions and behaviors, doing so can bring about the end of a relationship or marriage.

Do you think that human beings are designed biologically to be monogamous, or is this solely a social construct? Would you say that it is different depending on the biological sex of the person? Why or why not? And if monogamy is solely a social construct, what purpose(s) would it have served when it was first created? Do those same purposes apply today in the early twenty-first century?

Suggested Readings

D. M. Anapol, *Polyamory: The New Love Without Limits: Secrets of Sustainable Intimate Relationships*. San Rafael, CA: Intinet Resource Center, March 1997.

D. P. Barash and J. E. Lipton, *The Myth of Monogamy: Fidelity and Infidelity in Animals and People*. New York: W. H. Freeman, 2001.

C. Coontz, *Marriage, a History: From Obedience to Intimacy, or How Love Conquered Marriage*. New York: Viking Adult, 2006.

H. E. Fisher, *Anatomy of Love: The Natural History of Monogamy, Adultery, and Divorce*. Darby, PA: Diane Books Publishing Company, 1998.

M. Lamanna and A. Riedmann, *Marriages & Families: Making Choices in a Diverse Society,* (9th ed.). Belmont, CA: Wadsworth Publishing, 2005.

W. Matik, *Redefining Our Relationships: Guidelines for Responsible Open Relationships.* Oakland, CA: Defiant Times Press, 2002.

L. Miles and R. Miles, *The New Marriage: Transcending the Happily-Ever-After Myth.* Fort Bragg, CA: Cypress House, 2000.

A. A. Ravenscroft, *Polyamory: Roadmaps for the Clueless & Hopeful.* Santa Fe: Crossquarter Publishing Group, 2004.

ISSUE 16

Does Pornography Reduce the Incidence of Rape?

YES: Anthony D'Amato, from "Porn Up, Rape Down," Northwestern University School of Law, Public Law and Legal Theory Research Paper Series (June 23, 2006)

NO: Judith Reisman, from "Pornography's Link to Rape," WorldnetDaily.com (July 29, 2006)

ISSUE SUMMARY

YES: Professor of law Anthony D'Amato highlights statistics from the most recent National Crime Victimization Survey that demonstrate a correlation between the increased consumption of pornography over the years with the decreased incidence of rape. Some people, he argues, watch pornography in order to push any desire to rape out of their minds, and thus have no further desire to go out and actually do it.

NO: Judith Reisman, president of the Institute for Media Education, asserts that sex criminals imitate what they see depicted in the media, providing examples of serial rapists and killers who had large stores of pornography in their possession, and research in which approximately 33 percent of rapists said that they had viewed pornography immediately prior to at least one of their rapes.

$\mathbf{S}$ince the creation of the Internet, the world has seen a huge increase in the amount and manner in which information is exchanged with others. This includes the adult entertainment industry, which has become an enormous, multi-billion dollar industry thanks in part to the anonymity and privacy that online pornography provides adults. One challenge, many argue, is that adults are far from the only ones who are able to access porn sites online. Children as young as middle school-age are accessing images online, some of which they search for and some of which is targeted to them through SPAM e-mails or pornographic Web sites that purchase the domain of a similarly sounding Web site, counting on minors to arrive at their sites by accident.

The debates about the effects of porn on its users are nearly endless: Does viewing porn encourage young people to become sexually active at earlier ages? Does viewing porn psychologically damage kids? Do adults who view porn develop unrealistic expectations of beauty and sexual expression in their own relationships? And so on.

This issue looks at the effects of visual pornography on the incidence of rape in the United States. Since pornography became available, there are many proponents who maintain that by depicting certain sexual acts, sexually explicit media encourages people to try these acts out. In particular, they say, porn that shows rape makes this type of behavior real and, in the rapists' mind, acceptable, thereby encouraging rape. Others maintain that there is no causality between viewing Internet porn and the incidence of rape, that people are exposed to a wide range of information, images, and behaviors every day and do not engage in all of the behaviors they see. These include, they say, sexual behaviors.

Still others, like one of the authors who appears in this issue, maintain that having pornography available actually *decreases* the incidence of rape. Depicting rape, which is a socially unacceptable (and criminal) behavior, this author argues, actually provides a potential rapist with an outlet for his unacceptable fantasies, thereby keeping him from acting upon them. In the following selections, Anthony D'Amato analyzes data that correlates a decrease in rapes in the United States with the increase of pornography availability. Judith Reisman counters with stories from actual rapists who discuss viewing porn immediately before raping a victim.

YES ⬅

Anthony D'Amato

Porn Up, Rape Down

Today's headlines are shouting RAPE IN DECLINE![1] Official figures just released show a plunge in the number of rapes per capita in the United States since the 1970s. Even when measured in different ways, including police reports and survey interviews, the results are in agreement; there has been an 85% reduction in sexual violence in the past 25 years. The decline, steeper than the stock market crash that led to the Great Depression, is depicted in this chart prepared by the United States Department of Justice:

Rape rates
Adjusted victimization rate
per 1,000 persons age 12 and over

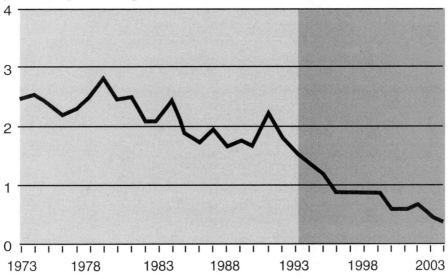

Source: *The National Crime Victimization Survey.* Includes both attempted and completed rapes.

As the chart shows, there were 2.7 rapes for every 1,000 people in 1980; by 2004, the same survey found the rate had decreased to 0.4 per 1000 people, a decline of 85%.

Official explanations for the unexpected decline include (1) less lawlessness associated with crack cocaine; (b) women have been taught to avoid unsafe situations; (c) more would-be rapists already in prison for other crimes; (d) sex education classes telling boys that "no means no." But these minor factors cannot begin to explain such a sharp decline in the incidence of rape.

There is, however, one social factor that correlates almost exactly with the rape statistics. The American public is probably not ready to believe it. My theory is that the sharp rise in access to pornography accounts for the decline in rape. The correlation is inverse: the more pornography, the less rape. It is like the inverse correlation: the more police officers on the street, the less crime.

The pornographic movie "Deep Throat" which started the flood of X-rated VHS and later DVD films, was released in 1972. Movie rental shops at first catered primarily to the adult film trade. Pornographic magazines also sharply increased in numbers in the 1970s and 1980s. Then came a seismic change: pornography became available on the new internet. Today, purveyors of internet porn earn a combined annual income exceeding the total of the major networks ABC, CBS, and NBC.

"Deep Throat" has moved from the adult theatre to a laptop near you.

National trends are one thing; what do the figures for the states show? From data compiled by the National Telecommunications and Information Administration in 2001, the four states with the *lowest* per capita access to the internet were Arkansas, Kentucky, Minnesota, and West Virginia. The four states with the *highest* internet access were Alaska, Colorado, New Jersey, and Washington. (I would not have guessed this.)

Next I took the figures for forcible rape compiled by police reports by the Disaster Center for the years 1980 and 2000. The following two charts display the results:

Table 1

States with Lowest Internet Access[2]

State	Internet 2001	Rape 1980	Rape 2000
Arkansas	36.9	26.7	31.7
Kentucky	40.2	19.2	27.4
Minnesota	36.1	23.2	45.5
W. Virginia	40.7	15.8	18.3

All figures are per capita.

While the nationwide incidence of rape was showing a drastic decline, the incidence of rape in the four states having the *least* access to the internet showed an actual *increase* in rape over the same time period. This result was almost too clear and convincing, so to check it I compiled figures for the four

Table 2

States with Highest Internet Access[3]

Alaska	64.1	56.8	70.3
Colorado	58.5	52.5	41.2
New Jersey	61.6	30.7	16.1
Washington	60.4	52.7	46.4

All figures are per capita.

states having the *most* access to the internet. Three out of four of these states showed declines (in New Jersey, an almost 50% decline). Alaska was an anomaly: it increased both in internet access and incidence of rape. However, the population of Alaska is less than one-tenth that of the other three states in its category. To adjust for the disparity in population, I took the combined population of the four states in each table and calculated the percentage change in the rape statistics:

Table 3

Combined Per Capita Percentage Change in Incidence of Rape

	Aggregate per capita increase or decline in rape.
Four states with lowest internet access	Increase in rape of 53%
Four states with highest internet access	Decrease in rape of 27%

I find these results to be statistically significant beyond the 95 confidence interval.

Yet proof of correlation is not the same thing as causation. If autumn regularly precedes winter, that doesn't mean that autumn causes winter. When six years ago my former Northwestern colleague John Donohue, together with Steven Levitt[4], found that legalized abortion correlated with a reduction in crime, theirs would have only been an academically curious thesis if they had not identified a causal factor. But they did identify one: that prior to legalization there were many unwanted babies born due to the lack of a legal abortion alternative. Those unwanted children became the most likely group to turn to crime.

My own interest in the rape-pornography question began in 1970 when I served as a consultant to President Nixon's Commission on Obscenity and Pornography. The Commission concluded that there was no causal relationship between exposure to sexually explicit materials and delinquent or criminal behavior. The President was furious when he learned of the conclusion.

Later President Reagan tried the same thing, except unlike his predecessor he packed the Commission with persons who passed his ideological litmus test (Small wonder that I was not asked to participate.) This time, Reagan's Commission on Pornography reached the approved result: that there does exist a causal relationship between pornography and violent sex crimes.

The drafter of the Commission's report was Frederich Schauer, a prominent law professor. In a separate statement, he assured readers that neither he nor the other Commissioners were at all influenced by their personal moral values.[5] . . .

Although the Reagan Commission had at its disposal all the evidence gathered by psychology and social-science departments throughout the world on the question whether a student's exposure to pornography increased his tendency to commit antisocial acts, I found that the Commission was unable to adduce a shred of evidence to support its affirmative conclusion. No scientist had ever found that pornography raised the probability of rape. However, the Commission was not seeking truth; rather, as I said in the title to my article, it sought political truth.

If pornography does not *produce* rape, I thought, then maybe it *reduces* rape. But no one apparently had any incentive to investigate the latter proposition. But the just-released rape statistics provide the necessary evidence.

Although neither Professor Schauer nor the other Commissioners ever responded to my William & Mary article, now they can forget it. For if they had been right that exposure to pornography leads to an increase in social violence, then the vast exposure to pornography furnished by the internet would by now have resulted in scores of rapes per day on university campuses, hundreds of rapes daily in every town, and thousands of rapes per day in every city. Instead, the Commissioners were so incredibly wrong that the incidence of rape has actually declined by the astounding rate of 85%.

Correlations aside, could access to pornography actually reduce the incidence of rape as a matter of causation? In my article I mentioned one possibility: that some people watching pornography may "get it out of their system" and thus have no further desire to go out and actually try it. Another possibility might be labeled "Victorian effect" the more that people covered up their bodies with clothes in those days, the greater the mystery of what they looked like in the nude. The sight of a woman's ankle was considered shocking and erotic. But today, internet porn has thoroughly de-mystified sex. . . .

I am sure there will be other explanations forthcoming as to why access to pornography is the most important causal factor in the decline of rape. Once one accepts the observation that there is a precise negative correlation between the two, the rest can safely be left to the imagination.

Notes

1. E.g., *Washington Post,* June 19, 2006; *Chicago Tribune,* June 21, 2006.
2. Statistics on Internet Access compiled from National Telecommunications and Information Administration. . . .
3. Statistics on forcible rape compiled from. . . .
4. Author of *Freakonimics* (2005).
5. U.S. Dept. of Justice, Final Report: Attorney General's Commission on Pornography 176–79 (1986) (personal statement of Commissioner Schauer).

Judith Reisman   **NO**

Pornography's Link to Rape

Would you try to put out a fire with gasoline?

No? Then you might disagree with an MSNBC online article, "Porn: Good for America!" by Glenn Reynolds, a University of Tennessee law professor. Reynolds suggests that pornography *reduces* rape!

As proof, Reynolds quotes a U.S. Department of Justice claim that in 2004 rape of "people" *over age 12* radically decreased with an "85 percent decline in the per-capita rape rate since 1979" (DOJ's National Crime Victimization Survey of "thousands of respondents 12 and older").

But the FBI also estimates that "34 percent of female sex assault victims" are "under age 12" (National Incident-Based Reporting System, July 2000).

Since the DOJ data *excludes rape of children under age 12*, child rape may be *up 85 percent*, for all we know.

Although the FBI and local police departments are now swamped with teachers, police, professors, doctors, legislators, clergy, federal and state bureaucrats, dentists, judges, etc., arrested for child pornography and for abusing children *under age 12*, the Department of Justice excludes those small victims from its "rape" rates. Why?

Do DOJ, FBI Harbor Pedophiles?

You have to wonder: Are there pedophiles and other sexual predators in the governmental woodpiles?

When I worked for DOJ's Juvenile Justice and Delinquency Prevention in the 1980s, someone high up killed the order to collect crime-scene pornography as evidence in prosecutions. No Democrat or Republican administration has yet mandated such on-site pornography collections. Whom is DOJ protecting?

Reynolds, writes less like an objective scholar than a pornography defender:

> Since 1970 porn has exploded. But rape has gone down 85 percent. So much for the notion that pornography causes rape. [I]t would be hard to explain how rape rates could have declined so dramatically while porn expanded so explosively.

He opines that pornography possibly prevents rape (the old discredited "safe-outlet" theory).

The DOJ's preposterous "85 percent" decrease in rape ignores the obvious. The U.S. FBI Index of Crime reported a *418 percent increase* in "forcible rape" from 1960 to 1999. That fear means we now keep our doors, windows and cars locked. Women seldom walk alone at night. Parents rarely let children go anywhere unaccompanied. Many states let people carry guns for self-defense. Rape Crisis Centers do not report rapes to police. More women perform as sexually required. A conflicting DOJ 2002 report says "almost 25 percent of college women have been victims of rape or attempted rape since the age of 14."

Why Don't the Feds Call Child-Rape 'Rape'?

In 1950, 18 states authorized the death penalty for rape; most others could impose a life sentence. Following Alfred Kinsey's "scientific" advice in 1948, many states redefined "rape" so the crime could be plea-bargained down to a misdemeanor like "sexual misconduct."

Missouri redefined rape to mean 11 different crimes for 11 different sentences, magically lowering "rape" rates. Like all states that have trivialized rape, Missouri relied on the Kinsey-based 1955 American Law Institute Model Penal Code.

"Rape" was eliminated from New Jersey's laws and replaced with a variety of terms during a 1978 penal law revision.

For example, Dr. Linda Jeffrey notes that the charge to which child-molesting teacher Pamela Diehl-Moore pleaded guilty was reduced to a second-tier crime, "sexual assault"—i.e., sexual contact with a victim under 13, or penetration where the "actor" uses physical force or coercion, but the victim doesn't suffer severe personal injury, or the victim is 16 or 17, with aggravating circumstances, or the victim is 13 to 15 and the "actor" is at least four years older. (Whew!)

Sex Criminals Copy What Porn Depicts

DOJ experts should read reports such as "Sex-Related Homicide and Death Investigation" (2003). Former Lt. Comdr. Vernon Geberth says today's "sex-related cases are more frequent, vicious and despicable" than anything he experienced in decades as a homicide cop.

In "Journey Into Darkness" (1997), the FBI's premier serial-rape profiler, John Douglas wrote, "[Serial-rape murders are commonly found] with a large pornography collection, either store-bought or homemade. Our [FBI] research does show that certain types of sadomasochistic and bondage-oriented material can fuel the fantasies of those already leaning in that direction."

In "The Evil That Men Do" (1998), FBI serial-rape-murderer-mutilator profiler Roy Hazelwood quotes one sex killer who tied his victims in "a variety of positions" based on pictures he saw in sex magazines.

"Thrill Killers, a Study of America's Most Vicious Murders," by Charles Linedecker, reports that 81 percent of these killers rated pornography as their primary sexual interest. Dr. W.L. Marshall, in "Criminal Neglect, Why Sex

Offenders Go Free" (1990), says based on the evidence, pornography "feeds and legitimizes their deviant sexual tendencies."

In one study of rapists, Gene Abel of the New York Psychiatric Institute cited, "One-third reported that they had used pornography immediately prior to at least one of their crimes." In 1984, the U.S. Attorney General's Task Force on Family Violence reported, "Testimony indicates that an alarming number of rape and sexual assault offenders report that they were acting out behavior they had viewed in pornographic materials."

More pornography equals more rape of children and women. We need to ask whether Big Government is now selling out to Big Pornography as it did to Big Tobacco for half a century.

POSTSCRIPT

Does Pornography Reduce
the Incidence of Rape?

Throughout history, people have looked for answers to why people perpetrate violent crimes on others. Mental health professionals, law enforcement officials, politicians, parents, and others have pointed fingers at many different potential causes without coming up with a clear answer. Is a person biologically determined to be a rapist? Is a rapist "created," and if so, by what or by whom?

One of the first sources people go to for these reasons is the media. One type of indictment against the media has been made since it has existed that it causes viewers to take actions that they would not otherwise take. Some argue, for example, that depictions of violence in the media leads to greater violence in real life. These arguments have even been brought to the legal system, and used during trials. In a well-known court case at the time (*Huceg v. Hustler Magazine,* 1983), a family brought suit against *Hustler,* an adult pornographic magazine, in which a description appeared of autoerotic asphyxiation, a sexual practice in a which a person restricts her or his breathing through partial hanging or other method, masturbates, and releases the air restriction at the moment of orgasm. The family's underage son tried this, did it incorrectly, and ended up hanging himself. The family sued *Hustler* magazine, arguing that if this had not been printed, their son would not have done it and died. The Court ruled for the magazine, saying that just reading a description of something does not necessarily encourage someone to do it—especially a young person for whom the material was not created.

To say, however, that the media has *no* effect on people's attitudes or behaviors would be inaccurate. Advertisers spend billions of dollars every year on television, print, Internet, and other ads to sell a wide variety of products. The ads are designed to influence people's behaviors—that if we see a particular commercial or hear a particular song, we will be more likely to purchase one product over another. If advertisers are successful at this—at actually influencing people enough to purchase something they may not have necessarily known they wanted—is it possible that the creators and producers of adult sexually explicit media could be doing the same?

For right now, the data are inconclusive—and there seem to be as many reports supporting each side of the debate. Be sure to consider a range of reasoning as you establish your own opinion on this topic. Is pornography always okay, as long as it's consumed only by adults? Is it never okay? Does it depend on what it depicts? And if there is some kind of causality shown, that pornography *does* indeed increase behavior, what role do you think the government should or should not play in regulating the industry?

Suggested Readings

M. Diamond, Pornography, Rape and Sex Crimes in Japan. *International Journal of Law and Psychiatry,* 1999, 22(1): 1–22.

S. Ehrlich, *Representing Rape: Language and Sexual Consent.* New York: Routledge Press, 2001.

D. Linz, N. M., Malamuth, and K. Beckett, *Civil Liberties and Research on the Effects of Pornography.* American Psychological Association. Accessible online at http://www.apa.org/divisions/div46/articles/linz.pdf

D. J. Loftus, *Watching Sex: How Men Really Respond to Pornography.* New York: Thunder's Mouth Press, 2002.

P. Paul, *Pornified: How the Culture of Pornography Is Changing Our Lives, Our Relationships and Our Families.* New York: Times Books, 2005.

D. E. H. Russell, *Dangerous Relationships: Pornography, Misogyny and Rape.* Thousand Oaks, CA: Sage Publications, Inc., 1998.

A. Soble, *Pornography, Sex, and Feminism.* Amherst, NY: Prometheus Books, 2002.

G. A. Walp, *The Missing Link Between Pornography and Rape: Convicted Rapists Respond With Validated Truth.* Ann Arbor, MI: ProQuest/UMI, 2006.

ISSUE 17

Should Men Who Have Sex with Men Be Allowed to Donate Blood?

YES: Bob Roehr, from "The Gift of Life: Gay Men and U.S. Blood Donation Policy," *Liberty Education Forum* (2006)

NO: Marc Germain and Graham Sher, from "Men Who Have Had Sex with Men and Blood Donation: Is It Time to Change Our Deferral Criteria?" *Journal of the International Association of Physicians in AIDS Care* (July/September 2002)

ISSUE SUMMARY

YES: Journalist and medical writer Bob Roehr believes that the 30-year blood donation policy that continues to ban men who have sex with other men is irrational, because it discriminates based on a behavior, not on risk factors. Why, for example, is a heterosexual woman who has unprotected intercourse with many male partners allowed to donate blood but a man who is in a monogamous relationship with only one other man in which they use condoms consistently is not?

NO: Dr. Marc Germain, medical director of microbiology and epidemiology at Héma-Québec, and Graham Sher, chief executive officer of the Canadian Blood Services, cite data that show a small increase in risk of transmitting HIV between men who have sex with other men, and that even this small increase merits restricting who can donate blood in order to serve the safety of the greater society. The expectation of the people receiving a blood donation that their blood will be disease-free outweighs, they say, the rights of those who are seen as high risk for HIV and other transfusion-transmitted diseases.

$\mathbf{T}$he practice of attempting blood transfusions can be traced to as early as the late fifteenth century in Europe, where even the most rudimentary attempts were done poorly and unsuccessfully. Learning, however, that this could be seen as a way of saving a person's life, scientists and medical professionals did not give up, and the first known blood transfusion took place in the United States in 1795. In 1932, the first blood bank was established in Russia, and in 1947 the American Association of Blood Centers.

According to the New York Blood Center (www.nybloodcenter.org/press/factsheets/index.do?sid0=8&sid1=41&page_id=88), approximately 38,000 pints of red blood cells are transfused in the United States every day to accommodate the transfusions that are needed every three seconds. To keep the blood supply safe, prospective donors are asked a long series of questions, so that people who may know even before their blood is taken that there is any reason why they should not donate blood will be excluded.

When the human immunodeficiency virus (HIV) was discovered, it was believed to exist only in gay men. Initially called "gay-related immune disorder," medical professionals quickly discovered that anyone who has HIV can pass it to someone else through blood, semen, vaginal fluids, or breast milk. That notwithstanding, gay men are still seen as the primary risk group for HIV, despite statistics showing that, worldwide, HIV is being found much more commonly in heterosexual populations. As a result, the screening procedure for blood donation asks specifically whether a male prospective donor "has had sexual contact with another male, even once, since 1977." This means, basically, that gay men have not been allowed to donate blood for several decades.

Supporters of this ban argue that, even as the face of HIV changes, men who have sex with men are at high risk of contracting HIV and therefore transmitting it to others. Opponents to the ban argue that the ban itself and the screening question is too broad—what, for example, does "sexual contact" mean? What if a man has only had non-penetrative sex? Or if he has had penetrative intercourse, what if he has always used latex condoms?

In the following selections, Bob Roehr argues that behaviors, not sexual orientation, should determine whether someone is at risk for HIV—that plenty of men who have sex with other men practice safer sex and are at lower risk than their heterosexual counterparts. Marc Germain and Graham Sher counter by pointing out that even when there is lower risk, the risk exists—and that with HIV still being a relatively young disease, there is much to learn. It is, therefore, not worth putting the general population at risk for contracting HIV just to allow this particular population to donate blood.

YES ⬅

Bob Roehr

The Gift of Life: Gay Men and U.S. Blood Donation Policy

Introduction

The U.S. Food and Drug Administration (FDA) establishes and administers policy with regard to all blood products used within the United States. The purpose is to ensure availability and uniformly high standards that guarantee safety and minimize the possibility of transmission of blood-borne infectious diseases in those blood products. About 14 million units of blood will be donated in the U.S. in 2001.

Most people who have not yet gone through the screening process to donate blood are surprised to learn that there are pages of exclusionary factors that may keep one from making a donation. Writing in the November/December 2000 edition of *GMHC Treatment Issues,* published by the Gay Men's Health Crisis in New York City, Derek Link listed some of the top 52 reasons for not being able to donate blood. And at least one more has been added since that date. The net result of these exclusionary screening procedures is that an estimated 30–40 percent of the American public is prohibited from donating blood for one reason or another.

The system relies on screening at three different levels in order to minimize the possibility of disease transmission through blood products. It encourages certain individuals, such as gay men, to self-select and not even show up to donate; it administers an elaborate questionnaire and on paper rejects those who may be at risk of carrying a blood-borne disease; finally, it submits every unit of blood that is drawn to an elaborate series of chemical tests for HIV, hepatitis B and C, syphilis, and other infections. That process takes about three days to perform.

Blood found to carry any of these infectious agents is removed from the system and destroyed. Donors are notified that their blood tested positive for specific infections, counseled as to what that means, and are encouraged to see their physician.

None of these efforts are failsafe, but the redundancy of overlapping systems has proven remarkably effective. So much so that the American Red Cross states in one of its "Frequently Asked Questions" prepared for consumers: "The risk of not getting a blood transfusion when it's needed is infinitely greater than the risk of infection from receiving one."

Most of the blood that is donated comes from a loyal 5 percent of the population that donates repeatedly throughout the year. But that group of repeat donors has been slowly shrinking, while the development of new medical procedures has increased the need for blood. The need has outpaced supply so that seasonal shortages and emergency appeals have become annual rituals in most major American cities.

History & Science

The current blood donation policy excludes all men who have had sex with another man since 1977. It is important to understand the context within which the ban was adopted, and how that context has changed over the ensuring years.

What came to be known as AIDS was identified in the United States in the early 1980s, first as a disease that affected gay men. As early as 1983 they were asked to refrain from donating blood. The FDA adopted the current policy in 1985, soon after HIV was identified as the virus that causes AIDS, and a test was developed to identify the antibody to that virus in blood. It was thought that HIV was not present or at least not widely prevalent in the United States prior to 1977, which explains why that date was chosen.

No one challenges the fact that people who know that they are HIV-positive should refrain from donating blood. And most people, including gays, believed that the draconian policy made sense in light of the devastating nature of HIV infection; the then limited epidemiological data and knowledge of how HIV is transmitted; and the relatively crude tools available to detect the virus in blood. Those conditions have changed substantially since 1985, but the policy has not.

The most recent research concludes that there is virtually no risk of transmission of HIV through oral sex, regardless of which end of the transaction one is on. Data from heterosexual couples in Uganda indicates that those with a sufficiently low viral load only rarely transmit HIV through vaginal sex. And proper, consistent use of condoms and lubricant is highly effective in preventing transmission of the virus when engaging in either vaginal or anal sex.

What policymakers have been most worried about is the window of time between the point of infection with HIV and when screening tests can detect that infection in a blood donation of that person. The early laboratory tests that screened blood for HIV looked for antibodies to the virus, which take several weeks, and in some individuals several months to develop. Blood policymakers worried that during this window HIV-tainted blood might slip through the screening mechanism.

This is where conditions have changed most dramatically since 1985—the window has closed to the point where it is barely open. The nucleic acid test (NAT) has become the standard by which all blood donations are screened in the U.S. It amplifies and looks for small fragments of HIV RNA in pooled samples from 512 units of donated blood at a time. It is virtually foolproof, able to detect HIV in pooled blood within 12 days of infection, says the FDA. If the technology is used on individual rather than large pooled samples, NAT can detect HIV within 4–5 days, according to testimony before the FDA by Michael Busch, MD, with the Blood Centers of the Pacific.

Another simple screening technique already in place is likely to catch many of these very early infections even before donors roll up their sleeves. Standard procedure calls for taking the temperature of every donor and turning away those with a fever as an indication of some sort of infection, even a common cold. Primary HIV infection often will result in such a fever. There also is some evidence supporting the view that the form of virus during this very early stage of infection may not be very capable of transmission to a third party.

The gay ban differs from every other blood policy exclusion in two significant ways. First, it is based on a person's status rather than acts that put them at risk for infection. Second, it reflects a double standard where the same risky acts performed by heterosexuals brings a temporal restriction that generally is limited to 12 months, while a gay man is banned for life.

Thus monogamous gay couples in stable long-term relationships, who have little risk of recent HIV infection, are barred from donating blood. However, a single heterosexual female who is dating around may be allowed to donate blood, or at worst will be deferred from doing so for a year after her sexual pattern stabilizes.

The discriminatory character of this policy has long been noted both outside the FDA and within it. Justification for the policy became increasingly difficult as blood screening technology improved and the chance of a tainted unit slipping through declined. Most experts in the field understand these changes since 1985 and have been willing to modify the de facto lifetime ban on gay men donating blood.

Reconsideration

The FDA professional staff administers policy, but that policy is set through public comment, the most visible portion of which is the consultation mechanism of an advisory committees meeting in public session. It is an opportunity for professional experts and the interested public to participate in the rule-making process. The FDA uses it to solicit input, educate the general and targeted publics, and often to take some of the heat on controversial policy issues. A solid consensus recommendation from an advisory committee inevitably is embraced by the agency, while a divided committee sometimes is overruled. Regardless, the final decision on all policy rests with the FDA.

The September 14, 2000 meeting of the FDA Blood Products Advisory Committee (BPAC) was a watershed event in reconsidering the policy of blood donations by gay men. For purposes of discussion, the FDA proposed changing the ban on donation by men who have had sex with another man from 1977 to a more flexible standard of having had sex with another man within the last five years.

By posing the question, and through its presentation in suggesting such a relaxation, the FDA professional staff indicated that it was predisposed to loosening the policy. There also was a strong suggestion that the FDA was willing to go farther in changing restrictions, but that their proposal was a compromise made with the hope of gaining support from those most opposed to any change.

FDA medical officer Andrew Dayton, MD, presented a worse case scenario model of how many additional units of HIV contaminated blood might slip through by relaxing the standard to a five-year deferral of donations. He estimated the risk at "around 1 in 750,000" units.

In reviewing data from hospitals in New York that process their own blood, Dayton found that even though they process just 10 percent of the volume of blood drawn, they produced 80 percent of the errors in the region. "He concluded, inappropriate release [of tainted blood] primarily due to non-automated blood handling systems, remains the biggest problem," far exceeding any risk from letting gay men donate blood.

At the BPAC meeting, the American Association of Blood Banks (AABB) went farther than the FDA and called for "modifying the deferral time period for male to male sexual contact to 12 months" to make it "consistent with those for other high risk sexual exposures." It has held that position since 1997.

By changing the policy, "The potential donor will be directed to focus on recent rather than remote risk behaviors and should have better recall for answers to the screening questions," said Louis Katz, MD, in speaking for the AABB. The organization represents professionals and facilities responsible for virtually all of the collection and more than 80 percent of the transfusion of the nation's blood supply.

America's Blood Centers (ABC) reinforced that same message. The association of 75 not-for-profit, community based blood centers collects nearly half of the nation's blood each year. Executive vice president Celso Bianco, MD, said, "I believe that we would not see a real difference between the five year and the one year" deferral standard.

He called the current policy counterproductive because "the question focuses attention on events that occurred more than twenty years ago instead of events that occurred within the currently known window period of days or weeks" when the technology may not detect early HIV infection.

"Like risks should be treated alike," said Adrienne Smith, MD, in testifying on behalf of the Gay and Lesbian Medical Association and other gay organizations. "This maxim exposes the central flaw in the current donor deferral policy which tolerates a wide range of risks associated with heterosexual sex while imposing a zero tolerance attitude toward MSMs [men having sex with men], regardless of the risk associated with individual behavior."

"By focusing on the source of the risk rather than the size of the risk, the current policy stigmatizes gay men." Smith urged a revised policy and screening questionnaire that focuses on recent behaviors and risks.

Only the American Red Cross (ARC) opposed changing the policy. It collects nearly half of the nation's blood. Rebecca Haley, MD, called changing the deferral question "a public health issue, not a social policy issue. . . . Modifying the MSM deferral criterion to five years would result in a small but measurable increase in the possibility that infectious blood might be released."

"Until data are available to show that changing the MSM deferral criterion will not elevate the risk to the nation's blood supply, we cannot support this change," said Haley. . . .

Motivations

A recounting of events over the last few years clearly indicates that opposition to changing the policy on blood donation by gay men does not come from the FDA staff, the association representing professionals in the field, or the association representing agencies that collect about half of the blood in the United States. Opposition to changing the policy comes primarily, one is tempted to say solely, from the American as arrogant in dealing with their colleagues in the industry. . . .

Changing Policy

Attempts to modify the current policy that bans donation of blood by gay men should start by proposing to amend the policy to a 12 month deferral, the same policy as with other risky behavior. It is the policy advocated by the American Association of Blood Banks and America's Blood Centers.

But the community should not stop there, it should seek parity with heterosexuals at all levels based upon the element of risky behavior.

Couples in monogamous, long-term relationships where both are HIV-negative should be held to the same standards, whether heterosexual or homosexual.

Consideration should be given to removing oral sex as a category of risky behavior.

The consistent use of condoms in anal sex, and whether the donor is exclusively insertive or receptive (top or bottom) are also factors worthy of consideration in reexamining the policy.

Alternative handling of a blood donation also should be explored. It may make sense, and be cost effective, to segregate blood from higher risk donors and screen them individually or in smaller pools.

Gay organizations may want to organize recruitment drives for first time donors, perhaps where donors are prescreened for pathogens weeks before being allowed to donate, or where the initial donation receives special handling. After that initial donation has cleared screening, the donor will be entered into the standard registry and mainstreamed, as it were into the donor network.

Regardless the course taken, it seems likely that internal and external pressure will have to be brought to bear on the American Red Cross for it to abandon its lone opposition to changing the policy. Even if the FDA decides to modify the policy, the ARC can always undercut it by maintaining its own, stricter policy. The most effective public argument in moving the ARC is likely to be one of identifying their position as one adopted for strictly for financial reasons, to save processing costs, while discriminating against a segment of American society when there is no valid scientific reason to do so.

Marc Germain and
Graham Sher

 **NO**

Men Who Have Had Sex with Men and Blood Donation: Is It Time to Change Our Deferral Criteria?

Men who have had sex with other men even once, since 1977, are permanently deferred as blood donors. This policy was put in place several years ago when it was recognized that men who have sex with men (MSM) represented a group at risk for HIV. The policy is not unique to the United States and Canada, since most industrialized countries apply the same rule, or one that is very similar. Many have expressed the view that such a policy, while it may have been justified in the early days of the HIV epidemic, is now overly cautious and has the unfortunate effect of stigmatizing gay men who would donate blood.

According to some, the policy is biased because it appears to be based on a person's sexual preferences rather than the sexual practices and partners that might put someone at risk for infection. It is also seen as setting a double standard by which certain behaviors in heterosexuals only bring a temporary deferral, while male-to-male sex entails lifetime exclusion.

The American Association of Blood Banks (AABB), an independent organization that represents the transfusion community, endorses a relaxation of the current deferral policy for MSM.[1] The AABB argues that highly sophisticated tests are now used to screen blood donations for HIV and other transfusion transmitted diseases (TTDs), making it unnecessary to apply such a restrictive policy. It suggests imposing a temporary deferral of one year for male-to-male sex, similar to deferrals that are applied for other activities at risk for TTDs. In theory, asking donors to focus on the recent past might also improve their ability to recall events that are more relevant to the risk posed by window period donations. This revised policy would also have the benefit of increasing the pool of eligible donors.

Not surprisingly, this question of MSM and blood donations is rather controversial, and it has been the object of heated debates for a number of years and in various jurisdictions. While recognizing the following discussion will most certainly not put an end to the argument, it represents our personal opinions and positions on this issue, not that of the organizations we represent.

From *Journal of the International Association of Physicians in AIDS Care*, Vol. 1, No. 3, (2002), pp. 86–88.
Copyright © by Sage Publications. Reprinted by permission.

All blood donations are tested for the presence of antibody and/or antigen of transfusion-transmitted infections, including hepatitis C virus (HCV), HIV, hepatitis B virus (HBV), syphilis, and human T-lymphotrophic virus (HTLV). In recent years, nucleic acid testing (NAT) for HCV and HIV has been added to the traditional arsenal of serological tests, as an attempt to reduce the risk of transfusing blood collected from donors who might be in the early phase of infection.[2] The transfusion industry has also been transformed into a highly regulated environment, in which processes are highly controlled and safeguards are put in place to make sure that these screening tests are being performed and documented with the highest possible level of proficiency.[3]

Given all that, one may ask whether current tests are more than sufficient as a way of safeguarding the blood supply. Why bother screening donors on the basis of their self-reported risk factors, if testing has become so effective? One obvious answer is the health questionnaire currently remains our only line of defense against certain TTDs, such as malaria and Chagas disease, but also for other conditions that may be detrimental to transfusion recipients or to the donors themselves. If only for this reason, the health questionnaire will always remain a necessary step in the donor screening process. The second reason is, even with the advent of nucleic acid testing, there remains the possibility that some donors will test negative if they donate during the window period of early infection. Recent experience has shown that this can happen even with all donations being subjected to NAT.[4,5] This is due to the intrinsic limit that nucleic acid tests have in their ability to detect infections in the earliest phase of viremia.

It is widely agreed, even with the most sensitive screening assays in place, donors should be deferred temporarily if they report recent behaviors that put them at risk for certain TTDs. Why impose a permanent deferral for behaviors that may have happened only once or a few times in the distant past in the case for male-to-male sex? The transfusion community remains divided on this particular issue.

Some argue the goal of the donor interview is not only to exclude donors who are in the window period of infection, but also to reduce as much as possible the prevalence of TTDs in the donor population, even if screening tests can easily detect such donors. The main contention is there should be an effort to reduce as much as possible the number of infected donations that come into the system in the first place because of potential failures of the overall screening process. Since the prevalence of HIV is much higher in MSM in comparison with the general population, a more inclusive deferral policy should be applied to this group of people. In fact, other groups at higher risk for TTDs, such as intravenous drug users and those who accept money or drugs in exchange for sex, are also permanently deferred for similar reasons. In spite of the apparent discrepancy in the level of stringency that is imposed on the MSM population in comparison with other groups at risk for TTDs, the proponents of the current policy believe that it remains a sensible risk reduction strategy. Is this a legitimate argument?

Published data shows that the process of screening blood donations is fallible. Testing errors can produce false-negative test results.[6] Clerical and administrative errors may lead to the inappropriate release of infectious blood components.[1] Such errors are now extremely rare because of the increasing level of control in the process of screening and handling donations. On the other hand, one cannot assume that these mishaps never happen. Blood products sometimes need to be transfused on an emergency basis, prior to laboratory screening for transmissible diseases. One of us (M.G.) conducted an analysis in which the impact of a relaxation of the current deferral policy for MSM was modelled, taking into consideration these various factors.[7] The results showed, if 12-month abstinent MSM were allowed to donate blood, the additional number of HIV-positive donations that would escape detection and find their way into the inventory would be extremely small, in the order of 1:11,000,000. Consider the following to put this estimate in perspective. With current test procedures, the residual risk of acquiring HIV from a blood transfusion is estimated at 1:1,000,000, at worst.[2] The risk of changing to a 12-month deferral policy for male-to-male sex represents less than 10 percent of that current risk. A more lenient deferral policy for MSM would also have the benefit of increasing the number of eligible donors by about 1 percent. This is small but maybe not insignificant, considering the difficulties recruiting and retaining a stable number of active blood donors.

With these numbers in hand, what should be done about the current deferral policy for MSM? Given today's paradigm in blood safety, even the minuscule increment in risk that would result from the revised policy appears unjustified and undesirable to many, especially to those in need of blood. Even the prospect of a positive impact on the availability of blood donors does not appear to make a difference to those who are exquisitely concerned about blood safety. In this context, it becomes very difficult for those who manage and regulate the blood system to make a strong argument in favor of a change in the MSM deferral policy, considering the perspective of those in need of blood products.

In November 2001, Canadian Blood Services and Héma-Québec hosted a consensus conference that addressed the broader question of blood donor screening based on reported risk factors for TTDs. Not surprisingly, the controversial question of male-to-male sex and blood donation was one of the issues that triggered the conference. A panel of experts and stakeholders was asked to reflect on these issues and produce a consensus statement that could guide the policy makers in their decision-making process. In that statement, which will soon be published in its totality along with the proceedings from the conference, the panel did not make any specific recommendation concerning the MSM deferral policy. However, the panel did provide some guidelines as to the scientific, societal, and ethical principles upon which the donor screening process should be based. It was agreed that certain constraints could be imposed on individuals when a significant risk exists, on condition that the risk can be effectively mitigated by such constraints. In addition, the economic costs and the burdens to certain individuals or groups of individuals should be reasonable when compared with the benefits that these constraints will bring to society in general. Finally, these restrictions should be fairly distributed among the general population.

Without trying to second-guess the consensus panel, it is our opinion that the current MSM deferral policy adheres to these principles, albeit tenuously in some respects. We firmly believe that a temporary deferral of male-to-male sex will always remain a minimum requirement to safeguard the blood supply, as long as sexually transmitted diseases and the HIV epidemic continue to disproportionately afflict the MSM population. On the other hand, we also believe that the calculable margin of safety that is gained by the current policy is extremely small when compared to a policy that would only impose a temporary deferral for male-to-male sex. This safety margin also comes with the cost of having to defer a fairly large number of men who could potentially contribute safe donations to a blood supply that is periodically difficult to sustain. This balance between safety increments (even marginal ones) and adequacy of the donor base will continue to challenge the transfusion industry, including operators, regulators, and stakeholders. Prior to any change to the current policy regarding MSM being promoted or imposed, there should be a very clear consensus that such a change is both justified and necessary. This consensus must be broadly based, and should not only come from those who feel unjustly treated by the current policy. In seeking such consensus, we believe that if priority should be given anywhere, it should be to the opinion of those who have the most to lose or to gain from this change, namely the transfusion recipients themselves. This is reasonable, given the rights of recipients of blood transfusions to expect their therapeutic intervention to be optimally safe.

References

1. Blood Products Advisory Committee. Gaithersburgh, MD, September 14–15, 2000. . . .

2. Busch MP. Closing the windows on viral transmission by blood transfusion. In: Stramer SL, ed. Blood safety in the new millennium. Bethesda, MD: American Association of Blood Banks, 2001. Pp. 33–54.

3. Quality Systems. In: Vengelen-Tyler V, ed. Technical Manual. 13th ed. Bethesda, MD. American Association of Blood Banks, 1999. Pp. 1–36.

4. Schüttler CG, Caspari G, Jursch CA, Willems WR, Gerlich WH, Schaefer S. Hepatitis C virus transmission by a blood donation negative in nucleic acid amplification tests for viral RNA. Lancet 2000;355(9197):41–42.

5. Delwart E, Kalmin N, Jones S, Ladd D, Tobler L, Tsui R, Busch M. First case of HIV transmission by an RNA-screened blood donation. 9th Conference on Retroviruses and Opportunistic Infections. Seattle, WA, February 24–28, 2002. (Abstract 768-W).

6. Busch MP, Watanabe KK, Smith JW, Hermansen SW, Thomson RA. False-negative testing errors in routine viral marker screening of blood donors. For the Retrovirus Epidemiology Donor Study. Transfusion 2000;40(5):585–589.

7. Germain M, Delage G. Men who have sex with men (MSM) and blood donation: a risk-benefit assessment of adopting a less stringent deferral policy. VII European Congress of the International Society of Blood Transfusion. Paris, France, July 15–18, 2001. Abstract in Transfus Clin Biol 2001 June;8 Suppl 1:198s.

POSTSCRIPT

Should Men Who Have Sex with Men Be Allowed to Donate Blood?

The debate about whether men who have sex with men can donate blood has become more and more heated as the HIV pandemic has gone on and it has been demonstrated, clearly, that as a group they are not putting themselves at risk—only those who have unprotected sex with partners they do not know well are. Yet at the same time, news reports continue to demonstrate that men who have sex with men, if they are not using latex condoms, may be engaging in anal intercourse—a behavior that is extremely high risk for transmitting HIV due to the lack of natural lubrication in the rectum. The chances of even slight tears inside the rectum, introducing blood into the rectum as well as creating openings, highlights the ongoing existence of such a risk.

Then again, sexuality education professionals have been seeing an increase in the number of different-sex young people who are having unprotected anal sex. More concerned with avoiding pregnancy than sexually transmitted infections (STIs), are these young people not also putting themselves at equally high risk?

Among the reasons why this remains so controversial is that it is so difficult to know who has an STI, including HIV, and who does not. Considering that so many STIs, including HIV, can be asymptomatic, it is nearly impossible to tell whether a prospective sex partner is infected without asking her or him. And even if that person is HIV+ (or has any STI), what is the likelihood that they will be honest, if doing so would mean that they would not end up having this sexual encounter?

So, does this policy protect the general public, or discriminate? If you were desperate for a blood transfusion, would you be willing to have blood donated to you by a gay man? What if you knew that he had only had one partner for the last 20 years? Or if he'd always used a latex condom? Would you be more or less likely to accept blood from a heterosexual person who had had many sex partners but never used a condom in her or his life?

Suggested Readings

The Associated Press, *Scientists Reject Easing Ban on Gay Male Blood Donors.* September 14, 2000. Accessible online at http://archives.cnn.com/2000/HEALTH/AIDS/09/14/blood.gaymen.ap

S. Bodzin, "Students Press to End Ban on Gay Male Blood Donors: College Activists Take Plea Directly to the Red Cross." *Los Angeles Times,*

July 11, 2005. Accessible online at http://www.boston.com/news/nation/articles/2005/07/11/students_press_to_end_ban_on_gay_male_blood_donors

Express Gay News, "Russia, France Said to Lift Bans on Blood Donations by Gay Men: Australia May Be Next." *Express Gay News,* July 17, 2006. Accessible online at http://www.expressgaynews.com/thelatest/thelatest.cfm?blog_id=8186

M. Germain, R.S. Remis, and G. Delage, "The Risks and Benefits of Accepting Men Who Have Had Sex with Men as Blood Donors." *Transfusion,* January 2003, vol. 43, no. 1.

M. Hutchens, "Washington State U. Blood Centers Ban Gay Men from Donating." *Daily Evergreen* (Washington State University), October 9, 2002. Accessible online at http://www.uwire.com/content/topnews100902001.html

A. Keegan, "FDA to Revisit Bans on Blood Donors: Prohibition on Donations from Gay Men May Be Up for Review This Week." *Southern Voice,* March 6, 2006. Accessible online at http://www.sovo.com/thelatest/thelatest. cfm?blog_id=5431

D. Link, "Should Gay Men Be Allowed to Donate Blood?" *GMHC Treatment Issues,* November/December 2000. Accessible online at www.thebody.com/gmhc/issues/novdec00/blood.html

E. Resnick, "Blood Donation Ban Puts the Red Cross in a Hot Spot." *Gay People's Chronicle,* August 26, 2005. Available online at www.gaypeopleschronicle.com/stories05/august/0826053.htm

ISSUE 18

Are Statutory Rape Laws Effective at Protecting Minors?

YES: Sherry F. Colb, from "The Pros and Cons of Statutory Rape Laws," CNN.com (February 11, 2004)

NO: Marc Tunzi, from "Curbside Consultation: Isn't This Statutory Rape?" *American Family Physician* (May 1, 2002)

ISSUE SUMMARY

YES: Sherry F. Colb, columnist and law professor, uses a case study involving a statutory rape case to raise concerns about whether rape and assault cases would be prosecuted sufficiently without statutory rape laws. Although not perfect, statutory rape laws can be assets in such rape cases as when the older partner denies the rape occurred or denies responsibility for a resulting pregnancy or infection.

NO: Marc Tunzi, a family physician, believes that statutory rape laws are ineffective because people can get around them too easily. These laws, he argues, require that an otherwise healthy relationship between two people of different ages be criminalized, solely because there is some kind of sexual activity involved. As a result, medical and other licensed professionals do not want to break up these relationships that, in their professional opinion, are not problematic solely because of the age difference between the two partners.

$\mathbf{T}$he term "rape" refers to forced sexual contact between two people that usually involves the insertion of a penis or inanimate object into another person's vagina, anus, or mouth. Rape is against the law in every state in the United States, and usually results in heavy penalties on the rapist.

Statutory rape laws say that sexual behavior between two people when there is a significant age difference is against the law, even if there was no force involved. These laws, which were originally created to protect adolescent girls from predatory adult males, are different in every state. The age at which a person is considered legally able to engage in sexual behavior, called the "age of consent," is different in every state, too. Most state laws are no longer restricted to a female victim and male perpetrator; they now apply to couples of any gender combination, including same-sex relationships. Most recently, the media has carried news of former schoolteacher Mary Kay Letourneau, an adult who was convicted of statutory rape for having a sexual relationship with an adolescent student. Even though the two claimed then (and maintain now) that they were in love, the law said that this relationship was illegal, and Ms. Letourneau went to prison.

People who support statutory rape laws argue that in any relationship where there is a significant age difference, the older of the two people has an inherent power advantage over the younger. Even if the younger partner agrees to have sex, statutory rape law supporters argue, that person was not old enough to make a well thought-out decision—and may have been coerced emotionally, even if not physically. What an older partner has can be very seductive—power, money, a job, a car, and more. These tangible things, they argue, play a powerful role in a younger person's decision-making process. In addition, it is quite flattering for a 14-year-old to have a 24-year-old person interested in her or him. One wonders, however, what a 24-year-old could possibly have in common, developmentally and experientially, with a 14-year-old. Statutory rape laws are designed, in part, to keep these types of unequal relationships from becoming sexual in nature.

Others disagree, saying that statutory rape laws are ineffective, judgmental, patronizing, and sexist. Opponents to statutory rape laws argue that adolescents and teenagers are able to make their own decisions about their sexual behaviors, even if their partner is older. Opponents maintain that relationships are about much more than sexual behavior, and that if a relationship is otherwise healthy and loving, penalizing the couple for their age difference does more to ruin lives than save them. There are young men, they argue, who have gone to jail because the parents of their younger partners learned that they were having sex, and wanted to punish them. As a result, these young men have a jail sentence on their records forever, solely because of an age difference.

What do you think about statutory rape laws? Do they protect, or do they discriminate? Do you think that an adult has more power than a teenager just because she or he is older? If so, is this power strong enough that the adolescent or teen could not say whether she or he wanted to have sex with that adult? What are some of the inherent problems with a significant age difference in a relationship? What are some of the positive things that can happen from two people of different ages having a relationship?

In the following selections, Sherry F. Colb takes the side of the victim, arguing that statutory rape laws, while inherently imperfect, do much more good than harm. For the number of young adolescents who claim they were forced to have sex (particularly by a known assailant), when the situation is often a simple matter of believing one person over the other, statutory rape laws give young rape victims voice. Dr. Marc Tunzi raises the concern that other health professionals have, how statutory rape laws affect a health professional's guarantee of confidentiality and informed consent to their patients. These laws, he argues, are discriminatory against young men (since these cases most commonly involve an older male partner and a younger female partner), condescending to young women, and sometimes culturally disrespectful, if there is a value that early sexual relationships are appropriate within the couple's particular cultural group.

YES

Sherry F. Colb

The Pros and Cons of Statutory Rape Laws

A 10 Year Sentence for Marcus Dwayne Dixon

> Recently, the Georgia Supreme Court heard arguments in Dixon v. State. The case involves the conviction of Marcus Dwayne Dixon for statutory rape and aggravated child molestation. (Dixon was acquitted of rape and several other charges.)

Statutory rape is sex between an adult and a minor, while aggravated child molestation also involves an injury. At the time of his offense, Dixon was an 18-year-old high school football player who had sex with a 15-year-old female classmate. The aggravated child molestation statute mandates a ten-year minimum sentence, and Dixon challenges the harshness of the resulting penalty.

The case has attracted claims of racism, because the victim was a white girl and the convict an outstanding African-American student with a football scholarship to Vanderbilt.

One provocative underlying (though unstated) question that has contributed to the notoriety of this case is whether the law can legitimately send teenagers to prison for having sex with other teenagers, in the absence of force. Because every state has a statutory rape law in some form, this case presents a challenge to a long and continuing tradition of criminal laws that confine men for what could be consensual sex with minors who are close to the age of majority.

Such liability is controversial in a number of ways, but it also has some benefits that are often overlooked by critics, thus leaving us with a difficult dilemma that admits of no easy answers.

Statutory rape laws have a checkered past. A primary purpose was to guard the virginity of young maidens against seduction by unscrupulous cads. To give up one's "virtue" to a man who was unwilling to pay with his hand in marriage was foolish and presumptively a product of youthful, poor judgment.

Such laws had more to do with preserving female virginity than with the force and violence that define rape. One sign of this is the fact that a man could (and in some states still can) defend himself against statutory rape charges by proving that his victim was already sexually experienced prior to their encounter (and thus not subject to being corrupted by the defendant).

Justifications for Statutory Rape Laws

Despite their unsavory beginnings, however, some feminists have favored these laws as well. Progressive women supported such statutes mainly as measures to help combat the sexual abuse of young girls.

Though a statutory rape charge would not require proof of force or coercion, feminists observed, young girls were (and may continue to be) especially vulnerable to being raped by the adults in their lives. In one study, for example, seventy-four percent of women who had intercourse before age fourteen and sixty percent of those who had sex before age fifteen report having had a forced sexual experience.

In addition, prosecutors attempting to prove rape in court have historically faced significant burdens, such as corroboration requirements premised on the complaining witness's presumptive lack of credibility.

For many years, legal thinkers like Eighteenth Century British Jurist Sir Matthew Hale were convinced that rape "is an accusation easily to be made and hard to be proved, and harder to be defended by the party accused, though never so innocent." Thus, rape law did not provide a reliable or efficacious vehicle for addressing most sexual violence, and it continues to be of limited utility for acquaintance rapes. . . .

For this reason too, feminists may have viewed statutory rape laws as a godsend. As long as there was sexual intercourse and an under-age victim, the jury could convict. And more importantly, that possibility itself might deter real sexual abuse.

Is Statutory Rape Just Rape Without Proof of One Element?

Viewing statutory rape laws as salutary in this way does raise a serious problem, however. In *In Re Winship*, the U.S. Supreme Court required that prosecutors prove every element of a crime beyond a reasonable doubt before a conviction can be constitutionally valid. Removing the "force" element of rape and leaving only intercourse and age might seem to amount, from some perspectives, to a presumption that the force element of rape is established, without the prosecutor's having to prove it and without the defense even having the option of affirmatively disproving it.

Such a presumption allows for the possibility that a fully consensual sexual encounter will be prosecuted and punished as rape. Some might understandably believe that this unfairly subjects essentially innocent men to unduly harsh treatment, simply in the name of deterring other, unrelated men from engaging in very different and far more culpable sorts of conduct.

Responses to Concerns About Prosecuting Consensual Sex

There are two potential responses to this concern. First, at some level, we might have doubts about the competence of a minor to "consent," in a meaningful way, to sexual activity. Because of her youth, the minor might not fully appreciate the full physical and emotional implications of her decision (including the possibility of offspring for which she will likely have little means of support).

Of course, many adults might also fall into this category, and the decision to treat intercourse as distinctive in this way may simply represent a revival of the old view that maidens should be protected from the corruption of their virtue. Why, otherwise, should girls who are sexually attracted to men be considered the men's victims rather than participants in arguably unwise and socially costly but mutually gratifying activity?

Another response to the concern about innocent men is more in keeping with feminist concerns. It is that when sexual activity with a minor is truly consensual, the activity is unlikely, at least in modern times, to be prosecuted. In other words, to the extent that statutory rape is truly a consensual and therefore victimless crime in a particular case, it is highly unlikely to generate a criminal action.

In the Dixon case, for example, the 15-year-old victim claimed that the defendant "tracked her down in a classroom trailer that she was cleaning as part of her duties in an after-school job, asked if she was a virgin, grabbed her arms, unbuttoned her pants and raped her on a table." This description renders the statutory rape and aggravated child molestation prosecution something other than the state targeting consensual activity for unduly harsh punishment.

Though Dixon was acquitted on the rape charge, that fact does not rule out the possibility of sexual assault. It means only that the jury was not convinced beyond a reasonable doubt that Dixon forced the 15-year-old girl to have sex against her will.

The normative question, then, becomes this: Is the likelihood that consensual sex will be punished by imprisonment sufficient to override the benefits of statutory rape legislation in facilitating the fight against actual sexual abuse of young adults?

Is Convicting in the Absence of Force Unacceptable?

One reaction to this question is that even the theoretical possibility of convicting in a case of consensual sex is unacceptable and unconstitutional. Prosecutors and juries, on this reasoning, should not have the option of finding a person guilty in the absence of force, regardless of how unlikely they are to exercise that option. Consensual sex is not criminal, period.

The assumptions underlying this reaction, however, though understandable, are at odds with other areas of the criminal law. Consider drug laws.

Possession of a large quantity of narcotics is regularly treated as a far more serious offense than possession of a smaller quantity. One reason is that the first is viewed as possession with the intent to distribute (that is, drug dealing), while the second is thought to be consistent with personal use. Since legislators and others view dealing as much more harmful than mere possession, the penalties are accordingly more severe.

Yet possession of a large quantity of drugs, though highly suggestive, is not necessarily accompanied by an intent to distribute. A person might, for example, possess large amounts of drugs to avoid having to risk apprehension or sources drying out, through repeated purchases.

Suppose the drug statute did require proof of intent to distribute. If so, then the judge would, on request, have to instruct the jury that the bare fact of quantity alone is enough for a conviction only if the jury draws the inference, beyond a reasonable doubt, that the defendant intended distribution. Without such a finding of intent, the jury would have to acquit.

With the statute providing instead that quantity is the sole element, however, intent becomes legally irrelevant. As a result, even the prosecutor and jury who know that the defendant is simply saving up for an anticipated heroin shortage rather than planning to deal drugs, can convict the defendant of the more serious felony without giving rise to any grounds for appeal.

By crafting a statute without an "intent to distribute" element, in other words, legislators target distribution without requiring its proof (or even allowing for its disproof). One might characterize this as an end-run around the constitutional requisite of proving every element of guilt beyond a reasonable doubt.

The same "end run" accusation can be leveled against statutory rape laws. Young girls may represent a substantial portion of rape victims, perhaps because they are vulnerable and have not yet become sufficiently suspicious of the people around them. In most cases, moreover, a truly consensual encounter with a minor will probably not be brought to a prosecutor's attention or trigger the prosecutorial will to punish.

As with drug possession laws, then, the omission of a requirement that would pose proof problems might generally serve the interests of justice, despite appearances to the contrary.

Consensual Sex With Minors Is Not a Fundamental Right

What permits legislatures the discretion to enact such laws, ultimately, is the fact that (like drug possession), consensual sex with minors is not a constitutionally protected activity. Even if it is victimless, sex with a minor may be criminalized and punished severely without resort to a force requirement. Indeed, it once was punished routinely in this way, because of misogynist concerns about preserving female purity.

In modern times, though, when consensual sex among teenagers is generally understood to be both common and profoundly different from the crime of rape, there might still be a role for statutory rape laws in protecting young girls from actual rapists, through deterrence and through the real possibility of retribution.

Racism Raised in the Dixon Case

A remaining concern is the worry about racism specifically, and discrimination more generally, that arises whenever officials are vested with a large amount of discretion. In Dixon's case, one witness testified that the victim said that the sexual intercourse in question was consensual but that she claimed it was rape to avoid the wrath of her violent, racist father. This testimony may have given rise to reasonable doubt in the jury on the rape charges.

In easing the burden of proof at trial by eliminating the requirement of proving force, then, the law does permit unscrupulous prosecutors and complainants to bring charges on the basis of what is truly victimless behavior.

One does wonder, though, why a girl would tell a violent and racist father about a sexual encounter with a black man in the first place, rather than simply keeping the information from him, if the encounter were actually consensual.

Are Statutory Rape Laws Worth Their Cost?

In short, the crime of statutory rape may have originated from repressive and misogynist conceptions of sexuality. Nonetheless, it has (and may always have had) redeeming characteristics, even from an enlightened perspective that takes into account the realities of prosecuting rape and of women's equality. It makes it easier, for example, to prosecute and thus to deter real rapists who count on jury skepticism about acquaintance rape allegations.

Still, reducing burdens of proof relies a great deal on trust—in victims and in prosecutors—that the omitted element will truly be present when cases come to trial. If and when that trust is misplaced, . . . a grave injustice can result.

Marc Tunzi

NO

Curbside Consultation:
Isn't This Statutory Rape?

Case Scenario

Several pregnant teenagers in my practice are underage and have boyfriends older than 18. Isn't this statutory rape? Some of these patients are immigrants who prefer to keep a low profile, not calling the attention of local authorities to themselves or their boyfriends. In most cases, the sex is consensual, and the teens involved don't particularly care about legal fine points. However, I do, because I have often seen older boyfriends disappear, becoming "deadbeat dads." If I reported these young men, maybe they would be forced to fulfill their obligations. On the other hand, reporting them might disrupt a potentially viable relationship. What is my obligation?

Commentary

"Isn't this statutory rape?" our colleague asks. The answer is . . . "maybe." Statutory rape laws were first enacted to protect minors from older predators. States differ considerably in the legal definition of statutory rape.[1] For example, in California, where my practice is located, the age of consent for lawful sexual relationships is 18. If the age difference between the adult and the minor victim is more than three years, the charge is a felony; if three years or less, it is a misdemeanor. In Hawaii, the age of consent is 14. In other states, the age of consent ranges from 15 to 18 years, and many states have associated provisions that specify the level of offense depending on age differences and other factors.

Consideration of the legal fine points of statutory rape requires knowledge of specific state laws. Most states require that health care providers report injuries related to criminal violence regardless of the age of the victim, and four states (California, Colorado, Kentucky, and Rhode Island) require health professionals to report domestic violence.[2] While reporting violent injuries is a well-accepted practice, there continues to be controversy about domestic violence laws (for example, what if the victim doesn't want the abuse reported?). Most experts, however, believe that unreported domestic violence simply breeds more violence and that it should be reported in most cases.

Whether statutory rape is considered violence may depend on the consent of the minor involved. From a strictly legal standpoint, minors are unable to give consent, which is exactly the reason statutory rape laws exist. However, in the majority of statutory rape cases, minors have given consent (legally or not) to having sex, limiting any potential criminal charge to that of domestic violence rather than the more serious charge of child abuse.

In fact, whether health care professionals are required to report consensual statutory rape to authorities really depends on whether the specific state considers it a type of child sexual abuse, which is reportable in all states. Unfortunately, laws on mandatory statutory rape reporting are confusing and often do not appear to be enforced even where they exist.[3-5] California child abuse law requires health practitioners and other child-related professionals to report statutory rape only when the adult is 21 years or older and the minor is younger than 16 years.[6] California law also specifically states that "the pregnancy of a minor does not, in and of itself, constitute a reasonable suspicion of child abuse."[6]

Many people believe that enforcing statutory rape laws will decrease the teen pregnancy rate and the number of young families needing public support because of "deadbeat dads." In fact, part of the 1996 federal welfare reform law specifically directed state and local governments to develop and enforce strict measures against statutory rape for those very reasons. California's response was a multimillion-dollar vertical prosecution program that allows the same prosecutor and investigator to remain on a case from beginning to end, while other states have developed their own programs.[4]

Even though more statutory rape convictions have resulted from these efforts, there is no real evidence that any of the programs have been the effective deterrents that Congress intended. In fact, there are still a lot of 16- and 17-year-olds on my hospital's labor and delivery unit. What these laws may have influenced is the unwillingness of pregnant teens to seek early prenatal care. While knowledge of statutory rape laws does not appear to prevent adult-minor relationships from occurring, fear of these laws may keep some young women from seeking prenatal care as a means of protecting their boyfriends from incarceration or deportation. Many professionals who work with pregnant adolescents are beginning to collect evidence supporting this concern.[1,4]

Another issue for family physicians is that statutory rape laws seem to conflict with the law as it applies to our practice and our understanding of informed consent for adolescents in other situations. Many teens have the capacity to participate in their own health care decision-making, even regarding serious and terminal illnesses. For example, teens are specifically able to consent for contraception, STD treatment, and pregnancy care in nearly all cases. The only illegality may be actually having sex.

The problem is that not all teens and situations are the same. Some teens are much more mature than others of the same age and are as able to consent to sex as an 18- to 20-year-old. At the same time, I think all of us would question a relationship between even the most mature 15-year-old and a 25- or 30-year-old. My own experience is that many teens of 16 and 17 know the emotions and consequences of having intercourse just as well as many teens of 18 and 19. In some of my Latina patients, becoming sexually active at a young age seems culturally acceptable and, at times, even encouraged within their culture. I, however, discourage it quite strongly. The question is whether enforcing laws against it is the right approach.

What is the right thing for a family physician to do when caring for a patient who has been involved in statutory rape (as defined by state law)? Not all young men are "deadbeat dads"—many work and are as responsible and dedicated to their partners and children as older men with older partners. Removing a source of financial and emotional support by incarcerating a young man in this situation would probably not help the young woman and her baby; in fact, it might possibly harm them.

If criminal violence has been involved, it must be reported to authorities. If domestic violence has been involved and the victim is a minor, I would report it as a case of child abuse even if the state does not have a mandatory domestic violence reporting law. If it is not violence, given the fact that mandatory statutory rape reporting laws are confusing and not necessarily enforced, I believe that a physician should report only after carefully considering several factors.

How mature is the minor? Is he or she in school and responsible in other matters? Does the minor have the capacity to consent to intercourse? Is she or he using contraception? Does the minor understand the consequences of pregnancy?

Is the couple's relationship truly consensual? What is the couple's age difference? Are they 16 and 36 (an older predator), or are they 16 and 19? Is the adult partner using physical or other power to take advantage of the minor?

If the patient is a pregnant minor, is her adult male partner emotionally and financially responsible and supportive? Is this a potential family in the making, or has the man already abandoned the patient?

Family physicians will probably not report most cases to authorities, believing instead that building patient trust and making appropriate referrals to social services and other allied health professionals are the right things to do for the patient and family involved.

References

1. Donovan P. Can statutory rape laws be effective in preventing adolescent pregnancy? Family Planning Perspectives 1997; 29:30-4, 40.

2. Rodriguez MA, McLoughlin E, Nah G, Campbell JC. Mandatory reporting of domestic violence injuries to the police. JAMA 2001; 286:580-583.

3. Madison AB, Feldman-Winter L, Finkel M, McAbee GN. Commentary: consensual adolescent sexual activity with adult partners—conflict between confidentiality and physician reporting requirements under child abuse laws. Pediatrics 2001; 107(2). . . .

4. Oliveri R. Statutory rape law and enforcement in the wake of welfare reform. Stanford Law Review 2000; 52:463-508.

5. Leiter RA, ed. National survey of state laws. 2d ed. Detroit-Gale, 1999; 313-30.

6. California Penal Code section 261.5 (Unlawful sexual intercourse with a minor) and California Penal Code sections 11165.1 and 11166 (Child Abuse and Neglect Reporting Act).

POSTSCRIPT

Are Statutory Rape Laws Effective at Protecting Minors?

The combination of age and sexuality is a sensitive subject in many cultures and societies. In the United States, we have many double standards about the age difference between sexual and romantic partners, and the gender of the people involved in the relationship. An older man with a much younger woman is much more commonplace than an older woman with a much younger man. An adult male pursuing a teenage girl is seen as a predator, while an adult female doing the same is seen as much less threatening. Even in some court cases, judges have dismissed charges in cases where the older partner was female and the younger one male. It is as if the law does not see an adolescent girl as being able to consent, but that a younger male is simply "coming of age" by being sexual with an older partner. In our mainstream society's eyes, an adolescent girl has lost something by being sexual so young; she has shown poor judgment and has been taken advantage of by this terrible older male. An adolescent male in the same situation with an adult woman, however, is often seen as having gained from the relationship—respect and experience. These assumptions are as prejudicial to boys as they are to girls.

What about same-gender relationships? In the well-known play, "The Vagina Monologues," a 15-year-old girl talks about her first sexual experience with an adult woman in town. The description is very loving, empowering, and positive. When I heard it read in the theater, the audience made sounds of appreciation and approval. All I could think was, "But isn't this statutory rape? Would anyone be smiling at this coming-of-age story if the 15-year-old girl had done the exact same things with a 30-year-old man?"

There are far too many unhealthy and abusive relationships in the United States. People bring different things to their relationships, including different levels of power. In some cases, age brings power with it; in others, money and experience; race or ethnicity; physical ability—the examples can continue almost endlessly. The questions that remain are, in what way can people have healthy, respectful, equal relationships given the inherent power differences that are there? To what extent can and should personal relationships be governed by law? As you read in Issue 11, there used to be laws dictating whether people of different races could marry (and, implicitly, be sexual together). In what ways is it different to govern who can be sexual together based on the ages of the people involved?

Contributors to This Volume

EDITOR

ELIZABETH SCHROEDER, EdD(c), MSW, is an international trainer and consultant in the areas of sexuality education, curriculum development, counseling, and facilitation skills. She has provided trainings throughout the United States and overseas to thousands of youth-serving professionals, adolescents, and parents presented at national conference. She is the co-founding editor of the *American Journal of Sexuality Education,* co-author of *Making SMART Choices: A Curriculum for Young People,* and "Being Out, Staying Safe: An STD Prevention Curriculum for LGBQ Youth," editor of *Taking Sides: Clashing Views in Controversial Issues in Family and Personal Relationships,* 5th and 6th editions, and author of chapters in *Health Counseling: Applications and Theory* and *The Continuum Complete International Encyclopedia of Sexuality.*

As a trainer and educator, Ms. Schroeder specializes in facilitation and presentation skills, adolescent sexuality, lesbian, gay, bisexual and/or transgender issues, and depictions of sexuality in the media. She also serves as a sexuality expert for the Web sites SEX, ETC, and the Internet Friends Network.

Before becoming a consultant, Ms. Schroeder was the associate vice president of education and training at Planned Parenthood of New York City, where she established the agency's first professional training institute for social service and school professionals. Before that, she was the manager of education and special projects at Planned Parenthood Federation of America, where she coordinated the production of their multiple award-winning video kit for families with adolescent children, "Talking About Sex: A Guide for Families."

STAFF

Larry Loeppke	Managing Editor
Jill Peter	Senior Developmental Editor
Susan Brusch	Senior Developmental Editor
Beth Kundert	Production Manager
Jane Mohr	Project Manager
Tara McDermott	Design Coordinator
Nancy Meissner	Editorial Assistant
Julie Keck	Senior Marketing Manager
Mary Klein	Marketing Communications Specialist
Alice Link	Marketing Coordinator
Lori Church	Pemissions Coordinator

Elizabeth Schroeder is a recipient of the Mary Lee Tatum award, which is given to the person who most exemplifies the qualities of an ideal sexuality educator, and of the Apple Blossom Award, which recognizes a Planned Parenthood Education or Training Director who has "risen quickly to the forefront with new ideas, energy, and commitment." An adjunct professor at Montclair State University, she earned a master's degree in social work from New York University and is completing a doctorate in human sexuality education at Widener University.

AUTHORS

SUE ALFORD is the director of public information services at Advocates for Youth, providing editorial oversight for Advocates' publications and Web sites, and researching and writing documents for the organization. She is the author of *Science & Success: Sex Education and Other Programs That Work to Prevent Teen Pregnancy, HIV & Sexuality Transmitted Infections* (Advocates for Youth, 2003) as well as *Science & Success in Developing Countries* (in press).

RACHEL L. BERGERON is an assistant clinical professor of psychiatry at the Yale University School of Medicine.

JOAN BISKUPIC is the Supreme Court correspondent for *USA Today*. She has also served as the Supreme Court reporter for the *Washington Post* and the legal affairs writer for *Congressional Quarterly*. The author of several reference books, she recently completed a biography of retired Justice Sandra Day O'Connor.

JEANNE BROOKS-GUNN is Virginia and Leonard Marx professor of child development and education at Teachers College, Columbia University. As a developmental psychologist, Brooks-Gunn serves as consultant to and trainer of in-house researchers, faculty, and students in areas of child development. Brooks-Gunn is a member of the National Advisory Committee of the Institute for Research on Poverty, an advisory board member of Substance Abuse and Sex of the National Center on Addiction and Substance Abuse, and a senior faculty affiliate of the Joint Center on Poverty Research, Northwestern University/University of Chicago.

B. CHERTIN is on the faculty of health science at Ben-Gurion University in Jerusalem, Israel.

SHERRY E. COLB is a professor at Rutgers Law School in Newark, New Jersey, where she has taught courses in criminal procedure, evidence, mental health law, and feminist legal studies. She has published articles in a variety of law reviews, covering such areas as Fourth Amendment privacy, Fourteenth Amendment liberty from physical confinement, and the role of personal character in criminal culpability.

TERESA STANTON COLLETT is a professor of law at University of St. Thomas School of Law in Minneapolis, Minnesota, and has taught courses in property, professional responsibility, legal limits of medical decision making, constitutional law, church-state relations, and religion, law, and ethics. Recent publications relating to family issues include *Recognizing Same-Sex Marriage: Asking for the Impossible, Seeking Solomon's Wisdom: Judicial Bypass of Parental Involvement in a Minor's Abortion Decision,* and *Independence or Interdependence? A Christian Response to Liberal Feminism.*

TIMOTHY J. DAILEY is a senior research fellow at the Center for Marriage and Family Studies at the Family Research Council, where he specializes in "issue threatening the institutions of marriage and the family." His experience includes college-level instruction both at home and abroad, including several years in Israel teaching the historical, geographical, and archaeological background of the Bible.

ANTHONY D'AMATO is the Leighton professor of law at Northwestern University School of Law, where he teaches courses in international law, international human rights, analytic jurisprudence, and justice. He was the first American lawyer to argue and win a case before the European Court of Human Rights in Strasbourg, and is the author of over 20 books and over 110 articles.

NORMAN DANIELS is the Goldthwaite professor of philosophy at Tufts University. He is a former senior fellow at the NIH Clinical Bioethics Center, and co-author of *Setting Limits Fairly: Can We Learn to Share Medical Resources?*

AMICUR FARKAS is the director of the Urology Department at Shaare Zedek Medical Center. Farkas is also on the faculty of health science at Ben-Gurion University in Jerusalem, Israel.

MARC GERMAIN is a physician who is currently the vice president and medical director, human tissues, for Hema-Quebec. He is also the scientific advisor, Microbiology and Epidemiology for Hema-Quebec and associate professor of Social and Preventive Medicine at Laval University, also in Quebec.

JONAH GOLDBERG is editor-at-large of *National Review Online* and a syndicated columnist. He is also the media columnist for *The American Enterprise Magazine,* and a CNN contributor and regular panelist on *Late Edition with WolfBlitzer.*

EZRA E. H. GRIFFITH is the deputy chair for clinical affairs and professor of Psychiatry and African-American Studies in the Psychiatry Department at the Yale University School of Medicine.

IRITH HADAS-HALPREN is director of the radiology and imaging department at Shaare Zedek Medical Center and is on the faculty of health science at Ben-Gurion University in Jerusalem, Israel.

WEN-JUI HAN is an associate professor at the Columbia University School of Social Work, where she focuses on such topics as social welfare policy, with an emphasis on children and families, the effects of maternal employment and child care on children's cognitive and behavior outcomes, the impact of welfare reform and child care subsidies on families, work schedules and child care use of low-income and welfare families, and child care issues facing immigrant families.

LESLIE DOTY HOLLINGSWORTH is an associate professor in the University of Michigan's School of Social Work. She is a certified social worker in Michigan, a clinical member of the American Association of Marriage and Family Therapists, and a member of the National Association of Social Workers, the Academy of Certified Social Workers, the National Council on Family Relations, and the Society for Social Work and Research.

THE HUMAN RIGHTS CAMPAIGN (HRC) is the country's largest gay and lesbian organization, providing a national voice on gay and lesbian issues. HRC effectively lobbies Congress, mobilizes grassroots action in diverse communities, invests strategically to elect a fair-minded Congress and increases public understanding through innovative education and communication strategies.

IRWIN A. HYMAN is a professor of school psychology and the director of the National Center for the Study of Corporal Punishment and Alternatives at Temple University. He is the author of numerous books and articles, including *School Discipline and School Violence: The Teacher Variance Approach* (Allyn & Bacon, 1997).

CHRIS JEUB is the founder and president of Training Minds Ministry, which works to provide educational opportunities to families participating in speech and debate. He previously worked as an editor and freelance writer for Focus on the Family and as a public school teacher.

STANLEY KURTZ is a contributing editor to the National Review Online and a fellow at the Hoover Institution. His writings have also appeared in *Policy Review*, the *Wall Street Journal*, and *Commentary*. He received his Ph.D. in social anthropology from Harvard University and later taught at Harvard, and was also Dewey Prize lecturer in psychology at the University of Chicago.

KATHY LABRIOLA is a counselor and nurse in the Berkeley, California area who specializes in working with polyamorous individuals and families.

WALTER L. LARIMORE is Focus on the Family's (FOTF) award-winning vice president for medical outreach. He is a former family physician with 20 years' experience, frequent interviewee for national and cable television news programs, and author of nearly a dozen books for FOTF.

BRIDGET E. MAHER is a policy analyst in the Center for Marriage and Family Studies at the Family Research Council, where she researches, writes, and offers expert commentary on the issues of marriage, divorce, cohabitation, adoption, family structure, and abstinence.

MARY B. MAHOWALD is a professor at the Pritzker School of Medicine at the University of Chicago. She is the author of *Women and Children and Health Care: An Unequal Majority; Disability, Difference, Discrimination: Perspectives on Justice in Bioethics and Public Policy;* and *Genes, Women, Equality.*

PAUL MCHUGH is the director of the Department of Psychiatry and Behavioral Sciences and the Henry Phipps professor of psychiatry at the Johns Hopkins University School of Medicine, the psychiatrist-in-chief of the Johns Hopkins Hospital, and co-chairman of the ethics committee of the American College of Neuropsychopharmacology.

THE NATIONAL REVIEW is a magazine "of Conservative opinion." Accessible in print version and online, it addresses a wide range of topic areas relating to family and personal relationships, as well as a myriad of other issues.

PLANNED PARENTHOOD FEDERATION OF AMERICA, INC., is the world's oldest and largest voluntary reproductive health care organization. Founded by Margaret Sanger in 1916 as America's first birth control clinic, Planned Parenthood believes in the fundamental right of each individual, throughout the world, to manage his or her fertility, regardless of the individual's income, marital status, race, ethnicity, sexual orientation, age, national origin, or residence.

JUDITH REISMAN is president of The Institute for Media Education, author of, among other publications, the U.S. Department of Justice, Juvenile Justice study, *Images of Children, Crime and Violence in Playboy, Penthouse and Hustler* (1989), *Kinsey, Sex and Fraud* (Reisman, et al., 1990) and *Soft Porn Plays Hardball* (1991), and *Kinsey, Crimes & Consequences* (1998, 2000). She is also a news commentator for *WorldNetDaily.com* and has been a consultant to four U.S. Department of Justice administrations, The U.S. Department of Education, and the U.S. Department of Health and Human Services.

JOHN A. ROBERTSON is the Vinson and Elkins chair at The University of Texas School of Law at Austin. He served as professor at the University of Wisconsin Law School and as the Russell Sage fellow in Law and Social Science at Harvard Law School. He is the author of two books in bioethics, *The Rights of the Critically Ill* and *Children of Choice: Freedom and the New Reproductive Technologies*. He currently serves as the chair of the ethics committee of the American Society for Reproductive Medicine.

BOB ROEHR is a biomedical and freelance writer, with a focus on HIV and infectious disease, who is based in Washington, DC. He serves on the Council of Public Representatives (COPR), an advisory body to the director of the National Institutes of Health.

MARK V. SAUER is the vice chair of Academic Affairs at Columbia University Medical Center in the Department of Obstetrics and Gynecology. Dr. Sauer also chairs Sloane Hospital's medical ethics committee.

GRAHAM SHER, the chief executive officer of Canadian Blood Services, is an expert in the field of transfusion science who was directly involved in the evolution of Canada's blood system. Dr. Sher has taught at the University of Toronto, served as the medical director of blood transfusion services at the Toronto Hospital/Princess Margaret Hospital, and was a staff physician in the Hematology/Oncology Division at the Toronto Hospital.

PETER SPRIGG is the director of the Center for Marriage and Family Studies at the Family Research Council (FRC) having been senior director of culture studies for two years prior to his appointment. He oversees FRC's efforts to analyze and influence our culture as it relates to "marriage and family structure; education; human sexuality and the homosexual agenda; religion in public life; and the arts and entertainment." He also serves as executive editor of the monthly e-mail newsletter *Culture Facts.*

CARSON STRONG is a professor in the Department of Human Values and Ethics at the University of Tennessee College of Medicine in Knoxville.

JINI PATEL THOMPSON is the author of books and articles on natural healing, including *Listen To Your Gut: Natural Healing & Dealing With Inflammatory Bowel Disease & Irritable Bowel Syndrome.* Jini Patel Thompson is not a licensed health care professional of any sort (nor medical or naturopathic doctor), but consults with people simply for her personal opinion, ideas, and personal experience. She has worked as a journalist and magazine editor and in the music business, and currently runs her own publishing/consulting business. Jini Patel Thompson is a health journalist who specializes in natural healing for digestive diseases: www.JiniPatelThompson.com.

MARC TUNZI is director of the Family Practice Residency Program at Natividad Medical Center, Salinas, California, and associate clinical professor of family and community medicine at the University of California, San Francisco, School of Medicine. He received his medical degree from the University of California, San Diego, School of Medicine.

THOMAS M. VANDER VEN is an associate professor in the Sociology Department at Ohio University specializing in the areas of Crime and Delinquency; Work, Family, and Crime; Criminological Theory; and the Sociology of Social Problems.

JANE WALDFOGEL is professor of social work and public affairs at the Columbia University School of Social Work, and a research associate at the Centre for Analysis of Social Exclusion at the London School of Economics. Dr. Waldfogel currently is a member of the National Academy of Science's Committee on Family and Work Policies and the author of *The Future of Child Protection: How to Break the Cycle of Abuse and Neglect* (Harvard University Press, 1998).

STEPHEN O. WATTERS was, as of 2001, the internet research analyst for the Department of Legislative and Cultural Affairs at Focus on the Family. He has written several articles about the pitfalls of the Internet for Focus on the Family.

JOHN PAUL WRIGHT is a professor of life-course criminology, biosocial criminology, life-course criminology, and juvenile justice at the University of Cincinnati's Corrections Institute. He has taught at East Tennessee State University in the Department of Criminal Justice and Criminology and published in leading criminal justice journals. Dr. Wright is also a developmental criminologist whose work integrates findings from a number of disciplines, including human behavioral genetics, psychology, and biology. He is the cofounder of the Crime Adaptation Network, which includes a group of scholars from around the world who apply dynamic systems theory to crime and offending.

FERDINAND D. YATES, JR., a fellow at the Center for Bioethics and Human Dignity, is the senior pediatrician and co-founder of Genesee-Transit Pediatrics. He is also a fellow of the American Academy of Pediatrics and he presently serves as a member of the Executive Committee for the Section on Bioethics. He also serves on ethics committees for several hospitals and health care settings.

Index